EARLY RYUKYUAN HISTORY

EARLY RYUKYUAN HISTORY

A New Model

Gregory Smits

University of Hawai'i Press

Honolulu

First printed, 2024

Library of Congress Cataloging-in-Publication Data

Names: Smits, Gregory, author.
Title: Early Ryukyuan history : a new model / Gregory Smits.
Description: Honolulu : University of Hawai'i Press, [2024] | Includes
  bibliographical references and index.
Identifiers: LCCN 2023045368 (print) | LCCN 2023045369 (ebook) | ISBN
  9780824897635 (hardcover) | ISBN 9780824898212 (epub) | ISBN
  9780824898229 (kindle edition) | ISBN 9780824898205 (pdf)
Subjects: LCSH: Ryukyu Islands—History—To 1879.
Classification: LCC DS895.R97 S63 2024 (print) | LCC DS895.R97 (ebook) |
  DDC 952./29—dc23/eng/20240130
LC record available at https://lccn.loc.gov/2023045368
LC ebook record available at https://lccn.loc.gov/2023045369

Cover Photograph: Portion of the Kasari Peninsula, Amami-Ōshima.
Photograph by Gregory Smits.

For my parents,
Mary and Stanley Smits,
who encouraged inquiry
from an early age

CONTENTS

Acknowledgments   ix

Introduction   1

Chapter One
A New Model of Early Ryukyuan History   21

Chapter Two
Well-Traveled Routes   52

Chapter Three
The Land, First Peoples, and the Shellmound Era   64

Chapter Four
Kikaijima and the Start of Japonic Ryukyu   89

Chapter Five
Spokes and Hubs: Modeling East China Sea Regional Trade   106

Chapter Six
Sacred Groves, Fortresses, and More: The Korean Impact   117

Chapter Seven
Agriculture   137

Chapter Eight
Trading and Raiding Intensify: The Late *Gusuku* Era   156

Chapter Nine
The Geopolitical Landscape   180

Chapter Ten
Many More than Three: The Tumultuous Sanzan Era in Okinawa   196

Chapter Eleven
Era of the First Shō "Dynasty"   222

Chapter Twelve
The Second Shō Dynasty and the Creation of a Centralized State   246

Chapter Thirteen
Early Ryukyu in Regional History   259

   Notes   273
   Works Cited   299
   Index   317

Acknowledgments

I began writing this book at the peak of the COVID-19 pandemic in the summer of 2020. Although much of the academic world was in suspended mode, Penn State's magnificent interlibrary loan staff quickly developed a way to keep myself and others supplied with needed materials. At Penn State, I thank Michael Kulikowski, long-serving head of the Department of History, for his strong support for my work over the years. I also thank Erica Brindley, currently head of Asian Studies, and my Japanese history colleagues Jess Abel and Ran Zwigenberg for their enthusiastic support for my work over the years.

I spent the spring semester 2022 at the University of Hawai'i at Mānoa (UHM) as the Arthur Lynn Andrews Visiting Professor in Asian Studies. This book benefited from access to UHM library resources and discussions with interested faculty and students. I would especially like to thank Masato Ishida, director of the Center for Okinawan Studies, and the center's Ella Camacho, as well as Cathryn Clayton, chair of the Department of Asian Studies, and Tess Constantino for bringing me to UHM and making all the many necessary arrangements after I arrived. In Honolulu, it was a pleasure to work with longtime friend Shari Tamashiro, whose labor has been instrumental in preserving local culture.

Over the past few years, I have benefited from comments, questions, and discussions with scholars in the aftermath of the publication of *Maritime Ryukyu* in 2019. These scholars include Fabian Drixler, Gerald Figal, Mark Hudson, Bob Huey, Thomas Monaghan, Scott O'Bryan, Morten Oxenboell, Len Schoppa, Timon Screech, Travis Seifman, Nozomi Tanaka, Marco Tinello, Watanabe Miki, Yoshinari Naoki, and many others.

Masako Ikeda, executive editor of University of Hawai'i Press, provided invaluable support for this project. I would also like to thank Gianna Marsella, managing editor, and Wendy Lawrence, copy editor. Two outside readers for the press provided detailed comments and criticism, which have greatly improved the book. I am grateful for the time and effort they put into this project. Needless to say, any remaining shortcomings are entirely my own.

Although they are not direct contributors to this book, I am always grateful to my network of music friends for helping maintain my mental well-being.

During the time I was working on this book my wife, Akiko, became interested in the history and culture of the Ryukyu Islands. She sent me all manner of video links and book references, some of which have contributed to this book or potential future books.

EARLY RYUKYUAN HISTORY

Introduction

In late May 2022, several Japanese news outlets ran a story about three sets of skeletal remains discovered in a stone ossuary in Fusato, southern Okinawa. The remains were from the fifteenth or sixteenth century, but the ossuary was made in 1706. It is therefore likely that the remains had been reinterred, complicating any speculation about a relationship between the three sets. News reports stressed that mitochondrial DNA (mDNA) analysis of the remains indicated a Japonic maternal ancestor,[1] as well as maternal ancestors from Europe or central Asia and the Korean Peninsula. Some or all of those interred in the ossuary may have come from first-generation immigrants or been the mixed-race offspring of such immigrants. Especially noteworthy is that two of the sets of remains indicate a movement of women from the Eurasian continent into the Ryukyu Islands (*Okinawa taimusu* 2022). The three sets of remains in Okinawa, each with maternal ancestors from vastly different places, nicely encapsulate much of the content of this book, *Early Ryukyuan History: A New Model*.

Although the detailed histories of these three skeletons remain obscure, work in a variety of academic disciplines has revealed the movement of people into the Ryukyu Islands at different points in the distant past. This book tells that story in detail, beginning with the earliest extant human remains (ca. thirty-five thousand years ago) and ending in the sixteenth century with the establishment of a centralized Ryukyuan state. Multidisciplinary in its approach, *Early Ryukyuan History* is grounded in the work of archaeologists. It also incorporates evidence and insights from DNA studies, soil science, anthropology, traditional document-based history, the analysis of myths and legends, and other academic fields. Its most basic narrative is a description of the peopling of the Ryukyu Islands with respect to the questions of who, where, and when. At approximately the eleventh century, the narrative expands to explain why certain groups came to the Ryukyu Islands, what they did to sustain themselves economically, and the nature of their societies, cultures, and conflicts.

My approach to the topic is unique in that it is grounded in multidisciplinary scholarship and informed by an original theoretical framework. This framework constitutes a new model of early Ryukyuan history. The findings in these pages derive from this new model and establish an argument for its usefulness and necessity.

Readers familiar with the approach to early Ryukyu found in books such as George H. Kerr's ([1958] 2000) *Okinawa: The History of an Island People*, Mamoru Akamine's (2017) *The Ryukyu Kingdom: Cornerstone of East Asia,* or any of the many Japanese-language survey histories of Okinawa or Ryukyu will notice that this book differs significantly in its overall outlook and specific conclusions. It is not the case that the authors of survey histories of the Ryukyu Islands all agree with each other. Nevertheless, when dealing with time periods before the sixteenth century, most modern histories adopt the framework of the official histories of the Ryukyu Kingdom, which were produced between approximately 1650 and 1750. For simplicity, in this introduction I call this modern metanarrative based on the official histories the "standard narrative." Chapter 1 examines historiographic matters in greater detail.

Comparison with Previous Work

I began my rethinking of early Ryukyuan history in a previous book, *Maritime Ryukyu, 1050–1650* (2019). *Early Ryukyuan History* moves that process much further along, in part by following up on questions raised in *Maritime Ryukyu* or on points mentioned in those pages but not thoroughly discussed. This book also includes much entirely new and original material.

Because this book advances a fundamentally new model of early Ryukyuan history, I discuss historiographic issues at some length. Chapter 1 examines the major trends and approaches to early Ryukyuan history from approximately the 1930s to the present. I explain that the model of early Ryukyuan history dominant today dates from about 1980 and made good sense at that time. However, archaeology especially, along with findings from other academic disciplines, has undermined this current model enough that it no longer works well for material before the sixteenth century. The new model I propose to replace it is arguably the most important contribution of *Early Ryukyuan History*.

Putting this new model to use, I reconceptualize the political, economic, and military history of the fourteenth and fifteenth centuries, especially the situation during the so-called Three Principalities (Sanzan) era in Okinawa and during the first Shō "dynasty." I also provide new insights into the origins of the second Shō dynasty and the eventual consolidation of power by Shō Shin and his successors.

After examining this long span of history, I conclude by reflecting on the East China Sea region's impact on the Ryukyu Islands and in turn the Ryukyu

Islands' impact on the region. I describe how and why the history of the early Ryukyu Islands is distinctive, not simply a late-developing, small-scale version of Japanese history. Moreover, the case of the Ryukyu Islands provides insights into environmental history, the nature of agriculture, state formation, migration, and the interconnected relationship between peripheral regions ("barbarian zones," following James C. Scott) and states. I also consider the question of Ryukyuan ethnogenesis and note some of the difficulties inherent in aligning the complex premodern Ryukyuan past with modern ways of conceiving of identities.

Select Arguments in *Maritime Ryukyu*

For those unfamiliar with *Maritime Ryukyu,* here I briefly state the major arguments from that book, which are also relevant to this one. In the next section, I list the major arguments in *Early Ryukyuan History.*

In *Maritime Ryukyu* I argue for a version of early Ryukyuan history that is both broader and more complex than the standard narrative. The breadth component is that the Ryukyu Islands did not develop in isolation. Maritime networks connected them with the Japanese Islands, the Korean Peninsula, and parts of coastal China. The complexity component is in part aimed at reducing Okinawa-centrism, the problematic tendency to equate the island of Okinawa with the Ryukyu Islands as a whole. The Ryukyu Islands were not a singular, natural political and cultural community. Each major island or group of islands possessed its own language, customs, economic dynamics, and so forth. The "Ryukyu Kingdom" was actually a maritime empire created by Okinawan subjugation of the other Ryukyu Islands.

CENTRALITY OF KIKAIJIMA AND PROBLEMATIC OFFICIAL HISTORIES

In the standard narrative, early Ryukyuan history starts in Okinawa. In *Maritime Ryukyu,* I argue that Ryukyuan history started in Kikaijima, a small island off the northeast coast of Amami-Ōshima. Similarly, I stress the importance of the Northern Tier islands of Kikaijima, Amami-Ōshima, and Tokunoshima within the cultural and economic history of the Ryukyu Islands as a whole. The modern tendency to regard Okinawa as central to the early history of the Ryukyu Islands in part reflects that island's relative prominence today. It is also a legacy of the official histories, which have framed the basic narrative ever since their creation in the seventeenth and eighteenth centuries. Even when dealing with ancient material, the official histories reflect the circumstances and ideologies of the early modern era. Among other things, *Maritime Ryukyu* was an attempt to write a history of the Ryukyu Islands that does not depend on the official histo-ries for periods prior to the sixteenth century.

OMORO SŌSHI AS HISTORICAL SOURCE

Instead of the official histories, *Maritime Ryukyu* makes extensive use of the songs in a collection known as *Omoro sōshi*, the first volume of which appeared in the early 1530s. Although difficult to use as historical sources, when read in conjunction with recent scholarship from disciplines such as anthropology, archaeology, and linguistics, *Omoro sōshi* songs shed much light on the early Ryukyuan past. For example, they reveal a web of maritime routes connecting the southern parts of the Korean Peninsula with the Ryukyu Islands via the islands of Tsushima and Iki and the western coast of Kyushu. This route formed the core of what I call the East China Sea Network.

CENTRALITY OF WAKŌ

I also argue that the most important group of people to move through the East China Sea Network and set up bases in its harbors were *wakō*. Conventionally translated as "Japanese pirates," fourteenth- and early fifteenth-century *wakō* included large numbers of Koreans and other non-Japanese. Moreover, although they often engaged in marauding, especially in Korea, *wakō* overlapped signifi-cantly with maritime merchants. *Wakō* also performed other functions such as the transfer of culture and technologies.

To a large extent, *wakō* made early Ryukyuan history. Indeed, upon close inspection it is often difficult to distinguish between *wakō* and "Ryukyuans" prior to the sixteenth century. The generous tribute trade terms that the Ming dynasty extended to local powers in Okinawa, starting in the early 1370s, were part of the Chinese court's *wakō* control policy. The basic plan was to make par-ticipation in the tribute trade so profitable for *wakō* in the Ryukyu Islands that they came to depend on it. Dependence on Ming tribute trade would, in effect, tame *wakō* and curtail their threat. At the same time, tribute trade via the port of Naha became a way for the Ming court to circumvent its own maritime prohibi-tions in a controlled manner.

REVISED STATE FORMATION NARRATIVE

Finally, *Maritime Ryukyu* questions and revises the standard narrative of state formation. Owing to the influence of the official histories, the standard narrative describes the rise of local rulers (*aji*) in harbors. Leagues of these local rulers had coalesced into three territorial states by the early 1300s, the so-called Three Prin-cipalities of Sannan (or Nanzan), Chūzan, and Sanhoku (or Hokuzan). The heads of these principalities became "kings" with the start of formal tribute trade with China in the 1370s. By the early 1400s (precise dates are unclear), Shō Hashi of Chūzan, originally of Sannan, succeeded in defeating the other principalities on the battlefield and became the first king of a united Okinawa.

Contrary to this standard narrative, I argue that the Three Principalities appear to have been the creation of Chinese merchant-officials who handled the tribute trade at Naha harbor. Never mentioned in *Omoro sōshi* songs, the Three Principalities seem to have functioned more as dummy corporations to facilitate diverse Okinawan powers participating in the trade. There is no strong evidence to suggest that they were territorial states and much to suggest that they were not. Moreover, even after Shō Hashi's rise to prominence in the early decades of the fifteenth century, his control—or nominal control—was over the port of Naha and the tribute trade. He was not a king in the sense of a monarch ruling over a centralized state. That centralized state, a "Ryukyu Kingdom" in the full sense of the term, came into existence during the latter part of the reign of Shō Shin, circa the 1520s. It resulted from decades of warfare and institutional reforms. In short, I locate the rise of a strong centralized monarchy based at Shuri approximately a century later than does the standard narrative. It is also important to note that it was only during the early 1500s that most of the Ryukyu Islands came under Shuri's control. The result was a maritime empire extending from Kikaijima in the north to Yonaguni in the south.

I advance other arguments in *Maritime Ryukyu*—for example, about the causes of the 1609 war between Ryukyu and Satsuma—but the points above are particularly relevant to the content of this book. In these pages I refine and expand on many of the arguments in *Maritime Ryukyu,* and I advance new ones.

Major Arguments in *Early Ryukyuan History*

From the time of the earliest extant human remains to the formation of a centralized monarchy, the Ryukyu Islands were never isolated. People from outside the islands journeyed to them for reasons that included pursuing economic gain or fleeing political or military defeat. This book's main argument is that newcomers to the Ryukyu Islands functioned as the principal drivers of early Ryukyuan history.

Gusuku Era as Reset

The diverse range of peoples who dwelled in the Ryukyu Islands did not necessarily merge into a single population or ethnos over time. Sometimes outside arrivals did blend into larger populations over one or more generations, but there were also discontinuities with respect to the human population. The most important example of outsiders migrating to the Ryukyu Islands and displacing the previous population is the early *gusuku* era. The standard narrative tends to assume that the Ryukyu Islands were a closed system and that the modern or contemporary population of the islands is the product of a gradual, linear, internal development extending thousands of years into the past.

The *gusuku* era, however, was a massive resetting of the population. By about the mid-1990s, some researchers were becoming aware of this point, and recent findings in archaeology, physical anthropology, and DNA studies have reaffirmed and refined it. Stated simply, starting in the eleventh century and continuing into the twelfth, waves of Japonic migrants settled in the Ryukyu Islands and swamped the small and declining indigenous population. The eleventh century marked the most significant discontinuity in the known history of the islands—namely, the replacement of non-Japonic peoples with northern migrants. The base culture of the Ryukyu Islands became Japonic at this time and has remained so ever since.

REVISION OF THE DUAL STRUCTURE HYPOTHESIS

Within the past two decades, the quantity of unearthed skeletal remains from around the Ryukyu Islands has increased significantly, and laboratory techniques for extracting and analyzing DNA continue to improve. Recent DNA results have undermined the widespread view that the pre-Japonic Ryukyu Islands were split between an Austronesian population (probably from Taiwan) living in the southern Ryukyu Islands and a Jōmon population (from Kyushu) in Okinawa and northward. It now appears that most or all of the people who dwelled in the southern Ryukyu Islands were genetically Jōmon, not Austronesian. In any case, during the eleventh and twelfth centuries, the population of the Ryukyu Islands came to resemble closely that of the larger Japanese Islands to the north, as it does today.

The dual structure hypothesis posits that the modern population of the Ryukyu Islands is of Jōmon derivation. It was first proposed by anthropologists in the early twentieth century and most famously advanced by Hanihara Kazurō in the late 1980s. The hypothesis that Jōmon people once populated the Ryukyu Islands by now appears to have been correct. However, it is incorrect in concluding that the modern population of the Ryukyu Islands is mainly of Jōmon derivation.

DIVERSE POPULATION INPUTS

The Japonic foundation of the Ryukyu Islands was able to absorb inflows of non-Japonic peoples. These peoples included Mongols and Alans in the mid- to late fourteenth century, one possible source of the western European or central Asian mDNA reported in 2022 in connection with the stone ossuary. By far the most important of these non-Japanese groups were people from the Korean Peninsula or nearby islands, such as Jeju. They exerted a profound cultural influence not only on the Ryukyu Islands but on western Kyushu and other parts of western Japan. The modern and contemporary tendency to depict the Ryukyu Islands as having existed within a political and cultural tension between Japan to the north and China to the southwest is reasonable for the early modern situation, between circa 1630 and 1880, but not for the period covered in this study.

The long early history of the Ryukyu Islands was punctuated by at least one major discontinuity and several subsequent periods of intense change, all driven by migrations. Groups of people arriving from Japan, Korea, and other places helped shape local communities and cultures. In this context, it is important to bear in mind that the Ryukyu Islands did not constitute a single political or ethnic community. Various groups and communities dwelled in the islands or harbors at different times and they frequently relocated. The ocean around the Ryukyu Islands did not act as a barrier to isolate them. On the contrary, it functioned as connective tissue, linking the Ryukyu Islands with other locations around the East China Sea, especially those to the north. Indeed, one generalization we could safely make about classical Ryukyuan culture is that it came into the islands from points to the north, along with people.

Eventually, the Ryukyu Islands did become relatively isolated, but not until the 1630s. Many cultural phenomena now regarded as distinctively Ryukyuan developed during the roughly two and a half centuries of isolation between the 1630s and the 1880s. During the period covered in this book, however, the Ryukyu Islands were closely linked with the East China Sea region and, indirectly, to places even farther afield.

HUB-AND-SPOKE MODEL FOR REGIONAL INTERACTIONS

In these pages I present a hub-and-spoke model as a way to visualize the web of regional exchanges in which the Ryukyu Islands were enmeshed. This approach helps clarify the situation at any given time. Changes to the hub-and-spoke configuration reveal, among other things, the impact of major regional political upheavals on the Ryukyu Islands. By zooming in for a close-grained look, a modified version of the hub-and-spoke model illuminates the political geography of the Ryukyu Islands during the fourteenth and fifteenth centuries.

HARBOR-FORTRESS UNITS, NOT LAND-BASED POLITIES

The standard narrative regards regional powers in Okinawa as small territorial states or confederations of local rulers. However, I argue that the main political and economic unit during the fourteenth and fifteenth centuries was a harbor linked with a fortress on high ground above the anchorage. These harbor-fortress units communicated with and often competed with other such units in Okinawa. However, their main economic connections were with harbors in other Ryukyu Islands and beyond, to points in Japan, Korea, and China. In other words, this book advances a new conception of political geography in the Ryukyu Islands during the fourteenth and fifteenth centuries.

Reassessment of the Sanzan and First Shō Dynasty Eras

Harbor-fortress combinations were trading and raiding units with an orientation outward, across the sea. The focus in these pages on harbor-fortress units linked into regional networks permits a fundamental reassessment of the era of the Three Principalities and first Shō "dynasty" (ca. 1370–1470). By integrating diverse sources of evidence, it is possible to identify specific trading groups in Okinawa and sometimes to map out parts of their networks.

In a fine-grained assessment, I pay close attention to each "king" during the Three Principalities and First Shō dynasty eras. Some were actual people, but many are so obscure that we cannot be sure they existed as more than names in official documents. Although the standard narrative characterizes Okinawa as having been divided into three territorial states, I portray the political geography as a much more complex array of harbor-fortress units. Similarly, I argue that the warfare of this era, which was extensive, should be understood as competition among different trading and raiding groups to gain a more beneficial purchase on the lucrative tribute trade with the Ming dynasty.

The standard narrative tends to view the development and emergence of small territorial states, and ultimately of a centralized kingdom, as the result of internal developments within Okinawa. In this view, widespread international trade was one *result* of the emergence of Okinawan states. By contrast, in this book I argue that widespread international trade was the main *cause* of the emergence of local powers and eventually a centralized state.

Importance of Korea

Ryukyu's official histories occasionally mention Korea. However, insofar as they discuss international relations, the official histories situate the Ryukyu Islands between Japan and China. It is not surprising, therefore, that so, too, does the modern standard narrative. While an emphasis on Japan and China makes sense for the early modern era, when the official histories were written, it is problematic for earlier eras. China was certainly important in the development of the early Ryukyu Islands but mainly as a source of wealth and goods.

For the most part, China was a source of neither people nor culture for early Ryukyu.

The main source of people, culture, and technology was Japan, especially the island of Kyushu. Next in importance was Korea, either directly or indirectly via western Kyushu. Sacred groves (*utaki*), a foundation of Ryukyuan religion, are of Korean origin. So, too, are the stone-walled fortresses (*gusuku*), some of which have become World Heritage sites. The first person to hold the title "king" in Okinawa came from Korea. So important was Korean influence on the development of early Ryukyu that this book devotes a full chapter to that topic (chapter 6).

IMPACT OF GEOGRAPHY AND THE PHYSICAL ENVIRONMENT

Although I generally use the term "external agents" to refer to groups of people, the physical environment of the Ryukyu Islands constitutes a crucially important force in early Ryukyuan history. Every group of people who settled in the Ryukyu Islands became subject to the advantages and disadvantages this environment afforded. By virtue of their location and the presence of numerous harbors, the Ryukyu Islands were ideal for maritime trading and raiding. Stated using James C. Scott's terminology, the Ryukyu Islands were ideally situated to function as a barbarian zone vis-à-vis the region's states.[2] On the other hand, the soil, terrain, and weather patterns in and around the Ryukyu Islands made them poorly suited for agriculture, especially on a scale that could support centralized states.

A DISTINCTIVE HISTORY, NOT A SMALL-SCALE REPLICA OF JAPAN

Many historians of the Ryukyu Islands writing in Japanese have treated the islands as a late-developing, small-scale version of mainland Japanese society. In the standard narrative, agricultural surpluses led to increasing social complexity in both places. In mainland Japan the process of building an agricultural society began during the Yayoi era. In the Ryukyu Islands, it began during roughly the eleventh century, at least according to recent reckoning. The idea that Okinawa, or the Ryukyu Islands in general, became a society based on agriculture remains a foundational assumption of the standard narrative. It also reflects a Marxist-inflected assumption that human history develops in set stages.

Following a small number of Japanese historians, I question whether the early Ryukyu Islands were ever an agricultural society. There is no doubt that agriculture existed and that it began during the eleventh century (and possibly earlier in a few locations). Moreover, agricultural cultivation provided an important source of food. These matters are not in dispute. The main question I take up is whether agricultural surpluses powered state development. My conclusion is that agriculture was not the economic driver of state development. Instead, agriculture supplemented what was fundamentally a trading and raiding society. In other words, mainly in response to the physical environment, early Ryukyuan society developed in a manner fundamentally different from that of Japan, Korea, or the other large agricultural societies of the region. Although culturally akin to Japan, the Ryukyu Islands were not simply a late-developing offshoot of Japan. They grew into a unique society that differed significantly from the ancestral homelands of most of the people who eventually settled the islands.

NEED FOR A NEW MODEL

In my view the standard narrative is no longer viable. In chapter 1, I examine the history of the historiography of early Ryukyu in some detail. Very briefly, the standard narrative assumes Okinawa is the geographic origin of Ryukyuan history and stresses internal development from an early, Japonic seed population. This internal development culminated in an impressive kingdom, created by successive generations of Okinawans and made possible by agricultural surpluses. In most versions of the standard narrative, Shō Hashi founded the Ryukyu Kingdom after decades of increasing social complexity. After coming into existence, the Ryukyu Kingdom supplemented its wealth by engaging in international trade. In this narrative the other Ryukyu Islands tend to be an afterthought.

The standard narrative, and the model upon which it is based, is incompatible with a large and growing body of data from archaeology and other fields. In these pages, therefore, I propose a new model of early Ryukyuan history. This new model better accommodates the findings and insights of diverse academic disciplines, and it provides greater explanatory power. Moreover, it situates the history and development of the Ryukyu Islands firmly within the context of East Asian and world history. The new model also calls for revised periodization and more precise terminology.

Importance of Early Ryukyuan History

It is commonplace for politicians, journalists, social activists, and scholars to invoke the ancient Ryukyuan past to bolster arguments or policies about the present and future. To take one example, in *Tatakau Okinawa, hondo no sekinin: Takakuteki ronten maruwakari* (Okinawa in conflict, the mainland's fault: A full understanding of multifaceted issues), Toki Naohiko (2018) writes about topics and causes such as recent and contemporary antibase activism, discrimination against Okinawa and its people in the modern era, and the excessive power of the United States and Tokyo vis-à-vis Okinawa Prefecture. His book is representative of a large body of literature on recent and contemporary issues and problems in Okinawa Prefecture. Like most writers on contemporary topics, Toki makes historical arguments and uses history to support them.[3] In this context statements like "Ryukyu was once the Ryukyu Kingdom, unconnected with the [Japanese] emperor or the emperor system" are typical (Toki 2018, 90).

Toki's book begins with a five-page preface titled "A Brief History of the Ryukyu Kingdom" (Ryūkyū ōkoku shōshi), which closely follows the standard narrative. The preface closes by noting that the inscription on Shō Taikyū's 1458 Sea Bridge to the Many Countries Bell (Bankoku Shinryō no Kane) adorns a folding screen in the governor's reception office, "demonstrating Okinawa's tradition of peaceful interaction" (Toki 2018, 13). As we will see, however, that bell inscription resulted directly from the warfare that Taikyū waged (chapter 11).

My purpose here is not to criticize Toki's book but to cite it as a typical example of the widespread use of Ryukyu's deep past to bolster contemporary political arguments. As with the invocation of Shō Taikyū's bell as a symbol of peace, many of these appeals to early Ryukyuan history are arguably inaccurate or problematic. The very sparse documentary record for early Ryukyu further encourages the appropriation of old inscriptions or monuments in the service of present-day politics. Insofar as my arguments in these pages are sound, this book is a foundation upon which to build a more nuanced, complex, and accurate history of the Ryukyu Islands, not only during the time period I cover but for the early modern, modern, and contemporary periods as well. Of course, it is also a starting point for further work on early Ryukyu.

This interdisciplinary book is the most detailed account of early Ryukyu in English. While thoroughly grounded in the relevant Anglophone and Japanese secondary literature and primary sources, it advances original models and conclusions with the potential to alter our fundamental understanding of the early history of the Ryukyu Islands. This altered understanding has implications for later periods of Ryukyuan history, several of which I note in these pages.

The Ryukyu Islands were an integral part of the fabric of maritime East Asia. This book examines the far-ranging movement of people, technology, culture, and goods from the East China Sea region into the Ryukyu Islands and, conversely, the impact of the Ryukyu Islands on the region. It therefore contributes to our understanding of regional history and dynamics. Especially important in this respect is the function of the early Ryukyu Islands as a zone in which mobile networks of nonstate actors interacted with the region's states, sometimes as competitors or marauders and sometimes as providers of valuable goods. In this capacity the Ryukyu Islands constituted an East Asian example of a zone occupied by people who preferred or actively sought to live outside state boundaries and control (cf. Scott 2017).

Conventions and Key Terms

In the interest of brevity and readability, I follow two general policies. First, I do not reargue points that are thoroughly discussed in *Maritime Ryukyu*. Instead, I state the main conclusion or conclusions and encourage interested readers to follow up using the relevant citations.

Second, for readers who are not familiar with archaeology the details of the evidence can present a forest-and-trees problem. In other words, the details can become overwhelming and obscure the larger point. Although academic writing in archaeology tends to place all the evidence and discussion within the main text, my policy is to place many of the details in endnotes. The result is a hybrid style of the in-line citations common in social sciences plus the extensive endnotes common in the humanities.

Given the topic of this book, many names have multiple possible pronunciations, and listing even a few would quickly become cumbersome. Therefore, I use what I regard as the most common or conventional pronunciation, listing one prevalent alternative in parentheses if appropriate. If necessary for clarity, I employ the abbreviations "J.," "Ch.," "K.," and "O." for Japanese, Chinese, Korean, and Okinawan, respectively. Except for the common place-names, dynasty names, or other terms found in English dictionaries, all Chinese names and terms include (modern) tone marks. Korean words appear in the revised romanization system.

Dates more specific than the year appear as "[Gregorian year].[lunar month]. [day]." For example, 1409.4.2 means "second day of the fourth lunar month, 1409," not April 2.

Certain key terms occur in these pages often. In the paragraphs below, I define them briefly.

ancient branch model: An older model of early Ryukyuan history that flourished circa the 1920s through the 1970s and that I discuss in detail in chapter 1. The internal development model replaced it.

early Ryukyu: In this book, "early Ryukyu" refers to the period starting with the earliest-known human habitation of the Ryukyu Islands up to the establishment of a strong, centralized state. Specifically, it refers to roughly 35,000 BP to approximately 1530. In these pages, early Ryukyu is not the same as the Japanese Ko-Ryūkyū (Old Ryukyu). Conventionally, the Japanese term refers to the start of the *gusuku* era, roughly the eleventh century, until the 1609 war with Satsuma.

early modern era: In the context of the history of the Ryukyu Islands, the early modern era is roughly the seventeenth through the nineteenth centuries. The key event was the 1609 war with Satsuma, which resulted in the Ryukyu Islands becoming the territory of the Shimazu daimyō. By the 1620s or 1630s, the initial framework of the postwar era was in place. In the form of institutions and customary practices, much of this framework persisted for several decades following the formal replacement of the Ryukyu Kingdom with Okinawa Prefecture in 1879. In my usage, early modern corresponds closely with the Japanese term *kinsei*.

external agents model: A new model of early Ryukyuan history for which I argue in this book.

centralized state: Defining precisely what is and is not a "state" is difficult and complex. For this book I adopt James C. Scott's (2017, 23) elegantly simple definition: "A polity with a king, specialized administrative staff, social hierarchy, a monumental center, city walls, and tax collection and distribution is certainly a 'state' in the strong sense of the term." In a Ryukyuan context, the only required modification is to substitute Shuri Castle for "city walls." In the Ryukyu Islands, such a state began to form in the late 1490s, and its framework was largely complete by the end of the 1530s.

internal development model: The currently dominant model of early Ryukyuan history, going back to approximately 1980. It is discussed in detail in chapter 1.

king and trade king: The term "king" is highly problematic in the context of early Ryukyu—so much so that it requires some modification. Chinese emperors bestowed the title *wáng* 王 (J. ō) on certain foreign rulers or warlords. The bestowal functioned partly like formal diplomatic recognition does in today's world. The title *wáng* was also a license to participate in formal state-sponsored trade with the Chinese court and de facto authorization to engage in a certain degree of private trade under the cover of state-sponsored trade. *Wáng* is always translated as "king" in English. However, the Chinese title said nothing about the extent of power that its holder wielded domestically or the structure of a *wáng*'s government.

Some of these *wáng* ruled centralized states as defined above. In the Ryukyuan case, however, many *wáng* were leaders of seafaring groups who emerged victorious in local warfare. The extent of their territorial control was limited to a subset of the island of Okinawa, sometimes only the Naha-Shuri area or some other harbor-fortress unit. Although undoubtedly assisted by trusted members of their groups, these *wáng* did not preside over bureaucracies or make use of written documents for domestic governance. Moreover, no evidence indicates that these seafaring *wáng* levied taxes in a systematic manner. In some cases, as we will see, *wáng* whose names appeared in Chinese and Korean records may not even have been actual people. Instead, they were names in documents under which certain Ryukyuans conducted official trade. These real or fictitious *wáng* were kings for trade purposes. In these pages I consistently refer to them with the term "trade king." By contrast, the term "king" (without scare quotes or modification by the word "trade") refers to rulers of centralized states. In this sense the first king in the Ryukyu Islands was Shō Shin (r. 1477–1527), and only toward the end of his long reign.

> *aji* 按司 (also *anji*): *Saikan* 寨官 (Ch. *zhàiguān*) is an older written term, common in Chinese documents, with the same meaning. Simply stated, *aji* refers to local warlords in the Ryukyu Islands. It is a term found in written documents, and it appears to date from the late fifteenth or early sixteenth century. A common equivalent term for *aji* or *saikan* in *Omoro sōshi* songs is *teda* (O. *tiida,* the sun) or *tedako* (child of the sun). The typical territory that an *aji* controlled was a harbor with a fortress (*gusuku*) located slightly inland and on higher ground. *Aji* who held the Chinese title *wáng* were trade kings. However, *aji* without this title were not necessarily less wealthy or powerful than trade kings. In this book I usually refer to *aji* as "warlords."
>
> *wakō* 倭寇 (Ch. *wōkòu,* K. *waegu*): The term *wakō* appeared in early thirteenth-century documents, although mariners engaging in piratical activities such as smuggling, marauding, and human trafficking obviously existed earlier. *Wakō* literally means "Japanese pirates," and many of these seafarers were Japanese and did engage in piratical activities. However, as Murai Shōsuke and other scholars of maritime history have noted, many thirteenth- and fourteenth-century *wakō* were Koreans, and *wakō* worked closely with networks of Korean collaborators (Murai 1988, 328–334; Ōta 2002, 7–8, 24–26). Moreover, *wakō* also functioned as merchants, diplomats, and security forces for hire. The distinction between seafaring merchants, who were almost always armed, and seafarers called *wakō* in documents is often unclear.

Peter D. Shapinsky has criticized my untranslated use of *wakō* in *Maritime Ryukyu,* noting the several entangled meanings the term has accumulated. The term *wakō* was a creation of scholar-officials in China and Korea, and the relevant seafarers did not self-identify as *wakō* (Shapinsky 2021, 193). Shapinsky's points are well taken, and the term *wakō* is far from ideal. However, any reasonably accurate translation would be awkward on account of the many modes in which *wakō* operated. The term *wakō* is used so widely that I am reluctant to attempt to coin a new word that might replace it. I discuss the wide range of meanings behind the term *wakō* in chapter 2 of *Maritime Ryukyu*, "*Wakō* and the Ryukyu Islands" (Smits 2019, 36–59).

> Gusuku: Capitalized and in normal (nonitalic) typeface, Gusuku refers to the Gusuku site complex (Gusuku Isekigun 城久遺跡群), a large cluster of eight archaeological sites on the island of Kikaijima.

> *gusuku:* Lowercase (usually) and italicized, *gusuku* (usually グスク; sometimes 城) refers to fortresses in the Ryukyu Islands during the period of roughly the twelfth through the fifteenth centuries. I discuss *gusuku* extensively in later chapters. Simply stated, there are two main types. The first, the stone-walled *gusuku,* were Ryukyuan versions of Korean mountain fortresses (K. *sanseong*). The largest of these *gusuku* are often called castles (J. *-jō*). The second type of *gusuku* was a trench-and-earthworks fortification of Japanese derivation. Although significantly different in terms of appearance, both types of fortifications are called *gusuku* in modern literature, which occasionally causes confusion. For clarity, therefore, I sometimes use the terms "stone-walled *gusuku*" and "trench-and-earthworks *gusuku*" to differentiate the two broad types.

> *gusuku* era: In lowercase (usually) and italic typeface, this term corresponds to *gusuku jidai* in Japanese, and its terminal dates are vague. In my usage it refers to approximately the middle of the eleventh century to the early fifteenth century. Japanese-language literature tends to emphasize the presence of *gusuku* (fortresses) as the defining feature of the era. In this book I focus on the migration into the Ryukyu Islands of northern people, mostly from Japan, as the defining feature. This migration transformed the population and culture of the Ryukyu Islands into something that I call Japonic.

> Japonic: In linguistics, this term refers to a family of languages spoken in the Japanese and Ryukyu Islands. However, here I use the term more generally to refer to culture and/or people from the Japanese Islands, often including some admixture of culture and/or people from the Korean Peninsula, especially in maritime areas. Prior to approximately the eleventh century, the peoples and cultures of the Ryukyu Islands were not Japonic (except, perhaps, in and around Gusuku). Waves of northern

immigrants arriving during the eleventh and twelfth centuries made the Ryukyu Islands culturally Japonic. Subsequent migrations of non-Japonic people (e.g., Mongols, Koreans, Alans) were not large enough to replace the Japonic base culture.

Ryukyu (琉球 J. Ryūkyū; Ch. Liúqiú): A term of convenience referring to the Ryukyu Islands as a geographic, cultural, or political entity. Geopolitical terminology for this region has been and remains complex. The term "Ryūkyū," especially, has undergone changes in meaning and reference over time. In old Chinese documents, Liúqiú often meant Taiwan, so care is required among historians when interpreting such material. For a thorough discussion of the geopolitical terminology of the region, see Smits (2019, 7–10).

omoro おもろ: Lowercase, italicized. There are a variety of terms for different types of ancient religious or folk songs (e.g., *kuena* or *niiri*), but genre details are beyond our scope. In these pages I use *omoro* as a generic term for ancient Ryukyuan songs, often of a religious nature. The individual songs in a collection like *Omoro sōshi* are *omoro*. Unfortunately, we know little or nothing about the sonic or melodic qualities of ancient *omoro*.

The Omoro: Another term for *Omoro sōshi* おもろさうし, a collection of *omoro* created by the royal court at Shuri, the first volume of which was published in the early 1530s.

Jōmon people 縄文人: Upper-Paleolithic people who migrated into the Japanese archipelago roughly fifteen thousand to sixteen thousand years ago. How and from where these people migrated is unclear. Recent DNA evidence indicates that a population of Jōmon people existed on the southern coast of Korea during the late Neolithic era, even though the present-day Korean population contains negligible Jōmon DNA (Robbeets et al. 2021, 619–620). Present-day mainland Japanese DNA includes approximately 10 percent Jōmon ancestry on average.

Yayoi people 弥生人: An ethnic group that migrated to the Japanese Islands via the Korean Peninsula roughly 3,300 years ago. The Yayoi were farmers based in the Liaodong-Shandong area before migrating to the Korean Peninsula and then to the Japanese Islands. Their arrival in the Japanese Islands triggered "a transition to full-scale farming, a genetic turn-over from J[ō]mon to Yayoi ancestry and a linguistic shift to Japonic" (Robbeets et al. 2021, 620). However, this transition took several centuries to play out fully. Present-day mainland Japanese DNA includes approximately 90 percent Yayoi ancestry on average. For residents of Okinawa and the southern Ryukyu Islands, it measures approximately 75–80 percent on average.

Book Layout

The chapters in this book proceed in roughly chronological order, although several are topical. Chapter 1 examines two approaches to early Ryukyuan history, the ancient branch model and the internal development model. It argues that the currently dominant internal development model is no longer adequate and that my proposed new approach, the external agents model, should replace it. Chapter 2 traces major maritime routes connecting the Ryukyu Islands with the East China Sea region. It covers a vast time span and emphasizes connections between the Ryukyu Islands, Korea, and Japan. Chapter 3 introduces relevant geographic features of the islands, examines the earliest-known human inhabitants, and provides a detailed account of the Shellmound era. The discussion brings a wide variety of evidence to bear on the dual structure hypothesis, significantly modifying it with respect to the Ryukyu Islands. Chapter 4 is a detailed account of the eleventh and twelfth centuries and the process by which the Ryukyu Islands became Japonic in terms of people and culture. Chapter 5 zooms out geographically to examine the details of regional trade during the early *gusuku* era. It features a hub-and-spoke model as a way of conceptualizing regional interactions.

Chapters 6 and 7 pause the chronology to examine two important topics rarely discussed in connection with early Ryukyuan history. Chapter 6 argues that Korea was the source of Ryukyu's sacred groves and the know-how for the construction of stone-walled fortresses (*gusuku*), among other forms of culture and technology. The Ryukyu Kingdom's official histories largely wrote Korea out of the story of early Ryukyu, and this book restores that omission. Chapter 7 takes up the question of whether and to what extent early Ryukyu was home to agricultural societies. (Because the Ryukyu Islands were not a single society at this time, I prefer to speak of "agricultural societies" in the plural.) Nearly all scholars writing about early Ryukyu assume that agricultural surpluses drove the process of state formation, but I and a few others argue that early Ryukyu was home to trading and raiding societies, not agricultural societies.

Chapter 8 examines the fourteenth and early fifteenth centuries, updating the hub-and-spoke model to reflect changed circumstances and explaining that political disruptions around the region sent people into the Ryukyu Islands.

Approx. Dates	Okinawa & Vicinity	Southern Ryukyu Islands	Japan	Korea	China
to 8,000 BCE	Paleolithic	Paleolithic	Early Jōmon, from ca. 12,000 BCE	Paleolithic	Pre-Han
7,000 BCE	Ealry Shellmound, ~7000 BC-300 BCE; Trade in shells etc., ~600 BCE-CE 1300; Late Shellmound, ~300 BCE-~CE 1050	Early Neolithic/ Shimotabaru ~2500-1500 BCE; GAP ~1500-800 BCE	Jōmon to ~300 BCE (overlap w/ Yayoi)		
5,000 BCE					
3,000 BCE					
2,000 BCE					
1,000 BCE			Yayoi, ~1000 BCE-CE 300	Ancient	
300 BCE		Late Neolithic ~800 BCE-CE 1100 (no pottery)			
CE 1				Three Kingdoms: Goguryeo, Baekje, Silla (57 BC-CE 935)	Han, 202 BCE-CE 220
CE 300			Kofun to 538		
CE 550			Asuka & Nara, 538-784		Sui & Tang, 581-907
CE 700					
CE 800					
CE 1000	Early gusuku era, ~1000-1250	Suku (Gusuku) era, ~1100-1500	Heian, 794-1185	Goryeo 918-1392	N & S Song, 960-1279
CE 1200					
CE 1300	Era of large *gusuku*		Kamakura & Muromachi, 1192-1573; N & S Courts, ~1335-1392 & later flare-ups		Yuan, 1271-1368
CE 1400	Sanzan (~1370s-1420s) & 1st Shō			Joseon 1392-1897	Ming, 1368-1644
CE 1450					
CE 1500	Kingdom & Empire (centralized state by ~1530)	Invasion of Yaeyama, 1500; Incorporation into Ryukyu empire, ~1500-1520; Okinawa Prefecture, 1879			
CE 1600	Early-modern Era (control by Satsuma); Okinawa Pref., 1879		Edo Period, 1603-1868		Qing, 1644-1911
CE 1700					
CE 1800					
CE 1900			Meiji, 1868-1912		

Figure I.1. Regional time line.

OFFICIAL REIGNS OF RYUKYUAN KINGS

BASED ON *GENEALOGY OF CHŪZAN* AND MING RECORDS (FOR SANNAN AND SANHOKU KINGS)

SHUNTEN LINE 舜天王統 (73 yrs)

Shunten 舜天
1187-1237 (51yrs / age 72*)

Shunbajunki 舜馬順凞
1238-1248 (11yrs / age 64)

Gihon 義本
1249-1259 (11yrs / age unstated)

EISO LINE 英祖王統 (90 yrs)

Eiso 英祖
1260-1299 (40 yrs / age 72)

Taisei 大成
1300-1308 (9 yrs / age 62)

Eiji 英慈
1309-1313 (5 yrs / age 46)

Tamagusuku 玉城
1314-1336 (22 yrs / age 41)

Sei'i 西威
1337-1349 (13 yrs / age 22)

SATTO LINE 察度王統 (56 yrs)

Satto 察度
1350-1395 (46 yrs / age 75)

Bunei 武寧
1396-1405 (10 yrs / age unstated)

SANNAN KINGS 山南王系 (~100 yrs)

Shōsatto 承察度
1337?-1396?

[Royal uncle] **Ōeiji[shi]** 汪英紫[氏]
1388-1402?

[Royal brother; king] **Ōōso** 汪應[応]祖
~1404-1414/1415

Tarumi (or Taromai) 他魯毎
1415?-1429

SANHOKU KINGS 山北王系 (~100 yrs)

Haniji 怕尼芝
1322?-1395?

Bin 珉
1396?-1400?

Han'anchi 攀安知
1401-1416

FIRST SHŌ DYNASTY 第一尚氏 (64 yrs)

Shō Shishō 尚思紹
1406-1421 (16 yrs / age unstated)

Shō Hashi 尚巴志
1422-1439 (18 yrs / age 68)

Shō Chū 尚忠
1440-1444 (5 yrs / age 50)

Shō Shitatsu 尚思達
1445-1449 (3 yrs / age 42)

Shō Kinpuku 尚金福
1450-1453 (4 years / age 56)

Shō Taikyū 尚泰久
1454-1460 (7 yrs / age 46)

Shō Toku 尚徳
1461-1469 (9 yrs / age 29)

2ND SHŌ DYNASTY 第二尚氏 (410 yrs)

Kanemaru 金丸 / **Shō En** 尚円
1470-1476 (7 yrs / age 62)

Shō Sen'i 尚宣威
1477 (6 months / age 48)

Shō Shin 尚真
1477-1526 (50 yrs / age 62)

Shō Sei 尚清
1527-1555 (29 yrs / age 59)

—*end of scope of this book*—

Remaining Kings: Shō Gen (1556-1572); Shō Ei (1573-1588); Shō Nei (1589-1620); Shō Hō (1621-1640); Shō Ken (1641-1647); Shō Shitsu (1648-1668); Shō Tei (1669-1709); Shō Eki (1710-1712); Shō Kei 1713-1751); Shō Boku (1752-1794); Shō On (1795-1802); Shō Sei (1803); Shō Kō (1804-1834); Shō Iku (1835-1847); Shō Tai (1848-1879)

* "age" = age at time of death

Figure I.2. Reigns of kings based on official sources.

Chapter 9 covers roughly the same time period and takes a close look at political geography, mostly on the island of Okinawa. It argues that local powers in Okinawa and elsewhere were not territorial states based on agriculture. Instead, they were maritime trading bases, with harbor-fortress pairs as the main political and economic units. With this point as background, chapter 10 presents a fundamentally new way of understanding the era of the so-called Three Principalities (Sanzan), circa the 1370s through the 1420s. Chapter 11 is a close look at the first Shō "dynasty." The era of the first Shō dynasty was similar in most important ways, I argue, to the Sanzan era, including the lack of a centralized state. One king, Shō Taikyū, successfully moved in the direction of creating a single state in Okinawa with his conquests of Nakagusuku and Katsuren in the 1450s. Building on this material, chapter 12 examines the process by which Shō Shin and Shō Sei created a centralized state and maritime empire, with Shuri as its strong center.

Chapter 13 brings the major points together to reinforce the main argument of this book: that people originating from outside the Ryukyu Islands were the main drivers of early Ryukyuan history. It examines the impact of the East China Sea region on the Ryukyu Islands, the impact of the Ryukyu Islands on the region, and the power of geography and the physical environment to shape historical development. The chapter, and the book as a whole, makes a strong argument for understanding early Ryukyuan history on its own terms, not as a late-developing small-scale replica of the Japanese Islands.

Time Line and List of Kings

For reference, figure I.1 is the overall periodization of the Ryukyu Islands and the major states in the region. When a more detailed time frame is required, it is provided in the relevant parts of the text.

Figure I.2 is a list of the names of the Okinawan kings and the reign dates typically assigned to them based on the official histories or Chinese records.

CHAPTER ONE

A New Model of Early Ryukyuan History

The currently dominant model of early Ryukyuan history dates from about 1980. I call it the internal development model. It was innovative in the 1980s, and it still works well for the early modern era and later. In my view, however, this model is no longer viable for early Ryukyu in light of a vast accumulation of archaeological evidence.

As one example, consider the small northern Ryukyu island of Kikaijima, just to the east of Amami-Ōshima. "Rethinking the Southern Islands from Amami's Archaeological Sites," read a July 31, 2006, headline in the *Yomiuri shinbun* newspaper about Kikaijima's newly excavated Gusuku Site Group (Gusuku Isekigun; hereafter referred to as Gusuku). That article, the first in a series of three, speculated that Kikaijima had once been the farthest extent of Dazaifu control.[1] The third article in the series noted that Gusuku might be the key to understanding the origins of the Ryukyu Kingdom (*Yomiuri shinbun* 2006.07.31, 08.02). Writing approximately a year later, journalist Itō Kazufumi used the term "Kikaijima shock." In his view the amazing finds at Gusuku undermined the dominant model of Ryukyuan history. That model emphasized the development of a kingdom from within Okinawa, largely independent of Japan. After that kingdom was in place, culture and political control flowed outward from Okinawa to various Ryukyu island peripheries. After the excavation of Gusuku, it became clear that Kikaijima, along with the northern Ryukyu Islands, laid the foundation for eventual state formation in Okinawa. Moreover, after the excavation of Gusuku it became clear that close connections with Japan and other countries of the region shaped the development of the ancient Ryukyu Islands (Tanigawa 2008, 8–12). The excavated ruins at Gusuku have undermined fundamental assumptions of the internal development model.

A Dearth of Conventional Historical Sources

Although Gusuku received widespread mass media attention, archaeologists had been uncovering important evidence regularly since the 1980s. This evidence is crucial for understanding the early history of the Ryukyu Islands, in part because of a lack of conventional historical documents from the time. There are some documents dating to the fifteenth century, but they are limited in scope. One is the diplomatic and trade correspondence preserved in *Precious Documents of Successive Generations (Rekidai hōan)*, initially produced and compiled by Chinese merchant-officials and later by their descendants at Kumemura in Naha. The documents in this collection cover the years 1424 to 1867. The other is the inscription on the 1458 Sea Bridge to the Many Countries Bell (Bankoku Shinryō no Kane).[2] Between 1497 and 1522, officials in Shō Shin's government erected eight major monuments, many of which praised Shō Shin's accomplishments (Smits 2019, 138–140). Neither the trade and diplomatic documents nor the monument inscriptions tell us much about the details of society or domestic government. Fortunately, several shipwrecked Koreans in the late fifteenth century wrote accounts of their time in the Ryukyu Islands, which shed useful light on social, technical, economic, cultural, and military matters.

It is common to speak of a "Ryukyu Kingdom" existing from the 1370s (or 1420s) onward, but this "kingdom" does not appear to have been a centralized bureaucracy until approximately the 1520s. The earliest extant domestic administrative document, at least at the time of this writing, is a writ of appointment (*jiresisho*) from 1523.[3] Approximately forty-six writs of appointment from the sixteenth century are still extant, a very small number of the total that must have been produced.[4] The other major written source from the early sixteenth century was the first volume of *Omoro sōshi*, a collection of songs circulating in oral traditions, edited and written down by the early 1530s. Like the monument inscriptions, many of these songs celebrate the greatness of Shō Shin. The monuments and the *Omoro* were products of the rise of Shuri as the center of a maritime empire. As such, they reinforce an Okinawa-centric or Shuri-centric view of early Ryukyuan history.[5] The previously mentioned Kikaijima shock, and other archaeological evidence discussed in this book, has belied the long-standing idea that Ryukyuan history and culture began in Okinawa.

Prior to the sixteenth century, it was Chinese merchant-officials residing in the Naha area who produced the official letters and other documents connected with commerce and diplomacy. Otherwise, there are no extant domestically produced written documents, the typical sources upon which historians rely. Therefore, the Ryukyuan past prior to the 1500s is mainly prehistory, corresponding to the Japanese term *senshi*. In these pages, however, I use "Ryukyuan history" or "early Ryukyuan history" for any segment of the islands' past.

There were myths, legends, and songs purporting to describe matters prior to the sixteenth century, and it is likely that some household records contain accurate accounts of pre–sixteenth century events. It was from myths, legends, and memories passed down orally within prominent households that the writers of the royal court's official histories (ca. 1650–1750) filled in some of the details for the twelfth through the fifteenth centuries. With respect to their coverage of the Ryukyu Islands' distant past, the official histories were, in their day, *secondary* accounts based on relatively weak sources. Moreover, the narratives and interpretations of the official histories were shaped by the strictures of classical Chinese historiography. As time went on, these secondary accounts aged to become the major *primary* source base that most modern scholars have used, and continue to use, for writing histories of early Ryukyu.[6]

The official histories claim that Shunten began his reign as Okinawa's first king in 1187. Shunten's purported father, Minamoto Tametomo, briefly ruled Okinawa as well. In other words, the official histories cover over four centuries of time for which, at least from today's vantage point, we have no domestically produced documents dealing with government administration or topics other than trade and its attendant diplomacy.[7] Even if we were to accept much of the narrative in the official histories as roughly accurate, coverage is sparse. Skeptical readings of these texts render that coverage even more thin. How have historians and other scholars dealt with this large gap in conventional historical documentation for early Ryukyu (figure 1.1)?

This gap has tended either to severely restrict what past historians have said about early Ryukyu or, more commonly, to encourage speculation and creativity. Consider someone in the 1960s writing a history of early Ryukyu. For such a scholar, it was almost impossible to advance strong arguments about the precise nature of early Ryukyuan society. A common approach was to summarize passages from the scholar's preferred sources, typically either the official histories or *Omoro sōshi,* sometimes supplemented by local legends or official folktales in collections such as *Legends from the Elders* (*Irō setsuden* 遺老説伝, compiled between 1743 and 1745). One possibility was simply to present legendary material with little or no comment. Such a move, of course, would typically imply historical veracity. Another possibility was to read against the grain or otherwise engage the material critically. In the latter case, however, it would have been difficult to make strong, positive conclusions about Ryukyu's distant past.

The social and political circumstances surrounding specific scholars, of course, also had an impact on the way they interpreted early Ryukyuan history. After the establishment of Okinawa Prefecture in 1879, for example, Iha Fuyū (1876–1947), Higashionna Kanjun (1882–1963), and others among the first generation of modern historians sought evidence that Ryukyuans were a branch of the larger Japanese family. As I noted throughout *Maritime Ryukyu,* they were

Sources for Early Ryukyuan History

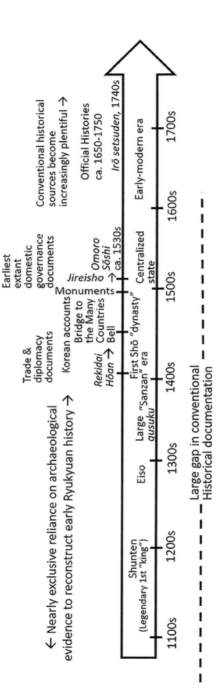

Figure 1.1. Major sources for early Ryukyuan history.

correct in a general way, even if certain specific claims, like the descent of ancient Okinawan kings from Minamoto Tametomo, lacked good evidence. During the period of direct U.S. Occupation and control of Okinawa and the southern Ryukyu Islands (1945–1972), many scholars pursued the task of placing Okinawa or Ryukyu firmly with the Japanese ethnos and nation with even greater urgency. By the 1980s, however, sociopolitical circumstances had shifted. With all the Ryukyu Islands securely within the Japanese state, a greater focus on Okinawan historical autonomy and distinctiveness became possible, leading to the internal development model.

Models of Ryukyuan History in Comparative Perspective

In this chapter I propose a new model of early Ryukyuan history, the external agents model. In subsequent chapters I demonstrate its usefulness. For this new model to make sense, however, some comparison with previous models is necessary. A comprehensive history of the writing of Ryukyuan history would require a book of its own, so my analysis here is brief. First, I explain the ancient branch model, which flourished circa the 1920s through the 1970s. Next, I explain the currently dominant internal development model, which dates from about 1980. The names for the various models and their conceptualization are my own, and I am not aware of any counterparts in the Japanese literature.

To facilitate clarity, I describe each model with respect to the same set of criteria. Below is a highly abbreviated summary, which I explain in the subsequent sections.

Ancient branch model (ca. 1920s–1970s)
Geographic origin: Japan/Okinawa
Focus: social development
Major change: primitive society to feudal society, ca. twelfth century; rise of *aji*
Major driving force: agricultural surpluses
Acknowledgment of external agents: yes
Role of geography and physical environment: minimal to moderate
Integration of other islands into the story: moderate
Integration of other states or territories into the story: moderate; China and Japan only
Centralized state established: early fifteenth century
Base culture: Japonic
Economic base: agriculture

Comparison with Japan: late developing, nearly identical society on a smaller scale

Big picture development trajectory: unbroken linear series of stages, unfolding naturally

Main intellectual framework: Marxist development stages

Role of warfare: moderate to extensive; frank acknowledgment

Sense of ethnic identity: local variety of the larger Japanese ethnos; stable and gradual

Sense of Ryukyu Islands: natural unit; subset of Japanese Islands

Internal development model (ca. 1980–present)

Geographic origin: Okinawa

Focus: political development

Major change: establishment of an autonomous kingdom

Major driving force: agricultural surpluses

Acknowledgment of external agents: minimal until kingdom established; material culture focus

Role of geography and physical environment: moderate

Integration of other islands into the story: minimal

Integration of other states or territories into the story: minimal; China and Japan

Centralized state established: early fifteenth century

Base culture: Japonic

Economic base: agriculture

Comparison with Japan: late developing, distinctive society (but with some tension regarding agriculture)

Big picture development trajectory: single line broken into stages; same population throughout

Main intellectual framework: the official histories with modification

Role of warfare: minimal

Sense of ethnic identity: related to Japanese ethnos but distinctively shaped by a separate history; stable and gradual

Sense of Ryukyu Islands: natural unit; independent of Japanese islands

External agents model (proposed replacement)

Geographic origin: Kikaijima and northern Ryukyu Islands

Focus: political development

Major change: Japonic (*gusuku*) era starting ca. eleventh century

Major driving force: trading and raiding; *wakō*

Acknowledgment of external agents: extensive
Role of geography and physical environment: strong
Integration of other islands into the story: extensive
Integration of other states or territories into the story: extensive; focus on Japan and Korea
Centralized state established: early sixteenth century
Base culture: Japonic
Economic base: trade
Comparison with Japan: different trajectory, distinctive society
Big picture development trajectory: discontinuities and periods of intense change and strife
Main intellectual framework: narrative derived from archaeology
Role of warfare: extensive
Sense of ethnic identity: unstable, variable
Sense of Ryukyu Islands: outer edge of East China Sea maritime region

Ancient Branch Model

If "Japan," however defined, is a tree, then the Ryukyu Islands constitute an ancient branch of that tree. The emphasis in the ancient branch model is on similarity. To continue the metaphor, a branch of a tree is of the same substance as the larger tree, even if the branch experiences somewhat different environmental conditions like more wind or greater exposure to the sun. Historians working in this model regard the early development of the Ryukyu Islands as mirroring that of Japan as a whole, but there is some room for environmentally induced local distinctiveness.

Geographic terminology is often awkward when writing about the Ryukyu Islands among these historians. In part because of the favorable overtones of the name "Okinawa Prefecture," combined with dislike for the U.S.-imposed name "The Ryukyus," scholars working in this model often lumped all the Ryukyu Islands together under the label "Okinawa." Nevertheless, often to a greater degree than more recent historians, scholars associated with this model paid some attention to events in Ryukyu islands other than Okinawa.

In this section I focus on the work of three representative ancient branch model scholars, Nakahara Zenchū (1890–1964), Inamura Kenpu (1894–1978), and Higa Shunchō (1883–1977).[8] All these scholars were eclectic in their background and careers and multidisciplinary in their approach to Ryukyuan history.

NAKAHARA ZENCHŪ

Nakahara worked extensively in mainland Japan and published books on world history, East Asian history, and Japanese history before turning his attention to Ryukyuan culture and history in the 1950s. His major work in this realm was *History of Ryukyu* (*Ryūkyū no rekishi*), intended as a textbook and published in two volumes in 1953 and 1954. Significantly, Nakahara followed up with *How to Think about Okinawan History* (*Okinawa rekishi no kangaekata*), which explains the ideas behind his textbook. Thoroughly at home with Marxist ideas of historical progress, Nakahara stressed the similarity between the development of Ryukyuan history and that of other parts of the world, especially mainland Japan. Nakahara (and Inamura) focused attention on the ordinary people who constituted society, not on real or putative royal reigns. In this sense Nakahara rejected the framework of the official histories.

Nakahara's bare-bones periodization and flow of history was the following:

Primitive Hunter-Gatherer Society (ca. 2000+ BP-third or fourth century)
Ancient Agricultural Society, or Time of Settlements (ca. fourth through eleventh centuries)
Medieval Early Feudal Society, or the Rise of *Aji*, through the Sanzan Era
Latter Feudal Society, or Era of the Kingdom, phases one, two, and three (three = after 1609)
Modern Society (1879–present)

Nakahara was aware that were we to privilege political power, then the periodization would be different (Nakahara 1969, 206). Importantly, Nakahara and all other scholars associated with the ancient branch model saw Okinawan or Ryukyuan history as a *long, unbroken continuum*. There were turning points and times of change, of course, but the people involved were all of the same Japan-derived ethnos from the primitive era to the present.

Nakahara explicitly considered whether Okinawan history developed based on an internal logic or as a result of external forces. He concluded that internal development was the dominant force but acknowledged that outside influences were strong at times (Nakahara 1969, 208).

As for sources, Nakahara stated that nothing is more important than the *Omoro sōshi*. Next in importance are castle/*gusuku* remains and local gazetteers, such as those compiled during the eighteenth and nineteenth centuries for the Miyako and Yaeyama Islands and Kumejima. Artistic works such as early *kumiodori* (an eighteenth-century dance and drama genre that drew on histori-cal events) can also be valuable sources. Significantly, Nakahara did not mention the official histories in his discussion of sources, although he occasionally referred to them (Nakahara 1969, 212).

Regarding the primitive period, based on the limited archaeological remains available at the time Nakahara wrote, he speculated that some kind of culture developed over two thousand years ago. Moreover, "it was of the same character as Japanese culture of the same era." In other words, ancient Oki-nawans were the same people as ancient mainland Japanese.[9] The only question was whether they came down from the north, as Iha Fuyū proposed, or up from the south, as Yanagita Kunio proposed.[10] In other words, the Ryukyu Islands might be the end segment of a north-to-south migration and settlement. Or the Ryukyu Islands might be the start of a south-to-north settlement of the Japanese Islands by ancient proto-Japanese migrating up from island Southeast Asia. Either scenario produced functionally the same result with respect to the relationship between Okinawa and mainland Japan (Nakahara 1969, 210–211).[11]

Looking at ancient Japanese history, Nakahara stressed the importance of iron from the continent, in the form of weapons, agricultural implements, and other tools, as the key to state formation in the Yamato area and in northern Kyushu. Nakahara noted that until the rise of warriors in the eleventh century, the Japanese state was loosely defined, and it sometimes suffered invasions. In this context it was only natural for the Yamato state and its successors in Japan not to incorporate small island groups. The Ryukyu Islands therefore did not become Japan's political territory, even though they were culturally and ethni-cally the same (Nakahara 1969, 211–212).

As they did in Japan, warrior leaders came to the fore in Okinawa at approxi-mately the same time, the twelfth century. In the Okinawan context, they were known as *aji*. The importation of iron tools resulted in agricultural surpluses and a population increase. Border conflicts within and between villages were one result of this larger population. The *aji* imposed order and presided over pieces of territory. In this way Okinawa became a feudal society, and we can trace the ori-gins of that society in local songs (*omoro*) and legends. Warriors formed groups under the *aji*, and they waged war with other communities. On the one hand, these warrior bands gave rise to an environment of constant battles over terri-tory. However, because they increased cultivation, communication, and the exchange of material resources, warrior bands also improved and solidified soci-ety. During the early decades of the Ryukyu Kingdom (ca. 1400), warfare sprang up like bamboo shoots after a rainfall. The root causes of this warfare were increases in production and changes to the social structure. Trade with China and goods imported from there added to the intensity of this warfare (Nakahara 1969, 212–222).

The fourteenth century was a time of great change and upheaval in the social structure and culture in Okinawa. This change reflected some of the developments in Muromachi-era Japanese society. Indeed, it is clear that the foundation of Okinawan material culture, such as clothing and dwellings, coalesced at this time, influenced by Muromachi culture. Politically, Shō Hashi unified Okinawa in 1406, and Shō Shin conquered all the way to Yaeyama and Hateruma starting in 1500. These kings accomplished what Japan had already achieved a thousand years earlier, with the advent of wet rice agriculture and iron tools. Why was Okinawa so late? Simply stated, because of geography: "It was way over there." Interestingly, Nakahara regarded the First Shō dynasty as a kingdom in name only and more akin to *aji*-dominated (early feudal) society. He saw the Second Shō dynasty as marking the start of mature feudal society (Nakahara 1969, 212–223).

With respect to people in ancient Okinawan history, Nakahara firmly rejected the Tametomo legend and claimed that Iha Fuyū, an initial advocate of it, later changed his mind. Nakahara also rejected the existence of the legendary figure Tenson, as well as Shunten's line of kings, noting that, among other things, the name "Shunten" really means *suiden* (wet fields) and that no such ruler's name appears in the *Omoro*. Among those traditionally regarded as early kings, Eiso was the first to actually exist. However, Eiso was ruler of the Urasoe area, not all of Okinawa. Perceptively, Nakahara (1969, 219–221) pointed out that the title "king" can be misleading because it is of Chinese origin and appears only in documents connected with trade and diplomacy.

Although he labored without the benefit of significant archaeological evidence, Nakahara's understanding of early history contains many insights. He identified a major change circa the twelfth century in connection with the appearance of warriors and *aji*. He even noted that many people crossed over to Okinawa from Japan at this time (Nakahara 1969, 212). In other words, Nakahara identified what archaeologists would now call the *gusuku* era. Only in the twenty-first century have scholars come to understand how radical a break with the past was the *gusuku* era. Nakahara also sensed that Shō Hashi was a king in name only, not the head of a centralized state. Nevertheless, Nakahara stated that Hashi united Okinawa in 1406. Finally, I highlight Nakahara's recognition that warfare was endemic to Okinawa starting in about the twelfth century. While archaeological and other evidence has confirmed this point many times over, the currently dominant internal development model minimizes the role of warfare. In the Anglophone world, especially, the myth of Ryukyuan pacifism remains strong (Smits 2010a, 2010b). Nakahara, however, had no such illusions.

INAMURA KENPU

A native of Miyako Island, Inamura Kenpu was a remarkable scholar. Among his several books is a 1957 monograph discussing the widespread evidence for the presence of *wakō* in early Ryukyuan history (Inamura 1957). Like Nakahara, Inamura focused on the lives and history of ordinary people. Here I concentrate on his 1969 book, *Research on* Makyo, *Ancient Okinawan Hamlets* (*Okinawa no kodai buraku makyo no kenkyū*). Although it is mainly a work of anthropology and folklore, Inamura frequently discussed his fieldwork in relationship to early Ryukyuan history.

Inamura's sense of the periodization of early Ryukyuan history was similar to that of Nakahara. Similarly, Inamura regarded the Ryukyu Islands and their people as having derived from the Japanese mainland. In the introduction he speculated that as far back as two thousand years ago, seafaring bands from northern Kyushu arrived at the Ryukyu Islands. Such travel and migrations continued, and from the medieval era onward, a north–south separation gradually developed (Inamura 1969, preface).

Inamura imagined a primitive past that included elements of Nakahara's Primitive Hunter-Gatherer Society (or Time of Settlements). The generic name for ancient settlements or villages in Okinawa is *makyo* or *kyoda*. They were founded by people sailing into the Ryukyu Islands from mainland Japan. The basic structure of *makyo* came from mainland Japan. However, mainland Japan was an agricultural society, whereas Okinawa, by necessity, was mainly a hunter-gatherer society, a significant difference. Because agriculture was, at most, a modest supplement to hunting and gathering, it was impossible to store up surpluses as a buffer against disasters, and the population remained small (Inamura 1969, 116–117). Notice that on this point Inamura recognized the power of the physical environment to modify lifestyles.

According to Inamura, the earliest social organizations in the Ryukyu Islands were consanguine communities of Japanese people. Although these communities often engaged in agriculture, they lacked iron tools and therefore supported themselves mainly by hunting and fishing. Population levels in such a society remain low in the absence of agricultural surpluses. During the thirteenth century, powerful local rulers known as *aji* established iron foundries at their fortresses, manufactured weapons and agricultural tools, distributed the tools to local communities, and created power centers based on agricultural surpluses. It was a significant new level of social organization that involved relocating or repositioning communities for ideal agricultural production.

Inamura sometimes referred to the thirteenth century as the agricultural era (*nōkō jidai*) or as a medieval agricultural society (*chūsei nōkō shakai*). Eiso, the earliest-known ruler to appear in *Omoro sōshi* songs, was probably a typical example of these new agriculture-based local lords. One type of evidence Inamura adduced is the ruins of seven iron forges that were known at the time he was writing. He also reasoned that insofar as *aji* existed, only agricultural societies could have supported them and their fortresses (Inamura 1969, 64–65, 72–73, 80, 84, 116–117, 165–166, 243–244, 254–272). Notice that like Nakahara, Inamura saw agricultural surpluses as the economic foundation, or force, that led to major change in early Ryukyuan society.

Regarding the overall geographic flow, for Inamura it was from north to south. For example, he pointed out that the northernmost part of the island is where people from Japan would have first arrived in Okinawa. The Amamikyo legend, in which the deity first established a sacred grove at Cape Hedo in the far north of Okinawa, probably reflects this situation (Inamura 1969, 309).

Recall that Nakahara emphasized internal development as the main driver of Ryukyuan history but acknowledged the influence of outside forces. Inamura gave greater weight to outside forces, albeit all from mainland Japan. He emphasized the rise of warriors after the Kamakura era and the importance of *wakō* in the development of Japan and the Ryukyu Islands. *Wakō* were the post-Kamakura pioneers of Japan's expansion and progress. Within the region, *wakō* stimulated development much as the invasions of Germanic tribes stimulated Europe's development (Inamura 1969, 470–472). Compared to Nakahara, Inamura appeared uninterested in fitting Okinawa or the Ryukyu Islands into a universal framework of historical development. Therefore, Inamura more frequently described distinctive characteristics of the culture and society that developed in the Ryukyu Islands, albeit within a broader Japonic framework.

Higa Shunchō

A native of Okinawa with aristocratic ancestry, Higa Shunchō worked as a teacher, journalist, and publisher. He was active in a variety of academic and political groups and published *History of Okinawa* in 1959 (revised editions were released in 1965 and 1970). The discussion here is based on the 1965 Okinawa Taimusu Sha edition.

Like Nakahara and Inamura, Higa saw Okinawan history as one long, unbroken line extending to the present: "We do not know when the first Okinawans, the ancestors of our ancestors, broke away from their ethnic brethren who had settled into the Japanese mainland. However, there is no doubt that these Ryukyu islands were well suited to their lifestyle at that time. Moreover, their coming to live in the Ryukyu islands initiated Okinawan history and determined the fate of we Okinawans, their descendants" (Higa Shunchō 1971, 1).

Like many scholars of his generation, Higa held to a strong sense of Okinawan identity while also claiming full membership in the larger Japanese national family. Just as Okinawans are part of the Japanese ethnos, the Ryukyu Islands are part of the Japanese Islands (Higa Shunchō 1971, 3).

Higa assumed, as did many scholars who matured during the prewar era, that the origins of those who became Japanese were mixed.[12] He speculated that people traveled to the Japanese Islands from the Asian continent, especially via Korea, as well as from southerly locations. They all mixed together during the Stone Age to create the "Japanese race" roughly four thousand to two thousand years before the common era. Japanese culture began to develop rapidly about two centuries before the common era, thanks to continental influence and technologies. Higa believed that as a subset of larger Japanese history, Okinawan origins followed a similar time line and trajectory. To support this conjecture, he noted that Chinese knife coins had been excavated at Gusukudake Shellmound (ca. second century BCE). In other words, continental influence reached as far as Okinawa while at the same time helping to transform all the Japanese Islands. Higa Shunchō (1971, 7–9) also noted that other Shellmound sites were being excavated and that the results of that work would provide many details about the earliest human settlements in Okinawa.

Despite the relative dearth of archaeological data, Higa creatively speculated in some detail about the nature of ancient Shellmound-era society, culture, and lifestyles. For example, he posited a society organized into kinship groups (*ketsuzoku shūdan*), which sometimes traded with each other. This relatively primitive lifestyle ended approximately during the twelfth century with the advent of agriculture. Agriculture both increased population levels and led Okinawan society to advance culturally. Society also became more complex, although the exact causal sequence is unclear in Higa's account. Nakahara, for example, posited that a greater quantity of iron tools resulted in better harvests, which increased the population. This increase led to boundary and other disputes. *Aji*, warriors, and warfare arose in this context.[13] In Higa's conception, the process was more orderly. As agriculture advanced, society adjusted—for example, by assigning cultivation allotments to each household (Higa Shunchō 1971, 15–18).

Nakahara, Inamura, and Higa all associated social development and increases in social complexity with agricultural surpluses. From about the twelfth century onward, the Ryukyu Islands were home to agricultural societies. Moreover, in their view the development of agricultural societies after the introduction of agriculture was a universal process. In Okinawa, Higa Shunchō (1971, 18) said, "the promotion and advancement of agriculture proceeded along the same course as agricultural societies in other countries." The idea that agriculture, once started, inevitably transforms society and leads to a society whose economic base is agriculture (i.e., an agricultural society) remains prominent to this day among historians of the Ryukyu Islands.

For Higa, agriculture caused social organization to shift from kinship groups to geographic groups (*chien shūdan*), ushering in an era of hamlets. Higa's description of society at this time included a relatively brief, idyllic age in the distant past, when agriculture improved everyone's lives but had yet to create a complex society. During the era of hamlets, all villagers cooperated, and "there were not yet any differences in wealth among the villagers, nor distinctions between governors and governed" (Higa Shunchō 1971, 20).

This placid society changed with the rise of *aji* and their fortresses, known as *gusuku*. The *aji* era began sometime between the tenth and twelfth centuries (Higa Shunchō 1971, 21, 50). In discussing stone-walled *gusuku*, Higa speculated that they were built between the eleventh and fourteenth century. These *gusuku* functioned as the abodes of *aji*.[14] During the hamlet era, each settlement was a self-contained society, and there was little contact between them. Higa speculated that as time went on, however, the population of each hamlet increased and began to compete for resources. Warfare broke out and some hamlets became wealthy and strong, whereas others became poor and weak. Warfare settled the differences between them and military leaders emerged. Powerful hamlets conquered the weak ones and imposed labor services and taxes on them. These labor services and taxes provided the means to build stone-walled *gusuku*. Clashes between *aji* had the power to alter society (Higa Shunchō 1971, 21–23, 46).

Inamura (1957) provided extensive anthropological and other evidence to argue that *wakō* inhabited the Ryukyu Islands during approximately the thirteenth through fifteenth centuries. Higa avoided the term *wakō* but noted a large overlap between *aji* and seafarers engaged in trade. Stating that trade with entities in Japan became common during the *aji* era, Higa proposed island-to-island and port-to-port exchanges between Ryukyu Islanders and harbors in Kyushu. The trade in palm fronds (*birō* or *kuba*) was one example. In this context Higa provided a long list of harbor-fortress pairs. (I will argue that harbor-fortress pairs were the main political unit in the Ryukyu Islands well into the fifteenth century.) According to Higa, some of the adventurous seafarers of this era later became *aji,* but for the most part, the seafarers remained under the control of the *aji.* These seafarers stimulated internal productivity and set the stage for cultural advances by sailing off to procure unusual items and new technologies. Thereby, they contributed to the improvement of lifestyles and the advancement of society (Higa Shunchō 1971, 27–29). Notice that although Higa attributed the rise of *aji* to agricultural surpluses, he gave considerable weight to trade as a force for social change.

In contrast with Nakahara, Higa tended to give the official histories greater credence and regard them as basically accurate regarding early historical figures. For example, Higa argued that "King Shunten" was a real person who controlled a portion of central and southern Okinawa. Higa disagreed to some extent with the official histories' Chūzan-centric accounts, which were based on the assumption that all Okinawa had been under a single ruler since the time of Shunten. His view of the Three Principalities era was also slightly at odds with the official histories. Higa stated that warfare during this era started as a result of the Ōzato *aji* (in the south) and Nakijin *aji* (in the north) becoming especially powerful and seeking to conquer other territories. The names Chūzan, Hokuzan, and Nanzan, Higa noted, were made up by Chinese officials. At the actual time of conflict, those names did not exist. Higa agreed with the conventional view of the Three Principalities as territorial states. However, he believed they had developed internally from local power bases that later expanded. They were not the remnants or pieces of an Okinawa-wide kingdom that broke apart, as the official histories claim. Moreover, it was the tribute trade with China that fueled the warfare of the Three Principalities era (Higa Shunchō 1971, 42–43, 71).

Summary

Naturally, the historians working within the ancient branch model did not agree on everything, and in the paragraphs above I noted some differences in interpretation or emphasis. Despite differences in emphasis regarding Ryukyuan distinctiveness, all three scholars featured here argued strongly that the Ryukyu Islands and their people were part of the larger Japanese national family—in essence an ancient branch of the Japanese tree. With respect to early Ryukyu, they focused on social development, not political history. The main driving force for social development was agricultural surpluses, although Higa also gave considerable weight to harbor-based trade. The three historians differ in the extent to which they focus on internal development versus external agents or forces. All of them acknowledge the importance of external agents, and those agents came exclusively from mainland Japan. The tribute trade with China was a background factor against which local warfare took place. Korea played no role in their narratives. Although all three focused on the island of Okinawa and often used the terms "Ryukyu" and "Okinawa" interchangeably, their accounts included extensive discussion of other islands.[15] One of the few commonalities in all three models is that the base culture of the Ryukyu Islands was and is Japonic. This point was strongly emphasized among scholars working in the ancient branch model.

In part because they constituted a branch on the Japanese tree, all three scholars believed the Ryukyu Islands developed in a manner similar to that of mainland Japan. For Nakahara, who also emphasized universal historical development in a Marxist mode, the developmental trajectory was nearly identical. For Inamura, by contrast, local environmental factors were sufficiently strong to place Okinawan society on a somewhat different developmental track. Higa's view of Ryukyuan distinctiveness fell in between those of Nakahara and Inamura. Although Nakahara and Higa sought to minimize the time lag vis-à-vis the mainland, once they got into the details it became clear that agricultural societies within the Ryukyu Islands developed at the time of the appearance of *aji* or slightly earlier. Okinawa may have developed exactly as did mainland Japan (according to Nakahara), but it did so much later. Significantly, all three scholars identified a major transformation of society occurring from the eleventh to thirteenth century. Without the benefit of archaeology, they had identified what today would be called the *gusuku* era.

As I explain in detail, the *gusuku* era was an even greater transformation than anyone working in the ancient branch model could have imagined. It was the *start* of Japonic Ryukyu, not an internal change within a longer Japonic history. For the scholars working in the ancient branch model, and even for many people today, "Okinawans" or "Ryukyuans" were the people who had always inhabited the Ryukyu Islands. Moreover, these Ryukyuans were Japonic in terms of ethnicity and culture. However, we now know that the *gusuku* era was a major discontinuity, marking a transition from non-Japonic inhabitants of the Ryukyu Islands to (mostly) Japonic inhabitants. This ethnic discontinuity contrasts with the views of all three scholars featured here, who assumed that stable "Ryukyuan" or "Okinawan" identities had persisted since the beginning of human habitation of the islands. Although they acknowledged Shuri's conquest of other islands, all three scholars regarded the Ryukyu Islands as essentially a single entity sharing much in common in terms of culture and ethnicity.

One important feature of Nakahara's and Higa's narratives is a frank acknowledgment of and engagement with warfare. Similarly, Inamura noted that regional strife resulted in a massive *wakō* presence in the Ryukyu Islands. The acknowledgment of warfare, and social strife more generally, makes sense in the context of Ryukyu as a late-developing small-scale version of mainland Japan and in the context of Marxist historiography. More broadly, and in contrast to the European-derived myth of Ryukyuan pacifism, these scholars' recognition of warfare indicates that they did not regard the Ryukyu Islands as exceptional. For all three, the motivation and behavior of people in the Ryukyu Islands and the societies they created were fundamentally similar to their counterparts elsewhere in the world.

Internal Development Model

Returning to the tree metaphor, for historians working in the internal development model the Ryukyu Islands did not constitute a branch of the Japanese tree. Instead, a seed from that tree blew or drifted into southern Okinawa. There it took root, slowly grew, and eventually flourished, becoming its own fully grown tree in the form of the Ryukyu Kingdom. In this model, although early Ryukyuans were related to mainland Japanese in some important sense, the two places developed along different historical trajectories. Whereas the ancient branch model stressed similarity with Japan while acknowledging some Ryukyuan distinctiveness, the internal development model stresses Ryukyuan distinctiveness while acknowledging some similarity with Japan.[16]

The internal development model celebrates the emergence of the Ryukyu Kingdom as an impressive achievement, in which today's Okinawans should take pride. Okinawans created the kingdom themselves, and they became the literal or figurative ancestors of many people residing in Okinawa today. There is, however, a problem with trying to combine a distinctive early history with the assertion that the Ryukyu Kingdom was the sole creation of Okinawans. The essence of that problem is agriculture. If the Ryukyu Kingdom had been built upon profits from trade, then by definition not only Okinawans but a vast network of trading partners from Korea and Japan in the North to island Southeast Asia in the south, as well as other Ryukyu Islands, would have built it. Therefore, a foundational claim for those working in this model is that agricultural surpluses powered increasing social complexity, culminating in the development of a kingdom. Trade was a secondary factor. However, after the kingdom became established, usually circa the 1420s in this model, the focus shifts to the kingdom's wide-ranging trading activities. Indeed, that is precisely what was so impressive about the early kingdom. It was built on a small island in the East China Sea with poor soil by the residents of those islands. Then, via trade, it became a hub or cornerstone for the East China Sea region.

Let us assume that Okinawa, or the Ryukyu Islands as a whole, became an agricultural society during the eleventh or twelfth century—precisely the claim of scholars working in this model. Moreover, a centralized bureaucratic state developed from within this agricultural society several centuries later. It is a narrative very similar to the rise of the Yamato state and Japan's imperial court but on a smaller scale and roughly seven centuries later. In other words, Okinawa or Ryukyu was, in the big picture, a late-developing, small-scale replica of Japan—essentially the same claim many scholars made while working in the ancient branch model.

It was precisely for this reason that Asato Susumu, whose early work scholars frequently cite to support the claim that early Ryukyu was an agricultural society, changed his mind. According to Asato (2010, 19), "The *aji* of the *gusuku* era and the economic foundation of the ancient Ryukyu kingdom were not the result of agricultural harvests but an accumulation of wealth from maritime trade." Moreover, "We should not use Japan, an agricultural society, as a standard by which to measure Okinawa, a society powered by trade, not by increases in agricultural productivity." Asato remains very much in the spirit of the internal development model, but he has had to reject one of its basic tenets. The tension between the claims made about agriculture for initial state development versus the focus on trade after the emergence of a centralized state remains a problem for this model.

Origins

Changing sociopolitical circumstances after 1972 set the stage for a reevaluation of Ryukyu's distant past. Consider the image of fifteenth-century Okinawa as an autonomous trade hub, which is prominent in the internal development model. Now consider the slogan on automobile license plates during most of the era of U.S. military control: "Keystone of the Pacific." It is hardly surprising that historians writing before 1972 would avoid portraying Okinawa or the Ryukyu Islands in precisely the way that U.S. officials did. However, a generation of historians during the 1980s and 1990s appropriated the keystone metaphor and reworked it to highlight the achievements of Okinawans far back into the past.

Visitors to Okinawa today are bombarded with images of a colorful, glorious Ryukyu Kingdom. In this context it is easy to forget that such images are quite new. For example, as a young scholar in the mid-1980s, I was struck by how many people outside of academic circles with whom I chatted in Okinawa (e.g., taxi drivers, shop clerks) expressed apparently genuine surprise that a sophisticated kingdom had once existed on the island. After all, much of that kingdom's physical infrastructure still lay in ruins at that time, and local history had rarely if ever been taught in schools. Though many of its tenets are common today, the internal development model was new and exciting in the 1980s. It not only provided a framework for excellent historical scholarship but also began to influence mass media portrayals of Ryukyu's distant past.

Two prominent early books that, in retrospect, initiated the internal development model were Takara Kurayoshi's (1980) *The Era of Ryukyu: In Search of the Big Historical Picture* (*Ryūkyū no jidai: Ōinaru rekishizō o megutte*) and Araki Moriaki's (1980) *New Okinawan History* (*Shin, Okinawa-shi ron*), a collection of previously published essays. Thanks in part to a compelling writing style, Takara's book became especially famous and influential. Takara also became a public intellectual, often appearing in interviews, documentaries, and films.[17] An explosion of scholarship in premodern Ryukyuan history occurred during the 1980s and beyond, much of it informed by the approaches and arguments of Takara and Araki.

Much of this scholarship focused on the early modern era, a time for which conventional documentary evidence is readily available. Because of the strong focus on the kingdom among internal development model historians, those who worked on topics prior to the early modern era typically focused on the fifteenth and sixteenth centuries.[18] Takara, for example, became known as the foremost analyst of writs of appointment (*jireisho*), the earliest genre of domestic government documents (Takara 1987a, 1987b). Another prominent historian, Dana Masayuki, specialized in household records (*kafu*). Although these records often purport to cover fifteenth-or sixteenth-century material, they were created during the early modern era. Therefore, most of Dana's work has focused on the early modern creation of Ryukyu's deeper past at the level of elite households, up to and including the royal family (Dana 1992). He has also worked on sixteenth-century monument inscriptions (Dana 2008). Tomiyama Kazuyuki, although mainly a historian of the early modern era, has effectively triangulated between Chinese and Korean documents and the earliest-known versions of royal rituals to contextualize changes in the nature of the royal government and to analyze relations with other countries (Tomiyama 1991; 2003; 2004, 1–110). More recently, Yano Misako has written a history of the royal government and royal power during the late fifteenth and sixteenth centuries using the official histories supplemented by other written sources such as writs of appointment and monument inscriptions (Yano 2014).

Perhaps scholars such as Takara, Dana, and Tomiyama and the many other historians working in the internal development model have exerted the most influence via the several general histories they have written collaboratively. These works, and indeed all general histories of Okinawa or Ryukyu from the 1980s onward, typically adopt a modified version of the narrative found in the official histories when covering time periods prior to the sixteenth century. The general focus in the coverage of early Ryukyu is contextualizing the rise of the kingdom.

Most scholars writing in the internal development model are professionally trained historians. They tend not to stray very far into other academic disciplines, such as literary studies or archaeology. Therefore, they tend to make sparse use of the *Omoro sōshi,* a text that has become the primary domain of literary scholars and linguists. One exception has been Asato Susumu, who has formal training in both history and archaeology. Much of his work is therefore directly relevant to this book (e.g., Asato 2010; Asato and Doi 2011). Asato has been a steadfast supporter of the idea that the official histories are accurate descriptions of early Ryukyu, even to the point of asserting that Eiso literally ruled over all the island of Okinawa (Asato [2006] 2010). Mainly for this reason, many of my conclusions differ from his. One important area of agreement, as we will see, is Asato's rejection of the idea that state formation in the Ryukyu Islands was based on agriculture.

Murai Shōsuke has written extensively about the Ryukyu Islands in the context of maritime history and interactions between the different regions of the East China Sea. His work, along with that of maritime historian Tanaka Takeo, informed *Maritime Ryukyu,* especially with respect to the role of *wakō.* Murai's work fits into the internal development model in many respects. However, his work tends to focus on how people, events, and culture outside the Ryukyu Islands affected early Ryukyuan history (e.g., Murai 2019). Therefore, in some respects Murai's work fits into the external agents model.

SUMMARY OF MAIN POINTS

Although Japan provided the seed population, the main geographic origin of Ryukyu in this model is the island of Okinawa. The focus is on political history, and the major change or turning point in society was the establishment of a kingdom in the early fifteenth century. The arrival of agriculture in the eleventh century and the rise of local rulers soon thereafter were important precursors of the kingdom. Despite a tendency to minimize the coercive power of the kingdom, it nevertheless conquered and ruled over the rest of the Ryukyu Islands. Therefore, the role of people outside the island of Okinawa in the narrative is minimal. While some writers highlight the impact of outside culture on early Ryukyu, their discussion is typically limited to material culture such as pottery or stone axes. The possible movement and migration of large groups of people are rarely if ever discussed.

Southern Okinawa is the origin point of Ryukyuan culture and society in the internal development model. The model readily acknowledges, and even celebrates, international trade, but typically only after the establishment of the kingdom or at least small kingdom-like states during the Three Principalities era. As noted above, there is a tension inherent in the claim that agriculture built the kingdom. On the one hand, the claim is necessary for the emphasis on internal development to ring true. Moreover, given the tendency to assume that agriculture is so powerful that its introduction leads to agricultural societies, the claim seems reasonable on the surface. On the other hand, however, an island kingdom built from agriculture can end up looking much like a small-scale, late-developing version of the Japanese Islands.

Like the ancient branch model, the internal development model tends to see the development of Ryukyuan history as a long, continuous, single line. In other words, people who lived in Okinawa during the Shellmound era were ancestors of *gusuku*-era Okinawans. However, vast archaeological and other evidence accumulated since the 1990s indicates that massive migration into the Ryukyu Islands occurred during the *gusuku* era, especially during its first century or so. It is now common, therefore, for general histories otherwise written in the spirit of the internal development model to acknowledge this point, although often only minimally. For example, a 2010 textbook for high school students says the following about the *gusuku* era: "For the most part this era corresponds temporally to the late Heian period through the early Muromachi period. Along with the rise of warrior authority [in Japan], for some reason (*nanraka no riyū de*), it is thought that many people migrated [into Okinawa] from the areas of Kyushu and the Amami islands" (Arashiro 2010, 40). This minimalist description of *gusuku*-era migrations, in a book that devotes over six pages to Paleolithic Minatogawa people, reflects an attempt to minimize discontinuities in the development of Ryukyuan history, particularly with respect to the human population.

The main source base that frames the narrative of early Ryukyuan history in the internal development model is the official histories. The general Shuri-centric focus of these works and their tendency to glorify the Ryukyu Kingdom fit well with the overall project of the internal development model. The official histories do not all agree with each other about the details of the narrative, leaving room for comparative discussion and differences of interpretation by modern scholars. However, the broad framework of modern narratives usually corresponds closely with that of *Reflections on Chūzan* (1650) and the two versions of *Genealogy of Chūzan* (1701 and 1725).

Scholars writing histories in the ancient branch model often made use of songs in the *Omoro sōshi* and other collections, as well as various sources from literature, folklore, and related fields. However, those working in the internal development model are usually formally trained academics who follow the protocols of professional historians. In the context of academic professionalization, texts such as the *Omoro sōshi* have become the province of literary scholars and linguists. Likewise, excavations of *gusuku* sites are now typically the province of professional archaeologists. (By contrast, recall that Nakahara specifically recommended the *Omoro* and *gusuku* sites as the best sources for Okinawan history.) Among other things, the internal development model reflects disciplinary specialization in modern academia.

All historians working in the internal development model recognize warfare in early Ryukyuan history, especially during the Three Principalities era and at crucial turning points. Nevertheless, compared with scholars working in the ancient branch model, discussion of warfare is usually infrequent and perfunctory. One reason may be the preferred source base. In general the official histories present, or try to present, a relatively smooth narrative of early Ryukyuan history that minimizes violence. Many *Omoro* songs, by contrast, celebrate violence and warfare. The myth of Ryukyuan pacificism is of European origin and is especially strong in Anglophone circles. However, the notion that the Ryukyu Islands were relatively peaceful, at least compared with mainland Japan, has also been prominent among many Japanese scholars.[19]

Finally, those working in the internal development model tend to regard "Okinawan" or "Ryukyuan" ethnicity as a stable entity that has developed and persisted over a vast span of time, reaching back at least into the Shellmound era. Similarly, they tend to regard the Ryukyu Islands as a natural, relatively homogenous cultural entity. In this context, conflict between islands tends to be minimized, and the island of Okinawa often stands in for the Ryukyu Islands as a whole.

External Agents Model

At almost the same time that the internal development model was gaining strength among historians, archaeologists began to unearth evidence that told a different story. The 1983 discovery of the first *kamuiyaki* kilns in Tokunoshima was an early indication that Ryukyuan history did not begin in Okinawa. *Kamuiyaki* is gray stoneware produced using technology that originated in the Korean Peninsula (figure 1.2).[20] By 2008, over one hundred kilns had been discovered in Tokunoshima, and *kamuiyaki* had been excavated from sites in western Kyushu and throughout all the Ryukyu Islands. The production of *kamuiyaki* dates from the eleventh century, a time when Gusuku was a thriving international trade center. Soapstone (steatite) cauldrons (*kasseki-sei ishinabe*) produced in the Nagasaki area, Chinese and Korean trade ceramics, and much other physical evidence began to show that the Ryukyu Islands, especially the northern Ryukyu

Figure 1.2. Gray stoneware (*kamuiyaki*) pot. *Source:* Yamazaki
2012, 144. Photo by Ikeda Yoshifumi.

Islands, were linked into regional and international networks centuries before
the emergence of a kingdom in Okinawa.

Excavated objects such as pottery, iron tools, weapons, iron slag and bellows
parts, ship anchors, human bones, and much more have provided concrete data
about ancient Ryukyu. Archaeological evidence is now of sufficient quantity and
quality to inform a detailed narrative of Ryukyu's early past. The broad outline of
this narrative differs significantly from the metanarrative for early Ryukyu in
the internal development model. Therefore, I argue that the time has come for a
new model of early Ryukyuan history and a new metanarrative.

Since the first decade of this century, Tanigawa Ken'ichi (1921–2013) and a
variety of other Japanese scholars have conducted innovative interdisciplinary
work foregrounding the role of external actors in early Ryukyuan history. Mark
Hudson, a multidisciplinary archaeologist writing in English, has been doing
similar work. Combining data from genetics, linguistics, and archaeology,
Hudson and his colleagues have provided important insights into the movement
of people and languages into the ancient Ryukyu Islands (Hudson 2020, 2022;
Robbeets et al. 2021). Similarly, archaeologist Richard Pearson's *Ancient Ryukyu*
is a thorough examination of early Ryukyu "from the point of view of the people
and things that came to them from outside." Pearson (2013, 4) describes "maritime communities, linked to each other and to adjacent land masses in variable
and constantly changing configurations." In that volume, Pearson highlights the
findings of many Japanese colleagues and provides extensive evidence that the
Ryukyu Islands were part of larger regional networks well before there was a
kingdom.

Historians working in the internal development model typically acknowledge a role for outside material culture in the early development of the Ryukyu Islands, with an emphasis on iron imported from Japan. While the external agents model is similarly concerned with material culture, it places a greater focus on people. Acknowledging the dynamic nature of populations in the Ryukyu Islands, the model seeks to determine who migrated to and resided in the Ryukyu Islands at what times and why.

Recall Inamura's (1957; 1969, esp. 470–472) argument that seafarers and *wakō* played a major role in the early history of the Ryukyu Islands. Drawing on Inamura and more recent work by Tanigawa, Fuku Hiromi, Yoshinari Naoki, and others, in *Maritime Ryukyu* I advanced a strong argument that *wakō* were the main drivers of early Ryukyuan history (Smits 2019). A related point, which I discuss in this book in detail, is that trading and raiding, not agriculture, was the economic basis for state formation in the Ryukyu Islands.

Both the ancient branch model and the internal development model regard the Ryukyu Islands as a singular, natural, political, and cultural entity. One result of this mindset is the tendency for Okinawa to stand in for all the Ryukyu Islands. Especially in the internal development model, the focus of most historians is on the Naha-Shuri-Urasoe area of Okinawa, the heartland of the Ryukyu Kingdom. In this approach the other Ryukyu Islands submitted to Shuri's power, willingly or otherwise, but they played no major role in the development of the kingdom beyond having been the objects of taxation. The role of people and forces external to Okinawa, or to the Ryukyu Islands as a whole, is minimized in the internal development model.

Yoshinari Naoki and Ikeda Yoshifumi have noted this strong internal focus and the tunnel vision resulting from the supposition that Ryukyuan history has been continuous and linear, without major discontinuities. They note a teleological assumption that earlier people and time periods must have been linked with or contributed to the kingdom that later developed. This assumption often shapes the conclusions of historians, archaeologists, and public intellectuals (Yoshinari 2020, 9–10). Similarly, historian Kurima Yasuo (2013a, iv) advocates discarding baseless "provincialism" and embracing the overwhelming evidence of outside influence in early Ryukyuan history that archaeology has provided.

In the external agents model, the Ryukyu Islands were never isolated prior to the seventeenth century.[21] The islands were linked to the East China Sea region via the ocean. At various times new groups of people swept into some or all Ryukyu Islands, sometimes in the pursuit of economic benefits or occasionally in response to political upheavals in the region (figure 1.3). Although people from many places made their way into the Ryukyu Islands, migrants from the

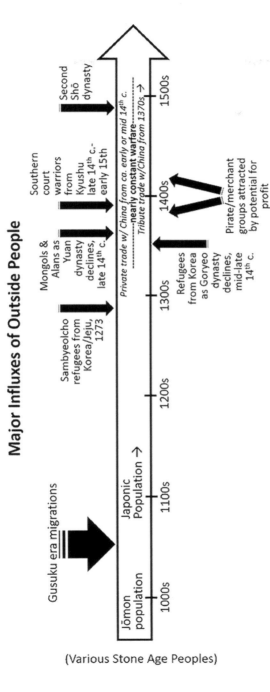

Figure 1.3. Major influxes of outside people.

Korean Peninsula and the Japanese Islands, often moving through western Kyushu, were inextricably and deeply connected with early Ryukyuan history.

In addition to people as external agents, the model stresses the powerful role of geography and the physical environment of the Ryukyu Islands. In this respect, the external agents model resembles the internal development model, but with an important difference. Writers working in the internal development model often link Ryukyu's distinctive history with its geographic remove from the main Japanese Islands. The point is typically to establish separation, often with the ocean acting as a barrier, not a bridge. In the external agents model, the East China Sea functioned to link the Ryukyu Islands to the broader region from the Stone Age onward (chapter 2). Moreover, the physical environments of the islands were suitable for certain economic activities and worked against others. Poor soil, severe typhoons, and problems with saltwater inundation, for example, inhibited cereal grain agriculture.

In the external agents model, early Ryukyuan history was dynamic, and the centers of political and economic power changed over time. During the eleventh and twelfth centuries, Kikaijima and Hakata in northwest Kyushu were the major centers of regional trade and technology diffusion. At this time the northern Ryukyu Islands were more advanced in terms of material culture and economic power compared with Okinawa and the southern Ryukyu Islands. The thirteenth century was a time of transition. The emergence of large fortresses (*gusuku*) in Okinawa at the start of the fourteenth century marked a shift in relative prominence. Places such as Nakijin, Katsuren, and Urasoe in Okinawa began to outpace harbors in northern islands in the accumulation of wealth and power. The rise of power centers in Okinawa resulted primarily from regional trade, legal and otherwise. Shuri emerged as the overwhelmingly dominant power center relatively late in the story. Shuri's dominance vis-à-vis other power centers began toward the end of Shō Taikyū's reign, around 1458, and was largely complete by the end of Shō Shin's reign in the late 1520s.

In this dynamic context, the category of people we could reasonably call Ryukyuans is difficult to fix or delineate clearly, at least prior to the sixteenth century. Groups who resided in the Ryukyu Islands included Jōmon people, Japonic people, people from in and around the Korean Peninsula, and even Mongols and Alans. Focusing on any point in time, it is possible to make distinctions between relative newcomers versus groups with deeper roots in the islands. For example, the early Okinawan trade kings Satto and Shō Hashi were new arrivals to Okinawa, from Korea and Japan, respectively. In the external agents model, neither the Ryukyu Kingdom nor local power centers developed independently or in isolation. East China Sea regional trade networks sustained them, and significant changes in the Ryukyu Islands often occurred in reaction to political conflict or major upheavals elsewhere in the region.

The external agents model rejects a strong sense of Ryukyuan or Okinawan exceptionalism. Of course, all local histories are distinctive by definition. Moreover, in the external agents model the geography and physical environment of the Ryukyu Islands is a major reason for their distinctive historical development. Nevertheless, the Ryukyu Islands and their inhabitants were subject to the same motivations and forces that affected people throughout the region and the world. One of my goals in *Maritime Ryukyu* was to integrate Ryukyuan history into the history of the East China Sea region. This book continues that process.

The broad argument of this book is that because the external agents model described above is a more powerful explanatory framework than the internal development model, it should supplant it with respect to early Ryukyuan history. Subsequent chapters function as support for this argument. They present a history of the Ryukyu Islands from the time of the earliest extant human remains until the establishment of a strong centralized state in approximately 1530. In the process I describe the diverse groups of people who have inhabited the Ryukyu Islands and advance new—sometimes radically new—reinterpretations of the traditional narrative. I also show that developments in the Ryukyu Islands shed important light on certain topics in world history, such as the role of nonstate peoples during what James Scott (2017, 33, 35, 222) has called the "Golden Age of Barbarians."[22]

Major Anglophone Books

The sections above describe, compare, and contrast the ancient branch model, the internal development model, and my proposed external agents model (figure 1.4). Here I briefly examine the four major English-language books covering early Ryukyuan history in whole or in part in light of these models. To state my conclusion in advance, these works are all idiosyncratic to some extent, and none of them are typical representations of the models.

George H. Kerr's *Okinawa: The History of an Island People,* published in 1958, was for decades the only systematic treatment of premodern Ryukyuan history available in English. Not surprisingly, therefore, its impact in Anglophone circles has been, and continues to be, powerful. Despite including some Japanese-language books in the bibliography, Kerr's book neither relies directly on Japanese sources nor indicates any familiarity with the academic debates about Ryukyuan history that were current either before or after the war.

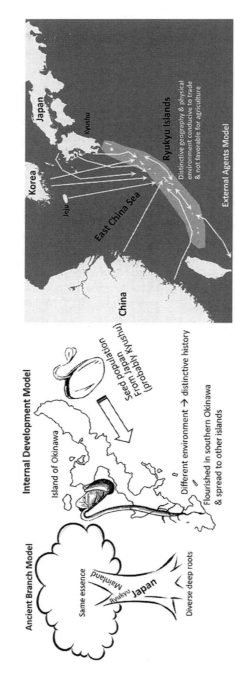

Figure 1.4. Three models of early Ryukyuan history.

Its content is more akin to the English-language materials assembled by U.S. research and information services in connection with the Battle of Okinawa.[23]

In other words, Kerr's *Okinawa* is not a representative example of the ancient branch model, especially given the interest of U.S. authorities during the 1950s in emphasizing differences between Okinawans and Japanese. In a general way, Kerr's narrative fits the broad framework of the official histories. Like other historians of the day, Kerr regarded Okinawan history as a single, continuous line of development. Similarly, he regarded Okinawans as a singular people whose identity persisted through centuries of time. To a greater extent than a typical historian working in the internal development model, Kerr stressed Okinawan exceptionalism. Again, such a focus was not surprising given U.S. interests at the time. In making the case for Okinawan distinctiveness, Kerr ([1958] 2000, 15) emphasized isolation, "poverty of human resources," and "an even greater poverty of material wealth." The latter included "harsh, thin soil, no metals, and little forest wealth."

Kerr's ([1958] 2000, 543–544) portrayal of the premodern Ryukyu Islands as a pacifist paradise has been especially influential, despite Mitsugu Sakihara pointing out its inaccuracy in a revised edition of *Okinawa*. Recall that historians writing in the ancient branch model often discussed warfare, and Kerr's denial of it was a continuation of the European-derived myth of Ryukyuan pacifism. Although Kerr applied this pacifist paradise description mainly to the Okinawa of the nineteenth century, there has been a strong tendency in Anglophone circles to generalize it far back in time as an essential quality of "Ryukyuans" (cf. Smits 2010a, 2010b).

My first academic book, *Visions of Ryukyu: Identity and Ideology in Early-Modern Thought and Politics* (Smits 1999), is mainly a study of royal ideology and social change during the era of Sai On (1682–1762). It mentions early Ryukyu only in passing. Nevertheless, my work was very much influenced by historians working in the internal development model, and I sought to highlight the distinctive history of Okinawa and the Ryukyu Kingdom. The major contents of this book have held up well over time, and it has been translated into Japanese (Smits 2011). If I were to revise it, I would reframe and recontextualize Ryukyu's early modern era in light of what I now know about earlier centuries.

A major focus of *Visions of Ryukyu* is Ryukyu's relationship with China with respect to politics, economics, technology, and ideas. Mamoru Akamine's (2017) *The Ryukyu Kingdom: Cornerstone of East Asia* also focuses extensively on Okinawan relations with China. Originally published in Japanese in 2004, *The Ryukyu Kingdom* focuses mainly on the early modern era, but it includes brief coverage of early Ryukyu. Akamine's narrative begins with the *gusuku* era. It fits the internal development model moderately well, although not perfectly. Akamine defines the *gusuku* era by the *gusuku* themselves and other new forms of material culture, but his account provides little or no indication of an influx of new people: "In the era prior to the Gusuku Period, the inhabitants of the Ryukyus and Amami led a primitive lifestyle centered on fishing, hunting, and gathering. At some point—and this is what marks the beginning of the Gusuku Period—they shed this lifestyle and began cultivating crops in earnest, eventually forming a stratified society of agricultural villages, each within recognized geographical boundaries and usually populated with people related by blood or marriage" (Akamine 2017, 11). In this typical approach, the denizens of the Ryukyu Islands are portrayed as a singular population that underwent internal change. The existing population took up farming, as opposed to farmers coming into the Ryukyu Islands from outside. Akamine's portrayal implies that agricultural surpluses led to a stratified, increasingly complex society.

Akamine mentions the major forms of material culture that characterized the *gusuku* era, such as *kamuiyaki*, soapstone cauldrons, and Chinese ceramics. Given the prevalence of these items, there must have been some external influence on the *gusuku*-era Ryukyu Islands. For Akamine, this influence was the vigorous trading activity of Song Chinese merchants: "The Gusuku Period did not simply come about as a result of naturally occurring phenomena within the Ryukyuan archipelago. Nor can its rise be attributed to the region's physical location within the Japanese cultural sphere of influence. It developed in the midst of a greater East Asian community with China at its center that was also undergoing systematic changes. Ryukyuan society received great stimulation from the movement of people and goods throughout East Asia, and it was this stimulus that brought about the Gusuku Period" (Akamine 2017, 15). Following this paragraph in Akamine's book is an extensive discussion of Chinese trade during the Song dynasty. In other words, outward-directed Chinese trade caused an invigorating ripple effect throughout East Asia. Although Akamine is vague regarding the specific mechanism, he notes the appearance of "Ryukyu" in Song and Yuan dynasty literary sources and suggests that whatever transformed *gusuku*-era society came from China—even iron (Akamine 2017, 18–19).[24]

This strong focus on (implied) direct Chinese influence during the *gusuku* era is unique to Akamine. *The Ryukyu Kingdom* contains a meta-argument that interactions with China created Okinawan civilization and sustained it. Moreover, Akamine (2017, 164–165) is very much an outlier among Japanese scholars in that he is sympathetic to the Beijing and Taiwan governments' claims to the Ryukyu Islands. In several important respects, therefore, *The Ryukyu Kingdom* is idiosyncratic.

Because there are so few books in English on Ryukyuan history, their impact on Anglophone readers, including scholars of East Asia, has been strong to the point of distortion. Akamine, a sinologist, provides fascinating details about elite Ryukyuan-Chinese interactions during the early modern era. In Japanese, his book takes its place among hundreds of others and makes a valuable, specialized contribution to our knowledge. In English, the combination of two monographs that extensively discuss elite Okinawan-Chinese interactions (*Visions of Ryukyu* and *The Ryukyu Kingdom*) has the unintended effect of exaggerating the extent of Chinese influence, cultural or otherwise, on the Ryukyu Islands. Even though both volumes focus on early modern–era elite Okinawans, readers are likely to generalize and extrapolate backward in time and beyond elite society.

Maritime Ryukyu, 1050–1650 acknowledges the importance of China as a source of wealth, but very few Chinese people ever migrated to the Ryukyu Islands. The key actors in *Maritime Ryukyu* are *wakō*, Japanese and Korean raiders and traders active throughout the East China Sea region.[25] These were the people who settled the harbors of the Ryukyu Islands during the *gusuku* era, displacing the indigenous population (much more on that process in this book). I began *Maritime Ryukyu* in the middle of the eleventh century precisely because that was the start of the *gusuku era,* the beginning of Japonic Ryukyu. If I were to revise the book, I would add a brief discussion of the situation before the start of the *gusuku* era to reinforce the eleventh century as heralding a major turning point and historical discontinuity.

Maritime Ryukyu, 1050–1650 is a revisionist history of early Ryukyu. As such, I understood that I was reacting to and rejecting much of the conventional narrative. This book goes further, replacing the very framework of the conventional narrative and facilitating a thoroughly new understanding of the early Ryukyu Islands and East China Sea maritime history.

CHAPTER TWO

Well-Traveled Routes

The early Ryukyu Islands were never isolated. Therefore, to understand their development through time it is necessary to map the major routes that conveyed people and culture. Archaeological artifacts are the main tool for such mapping, supplemented by genetic and documentary evidence. This chapter is an overview to set the stage. Later chapters discuss subroutes, trading ports, and other relevant topics in greater detail.

The Core Cultural Zone

The core cultural zone for early Ryukyu was an area of the East China Sea, extending from the southern Korean Peninsula through the Ryukyu Islands via western Kyushu.[1] Depending on time and circumstances, southwest Honshu can also be included within this zone. This area had been an active zone of exchange since the Jōmon era (figure 2.1).[2]

It is possible to sail from southern Korea to Okinawa, or vice versa, and remain within sight of land for most of the voyage. One crucial segment is the southern coast of Korea, the islands of Tsushima and Iki, and Hakata Bay in Fukuoka Prefecture. The southern coast of Korea is visible from parts of Tsushima in clear weather, and Iki is visible from high points in northwest Kyushu. Iki and Tsushima would not have been visible in a premodern sailing vessel, so modest navigational skills would have been required to make the crossing between Korea and Japan. Nevertheless, the passage from southern Korea to northwest Kyushu was well known to regional mariners since ancient times. In traveling between Kyushu and Okinawa, Michinoshima (the northern Ryukyu, Tokara, and Satsunan Islands) permits sailing with one island visible from the stern and the next island in the chain visible from the bow. From northwest Kyushu, the voyage to the Ryukyu Islands as far as Okinawa would have required only simple line-of-sight navigation, at least in good weather. Voyaging from the coast of Korea to an Okinawan harbor, although time-consuming, was not technically demanding. Importantly, a single vessel need not make the whole voyage because the entire route was full of good anchorages.

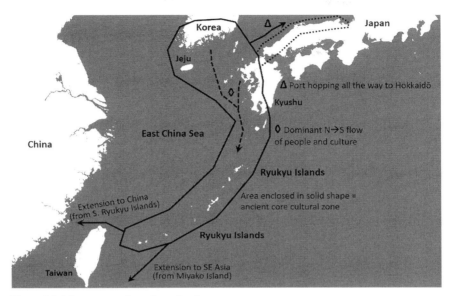

Figure 2.1. Movements of people and culture.

From the Korean Peninsula to the Ryukyu Islands

In the paragraphs below, I examine diverse evidence for the transmission of culture and people from the Korean Peninsula to the Ryukyu Islands, moving in approximate chronological order. This evidence shows that travel through the core cultural zone, especially between Korea and the Ryukyu Islands, took place from the Jōmon era onward.

Starting with genetic evidence, approximately 10 percent of the DNA in the present-day population of the main Japanese Islands is of Jōmon derivation. The people we now call "Jōmon" came into the Japanese Islands approximately fourteen thousand to sixteen thousand years ago, and their ultimate origins remain unknown.[3] Until recently, there was little or no evidence of a significant Jōmon population outside of the Japanese Islands. However, a recent analysis of prehistoric genomes at sites in Korea indicates the presence of a late-Neolithic Jōmon population at the southern edge of the Korean Peninsula and a heterogeneous (0–95 percent) presence of Jōmon ancestry in Neolithic Koreans (Robbeets et al. 2021, 619–620).[4] One possibility is that Jōmon groups moved from Japan to the southern coast of Korea, possibly in pursuit of trade. Another is that genetically Jōmon populations had deep roots in the Korean Peninsula (Hudson 2022, 5–6).

Moreover, we now know that Jōmon people populated not only the Japanese Islands but all or most of the Ryukyu Islands, including the southern Ryukyu Islands (Robbeets et al. 2021, 619–620; Hudson 2022, 5). Therefore, although many migration-related details remain unclear, Jōmon people were found in southern Korea, throughout the Japanese Islands, and throughout all or most of the Ryukyu Islands. The same can be said for Jōmon material culture. Jōmon-era Sobata-type pottery, excavated in Kyushu and the Ryukyu Islands, is a direct off-shoot of Korean comb-pattern pottery (figure 2.2).[5] It first appeared in the Korean Peninsula during the Neolithic era and spread to Okinawa via the west coast of Kyushu (Ikeda 2012b, 327–328). Many Jōmon people were seafarers, and a dugout canoe dating to approximately 2,000 BCE has been excavated at the Meebaru site in Okinawa (Kinoshita 2019, 316).

Knife coins from the Chinese state of Yàn (conquered 222 BCE), whose northeast border approached the Korean Peninsula, have been found in several sites in Okinawa. So, too, has pottery whose origin was the Lèlàng Commandery (103 BCE–313 CE), which included the northern part of the Korean Peninsula (Ikeda 2012b, 328–329). Products made from Ryukyu Islands cone snail shells (*imogai*) have been excavated from the Lèlàng area from approximately the same era. During Japan's Kofun period (ca. 300–538), the quantity of cone snail products in Korea increased significantly (Ikeda 2012b, 330–331, following Kinoshita Naoko).[6]

A similar situation occurred regarding products made from Ryukyu Island turbo shells.[7] Turbo shell spoons/ladles have been excavated from Silla and Gaya royal tombs. Where the ladles were actually made is unclear, but the raw material

Figure 2.2. Sobata-style pottery (*left*) and Korean Comb-pattern pottery (*right*). *Source:* Saigen Jiro, Wikimedia Commons; PHGCOM, Wikipedia.

had to have come from the Ryukyu Islands (Ikeda 2012b, 331–332). Ryukyu Island turbo shells made their way to Korea and helped fuel trade from approximately the late fifth century onward. They are found as funerary goods in the Goryeong Jisandong Tumuli (#44) and at four places as funerary goods in the royal tombs of Silla and Gaya. In Japan, Korean shell ornaments and earrings have been excavated at the Densayama *kofun* in Kumamoto Prefecture (lower Kikuchi River area), and Korean earrings have been excavated from the Daibō *kofun* (Tamana City, Kumamoto Prefecture). Korean-made earrings, belt and horse hardware, and funerary items have been excavated from the Etafunayama *kofun* (Tamana City). At all these tombs, shell ornaments, whose raw material came from the Ryukyu Islands, have been found along with Korean-made metal items. This situation indicates exchange and trade networks linking the Ryukyu Arc and the Korean Peninsula (Yoshinari 2018, 63–64).

Tensions between Korea and Japan were high during the period of unified Silla (668–935). During this time, for example, official Japanese voyages to China no longer proceeded along the Korean coast but instead used a southern route through some of the Ryukyu Islands. Significantly, no Korean items from this period have been excavated in the Ryukyu Islands. One conclusion is that entities in Japan were necessary intermediaries in moving goods between the Korean Peninsula and the Ryukyu Islands (Ikeda 2012b, 333–334).

Soon after Goryeo (918–1392) replaced Silla, agriculture began to spread throughout the Ryukyu Islands. Excavated Goryeo ware in the Ryukyu Islands is especially concentrated in Amami-Ōshima and Kikaijima. Given the quantity and dating of these Goryeo items, it is likely that traders from Goryeo traveled to Gusuku in Kikaijima during the eleventh and twelfth centuries. In addition to blueware, Goryeo pottery has been excavated at Kikaijima. It is likely that the technology for making pottery was imported from Korea in the form of the *kamuiyaki* (gray stoneware) kilns on Tokunoshima. The technology for *kamuiyaki* was Korean, and the actual *kamuiyaki* products reflect a Korean, Japanese, and Chinese influence. There had been no previous manufacture of pottery in Tokunoshima, and *kamuiyaki* appeared there suddenly. *Kamuiyaki* manufacture therefore likely included merchants or technicians from Goryeo (Ikeda 2012b, 334–335; Murai 2019, 74). In other words, during the early part of Ryukyu's *gusuku* era, Korean merchants and technicians visited, and probably resided in, Kikaijima and Tokunoshima. Genetic evidence attests to this likelihood as well.

The human leukocyte antigen (HLA) system is a group of related proteins responsible for the regulation of the immune system. Among the HLA gene class haplotypes for several major population groups in Northeast Asia is one that only Koreans and Okinawans share (Saitō 2005, 95).[8] This shared HLA haplotype indicates some degree of direct contact between the Ryukyu Islands and the Korean Peninsula since the Shellmound era. Possible agents of contact include merchants based in Gusuku, Korean technicians connected with the Tokunoshima kilns, and *wakō,* many of whom came from Korea (Yoshinari 2009, 274).

Additional genetic evidence indicates the direct movement of people from the Korean Peninsula into the southern Ryukyu Islands and from there northward. The Y chromosome haplogroup O2b is present in 51 percent of the population of the Korean Peninsula. Its incidence in the southern Ryukyu Islands is 67 percent, in the northern Ryukyu Islands, 30 percent, and in Tokyo, 26 percent (Sakitani 2008, 29; Yoshinari 2009, 272).[9] In this case we see a pattern of movement from Korea to the southern Ryukyu Islands and then northward into the Japanese Islands, a pattern that differs from the more common north-to-south flow described above. Peoples and cultures have traveled between the Korean Peninsula and the Ryukyu Islands via western Kyushu since prehistoric times. Although less common, there is also evidence for at least some direct travel from Korea to the southern and northern Ryukyu Islands.

MOVEMENT THROUGHOUT THE CORE CULTURAL ZONE MORE GENERALLY

Place-names, especially in the context of religiously significant mountains and groves, are another indication of movement through the core cultural zone. For example, the prominent religious site Mount Soto 卒土 in Tsushima resembles in name and appearance sacred groves in ancient Korea also called *soto* 蘇塗. Similarly, there is a group of sacred mountains in Tsushima called *-tansan* 壇山, a term synonymous with Korean sacred mountains called *dangsan* 堂山 (Okaya 2019, 140–142). Writing in 1941, Mishina Shōei noted a close similarity between the stone altar at Mount Soto in Tsushima and the altars in Korea under sacred trees. He also noted the frequent appearance of the name *-dan* in connection with sacred sites in Tsushima, which corresponded to sacred groves called *dan* (K. *dang* 堂) in Jeju Island (Mishina [1941] 1995, 165). Mishina ([1941] 1995, 178–182) noted other likely place-name connections linking sacred sites in Tsushima with Korea, blacksmiths, and the mariners' deity Hachiman.

In Iki Island, religious sites called *o-dō* (J. *dō* 堂 is the same character as the Korean *dang,* a type of sacred grove) rapidly faded in prominence during the postwar era. Before the 1940s, although ostensibly Buddhist, these sites featured shamanic religious performances by women known as *ichijō.* Like Korean *dang,* most of the participants in *o-dō* rites were women (Harajiri 2012, 84–90, 100). Insofar as these sites are identifiable today, several are sacred groves. *Dō* or *o-dō* exist elsewhere in Japan as small Buddhist shrines. In Iki, however, *o-dō* functioned as sacred groves, almost identically to their likely namesakes in Korea.

An entry in *Goryeo History* for 1260 notes that the Korean island of Jeju attracted many foreigners. Chinese merchants and "island *wajin*," meaning people from Iki and Tsushima, visited Jeju constantly (*Goryeo History* 1:61). It is likely that many of these island *wajin* from Iki and Tsushima were de facto *wakō*. Such mariners figured prominently in the core cultural zone from the thirteenth century onward (Smits 2019, 36–59). Moving forward in time, an entry in *Joseon Veritable Royal Records* for 1482 notes that Jeju Island is a gathering place for people from other regions who take to the sea. "They study the language and clothing of the *wajin* (Japanese or hybrid-Japanese) and plunder the people of the seacoast" (*JVRR-d* #29651).[10] In short, from the thirteenth century through the fifteenth, *wajin* and *wakō*, many of whom were Korean, connected coastal Korea, Jeju Island, Tsushima, Iki, and ultimately the entire core cultural zone.

Starting with the late fourteenth century, approximately fifteen cases of people from Jeju Island drifting or otherwise making their way into the Ryukyu Islands or vice versa were recorded (Chang 1973, 57; Okaya 2019, 151–152). During the 1870s and 1880s, fishermen from Itoman in Okinawa worked their way seasonally through the northern Ryukyu Islands, western Kyushu, Sasebo, the Gotō Islands, and then to the northern and southern parts of Tsushima. They also ventured as far as Hirado, the Oki Islands in Shimane, and Wakasa Bay in western Honshu. At Wakasa Bay they fished by beating the surface of the water with staves. The Itoman fishermen appeared with such regularity in the summer that the people of Obama in Fukui Prefecture regarded their arrival as marking the start of the summer season. Itoman fishermen also ventured southward to the Yaeyama Islands (Tanigawa 1992, 28–29). In other words, one community of itinerate fisher people based in Okinawa sailed throughout every part of the core cultural zone except Korea. The larger point behind all these examples is that the East China Sea had functioned to connect people from throughout the core cultural zone since prehistoric times.

The Shell Road: All the Way to Hokkaidō

One indication of the spread of material culture within the East China Sea region and even well beyond is what modern historians often call the "road of shells" (*kai no michi*). Trade in seashells and their products linked the ancient Ryukyu Islands to a network of exchange that included the island of Tsushima and southwest Honshu and extended as far north as Hokkaidō (Shirakihara 1992, 118). We can divide the shell trade centered on the Ryukyu Islands into two broad phases. The early phase began around the start of the Yayoi era, circa 1000 BCE, and it continued through the seventh century CE. The latter phase began in the ninth century and continued until the fifteenth (Kinoshita 2019, 326–327). The focus here is on the early phase. The basic process entailed the people in Okinawa and the northern Ryukyu Islands collecting valuable shells. Other groups transported the shells northward in small boats. In Kyushu, craftspeople then made the shells into bracelets and other products. In return for the shells, Ryukyu islanders received pottery, cloth, and other trade goods from Kyushu (Kinoshita 2019, 327, figure 17.9).

In 1988, seven cone shell fragments were excavated from a tomb in the Usumoshiri site at the mouth of Usu Bay in Date, Hokkaidō. The fragments were originally part of a shell bracelet, and they closely resemble fragments excavated in Aomori and Nagasaki Prefectures. These findings, together with excavations from sites in the Satsuma Peninsula, reveal the broad contours of a network that operated during the Yayoi era. Maritime bands traveled between southern Kyushu and the central and northern Ryukyu Islands to obtain shells. In places like the Takahashi site in Minami-Satsuma City, the shells were made into bracelets and moved northward along the coast of western Kyushu. The maritime distribution route continued along the coast of western Honshu to Tsugaru Bay in Aomori and across to Hokkaidō (Kinoshita 1996, 176, 201; Suzuki Yasutami 2020, 269–270). The demand for shell bracelets during the Yayoi era brought maritime traders from Kyushu into the Ryukyu Islands to procure the raw materials.

As the Yayoi era came to an end, the demand for shells dropped as bracelets began to be made from copper or other materials. However, the trade continued as other uses for shells developed. Cone shells, for example, became widely used for the manufacture of horse ornaments, which were consumed all over Japan during the sixth and seventh centuries (Yoshinari 2018, 57–58; 2020, 21–22; Shinzato Takayuki 2018, 39–40; Suzuki Yasutami 2020, 271).

A close correlation existed between the demand for shells north of the Ryukyu Islands and the consumption of northern goods, mainly pottery, within the Ryukyu Islands. For example, imported pottery in the northern Ryukyu Islands reached a nadir at the end of the Yayoi, which is also the approximate trough in Kyushu shell consumption. During the Kofun era, Tanegashima became a new nexus in a revitalized shell trade. Large quantities of conch and cone shells have been found at Tanegashima's Hirota site, in sites in Amami-Ōshima, and at sites in and around Okinawa (Yoshinari 2018, 58; Shinzato Takayuki 2018, 39–40). The most important axis of the shell trade during the Kofun era was the zone between Tanegashima and Amami-Ōshima (Yoshinari 2022, 19–20; figure 2.3).

The shell trade exposed the Ryukyu Islands to Yayoi pottery styles, transmitting and disseminating pottery information (doki jōhō) throughout the central and northern Ryukyu Islands (Shinzato Takayuki 2018, 41–42). In addition to consuming pottery from Kyushu, Ryukyu Islanders made their own in imitation of Yayoi styles. The Yayoi decorative patterns in Kyushu are found most abundantly in the local pottery of the Satsunan and northern Ryukyu Islands, and they

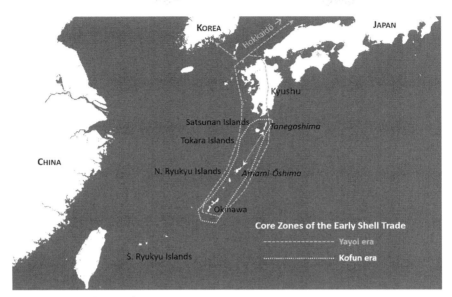

Figure 2.3. Early shell-trade core zones.

fade out in Okinawa. Large quantities of Yayoi goods came into Okinawa during the Yayoi and Kofun eras, but there is no evidence of the general adoption of Yayoi culture there (Yoshinari 2020, 25–29).[11]

As we have seen, cone and conch shells from the Ryukyu Islands were intermittently imported into Korea and have been excavated at tomb sites there, as have mother-of-pearl objects made from Ryukyuan turbo shells. The majority of these shell products probably arrived in Korea via Kyushu, with sea peoples from the coasts of Higo and Satsuma working as intermediaries. However, it is also possible that Korean merchants purchased the shells directly from Ryukyu Island locations (Yoshinari 2018, 59, 63; Suzuki Takayuki 2020, 272).

The economic activity connected with the shell trade produced and distributed objects throughout the core cultural zone and as far north as Hokkaidō. The ocean did not isolate the Ryukyu Islands. Instead, it linked the islands into networks of travel and exchange, connecting them with the Korean Peninsula and the Japanese Islands.

Ryukyu's Northern Orientation

The cultures and, for the most part, the people of the Ryukyu Islands arrived there from the north. With that point in mind, consider the Sea Bridge to the Many Countries Bell (Bankoku Shinryō no Kane) that King Shō Taikyū commissioned in 1458. Its classical Chinese inscription begins, "The country of Ryukyu is located favorably in the southern seas. It has gathered the excellence of the Korean kingdoms. It is a supplementary vehicle to the Great Ming. It is to Japan like teeth are to lips."[12] Significantly, Korea is first among the three countries listed. According to the bell, Ryukyu has concentrated (*zhōng*) the excellence or superiority of Korea. Some of the most iconic and foundational aspects of classical Ryukyuan culture, including sacred groves (*utaki*) and stone-walled *gusuku,* came from Korea (chapter 6). The devoutly Buddhist Taikyū may also have had the Korean-supplied Tripitaka in his mind as an example of Korean "excellence." By contrast, Ryukyu's relationship with Ming China was functional. Circa the 1450s the Ryukyuan royal court and the port of Naha operated much like a shipping company, with the Ming dynasty as its largest client (Smits 2019, 77–81). As a fundamentally Japonic society (*gusuku* era and later) with extensive human and cultural ties to the Japanese Islands, Ryukyu would indeed have been as close to Japan as teeth are to lips. The Ryukyu of this inscription has received superior culture and technology from Korea, maintains a good working relationship with China, and is culturally akin to Japan. What may be the most significant term in this passage is easy to overlook: "southern seas." The expression speaks to a *northern* frame of reference that pervades early Ryukyuan history (Yoshinari 2020, 305–307).[13]

Other northern frames of reference can be found in the songs of the *Omoro sōshi.* Consider, for example, the use of snow (*yuki,* spelled "yoki") as a metaphor. One *omoro* praises the rice grown in Sashiki as being "as white as snow," and several others praise top-quality rice as "snow" (*Omoro sōshi* 19–1287, 12–672, 673, 22–1511). Others refer to "snow beach" (*yuki no hama*) to praise the white sand of Yonaha beach and the white sand of Yonabaru beach (*Omoro sōshi* 1–39, 3–100). White horses are praised for their beauty and described as "the color of snow" or otherwise likened to snow (*Omoro sōshi* 10–541, 10–583). A deity of a sacred grove in Kumejima is called Venerable snow (*yuki-ganashi; Omoro sōshi* 13–955). Another *omoro* speaks of snow falling during the first lunar month (*mutsuki; Omoro sōshi* 14–1000). However, in the semitropical Ryukyu Islands, snow never accumulates. Even a few passing flakes are extremely rare, and no mountains are tall enough to have snow-covered peaks.[14] These snow references made sense to people whose roots were in places like Japan or Korea.

Myths, legends, and origin tales within the Ryukyu Islands indicate a north-to-south flow. According to the Ryukyuan court's creation mythology, deities from the north created the Ryukyu Islands. The version in *Reflections on Ryukyu* starts the process in northern Okinawa, with the deity Amamiku (Amamikyo in the *Omoro*) creating sacred groves (*utaki*) from Hedo southward. However, as Iha Fuyū has discussed in detail, the Amami component in these names refers to the northern Ryukyu Islands. In the Kasari Peninsula of Amami-Ōshima, there is a mountain, Amami-dake, where Amamikyo descended from the heavens according to local lore. Noting that crossing the seventeen *ri* of sea between the Satsunan and Tokara Islands was often called the Amami crossing (*Amami-shū no watari*), Iha (1974b) concluded, "In the Amami crossing, we are informed of the route that Amamikyo (meaning the Amami people) followed in a southward migration" (cf. Inamura 1969, 437).

Turning to the southern Ryukyu Islands, *Origins of Ryukyu* lists six sacred groves for Taketomi-son (Taketomi Island).[15] The deities for each grove arrived in Taketomi from north of the Kerama gap.[16] Moreover, the name of the sacred space (*ibe*) at the Kumabara grove and the Shikoze grove in Kabira (Ishigaki Island) is Tomori-Ōaruji (*Origins* [1713] 1988, 603–604). The Tomori surname, a variant of Tomari and closely associated with arrivals from Japan,[17] is found in the Yaeyama Islands of Hatoma, Taketomi, and Yonaguni. What these personal and place-names indicate is the process of northern peoples migrating into the southern Ryukyu Islands (Tanigawa 2010, 180). The archaeological evidence presented in this chapter and chapter 3 maps out that process with greater precision.

The Southern Ryukyu Islands to Island Southeast Asia

During the early fourteenth century and possibly slightly earlier, people from the island of Miyako in the southern Ryukyu Islands began sailing to island Southeast Asia to acquire valuable tropical products for trade. According to Chinese records, some Mìyágǔ 密牙古 (Miyako) people on their way to conduct trade in the Singapore area were caught in a storm, blown to China, and returned to their country in 1317. They were from Bora in eastern Miyako. The small vessel blown into China contained fourteen people. When someone who could understand their language was located, the survivors explained that approximately sixty people in total, some in a large ship and some in a small ship, had set out for Chèlìjí 撤里即 (here probably meaning the Singapore straits) to trade. In a storm the large ship was lost, and only the small ship holding fourteen people survived. The group was taken to Quánnán, where they waited until a vessel sailing in the direction of Miyako took them home (Gi 2007, 85; Shimoji 2008, 336–337; *Yuánshǐ* 26.7).

At the Boranomotojima site, the probable location of the base of these Miyako sailors, 5 percent of the excavated Chinese pottery is from the Southern Song-Yuan era, 35 percent is from the early Ming, and 60 percent is mid-Ming (fifteenth century). Some of the excavated pottery includes items from Korea, Vietnam, and other Southeast Asian locations. This Southeast Asian pottery is probably one category of items the rescued Miyako traders were seeking to acquire.

Notice that someone who understood the language of the islanders was found in China and that a ship sailed from China in the direction of Miyako. Most likely some direct trade between Chinese merchants and Miyako and/or Yaeyama was taking place by the early fourteenth century. Moreover, the original group of Bora sailors had consisted of sixty people in a large ship (lost) and a smaller one (rescued). Given this scale, it is likely that several communities in Miyako were cooperating in the trade (Shimoji 2008, 337–338). Two possibilities are Urukano-motojima and Tomorinomotojima, where quantities of blue- and whiteware on a par with Boranomotojima have been excavated (Okada 2000, 194).

Four early fourteenth-century sites are in the vicinity of Boranomotojima, all within an eight-kilometer zone. Chinese ceramics have been excavated from all of them. Today, Wēnzhōu is a coastal city in Zhèjiāng Province, just north of Fújiàn Province across from Taiwan. In *Chronicle of Wēnzhōu* (*Wēnzhōu fǔzhì* 温州府志), mentions of people from "Bora" can be found into the fifteenth century. Shipwrecked Koreans who came to Miyako in 1477 recorded the place as "Bora Miyako." As late as 1477, therefore, "Bora" stood for Miyako (Shimoji 2008, 338–339). The Chinese ceramics from Boranomotojima did not come from Fújiàn or Zhèjiāng, but those excavated from Sumiya and Uruka in Miyako include a high percentage from Fújiàn and Lóngquán. In every location in Miyako, the fourteenth and fifteenth centuries were a time when Chinese ware rapidly increased in quantity. Some might have gone to Miyako via trade with Okinawa, but not in such quantities. The most likely scenario is that most of this ware came from direct trade with Chinese merchants, which would technically have been illegal soon after the establishment of the Ming dynasty in 1368 (Shimoji 2008, 343). In this connection it is also important to note that the late fourteenth and early fifteenth centuries were a time of especially vigorous *wakō* activity in the southern Ryukyu Islands (Smits 2019, 53–59).

The term "Chūzan" refers to an Okinawan state or pseudo-state based in the Shuri-Naha-Urasoe area. It was one of the entities that participated in Chinese tribute trade from the 1370s onward, and it also engaged in official trade with Korea. Shimoji Kazuhiro points out that in 1390, for the first time, pepper and sappanwood were listed as items that Chūzan presented to China as tribute. Contact with the southern Ryukyu Islands enabled Chūzan to ship those items, which came from tropical Asia and were much valued in China. Moreover, these two products were listed in the items Chūzan sent to Korea in 1389, along with Koreans who had been captured by *wakō* (Hong-Schunka 2005, 126–127).[18] Connecting some dots, notice that the Bora Miyakoans traded as far afield as Southeast Asia at the start of the fourteenth century, and possibly earlier. The story in the official histories describes Miyako as presenting "tribute" to Chūzan in 1390, long before Miyako came under Shuri's control. What this story actually reflects is Chūzan obtaining pepper and sappanwood via trade with Miyako sailors, who obtained the items in Southeast Asia (Shimoji 2008, 342, 344, following Sunagawa Akifusa; Smits 2019, 54–55).

This chapter has sketched some of the flows of people, technology, and goods into and out of the Ryukyu Islands and the routes by which these exchanges took place at different points in time. Activity within the core cultural zone started during the Jōmon era. Later, during the Yayoi and Kofun eras, products made from Ryukyuan shells moved as far north as Hokkaidō. In the early fourteenth century, Miyako sailors traveled as far as Southeast Asia. These sailors almost certainly traded directly with merchants in Southeast China, and they also brought some of their goods to Okinawa. From Okinawa those tropical Asian products went to China and Korea. Later chapters examine this economic activity in greater detail. Chapter 3 zooms in on the Ryukyu Islands, examining the land itself and the earliest peoples who lived on it.

CHAPTER THREE

The Land, First Peoples, and the Shellmound Era

If by "Ryukyuan" we mean people residing in the Ryukyu Islands, then the population of Ryukyuans changed at certain points in the past as one group faded out and another replaced it. This chapter examines the earliest-known inhabitants of the Ryukyu Islands and the people who inhabited the Ryukyu Islands during the vast span of time from approximately 7000 BCE to the eleventh century CE. This period is called the Shellmound era (or Shellmidden era, J. *kaizuka jidai*). Before surveying these early Ryukyu Island inhabitants, I start with a description of the geology and land of the islands.

The Land

Each individual Ryukyu island is a closed system with a distinctive physical environment. Each island differs from the others in terms of hydrology, forest resources, soil quality, agricultural potential, and more. One important broad division is between high islands and low islands. High and low islands came into existence via different geological processes.

HIGH ISLANDS AND LOW ISLANDS

The high islands in the Ryukyu Arc include Yakushima, Amami-Ōshima, Kakeroma, Tokunoshima, Iheya, Kumejima, Tonaki, Kerama, northern Ishigaki, Iriomote, and Yonaguni. The northern part of Okinawa also has the characteristics of a high island. High islands feature continental topography and were formed from volcanic action. Rock formations in high islands are hard and nonporous, so water tends to flow along the surface. The hydrologic environment derives from streams and rivers, and the climate tends to be humid. Fruit trees grow well in the acidic soil of high islands. Water is usually abundant, but the soil quality and steep terrain make large-scale agriculture difficult (Ōshiro Itsurō 1992, 75–76; Takanashi 2008a, 127–129).

Low islands in the Ryukyu Arc include Tanegashima, Kikaijima, Okinoerabu, Yoron, central and southern Okinawa, Miyako and its surrounding islands, Irabu, Tarama, southern Ishigaki, Taketomishima, and Hateruma. Low islands consist mainly of limestone that formed 500,000–600,000 years ago. This limestone, from uplifted coral reefs, was a desirable building material for walls, roads, and tombs. Vegetation is typically sparse, and many low islands lack lumber for wood or fuel. Low islands are characterized by karst topography. Water tends to percolate through the limestone, resulting in depressions, caves, and springs, with little or no surface water accumulation. The limestone causes neutral or slightly alkaline soil. Grasses (especially sugarcane), root vegetables, and other vegetables grow relatively well in low islands, but intensive cultivation is necessary to compensate for soil problems such as a lack of organic material or the inability to retain water. Most low islands are without habu, a species of highly venomous snake found in the high islands (Ōshiro Itsurō 1992, 75–84; Takanashi 2008a, 127–129).

If for no other reason than the rugged, steep terrain, high islands are unlikely to support large or dense populations. Low islands, and the low areas of Ishigaki and Okinawa, typically face shortages of fuel, lumber, and water. This is one reason why the control of water became the hallmark of powerful rulers in Ryukyuan culture (Smits 2019). Another dynamic often resulting from this geography was the need for populations on low islands to control the resources of nearby high islands. For example, Gusuku developed on a low island, but it had to rely on resources from the nearby high islands and probably directly controlled the Kasari Peninsula of Amami-Ōshima (Takanashi 2005, 208–210). At the other end of the Ryukyu Arc, local powers in Miyako depended heavily on lumber from Iriomote in the Yaeyama Islands. This dynamic was a source of conflict and likely factored in the large-scale warfare of 1500 (Shimamura 2008, 308–311, 315).

Geography played a role in the island of Okinawa eventually dominating the other Ryukyu Islands. The port of Naha was especially suitable for large ships because fresh water from the flow of three rivers into the harbor suppressed the growth of coral. Crucially important was the presence of both high-island and low-island topography within the same landmass. Okinawa's central location within the Ryukyu Arc and its location at the end of the road of islands known as Michinoshima were also geographic advantages contributing to its potential power and prominence.

Looking more closely at the high-low division of Okinawa, the border is the Ishikawa isthmus (northern Uruma City; central Onna Village). To the north the elevation increases, and hilly and mountainous terrain composes more than 70 percent of the total area. To the south are plateaus or terraces (*daichi*) and lowland areas. South of the Ishikawa isthmus, mountainous terrain is a mere

0.2 percent of the total land, hills and terraces compose just over 40 percent, and lowland makes up just 15.2 percent. North of the isthmus, only 7.6 percent of the terrain is lowland. The sides of hills in the south of Okinawa usually feature gradual slopes. However, because they contain areas of clay that can swell with prolonged exposure to water, landslides are common (Hokama Kazuo 2015a, 57–58).

The Soil

The first people to arrive in Okinawa and the other Ryukyu Islands probably noticed the red earth. In Okinawa it is called *maaji* 真土. Red soil created from the weathering of limestone is called *Shimajiri-maaji*. Red or reddish soil created from other sources is called *Kunigami-maaji*. The former is common in the low islands (or low parts of islands); the latter, in the high islands. *Shimajiri-maaji* ranges from slightly acid to slightly alkaline. *Kunigami-maaji* is acidic. This difference in pH is mainly why pineapples grow well in northern Okinawa and sugar grows well in the south (Ōshiro Itsurō 1992, 81–82). The third and final major soil type is gray in color. It comes from the weathering of marl and is known as *jaagaru*.[1] There are more detailed ways to classify soils, which can become relevant when considering agricultural viability, but most discussions of soil refer to these three types.[2] Although most of the soil of the Ryukyu Islands comprises these three types, small areas of other soil types can be found, which can be significant at local scales.

Kunigami-maaji is clay soil, red or yellow-red in color. Its water permeability is poor. Very little rainwater seeps into it, most pooling at the surface or washing across it. Water-resistant aggregates are few, and its dispersion rate is high. The result is severe erosion potential. *Kunigami-maaji* is not well suited for agriculture. It composes 66.9 percent of the soil of Okinawa and 55.4 percent of the soil of Okinawa Prefecture. Only 9.3 percent of the cultivated land in Okinawa is *Kunigami-maaji* (Hokama Kazuo 2015a, 59–61).

Shimajiri-maaji contains the highest concentration of clay and is highly developed (structured). The result is good aeration (breathability) and water permeability. Fields can be worked one day after a rainfall. The soil bulges, so it is easy to till. However, the reverse side of its good permeability is poor water retention. Therefore, *Shimajiri-maaji* is subject to damage from drought. Water-resistant aggregates are numerous, and the dispersion rate is low, so the soil resists erosion. *Shimajiri-maaji* composes 15.2 percent of Okinawa's soil and 26.6 percent of the entire prefecture's soil. Approximately 40 percent of the land in Okinawa Prefecture under cultivation is *Shimajiri-maaji* (Hokama Kazuo 2015a, 59–61).

Jaagaru is poorly developed (structured) soil. It drains poorly but retains water well. *Jaagaru* contains relatively few coarse pores, which inhibits vertical water movement under the force of gravity. The base material is impermeable, so stagnant water accumulating in the soil layer can cause damage. After rainfall, the soil bulges and becomes very sticky, clinging to agricultural tools. It is necessary to wait several days after a rainfall before working *jaagaru* fields. After a hard rain, a subtle film forms on the surface, making aeration (breathability) and water permeability poor. This hard film on the soil can damage germinating plants. When dry, *jaagaru* contracts, causing hard fissures to form, which can damage roots. For Okinawa, 17.9 percent of the soil is *jaagaru,* as is 8.7 percent of Okinawa Prefecture's soil. Seventeen percent of the prefecture's cultivated land is this type. Despite its shortcomings, *jaagaru,* an alkaline (base) soil, can be suitable for agriculture using intensive cultivation. It is a very difficult soil to work, but it is the most fertile of the three types and has the best overall microbiome (Hokama Kazuo 2015a, 59–63).

Earliest Human Remains

Human remains, especially bones and teeth, are potentially capable of revealing much information. Unfortunately, bones degrade quickly in the hot, humid conditions of the Ryukyu Islands, and only recently have a fairly large number of analyzable samples from a variety of time periods been studied. Bones consist of inorganic compounds like calcium phosphate and organic compounds like collagen. Age determination and DNA analysis rely on the organic compounds. Soon after bones are unearthed, it is necessary to recover organic material that degrades with time. Collagen contains carbon, which comes in three isotopes: ^{12}C, ^{13}C, ^{14}C. Isotopes twelve and thirteen are stable. Carbon-14 is unstable, with a half-life of 5,730 years. This instability permits radiocarbon dating if sufficient testable material is recovered. DNA analysis imposes more severe conditions on samples (Doi 2018, 18–19). The scientific analysis of skeletal remains can shed useful light on Ryukyuan prehistory.

As of this writing, the oldest extant piece of human remains in Japan is small fossilized fragments of leg bone from a child. The fragments are approximately thirty-two thousand to thirty-five thousand years old and were found in Naha's Yamashita-chō Cave Site 1 (Pearson 2013, 39; Yamasaki 2018, 45). A skeleton found in a cave in Ueno Village in Miyako was dated to roughly twenty-five thousand years ago, and skeletons from roughly twenty thousand to thirty thousand years ago have been found throughout the Ryukyu Islands (Ōshiro Itsurō 1992, 85–87; Yamasaki 2018, 45). The most widely known human remains are from a limestone fissure in Minatogawa in southern Okinawa, the result of three excavations conducted in 1968, 1970, and 1974. They yielded bones, roughly twenty thousand years old, belonging to between five and nine people. Many of the remains were widely scattered, and some evidence suggests that these Minatogawa individuals met a violent death and may have been cannibalized. Two male and two female skeletons have been assembled from the remains (Pearson 2013, 38–41).

Because of the absence of artifact assemblages, it is virtually impossible to draw conclusions about the nature of the human population from which the Minatogawa and many other Paleolithic remains came (Pearson 2013, 40). Until recently, journalists and scholars commonly believed that the present-day population of Okinawa came from Minatogawa humans. For example, in 1982 Hisashi Suzuki, leader of the Minatogawa excavation teams, stated that "present day Okinawans are without doubt the direct descendants of Minatogawa humans" (quoted in Pearson 2013, 42). Bioanthropologist Hanihara Kazurō (1927–2004) agreed with Suzuki and further proposed that Minatogawa humans were remote ancestors of Jōmon people (Pearson 2013, 43). I discuss the Ryukyu-related portion of Hanihara's dual structure hypothesis for the peopling of the Japanese Islands at length later in this chapter. At this point I simply note that, in addition to much other evidence, our understanding of the eleventh and twelfth centuries (the start of the *gusuku* era) as a major discontinuity in the population of the Ryukyu Islands has undermined the idea of an "Okinawan" or "Ryukyuan" population that has persisted in the islands since the Stone Age.

Two of the most important sites for Paleolithic (and later) human remains are the Shiraho-Saonetabaru Cave Site (*Shiraho-Saonetabaru dōketsu iseki* 白保竿根田原洞穴遺跡) in Ishigaki Island and the Nagabaka site (*Nagabaka iseki* 長墓遺跡) in Miyako Island. The Shiraho-Saonetabaru site has yielded more than 1,150 human bone fragments and several partial skeletons. Carbon dating places many of the remains in the 10,000–20,000 BP range, with the partial skeletons ranging in estimated age from 27,685 to 19,791 BP. The position of the partial skeletons indicates that the site was probably a Paleolithic graveyard (Okinawa Kenritsu Maizō Bunka Sentaa 2017, 64–85; Doi and Kudaka 2017). The Nagabaka site contains a set of human remains dating from roughly 4000 to 1000 BP as well as a set of remains from the early modern era (seventeenth–nineteenth centuries). Both sets of remains have yielded full genomes, which I discuss in subsequent sections.

From 1957 through 1959, over one hundred skeletons from the Hirota site on the Satsunan island of Tanegashima were analyzed. The site consists of two main strata. The lower stratum corresponds approximately to the early Yayoi era and the upper to the late Yayoi through the Kofun eras (Ikehata 1990, 123–124). Although some scholars have characterized the human remains from Hirota as resembling the Yayoi population (e.g., Nakahashi 2005, 252), others have pointed out that the Hirota remains differ significantly from both mainland Yayoi and Jōmon examples. The overall height is significantly shorter, and the skulls are relatively small and round (Ikehata 1990, 127–128; Doi 1998, 99–100; 2018, 62–63). The distinctiveness of the Hirota skulls is striking when placed side by side with Yayoi and Jōmon skulls.[3] The Hirota remains closely resemble those excavated from other sites of similar vintage in Tanegashima (Ikehata 1990, 127). Two sets of Yayoi-era remains from Yomitan in Okinawa also morphologically resemble the Hirota sample (Doi 1998, 99–100; 2018, 64–65; Nakahashi 2005, 252). Two adult skeletons excavated in 1978 from Ushuku in northern Amami-Ōshima, both approximately two thousand years old, also resemble Hirota site remains (Kasari-chō 1997, 1–9).

From this sample we can draw two tentative conclusions. One is that human movement and a likely economic connection took place between parts of the Ryukyu Arc from Tanegashima to central Okinawa. Shell artifacts also support this point (Doi 2018, 74–76), as does the pattern of the shell trade (chapter 2). During the late Yayoi and early Kofun eras, Tanegashima became a major hub in the shell trade between the Ryukyu Islands and northern Kyushu (Yoshinari 2018, 58; Shinzato Takayuki 2018, 40). Second, whatever the mix of people living in the Ryukyu Arc circa 2,000 years ago may have been, it included some people who resembled neither the Jōmon nor Yayoi populations of Japan.[4]

The most commonly unearthed human remains in the Ryukyu Islands are from the early modern era. Significantly, these remains closely resemble mainland Japanese skeletons from the same era. Moreover, early modern Ryukyu remains are distinct from prehistoric Ryukyu remains. In other words, the greatest change in human morphology within the Ryukyu Islands was a function of time, not place (Doi 2018, 78–81). That period of major change was the *gusuku* era, roughly the eleventh through fifteenth centuries.

For example, when the Urasoe Yōdore mausoleum was excavated (1996–2004), remains from approximately 156 skeletons were recovered, but the bones and bone fragments were mixed and dispersed. The Eiso #2 tomb contained some especially well-preserved bones and fragments, and the team put them together in the manner of a jigsaw puzzle. The resulting skull was entirely unlike prehistoric Ryukyuan examples. It was elongated, with a flat face, and displayed characteristics typical of skulls from mainland Japan during the Kamakura and Muromachi eras (Doi 2018, 90–92). Such skulls are typical of the *gusuku* era, and they reflect a large influx of people from the Japanese mainland into the Ryukyu Islands.

In other examples, ten skeletons from the Yaeyama Kuramoto site in Ishigaki from the fifteenth to sixteenth century look exactly like other *gusuku*-era examples, the skulls featuring an elongated face and a protruding lower jaw (Doi 1998, 101; 2018, 116–117). Human remains dating from the fourteenth through sixteenth centuries have been found at three different sites in Miyako. Their skull morphology is similar to *gusuku*-era Okinawa examples, but with more variation (Doi 2018, 117–118).

Writing around 1995, physical anthropologist Dodo Yukio criticized the widely held notion that the populations of the Amami Islands and Okinawa are essentially of Jōmon ancestry and thus closely related to Hokkaidō Ainu. According to Dodo's analysis, which focuses on small variations in skull morphology as an index, the populations of the northern and central Ryukyu Islands are far removed from Jōmon people or Ainu. Instead, they have nearly a classic "Mongoloid" morphology similar to ancient Yayoi immigrants to Japan, modern residents of Honshu, northern Chinese, or Mongolians. He calls for a rethinking of the simplistic model whereby Yayoi people came into the central regions of the Japanese mainland, spread north and south, but did not reach Hokkaidō or the Ryukyu Islands (Dodo 1995, 170–171). In other words, Dodo calls into question the dual structure hypothesis with respect to the Ryukyu Islands.

The Dual Structure Hypothesis

In the 1920s anthropologist Torii Ryūzō (1870–1953) argued that the modern Japanese population derived from prehistoric mixtures of Ainu, a southern people, and a continental people. As part of his model of Japanese origins, Torii argued that Ainu once lived from Okinawa to Hokkaidō. One piece of evidence Torii cited was the distribution of what he called "Ainu pottery"—actually Jōmon pottery—throughout all of Japan from Okinawa through Hokkaidō. Torii's ideas were highly influential, and his overall argument about the diverse origins of the Japanese nation functioned in part to justify Japanese control over Korea (Oguma 2002, 129–131). Setting aside the bulk of Torii's argument, the key point for our purposes is his popularization of the idea of Ainu and Okinawans sharing a common ancestry, which would later become understood as a Jōmon ancestry.

The Jōmon people inhabited the Japanese archipelago, including the Ryukyu Islands, from roughly 14,000–400 BCE, "probably the longest archaeological period in the world." Jōmon people were hunter-gatherers and fishers. They also domesticated plants such as barnyard grass, perilla, and soybeans but did not rely on them as staple foods (Rhee and Aikens 2021, 45).

During the 1980s and 1990s, Hanihara Kazurō (1991) advanced a model of Japanese origins commonly known as the dual structure hypothesis. This hypothesis has been and remains highly influential, and it is also known as the Hanihara hypothesis. Simply stated, Jōmon peoples who migrated into the Japanese Islands developed into the Ainu in Hokkaidō and Ryukyuans in the Ryukyu Islands. These Jōmon people also contributed to the biological inheritance of modern mainland Japanese. However, Yayoi people migrated into the Japanese Islands from Northeast Asia via the Korean Peninsula.[5] Therefore, modern mainland Japanese are biologically a mixture of Yayoi and Jōmon heritage (figure 3.1). While today we know that the genetic contribution of the Jōmon component is only about 10 percent, Hanihara's model suggests that the Jōmon and the Yayoi were of roughly equal importance. Mark Hudson (2022a, 9–10) notes that Hanihara's model "quickly became the new orthodoxy" and contributed to a "view of Japanese culture as a 'harmonious' integration of Jōmon and Yayoi."

The Hanihara hypothesis may hold up well with respect to Ainu origins, but data from the Ryukyu Islands do not support its conclusions about the early

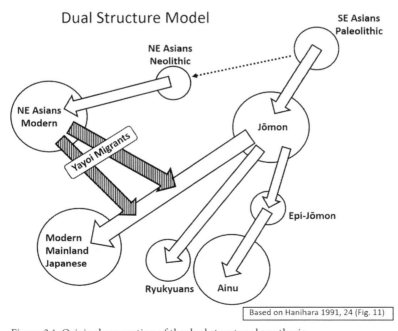

Figure 3.1. Original conception of the dual structure hypothesis.

modern and modern Ryukyuan population. It is unlikely that Hanihara was familiar with the literature in Ryukyuan history. Nevertheless, insofar as he imagines a singular "Ryukyuan" people who persist over time, Hanihara's sense of history is roughly consistent with the internal development model. The difference is that Hanihara's hypothesized Jōmon seed population was a non-Japonic group. Of course, the notion of a singular Ryukyuan people persisting over time is also a hallmark of the ancient branch model. In either context, the idea is problematic.

The main problem for the dual structure hypothesis is the *gusuku* era. As the skeletal evidence discussed above indicates, starting in the eleventh century people in the Ryukyu Islands began increasingly to resemble mainland Japanese. The simple reason is that people from the Japanese mainland swept into the Ryukyu Islands, swamping indigenous populations over a relatively short time of roughly two centuries (chapter 4). Anthropologist Takamiya Hiroto (2005, 185) points out with respect to human remains that the data "does not support Hanihara's conclusion. In other words, early-modern Okinawans are not in the same cluster as Ainu and Jōmon people; they clearly are a group closest to the cluster of Yayoi people who arrived [in the Japanese Islands] from abroad." Commenting on recent whole-genome genetic evidence, which indicates a close similarity between mainland Japanese and Ryukyu Islanders, Takamiya states that during the *gusuku* era, "farming people from the [Japanese] mainland colonized [the Ryukyu Islands], bringing with them proto-Ryukyuan." The recent genetic evidence "is especially valuable because it refutes the famous 'dual structure hypothesis of the Japanese'" (*Asahi Shinbun Digital* 2022).

DNA Evidence

DNA evidence is potentially much more powerful than morphological evidence in determining the biological affiliation or admixtures of ancient populations. Technical challenges in analyzing the relatively small sample of ancient human remains from the Ryukyu Islands have been a significant limiting factor, but recent advances in DNA analysis have provided important new evidence. DNA results are sensitive to sampling procedures and the selection of analytical methods. Interpreting DNA results usefully often requires a suitable comparative context. Moreover, DNA conclusions are often insufficiently precise in the temporal dimension to be more than suggestive with respect to the timescales of use to historians.[6] Compared with genetic evidence, archaeological evidence typically allows for the most precise dating, and the dating of human remains often depends on objects unearthed along with the bones.

Other problems with the use of DNA evidence for reconstructing human history are not technical in a narrow sense (experimental design, modelling, analytical methods, etc.). Instead, they involve unwarranted assumptions and a lack of appreciation for important contexts. The dual structure hypothesis has been so influential that many DNA studies presuppose it. For example, a study by Matsukusa et al. (2010, 221) assumes Jōmon-era ancestors for the Ryukyuan population as a starting premise.[7] Similarly, in their introductory material Sato et al. (2014, 2930) present Hanihara's dual structure model as widely accepted, as do other studies (e.g., Jinam et al. 2012, 787–788).

Additionally, it is not uncommon for DNA studies to begin with the unwarranted assumption that the Ryukyu Islands and their populations were "isolated," as if the seas around them functioned as a barrier (e.g., Bendjilali et al. 2014). Matsukusa et al. (2010, 221) also begin with this assumption, but they note that "puzzlingly, genetic data in this study show no evidence of isolation(s) in [Ryukyu] islanders." Indeed, the lack of isolation of the Ryukyu Islands is a conclusion reported in many DNA studies. This lack of isolation can be seen in genetic diversity levels, which are approximately the same within the Ryukyu Islands as in surrounding populations: "Ryukyu islanders and other East Asians had similar levels of within-island genetic diversity" (Matsukusa et al. 2010, 215). Similarly, "the mtDNA, Y-STR and A-STR analysis of the Ryukyu islanders showed no remarkable within-population diversity compared to other East Asians . . . suggesting no evidence for long-term genetic isolation" (219). Other genetic studies have reached similar conclusions.[8]

With respect to contextualizing DNA studies, the most important for our purposes is an awareness of the *gusuku* era. Recall that the implications of the *gusuku* era are awkward for the internal development model. The realities of the *gusuku* era also contradict the dual structure hypothesis, at least with respect to the Ryukyu Islands. Even studies that presuppose the dual structure hypothesis, and thus Jōmon ancestry, sometimes note that Jōmon traces are absent in modern populations. For example, "Because there have been recent migrations from Honshu to main-island Okinawa, and from main-island Okinawa to Sakishima [the southern Ryukyu Islands], any trace of a J[ō]mon-era common ancestor would have been eliminated" (Sato et al. 2014, 2933). "Recent" is a potentially misleading term in this context, and many readers might assume it refers to the early modern or modern era. However, the only migration large enough fundamentally to alter the genetic makeup of the population took place early in the *gusuku* era. Some genetic studies that are well informed historically do factor the *gusuku* era into their conclusions. For example, regarding the oldest of three waves of migration into Miyako and nearby islands and "considering the archaeological evidence and the results of haplotype sharing and D statistics analyses, the time of migration into Irabu/Ikema may date back to the Gusuku period (900–500 BP) as described in the introduction" (Matsunami et al. 2021, 2053).

Because of technical limitations, the majority of published research has focused on Y chromosome DNA, inherited from the male line, and mitochondrial DNA (mDNA or mtDNA), inherited from the female line, not full-genome studies. Neither type of DNA recombines, thus limiting the possible genetic information. As Kanzawa-Kiriyama et al. (2019, 84) note, mtDNA is "subject to chance events, such as random genetic drift, as well as gene flow and positive selection. The amount of information we can infer about social systems, such as kinship, origin, and the formation of past populations, using only mtDNA sequence is limited." What makes mtDNA useful is its high mutation rate. Mutations created new types of mtDNA, single lineages of which are called haplogroups. The frequency and locations of haplogroups can help determine ancient migration patterns.

Several studies based on mtDNA analyses (in whole or in part) have noted results consistent with the replacement of local indigenous populations of the Ryukyu Islands by northern migrants (e.g., Shinoda and Doi 2008, 16, 17; Matsukusa et al. 2010, 219).[9] Because we now have superior full-genome data, here I discuss only the mtDNA haplogroup M7a, which is associated with Jōmon populations. In Okinawa M7a occurs in 25 percent of the population, and in mainland Japan the frequency of M7a is about 7 percent (Yoshinari 2009, 244, 245, 248; Shinoda 2018, 75). Despite attempts to analyze the DNA of thirty-two skeletal samples at Ishigaki's Shiraho-Saonetabaru Cave Site, only five yielded results. Haplogroup M7a was found in three skeletons about four thousand years old. The most likely scenario for the M7a presence was the movement of Jōmon people into Ishigaki (Shinoda and Adachi 2017, 56; Shinoda 2018, 75–76, 78). The key point for our purposes is that some genetic evidence exists for a prehistoric Jōmon presence in Ishigaki Island in the Yaeyama group.

Recent DNA sequencing has yielded the first genome-wide data from the Ryukyu Islands (Robbeets et al. 2021, 620). This data partially refutes the Ryukyu portion of the dual structure model. It also refutes the hitherto widely held view that the population of the southern Ryukyu Islands was Austronesian during the Shellmound era. These new genetic data are so important that they were widely reported in the popular press (e.g., *Asahi Shinbun Digital* 2021). Let us examine the matter further.

The earliest-known Neolithic sites in the Yaeyama Islands date to approximately 4500–4200 BP (Summerhayes and Anderson 2009; Hudson 2017, 190). This early Neolithic population persisted until about 3500 BP and produced crude but functional pottery of the Shimotabaru type. After a roughly seven-hundred-year temporal gap, Yaeyama's late Neolithic phase began around 2800 BP and persisted until the *gusuku* era. The late Neolithic phase is characterized by a lack of pottery (the nonceramic period) and the presence of *Tridacna* shell and stone adzes. It is likely that the early Neolithic population died out and that roughly seven centuries later, another group settled into the islands (Hudson 2017, 190–200).

General histories of the Ryukyu Islands as well as more specialized studies have frequently characterized the late Neolithic inhabitants of the southern Ryukyu Islands as Austronesian on the basis of material culture, although Richard Pearson (2013, 77–80) has been skeptical of this portrayal. On the other side of the Kerama gap, the inhabitants of Okinawa and points northward were Jōmon people during this time (Shinzato Takayuki 2018, 20–21). Introductions to the era often feature graphic images deploying arrows and circles to indicate the flow of Jōmon people and culture coming down from the North versus Austronesian flow coming up from the South (e.g., Miyagi and Takamiya 1983b, 39; cf. figure 3.2).

Contrary to the situation depicted in figure 3.2, Bronze Age human remains from the Nagabaka site in Miyako Island are genetically 100 percent Jōmon. Moreover, "our results contradict previous assumptions of a northward expansion by Austronesian populations from Taiwan" (Robbeets et al. 2021, 620). It is

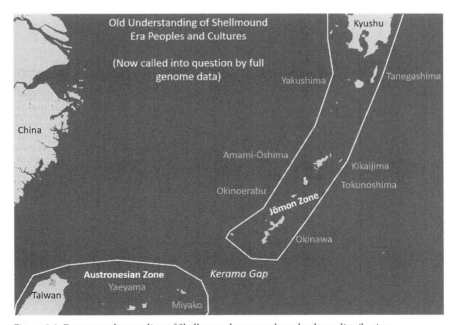

Figure 3.2. Former understanding of Shellmound-era people and culture distribution.

possible that future DNA research could indicate an Austronesian presence in the Yaeyama Islands, but the presence of the M7a haplogroup in Ishigaki and strong evidence of a Jōmon presence in Miyako make Jōmon settlement of the entire Ryukyu Islands likely.

The view of Austronesian settlement in the southern Ryukyu Islands has coexisted awkwardly with Hanihara's dual structure hypothesis and its claim of Jōmon settlement of the Ryukyu Islands. The latest genetic data support the part of the dual structure hypothesis positing Jōmon settlement. However, they contradict the claim that the modern population of the Ryukyu Islands is exclusively or largely of Jōmon derivation. As with mainland Japanese, there is indeed a Jōmon component to modern Ryukyuan genomes, but it is relatively small. Figure 3.3 summarizes the key data points for our purposes. Remains from post–*gusuku*-era Nagabaka are nearly the same as modern mainland Japanese, which constitutes further strong evidence for substantial population turnover during the *gusuku* era. Moreover, the genetic composition of modern Okinawan and Miyako populations, while containing a comparatively larger Jōmon component, is nevertheless similar to mainland Japanese, especially considering the time differences between the start of the Yayoi period and the start of the *gusuku* era.[10]

Given the overwhelming evidence from biological anthropology and genetics, it is necessary to modify the dual structure model with respect to the

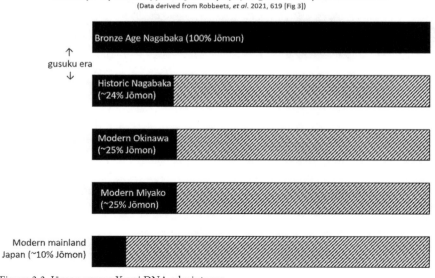

Figure 3.3. Jōmon versus Yayoi DNA admixtures.

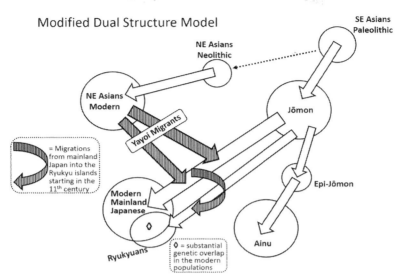

Figure 3.4. Revised depiction of the dual structure hypothesis.

population that Hanihara designated as "Ryukyuans" and depicted as separate from mainland Japanese. Figure 3.4 illustrates the key modification, whereby there is a substantial genetic overlap between mainland Japanese and Ryukyuan populations.

Austronesian Culture in the Ryukyu Islands

Writing in the early 1960s, anthropologist William P. Lebra noted a variety of cultural practices in the island of Okinawa with likely Austronesian roots:

> A few of the specific traits shared by Okinawa and Taiwan are sibling creator deities, dugout canoes (without outriggers), tattooing, red finger-nail coloring, postnatal "roasting" of mother and child, fermentation of ceremonial wine by chewing grain, banana cloth, ikat textiles, special houses for young unmarried adults, cockfighting, and bullfighting. Some of these are rare or moribund on Okinawa today but can be readily recalled by older informants.
> . . . It is not my intention to argue here for an Indonesian substratum in Okinawa but merely to indicate that the instances of shared traits are too numerous to be ignored and that these suggest lengthy contiguity and mutual influence. (Lebra [1966] 1985, 11)

The reference to postnatal "roasting" of mother and child refers to a lengthy fire-fueled sweat bath in a hut to restore the mother's health after giving birth. The practice was found throughout the Ryukyu Islands, and a physician noted it in Tokunoshima in 1798.[11] Postnatal sweat baths were also common in Austronesian Southeast Asia, including Taiwan (Kojima 1983, 57–59; 1990, 146–147; Nakayama Tarō [1929] 2012, 317).[12]

Other items could be added to Lebra's list, the most important of which is red rice and treading cultivation. Each year red rice (*akagome* or *akamai*) is planted in sacred paddyland belonging to the Hōman Shrine in the Kukinaga region of southern Tanegashima. Although now cultivated only in the shrine plots, in the past red rice was planted all over the island in both wet and dry fields. The red rice of Tanegashima is a southern rice cultivar similar morphologically, ecologically, and genetically to a variety of red rice called *bulu* in Indonesia (Watabe 1990, 386–388, 390–392). Before the 1920s, red rice was cultivated widely throughout the Ryukyu Islands.[13]

The distribution of red rice substantially overlaps the distribution of a distinctive method of cultivating rice. Called *tōkō* in modern Japanese and something different in each island, this method involves using horses or, more commonly, oxen to trample back and forth across fields in preparation for seeding or transplanting. It is found throughout much of Indonesia, the Philippines, and elsewhere in the western part of the Austronesian world. Trampling cultivation is also found throughout the Ryukyu Islands. In the southern Ryukyu Islands, a group of shipwrecked Koreans from Jeju Island noted the practice in 1477. In Yonaguni rice fields, "during the twelfth month, oxen are used to trample [the soil] and seeds are sown" (*JVRR-r*, 230). They observed the same method in Miyako (*JVRR-r*, 237). In Tanegashima, trampling cultivation usually involved teams of horses, and the method persisted there through the 1890s. Although a few early modern cases of it have been recorded in Satsuma, trampling cultivation is not found in mainland Japan (Watabe 1990, 392–395).

Not only red rice but other cultivars appear to have arrived in the Ryukyu Islands from Southeast Asia. Plant DNA studies indicate that tubers entered the Ryukyu Islands from Southeast Asia via Taiwan (Yoshinari 2018, 46–50). Moreover, taro-type tuber cultivation in wet fields is prominent in island Southeast Asia, especially around the Philippines. Taro cultivation spread north as far as the Tokara and Satsunan Islands, and it overlaps significantly with *bulu* rice and trampling cultivation (Ōbayashi 1990, 38). A wild tropical taro (*Colocasia esculenta* var. *aquatilis*) known as *fee-muji* in northern Okinawa is of Southeast Asian origin. As Matthews, Takei, and Kawahara (1992, 27) point out, "The abundance of var. *aquatilis* on Okinawa and Tanegashima in the ruderal habitat, and its absence from natural habitats, suggests that it spread with human settlement." In short, several varieties of cultivated food plants and treading cultivation appear to have entered the Ryukyu Islands from Austronesian cultures.

Southern mythology can also be found in the Ryukyu Islands. For example, in a tale from Shiraho in Ishigaki the solar deity ordered the deity Aman to create an island and people. Aman piled up stone and dirt in the sea to create an island. To seed it with humans, Aman placed a hermit crab on the island, which dug a hole. A man and woman were born from this hole in the earth and populated the island (Yamashita 2003, 86, 127, 131, 184–185; Yoshinari 2018, 256–257). Notice in the tale that the ancestral humans came forth from a hole in the ground dug by a hermit crab. That humans came from a hermit crab is perhaps the most pervasive Austronesian myth in the Ryukyu Islands. The word *aman-yo* (O. *aman-yū*) is found in all Ryukyuan languages. It means "long ago," similar to *ōmukashi* in Japanese. More literally, it means "age of the hermit crab."[14]

The presence of a wide range of culture and know-how of Austronesian origin in the Ryukyu Islands indicates contact with places like Taiwan, the Philippines, and Indonesia. Yoshinari Naoki has amassed an impressive array of evidence in support of an argument that Austronesian culture represents the deepest stratum of culture in the Ryukyu Islands. He argues not only that the pre-Japonic southern Ryukyu Islands were Austronesian in terms of population but that an Austronesian presence was in Okinawa and the northern Ryukyu Islands as well (Yoshinari 2018, 12–57). The full-genome genetic evidence described above, however, all but rules out the presence of significant Austronesian populations anywhere in the Ryukyu Islands. It is certainly possible that small groups of Austronesians could have resided in Tanegashima or other islands of the Ryukyu Arc during the Shellmound era, and there is evidence for such a scenario.[15]

However, it is likely that most of the Austronesian culture mentioned here came into the Ryukyu Islands after the *gusuku* era began, not as a result of large-scale migration but from contact in the context of trade. One likely route was via Miyako, as described in chapter 2. From the early fourteenth century, and possibly earlier, sailors based at Bora navigated to Southeast Asia to procure tropical trade goods. Another possible route during the fourteenth and fifteenth centuries was the port of Naha. Ships sailing to China to conduct tribute trade often continued their voyage south, into island Southeast and South Asia to conduct further trade. Moreover, ships from island and coastal Southeast Asia sometimes weighed anchor in Naha to conduct trade.[16]

Late Shellmound-Era Trade with Japan

Moving ahead to approximately the eighth through tenth centuries, the late Shellmound era was a time of extensive contact between the Ryukyu Islands and Japan. The islands were home to a variety of useful products that were either unique to the Ryukyu Islands or plentiful there compared to other locations.

Seashells were the most common economic product of the islands of the Ryukyu Arc. In addition to the cone, conch, and turbo shells discussed previously, giant trumpet shells (*gohoragai*) were a prized commodity found mainly in the Ryukyu Arc. Based in part on their alluring appearance, trumpet shells were in demand for use in the mantic arts from the Yayoi era onward (Ikehata 1990, 115). By themselves or with modification, shells could become a variety of fishing equipment and household items. They could be made into illumination plates, food-serving utensils, washbasins, water bowls for livestock, incense burners, vessels for boiling water, radish scrapers, ladles, tools for threading ramie, and pot cleaners and polishers. Shells also functioned as talismanic objects, as weasel repellents in chicken coops, and as decorative objects or the raw material for mother-of-pearl (Ikehata 1990, 116–117).

Another product of high value was the several varieties of tropical and semitropical bishopwood (J. *akagi; Bischofia javanica* and *Bischofia polycarpa*). A 927 entry in *Engishiki* indicates that bishopwood was shipped to Dazaifu from the southern islands each year and from there was sent to the court in Kyoto. At court, the trees went into a storehouse. As needed, government offices used bishopwood cores for bound volumes of official proclamations. The wood was also used in sutra scrolls and probably in the making of *kokto* (zithers). Bishopwood was also used for sword hilts. In 1984, two wooden tag fragments were found at Dazaifu, one with the name Amami-tō 俺美嶋 and the other with the name Iran [Irabu]-tō 伊藍嶋 (the latter referring to Okinoerabu). They date from the early eighth century and probably identified items in Dazaifu that originated from those islands. After the tenth century, Dazaifu's regular yearly intake of bishopwood faded, and ad hoc shipments from merchants doing business in the southern islands took its place (Yamazato Jun'ichi 2012, 82–87).

Other southern island products were palm fronds (*biro* or *binrō*; O. *kuba* 檳榔), hawksbill sea turtles (*taimai* 玳瑁; *Eretmochelys imbricata*), and later during the *gusuku* era, sulfur and horses. According to *Engishiki* (927), palm frond fans were used in the imperial kitchen to circulate air. The fans were also used to decorate the ox carts of nobles of the fourth rank and above. Dazaifu trade records also mention horse-riding capes made from palm fronds, and these capes made their way into several court offices dealing with elite ceremonial matters connected with the imperial family. In general, palm fronds were an elite item, whose use was limited to emperors and high nobles. Parts of the tree were also used for medicinal purposes. Seed kernels called *achimasa,* for example, were used to treat excess phlegm, abdominal pain, tapeworms, and colds (Yamazato Jun'ichi 2012, 106–110).

Hawksbill sea turtles are especially numerous in the Yaeyama Islands, where they lay eggs at Kuroshima. They also lay eggs in northern Okinawa, around Ōgimi and Kunigami villages. Hawksbill meat is not prized, but its shell and scales were used in turtle-shell crafts (*bekkō saiku*). The earliest shell fragments excavated in Nara and areas nearby date to approximately the seventh century (Yamazato Jun'ichi 2012, 110). Other valuable southern island products included sea cucumbers (*namako*), dugongs, animal hide, ramie, banana fiber cloth (*bashōfu*), shark fins, pearls, and medicinal plants (Ōhama 2008, 368). The Ryukyu Islands were home to a variety of valuable natural products, many of which were in high demand further north.

The Japanese Court and the Southern Route

Following the Yamato defeat in the 633 Battle of Baekgang (J. Hakusukinoe or Hakusonkō) on the Korean Peninsula, the court began sending embassies to China (*kentōshi*) as part of an effort to absorb as much useful, advanced technology as possible. Because of poor relations with Silla, the northern route to China via Korea was no longer viable. The eighth embassy (702) through the twelfth (752) used the southern islands route (modern name: *nantōro*). As it became aware of the Ryukyu Islands, the Japanese court sought bishopwood, palm fronds, shells, and other items from them, typically portrayed as "tribute" in official documents (Ōhama 2008, 350–351).

From as early as the seventh century, a southern route to China via the Satsunan and Ryukyu Islands was known in Japan. In 677, visitors from Tane no shima (Tanegashima) lodged at the Asuka temple (Matsuda 1981, 45–46). Treated to excellent lodgings and a banquet, these islanders probably swore allegiance to the court. In 681, court envoys sent to Tanegashima returned with a map and noted that the island was rich in marine products and grew rice, with one planting yielding two harvests per year (Matsuda 1981, 47). According to a 682 entry in *Chronicles of Japan,* "Tane people, Yaku people, and Amami people each received varying gifts from the court" (Matsuda 1981, 48). During Suiko's reign (592–628), all people south of Kyushu were "Yaku people." In other words, the Satsunan island of Yakushima stood for all the Ryukyu Islands. Afterward, the various islands gradually became distinguished from each other. During the reign of Tenmu (673–686), we find records of numerous envoys being dispatched to Tanegashima, and this situation continued during the reign of Jitō (690–697; Matsuda 1981, 48–49; Yamazato Jun'ichi 2012, 35–45).

Whereas Tenmu and Jitō sent envoys to Tanegashima (Tane-no-shima), Monmu (r. 697–707) sent them to "the southern islands" (*nantō*). Monmu sent envoys in 698 and again, three times in 699 and once in 700 (Matsuda 1981, 49–52). The second of these envoys discovered "Tokan"—that is, Tokunoshima. From around 699, Tokunoshima came into the orbit of the court as a nominal tributary.

These Yamato court envoys to the southern islands were operating several years prior to the 702 embassy to China, which used the southern island route. One of their tasks was probably to explore a new route to China via the southern islands. In 707 the court dispatched an envoy to Dazaifu, where people from the southern islands who had come to present tribute (i.e., had come to trade) received gifts and formal rank (Matsuda 1981, 53–54). In this case it is likely that the southern islanders made their way to Kyushu on their own and were thus not expected by the court. In 715 a total of seventy-seven people from Shigaki (Ishigaki), Kumi (either Kumejima or Kome on Iriomote), Amami, Yaku, and Tokan (Tokunoshima) plus *emishi* from Mutsu and Dewa were present at court, all of whom presented tribute. A follow-on entry for the fifteenth day stated that seventy-seven *emishi* and southern islanders received rank (Matsuda 1981, 54–55). Interestingly, no Okinawans are mentioned (Yamazato Jun'ichi 2012, 48–58). At least in the eyes of the Yamato court, Okinawa was not a major participant in southern island exchanges during this time.

In 735 Dazaifu dispatched officials to the southern islands to set up placards (*hai*) to assist navigation, but over the years they rotted away. In 754 the court sent a group to restore them (Matsuda 1981, 64–65). On each placard was written the name of the island, an indication of where a ship could dock, water conditions, and the distance to the next island. From context we know there was also such a marker in Okinawa, even though Okinawa was not represented by those presenting "tribute" to the court (Yamazato Jun'ichi 2012, 73–75).

Engishiki states that the Yamato embassies to China included two types of interpreters (*osa*), Silla interpreters and Amami interpreters. There is some disagreement about the significance of the Amami interpreters. Noting that until approximately the twelfth century, Ryukyuan languages and Japanese were nearly the same, Yamazato Jun'ichi (2012, 77–79) argues that the presence of Amami interpreters was probably a way for the Japanese court to demonstrate to the Tang court that it had subordinate "barbarians" in its entourage. Yamazato is probably correct regarding the status of Ryukyuan languages during the twelfth century, and he may also be correct about the prestige benefit of subordinate southern islanders. However, Yamazato seems to assume that the languages spoken in the central and northern Ryukyu Islands during approximately the eighth century were Japonic. In other words, like many scholars Yamazato mistakenly assumes a continuous line of culture in the Ryukyu Islands.

Yoshinari Naoki argues against the idea that any Japanese-based language was spoken widely in the Ryukyu Islands prior to the *gusuku* era. Certainly, trade linked the islands with Japan, but the large-scale movement of Japanese people into them had not yet happened. It is possible that a variety of Japanese was spoken earlier than the *gusuku* era in Kikaijima and in parts of Amami-Ōshima and Tokunoshima, in connection with trading posts. Even if some Japonic speakers existed within the islands, interpreters would have been needed to facilitate trade. The northern Ryukyu Islands would have received relatively more Japanese-language influence than places farther south, but non-Japonic languages were widely spoken throughout the Ryukyu Islands until the *gusuku* era (Yoshinari 2018, 27–28, 86–87; see also Ikeda 2019, 13–14).

The Southerners Attack

Japanese court envoys to the southern islands occasionally encountered hostility. For example, an envoy passing south through Satsuma on his way to the southern islands in 700 was attacked or intimidated by an armed band of "Hibito and others," a reference to Kumaso or Hayato, and in 702, Satsuma and Tanegashima rose in rebellion against the court (Matsuda 1981, 52–53). Overall, however, the documentary record suggests only a good relationship between the people of the southern islands and the Japanese court. This situation changed in 996 and 997, and it appears to have remained volatile for a least fifty years thereafter.

On the first day of the tenth month of 997, Fujiwara-no-Sanesuke (957–1046) recorded in his diary (*Ouki* or *Shōyūki*) that an emergency messenger from Dazaifu had arrived in the midst of a palace banquet. The messenger reported that Koreans ("Goryeo people") had attacked and pillaged Iki, Tsushima, and Hizen. Alarm spread through the group of high officials. Upon reading the report the messenger carried, however, they found that the marauders were "Amami people," who attacked the Kyushu provinces of Satsuma, Higo, Hizen, Chikugo, and Chikuzen; and the islands of Iki and Tsushima. The marauders set upon seafarer communities in these places, and according to the report, many attackers were hit by arrows. Nevertheless, they killed, pillaged, burned, and carried off some three hundred people. The report noted that the previous year (996) Amami marauders had attacked the Ōsumi Peninsula and carried off four hundred captives. However, Dazaifu officials did not report the matter to the court at that time (Matsuda 1981, 75–79). Fujiwara-no-Yukinari (Fujiwara-no-Kōzei, 972–1027) recorded in his diary (*Gonki*) that the marauders were "southern barbarians" (*nanbanjin*), the term also used in *Abbreviated History of Japan* (*Nihon kiryaku*, eleventh century; Matsuda 1981, 81–86).

Several points may not be obvious from the surface description. First, that the islanders attacked and carried off "seafaring people" (*kaifu*) is a meaningful detail. This term refers to the seafarers who conducted the trade discussed above. It is likely, therefore, that the violence resulted from something having gone wrong in the trade between the Ryukyu Islands and Kyushu (Yamazato Jun'ichi 2012, 138–139). The attackers would have been familiar with the trade routes from southern Kyushu through Tsushima. The force may have included Amami Islanders and probably had a base in the northern Ryukyu Islands, but it was an international group of traders whose mutual interests transcended place of origin or ethnic affiliation. Dazaifu had strengthened its participation in Amami (the northern Ryukyu Islands) during the ninth century, which encouraged island people to form separate relationships with outside groups. An "Amami-international traders combined military force" was one result (Kurima 2013a following Tanaka Fumio, 133–134).

Notice the numbers of people recorded as carried off by the raiders—four hundred in 996 and three hundred in 997. These numbers may well be exaggerated. If accurate, however, the size of the operation means that Amami islanders could not have been acting alone. Based on similar raids during this era, a force of at least ten seaworthy ships would have been required. The marauders encountered serious resistance, so they had to have been well armed. Notice also that the territory attacked was along the route between Korea and the Ryukyu Islands—precisely the route that had been in operation since the Jōmon era (chapter 2).

Initial Dazaifu suspicions of Korean ships were probably reasonable. By the tenth century, the trading base at Gusuku in Kikaijima had been established. During the following century, *kamuiyaki* kilns based on Korean technology would be established in Tokunoshima. Moreover, there were close, possibly direct ties in the shell trade between the northern Ryukyu Islands and Korea, indicated in part by the presence of a distinctive type of mother-of-pearl ladle found in both areas. In short, the attacks bring into relief most of the core cultural zone, the maritime network from the northern Ryukyu Islands to Korea via western Kyushu, Iki, and Tsushima (Yamazato Jun'ichi 2012, 139–141; Yoshinari 2018, 74–75; 2020, 20–21; Kurima 2013a, 130–131).

In 997 an iteration of this force attacked again. According to *Abbreviated History of Japan*, the next year Dazaifu ordered "Kikajima" 貴駕島 to apprehend the southern barbarians. In 999 a report from Kikajima to Dazaifu indicated that it had chastised the southern barbarians (Matsuda 1981, 86–87). There is no corroboration for any of these points. While it is possible that "Kikajima" could refer to Kikaijima, the name also commonly indicated Iōjima or other islands immediately south of Kyushu (Matsuda 1981, 86; Kurima 2013a, 129). By this time, Gusuku had become closely linked with the Korean-northern Ryukyu Islands trade network. Therefore, if indeed Dazaifu sent such a message to someone on Kikaijima in 998, the perfunctory reply the following year may have been nothing more than a formality.

In 1020 the diary of Minamoto-no-Tsuneyori (*Sakeiki*) reported a "southern barbarian" (*nanban*) attack on Satsuma. The reported response was to change the reign name and send a messenger to tell Dazaifu to chastise the marauders (Matsuda 1981, 87–88). Whatever the details, the 1020 incident probably indicated wider trade issues. Fujiwara-no-Sanesuke uncharacteristically reported no products from the southern islands arriving at court from 1020 until 1025 (Yamazato Jun'ichi 2012, 149). Indirect evidence also indicates an attack of some kind in 1054. This is because on the twenty-seventh day of the second month Dazaifu ordered the deities in its jurisdiction advanced in rank, citing the precedent of 997 (Yamazato Jun'ichi 2012, 149, 152; Kurima 2013a, 131).

Although these marauders preceded the advent of the word, multiethnic groups of armed seafarers who engaged in piracy, smuggling, human trafficking, and commerce would later become known in Korean sources as *waegu* (J. *wakō*, Ch. *wōkòu*). They played a major role in early Ryukyuan history, which I have written about extensively in *Maritime Ryukyu*. The main point here is that prior to the *gusuku* era, the northern Ryukyu Islands (not including Okinawa) became connected to the Korean Peninsula via western Kyushu in networks of trade. Moreover, trade conditions sometimes resulted in piratical violence. This general situation remained unchanged even after the start of the *gusuku* era.

Late Shellmound-Era Population Crash

Takamiya Hiroto (2005, 187–188) notes that the sudden onset of agriculture, the changes in skull morphology, the establishment of Okinawan (i.e., Japonic) dialects, and the origins of the modern Okinawan population were the result of an influx of agriculturalist colonizers at the start of the *gusuku* era. Here, summarizing Takamiya's analysis, I present a broad sketch of the population of Okinawa and nearby islands up to that point. Using the number of archaeological sites as a rough proxy for population showed a significant increase during the late Jōmon era, with the indigenous population peaking at the end of the Jōmon era, possibly

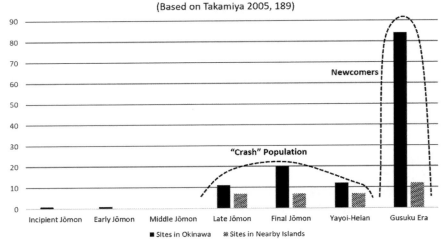

Figure 3.5. Crash of indigenous population and its replacement by newcomers.

supported by the practice of limited cultivation of plants and animals (figure 3.5). During the Yayoi to Heian periods, however, and despite trade with Kyushu, the indigenous population came under stress and began to decline precipitously (to crash). The result was a replacement of the indigenous population by agriculturalists from the north. The relatively small indigenous population eventually either died out or was absorbed (Takamiya 2005, 187–190).

Writing in the early 1990s in the context of a survey of the archaeological history of the central and northern Ryukyu Islands, Shirakihara Kazumi makes essentially the same point as Takamiya. Shirakihara notes that the period from approximately the Kofun era through the early Heian was a time of depopulation and relative quiescence in the Ryukyu Islands. He is puzzled by an apparent disconnect between this time of quiescence or decline and the vigor of the subsequent (*gusuku*) era. Shirakihara's puzzlement resulted from the tendency in both the ancient branch model and the internal development model to assume a continuous, unbroken evolution of people and society within the Ryukyu Islands since the Stone Age. Indeed, doubting the veracity of the archaeological record he had just explained, Shirakihara speculates that this apparently quiet and depopulated era must have really been more vigorous than the available evidence indicates. Otherwise, how could one explain the burst of activity and population growth that started around the eleventh century (Shirakihara 1992, 119–121)?

Shirakihara need not have doubted his own findings. The archaeological record he describes perfectly fits with later evidence, including morphological and genetic evidence, of the replacement of a declining population of hunter-gatherers with newcomers arriving from northern societies.

This chapter has covered a vast expanse of time, from approximately thirty-five thousand years ago to the start of the eleventh century. We have also examined a wide range of evidence. Simply stated, the peopling of the Ryukyu Islands included several entirely different groups, specifically:

1. Several Paleolithic populations of which we know very little. The bone fragments from the Yamashita-chō Cave Site in Naha are one example, and the more numerous Minatogawa remains are another.
2. Several Neolithic populations, most or all of whom were Jōmon people. In Okinawa the Shellmound era began roughly nine thousand years ago. The populations supported themselves by hunting, fishing, and gathering. Sometime during Japan's Yayoi Period, trading in shells and other southern island products also began. In the southern Ryukyu Islands, Neolithic people lived during the Shimotabaru Period, roughly five thousand to four thousand years ago, and then vanished. After a gap of about a millennium, a new group arrived. They were probably Jōmon people, and they lacked pottery.
3. Throughout all the Ryukyu Islands, these populations had declined significantly by the tenth century. Starting in the eleventh century, Japonic migrants began to replace them.

The Ryukyu Islands have been a maritime crossroads. This chapter should make clear that the population of the islands came from multiple sources over time and that a single population did not persist within the islands from the Stone Age to the present. This situation is one reason why Hanihara's dual structure hypothesis contains inaccuracies with respect to the Ryukyu Islands.

Hanihara was correct to posit that Jōmon people dwelled throughout the Japanese Islands, broadly defined, from Hokkaidō through the southern Ryukyu Islands. Genetic evidence now rules out a significant Austronesian presence in the Ryukyu Islands, at least from Miyako northward. However, genetic and morphological evidence ultimately refutes the dual structure hypothesis with respect to its conclusions about the modern population of the Ryukyu Islands. Biologically, it is very similar to that of mainland Japan. This is because of the population changeover that took place during the early centuries of the *gusuku* era.

Economically, the Ryukyu Islands became ever more closely connected with Japan starting in the Yayoi era, via trade in southern island products. These economic ties do not appear to have altered local culture in the Ryukyu Islands, except for pottery in some places. During the Heian period, demand for southern island products increased. As the Heian order broke down, northern migrants settled in the Ryukyu Islands. The Japonic culture of today's Ryukyu Islands has its roots in those *gusuku*-era northern migrants.

CHAPTER FOUR

Kikaijima and the Start of Japonic Ryukyu

The displacement of the sparse Jōmon population by northern migrants over the course of the eleventh and twelfth centuries was the most consequential transformation in early Ryukyuan history. These northerners came mostly from the Japanese Islands, and they brought Japonic language, agriculture, and important technologies such as ironmaking. By approximately the thirteenth century, the population of the Ryukyu Islands had come to closely resemble that of the Japanese Islands culturally and physically.[1] This chapter examines the early migrations of the *gusuku* era, with a focus on Kikaijima. In addition to explaining *what* happened, I also address possible reasons *why* the migrations took place, as well as their broader significance.

We have seen that ancient branch model historians assumed that Ryukyuan history consisted of a long, continuous line of development. Nevertheless, most of them identified the *gusuku* era in the sense of noting a major change around the eleventh or twelfth centuries. Nakahara Zenchū (1969, 212), for example, wrote that many people crossed over to Okinawa from Japan during approximately the twelfth century. Similarly, for Higa Shunchō (1971, 21, 50) the *aji* era began sometime between the tenth and twelfth centuries. Internal development model historians have recently come to use the term "*gusuku* period" (*gusuku jidai*), and like Nakahara and Higa, they note that the eleventh and twelfth entries were a time of major change. Nevertheless, few historians thus far have acknowledged the radical nature of this change.[2]

The *gusuku* era was a major discontinuity. The people who eventually created a centralized state and developed what we now call Ryukyuan culture were not descendants of Paleolithic groups such as the Minatogawa people. Neither were they descendants of the Jōmon hunter-gatherers who inhabited the islands during the early centuries of the shell trade. Instead they descended from the northern agriculturalists who replaced these earlier peoples, along with other groups of immigrants who arrived later during the *gusuku* era. The sections below describe the nature of the initial *gusuku*-era migrations and propose a theoretical framework for them.

General Characteristics of the Gusuku Era

Summarizing the *gusuku* era, Kurima Yasuo lists six characteristics. First is the emergence of locally powerful groups and their fortresses (*gusuku*).[3] Second is the emergence of agriculture, indicated by excavated carbonized grain and the bone fragments of livestock. Indeed, most scholars (but not Kurima) regard the Ryukyu Islands of the *gusuku* era as having become full-fledged agricultural societies. Third is the presence of soapstone (steatite) cauldrons from Nagasaki and *kamuiyaki* stoneware from Tokunoshima in all the Ryukyu Islands. Fourth is widespread trade, indicated by an abundance of Chinese trade pottery as well as items like metal tools, coins, and jewels. Fifth is the use of metal tools. Sixth is the inclusion of the southern Ryukyu Islands, as well as the central and northern Ryukyu Islands, into a single zone of common material culture (Kurima 2013b, 161).

Kurima also notes a tendency among archaeologists and others to transpose the basic narrative of mainland Japanese history when assessing *gusuku*-era Ryukyu. Japan became home to agricultural societies during the Yayoi era, which became the basis for the eventual emergence of a centralized state. Similarly, the development of the Ryukyu Islands is often assumed to have followed nearly the same course, only later. In this context the Ryukyu Kingdom looms large, in a problematic way, encouraging teleological interpretations of the pre-kingdom centuries (Kurima 2013a, following Ikeda Yoshifumi). I agree that the Ryukyu Kingdom, often in an idealized conception, tends to skew both early and modern (postkingdom) Ryukyuan history in problematic ways. In subsequent chapters I develop the argument that the Ryukyu Islands were not simply a late-developing, small-scale version of the Japanese Islands. At this point I simply note that a focus on the Ryukyu Kingdom directs attention to the Shuri-Naha area in the island of Okinawa. The deeper origins of the Ryukyu Kingdom, however, lie farther to the north, in the small island of Kikaijima, just across the sea from the Kasari Peninsula in Amami-Ōshima.

In the Beginning There Was Kikaijima

Kikaijima is a low island, but it is not uniformly flat. Moving westward, the terrain tends to slope downward toward Amami-Ōshima. Along much of the east side is a steep seaside cliff. The Gusuku Site Group (hereafter referred to as Gusuku) sits on a plateau about halfway between sea level and the highest point on the island. The sites in the group do not occupy the whole plateau, and they tend to be located around the edges. Outside Gusuku, several other sites from the same period are located on relatively high ground. The scale of Gusuku is strikingly large. Taken as a whole, at approximately 130,000 square meters, it is the largest archaeological site in the Ryukyu Islands. Adding coexistent sites on Kikaijima expands the scale further (Takanashi 2008a, 129–131, 138). On the eve of the *gusuku* era in the Ryukyu Islands, Kikaijima was the location of advanced technology, vast wealth, and potential power. The history of Japonic Ryukyu began in Kikaijima.

Only a few pieces of Kaneku-style pottery, the type truly local to the northern Ryukyu Islands, have been excavated from Gusuku. Most residents of Gusuku came from outside the Ryukyu Islands, and among the many imported items they brought were containers from Japan, Korea, and China. The one local variety of container pottery was *kamuiyaki,* the stoneware manufactured in Korean-style kilns in Tokunoshima.[4] Excavated pottery at Gusuku includes large quantities of Japanese-made *hajiki* and *sue* ware, soapstone cauldrons from Nagasaki, and high-quality imported wares from China and Korea. *Hajiki* and *sue* ware have all been excavated in Amami-Ōshima and Okinawa but in much lower quantities compared with Gusuku. Also, in Gusuku excavated jars or pots (for boiling) are numerous, whereas cups, bowls, and plates are few. In other words, Gusuku functioned in large part as a warehouse. Among the *sue* ware, jars and urns are the most numerous. Some were made in Higo Province (Kumamoto Prefecture in Kyushu) and some in Sanuki Province (Kagawa Prefecture in Shikoku), but most are of unknown provenance. The soapstone cauldrons, although manufactured in Nagasaki, came to Gusuku from Song merchants residing in Hakata (modern Fukuoka in northwest Kyushu). Gusuku and Hakata were closely connected. The high-quality imported trade ware also indicates connections with Dazaifu. Prior to Gusuku's discovery, the presence of Korean blueware and Korean unglazed ware in the Ryukyu Islands was thought to have been a fourteenth-century phenomenon. Because of the Gusuku excavations, we now know that these wares were present in quantity as early as the late eleventh century. The Gusuku excavations provide a glimpse into a society comprising people who were familiar with every country bordering the East China Sea (Takanashi 2008a, 132–134, 144).

Many round *suribachi*-style iron furnaces were discovered in the Gusuku sites. These furnaces and the technology they employed may have come from Bōnotsu in the southern Satsuma Peninsula. They were used to melt down old iron goods and iron sand to create iron for manufacturing new items (Tanigawa 2008a, 17; Ikeda 2019, 17). Similarly, tuyeres (stone bellows valves) have been excavated extensively in the northern (and other) Ryukyu Islands, and a large granite tuyere was found among the *kamuiyaki* kilns in Tokunoshima (Ōhama 2008, 355–356). Over one hundred sunken-pillar structures have been identified in Gusuku, many very large. The majority are thought to have been built from the late eleventh through the twelfth centuries, the peak period of Gusuku's prosperity (Takanashi 2008a, 135).

Being a low island, Kikaijima lacks significant forests. Therefore, the lumber for the Gusuku buildings had to be imported, almost certainly from nearby Amami-Ōshima. Takanashi Osamu points out that nearly all the ninth- and tenth-century shell trade sites in Amami-Ōshima are in the Kasari Peninsula, just across from Kikaijima, which also contains sites from this era. Mostly likely, Kasari and Kikaijima were part of the same geopolitical entity, which Takanashi calls the "Kikaijima orbit of power" (Kikaijima *seiryoku ken*).[5] Its characteristic feature was the presence of large quantities of nonlocal goods (Takanashi 2008a, 142–143; Smits 2019, 256n12). Eighty-five percent of Amami-Ōshima is forest. Its natural resources include manganese, copper, gold, silver, and coal. Indeed, mining continued on the island into the early twentieth century, and the ruins of old gold and silver mines remain. The Kasari Peninsula includes the largest area of land on Amami-Ōshima suitable for agriculture (Nakayama Kiyomi 2008, 198–199). The peninsula was the source of the raw material needed to sustain the massive commercial and manufacturing activity taking place next door, so to speak, in Kikaijima.

Domesticated cereal crops appeared in Kikaijima as early as the eighth century, about two centuries before the first cultivated grains appeared in Okinawa (Jarosz et al. 2022, 9). The Kikaijima-Kasari Peninsula zone appears to be the source from which agriculture disseminated southward to the rest of the Ryukyu Islands.

There are several periodization schemes for Gusuku, but the simplest will serve our purposes:

Phase 1: ninth through early eleventh centuries
Phase 2: mid-eleventh through twelfth centuries (early *gusuku* era)
Phase 3: thirteenth through early fifteenth centuries (late *gusuku* era)

Phase 2 was the peak of Gusuku's prosperity as well as a period of rapid population increase. During this time, Gusuku resembled a medieval Japanese city like Hakata or Kamakura, albeit on a smaller scale (Ikeda 2019, 15, 17).

Gusuku came into being through interaction with Dazaifu following the elimination of Tane-no-kuni (Tanegashima and Yakushima, an older commerce nexus) in 824. Both official and private trade took place during the ninth century, and indirect evidence shows that government officials resided on Kikaijima. During phase 2, Kikaijima broke with or drifted away from official Dazaifu control and began to flourish as an international commerce hub. It exerted great influence over Ryukyu-wide trade networks and was a hub for Japanese-Song trade. Chinese-made whiteware spread from Kyushu southward into the Ryukyu Islands at this time, but it is unlikely that Song merchants visited the Ryukyu Islands, even Kikaijima, directly. Similarly, there is no evidence for a south-to-north Chinese trade route via the Ryukyu Islands during the tenth or eleventh century. In other words, Chinese-made products came into the Ryukyu Islands via Japanese merchants and the port of Hakata (Yoshinari 2018, 70–71).

It is likely that Goryeo merchants and technicians did reside in Kikaijima. One reason to think so is the close connection between Korean pottery and *kamuiyaki*. Goryeo people came to Kikaijima to conduct trade, and a Goryeo community developed there. They created *kamuiyaki,* modeled after Goryeo pottery, and we find the vast majority of *kamuiyaki* in Tokunoshima and Kikaijima, with relatively little found in the southern Ryukyu Islands. Another indication of the connection between Goryeo and the northern Ryukyu Islands is that initially Dazaifu mistook the 997 Amami marauders as having come from Korea (Yoshinari 2018, 71–72, 75). Final and important pieces of evidence for the presence of Korean traders in the northern Ryukyu Islands are the blueware bowls made from kilns in Jeollanam (South Jeolla) Province and the Goreyo earthenware excavated at Gusuku. These items were daily-use goods, not trade ware, a strong indication of Korean residency (Ikeda 2012b, 334).

During phases 1 and 2 of Gusuku, the demand in Japan and the rest of East Asia for turbo shells steadily increased. Trade in turbo shells became especially active and lucrative from the tenth century onward. The hard caps of turbo shells were used in making mallets, the meat is edible, and the shells could be crafted into high-end drinking cups that became fashionable at the Heian court. The most important use for turbo shells, however, was as a source of mother-of-pearl (*raden;* MOP). Turbo shells from the Ryukyu Islands provided the raw material for expensive products. Chinese artisans consumed MOP from Japan, and Japanese artisans learned Chinese inlay techniques. By the tenth century, we find Japanese artisans producing MOP inlays in black lacquer, and in the early eleventh century, merging *makie* (gold and silver dust in lacquer) and MOP created unique Japanese designs. These objects were also prized in Korea and China.[6] Tens of thousands of turbo shells were exported from the Ryukyu Islands into Japan during these centuries (Takanashi 2008b, 225–228; Yamazato 2012, 90–93). Although turbo shells are found in Okinawa as well, Amami-Ōshima, especially the Kasari Peninsula, was the most important location for turbo shell collection during phases 1 and 2 of Gusuku (Yamazato 2012, 94–97; Yoshinari 2018, 63).

During the early *gusuku* era, the northern Ryukyu Islands of Tokunoshima, Amami-Ōshima, and Kikaijima constituted a region of intense economic activity. Gusuku was a thriving international trade hub. It received manufactured products and raw materials from all over the East China Sea region, and it was also a manufacturing site itself. Items shipped out of Kikaijima to the other Ryukyu Islands. In relative terms, the island of Okinawa was a backwater at the start of the *gusuku* era.

Migration into the Ryukyu Islands

We saw in chapter 2 that the sea connected the Ryukyu Islands with the rest of maritime East Asia. Moreover, from the Jōmon era onward, the Ryukyu Islands were never isolated. In chapter 3 we surveyed the early populations of the Ryukyu Islands, noting the strong genetic, morphological, and archaeological evidence for a new population of northerners coming into the islands during approximately the eleventh century and supplanting the sparse Jōmon population. This section examines early *gusuku*-era migration into the Ryukyu Islands in greater detail (figure 4.1).

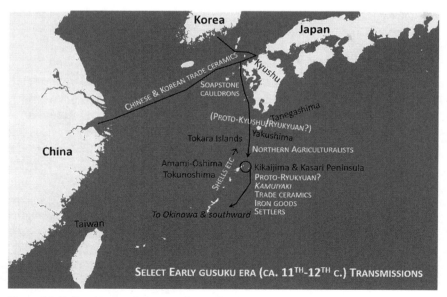

Figure 4.1. Cultural transmissions, early gusuku era.

In the broadest terms, the eleventh and twelfth centuries (earlier in the northern and central Ryukyu Islands; somewhat later in the southern Ryukyu Islands) saw a fundamental change in pottery from what Shinzato Akito calls "group A" to "group B." *Kubire-hirasoko* earthenware and other locally made Shellmound-era pottery is representative of group A. This type feels sandy, has grains of sand in the base soil, is red or contains red clay, and may flake off when touched. By contrast, group B pottery features gray minerals, phlogopite (magnesium mica), talc, or other minerals mixed into the base soil. Compared with group A, group B items are thicker and darker in color and smooth to the touch. From these characteristics, sherds lacking any design or indication of pot shape can still be categorized into one group or the other (Shinzato Akito 2018, 19–20).

Based on shape and type, group B ware resembles pottery imported from Kyushu and China. It is deeply connected with Japanese food utensil culture, which had spread over a wide area. During approximately the two millennia prior to the *gusuku* era, there was no pottery in the southern Ryukyu Islands. The appearance of group B items there brought the southern islands into a common material culture zone with the rest of the Ryukyu Islands. The replacement of group A items with those of group B indicates their introduction by outside groups, and this process took place in every part of the Ryukyu Islands (Shinzato Akito 2018, 41–42). In short, the spread of group B ware throughout the Ryukyu Islands is a proxy for the spread of a new group of people.

Ikeda Yoshifumi describes this process as starting with the building of a trading center at Gusuku during phase 1 and then spreading from Gusuku to all the Ryukyu Islands during phase 2. Starting with the Amami Islands, Japonic people spread to Okinawa, to the Miyako Islands, and finally to the Yaeyama Islands, bringing with them sunken pillar building consruction, Chinese trade ceramics, *kamuiyaki,* and the other items in the *gusuku*-era material culture package. It was a large-scale migration of people from the Japanese Islands into the Ryukyu Islands (Ikeda 2019, 18).

There is no documentary evidence connected with or describing the start of the *gusuku* era. The physical evidence indicates Kikaijima as the major staging area for migration farther south. Gusuku was the main source of the group B pottery, and *kamuiyaki,* white porcelain, and soapstone cauldrons (or pottery with ground-up soapstone powder in the clay) were the main components of a container package that spread southward throughout the Ryukyu Islands.[7] The components of this original container package are found most abundantly at Gusuku, again indicating Kikaijima as the local geographic origin of the migration.[8]

Overall, there is a significant group B pottery gradient during the eleventh and twelfth centuries, with the largest quantity found in the northern Ryukyu

Islands, a large but lesser quantity in Okinawa, and much less in the southern Ryukyu Islands (Shinzato Akito 2018, 79). After the twelfth century, the movement of people and things became more complex. Nevertheless, during the early centuries of the *gusuku* era new people and culture spread from north to south, with Kikaijima and other northern Ryukyu Islands serving as staging areas for southward migration.

The remains of communities that existed prior to the *gusuku* era are found along coastal low-lying areas. By contrast, *gusuku*-era settlements were mostly located atop limestone hills or on their slopes. The era gets its name from the fortresses (called *suku* in the southern Ryukyu Islands) associated with these settlements.

The Kian Gusuku site in Uruma, Okinawa, illustrates one possibility in the migration process and the interaction of migrants with the indigenous population. In this case, archaeological evidence indicates that two different populations, newcomers from Japan and an indigenous population, coexisted for a relatively long time: the late twelfth century until the late thirteenth or early fourteenth (Yoshinari 2022, 30–31). The indigenous population disappeared entirely in the fourteenth century (Ikeda 2019, 41).[9] The period of coexistence seen at Kian Gusuku is not the only possibility or pattern. Some early *gusuku*-era sites in Okinawa feature little or no indigenous pottery, and these sites were often organized for agriculture. They are examples of the newcomers setting up communities in which only they dwelled (Seto 2019, 49–51). The specific details of the newcomers and their interactions, if any, with the indigenous population differed significantly from one location to another (Yoshinari 2022, 31).

Zooming out for a broader view, the replacement of group A pottery with group B pottery indicates the arrival of new people, and we know from the excavation of carbonized grains that these newcomers brought agriculture. However, agriculture was not accompanied by a specific tool set or a specific set of domestic ceramics. High-quality imported trade wares dominated the ceramic assemblage of this era. Although the newcomers came from agricultural societies and continued some agricultural practices, they do not appear to have been farmers seeking new land to cultivate (Jarosz et al. 2022, 9, 16). Trade, not agriculture, probably motivated *gusuku*-era migrants.

In addition to agriculture, these *gusuku*-era migrants brought Japonic languages. Recent linguistic research has called into question the long-standing view that the first division within the Japonic language family is mainland versus Ryukyuan. Instead, it appears that there are as many as four major divisions of Japonic, and the ancestor of the Ryukyuan languages is a branch called Kyushu-Ryukyuan. Ryukyuan languages broke off from Kyushu-Ryukyuan and dispersed throughout the Ryukyu Islands. Those Kyushu-Ryukyuan speakers remaining in Kyushu eventually shifted to mainland Japanese because of extensive interactions with mainland Japanese speakers (Jarosz et al. 2022, 13; Yoshinari 2020, 43–47 following Igarashi Yōsuke). There is an especially striking seafood-related shared vocabulary between Kyushu and Ryukyuan, which permits "the conclusion that the Kyushu-Ryukyuan farmers developed a more maritime, seafaring culture after the breakup of Proto-Japonic" (Jarosz et al. 2022, 14).

Proto-Ryukyuan appears to have originated from southern Kyushu dialects. Proto-Ryukyuan was not a trading creole (e.g., in the context of the shell trade) nor a language spoken by isolated groups in Kyushu such as the Hayato (Jarosz et al. 2022, 14, 15). "The most plausible homeland for Proto-Kyushu-Ryukyuan is in southern Kyushu and the neighboring islands such as Tanegashima, Yakushima, Tokara, and Koshiki." Assuming that Proto-Kyushu-Ryukyuan is indeed a valid genealogical unit of the Japonic family, "the hotspot where we find the greatest linguistic diversity with regard to the Kyushu and Ryukyuan sub-branches would be located on the interface between the Tokara and Amami Islands, and Kikai Island would thus be a plausible homeland for Proto-Ryukyuan" (Jarosz et al. 2022, 15). More work is necessary before a strong conclusion is possible, but it may be that Kikaijima was the geographic source from which Proto-Ryukyuan dispersed southward.

Brief Synopsis of Gusuku-Era Migration

The initial wave of migration into the Ryukyu Islands took place during the eleventh through twelfth centuries. The migrants were mainly Japanese, although some direct contact may have occurred between Korea and the northern Ryukyu Islands. In any case this initial wave of migration was closely connected with the international trading center at Gusuku. At the start of the *gusuku* era, the northern Ryukyu Islands experienced the bulk of island economic activity, as indicated by the pottery gradient noted above. As time went on, the population of Okinawa increased. Over the course of the thirteenth century, Okinawa emerged as the most prominent island in the Ryukyu Arc. At the end of the thirteenth century and the start of the fourteenth, large-scale *gusuku* began to emerge in Okinawa.

By the early fourteenth century, many of these *gusuku* featured massive stone walls and other militarily effective construction features. The late thirteenth through the early fifteenth centuries was a time when *wakō* groups dwelled in the major Ryukyuan harbors and the fortresses associated with those harbors. As I discuss in later chapters, the fortunes of these groups were partly connected with the competition between them and partly connected with major political events around the region, such as the collapse of the Song dynasty in 1279, the breakup of the Yuan dynasty in the 1350s–1360s, the tumultuous final decades of the Goryeo dynasty in Korea circa 1350–1392, and the struggle between the Northern and Southern Courts in Japan, circa 1335–1392.

Most of this thirteenth- and fourteenth-century migration was to the island of Okinawa, where regional trade was flourishing. In addition to being the largest of the Ryukyu Islands in terms of land area, Okinawa had many other advantages vis-à-vis the other islands. Okinawa was centrally located yet well connected to Kyushu and Korea via line-of-sight navigation. Okinawa's coastline was well endowed with harbors, many of which became significant centers of power during the fourteenth century. The deepwater harbor of Naha could accommodate large Chinese ships. The island of Okinawa possesses the qualities of both a high island and a low island. It has good timber and water resources in the North, as well as large tracts of land in the south that can support a relatively large population. In general, the Ryukyu Islands are not well endowed with natural resources. Their main value was as an ideal location for trading and raiding—accessible to the ports of Japan, Korea, and China but outside the control of any of the region's states. Within the Ryukyu Islands, Okinawa was ideally located and equipped for such trading and raiding.

For these reasons the relative prominence of Okinawa began to increase soon after the arrival of the northern immigrants during the eleventh and twelfth centuries. During the thirteenth century, Okinawa became the most populous and economically significant island in the Ryukyu Arc. By the fourteenth century, local powers based at large fortresses (each with a harbor nearby) appeared along the eastern and western coasts of Okinawa.[10]

Reasons for Gusuku-Era Migrations

One or more waves of northern migrants swept into the Ryukyu Islands, starting in the eleventh century, displacing the preexisting Jōmon population. Based on a diverse range of evidence, we know *what* happened in some detail. Explaining *why* it happened is more difficult. There are no direct written records or other sources that enable a glimpse into the motives of those who moved south. According to Yoshinari Naoki (2022, 31), "The goal of those who immigrated from the northern Ryukyu Islands, with Kikaijima as the center, southward to Okinawa was to procure southern island products such as grey stoneware (*yamuiyaki*), bishopwood (*akagi*), and palm fronds (*birō*)." My view is the same. They came, at least initially, to profit from the trade in southern island products.

A common way of understanding migration is to analyze push-pull dynamics. In this view negative circumstances such as warfare or environmental decline "push" people away from their homelands, and potentially positive circumstances such as available lands for cultivation or valuable resources "pull" immigrants into a region (Rhee and Aikens 2021, 7). Pull factors seem mainly to have driven the *gusuku*-era migration of northern peoples into the Ryukyu Islands. Because there is no evidence of military or political upheavals driving people out of their homelands, or of natural disasters, the basic motivation for the early *gusuku*-era migrations must have been economic. In other words, the migrants saw relocation to the Ryukyu Islands as profitable. It is also possible, in this context, that they actively sought to remove themselves from state control—a push factor.

Important background factors include rising demand for luxury goods at the Heian court and increasing commercial activity during the eleventh century.[11] One of the characters in Fujiwara-no-Akihira's (989–1066) fictional *Shin-sarugaku ki* (ca. 1050s) is a master merchant called Hachirō-no-mahito. His peculiar name is typical of a fictional character, but his description is appropriate for merchants of that time. Hachirō-no-mahito conducted business from the Tōhoku region to "Kikaigashima" (Kikaijima or somewhere in the Satsunan Islands). The list of Japanese goods that Mahito traded includes gold, silver, copper, sulfur, quartz, amber, silk, cloth, thread, brocade, *kōkechi* (a type of dyed cloth), a variety of other types of cloth, sappanwood, pearls, and turbo shells. Of these items, those most desired by Song Chinese merchants were gold, silver, copper, sulfur, pearls, and turbo shells, the raw material for MOP (Batten 2006, 114; Tanigawa 2008, 21; Yamazato 2012, 160–162). It was merchants like Hachirō-no-mahito who connected Japan and the Ryukyu Islands during the eleventh century. Many of these merchants were based in Kyushu, especially in Hakata (Kurima 2013a, 252–254, citing Asato Susumu).[12]

Provincial powers began to challenge the Heian court during the tenth century, amid a "general militarization of society" (Adolphson 2007, 58).[13] Social unrest continued during the eleventh century, but there was no revolt, warfare, or similar upheaval strong enough to cause emigration to the Ryukyu Islands. We can assume, therefore, that Japanese migrants came to Ryukyu in pursuit of economic gain. As people from an agricultural society, is it possible that the newcomers to Ryukyu sought new land to cultivate? That possibility is highly unlikely. Land in mainland Japan was readily available at this time, with labor the limiting factor in agricultural production (Farris 2006, 9–10; Jarosz et al. 2022, 16). Japan's population during the eleventh century was stable, with a modest increase in the twelfth (Farris 2006, 10). As I describe in chapter 7, the Ryukyu

Islands are poorly suited for cereal agriculture. The only viable general explanation for Japonic people settling in the Ryukyu Islands at this time was their desire to profit from trade in southern island products and possibly other trading or raiding activities.

The demand for a variety of southern island products was high for a century or so before the *gusuku* era and remained so into the *gusuku* era. The demand for turbo shells, especially, increased sharply during the eleventh and twelfth centuries, and the Ryukyu Islands were the only practical source for them in the region. MOP had diffused into elite society in Japan and elsewhere in East Asia. The term often appears in twelfth-century diaries, and big projects like Konjikidō at Chūsonji in Hiraizumi and Minamoto Yoritomo's construction of Hiraizumi-shodō at Eifukiji in Kamakura required massive quantities. The Kamakura bakufu's need for large quantities of MOP added to overall demand. The popularity of *makie* (a lacquer decoration technique using MOP) was another source of demand for turbo shells (Takanashi 2008b, 227–228).[14]

Gusuku was located at the northern edge of the turbo shell range, as well as the fuzzy southern border of Japan. The Gusuku sites flourished during a time of rapidly growing demand for MOP. The sites on the Kasari Peninsula across from Kikaijima, probably part of the territory Gusuku controlled directly, are especially rich in turbo shells (Takanashi 2008a, 145). The high demand in Japan, Korea, and China for southern islands products resulted in the establishment of a new trade network during the eleventh and twelfth centuries, which extended all the way to the Yaeyama Islands. Kikaijima was the administrative center of this network (Yoshinari 2020, 31). The northern Ryukyu Islands, Kikaijima, Amami-Ōshima, and Tokunoshima, provided many of the material goods for this Ryukyu-wide trade network.

Another relevant point to consider is the breakdown of the Heian court's consistent ability to enforce its prohibition of Japanese subjects traveling abroad.[15] During the ninth and tenth centuries, the demand for luxury goods from abroad increased. One result was that Dazaifu officials often accepted flimsy excuses (typically that strong winds inadvertently blew a Chinese or Korean ship into a Japanese port) to permit more frequent trade than official regulations stipulated. In 1072, Korean records noted the arrival of two merchants from Japan. Subsequently, a "parade" of Japanese landed in Korea over the next two decades (von Verschuer [1988] 2006, 43). This direct trade with Korea at the end of the eleventh century appears to have been clandestine, and therefore it is not found in Japanese records. It was not until 1173 that a public figure, Taira no Kiyomori, conducted private trade with China in the open (von Verschuer [1988] 2006, 47). By that time, clandestine trade by unauthorized people, including the Japanese merchants traveling abroad, had been underway for at least a century.

The Heian court never officially rescinded its trade-related prohibitions. However, in the context of de facto loosening of trade restrictions and increased trade activity in the region, it made sense for ambitious Japanese trading groups to settle the Ryukyu Islands. The demand for Ryukyuan products remained strong throughout the eleventh century. Furthermore, recall that the indigenous population of the islands was in steep decline during the ninth and tenth centuries. It is entirely plausible, therefore, that local labor was insufficient to sustain the trade in shells and other valuable natural resources, thereby creating a labor gap for the newcomers to fill. Similarly, with respect to the Yaeyama Islands, Ōhama Eisen (2008, 357–358) argues that it was increasing Japanese demand for southern island products, from the tenth century onward, that caused settlers from mainland Japan to take up residence in the southern Ryukyu Islands. In any case, we know from the archaeological record that the Ryukyu Islands were linked to busy trade networks, the topic of chapter 5.

The Ryukyu Islands as a "Barbarian" Zone

In *Maritime Ryukyu* I argued that prior to the establishment of a centralized state, and even later, the Ryukyu Islands functioned as a frontier region of Japan (Smits 2019, 8, 156–157). In this section I refine this frontier region idea in the context of the early *gusuku*-era migrations, drawing on the work of James C. Scott and others. To start I question the common assumption that the establishment of agriculture inevitably leads to agricultural societies. One general point to remember is that Neolithic sedentary agricultural societies were detrimental to the health and well-being of individual cultivators.

Historically, the presence of agriculture did not necessarily lead to agricultural societies or to persistent agricultural societies. One possibility is for societies to practice agriculture only in certain times and circumstances. "In Greater Amazonia, such seasonal moves in and out of farming are documented among a wide range of indigenous societies and are of considerable antiquity" (Graeber and Wengrow 2021, 267).[16] Another possibility is that an agricultural society suddenly or gradually abandons agriculture in favor of other sources of food. For example, in the American Southwest "the overall trend for 500 years or so before Europeans arrived was the gradual abandonment of maize and beans, which people had been growing in some cases for thousands of years, and a return to a foraging way of life" (Graeber and Wengrow 2021, 254, 451).[17] Agriculture "was not a one-way process: there is a growing number of examples, over a timescale of several centuries, of people adopting aspects of agriculture alongside foraging, then reverting back to foraging, then turning to agriculture again" (Barker and Janowski 2011, 2). As Peter Bellwood (2005, 39) states, the many examples from around the world of hunter-gatherer societies that were once agricultural societies "can terminate forever the idea that evolution from foraging to farming is a one-way street."[18]

Farming does not always work out in the long run. A particularly dramatic example is the first arrival of farmers in central Europe, the bearers of Linear Pottery. Their settlement in central Europe initially resulted in a massive population increase. However, this farming population crashed dramatically, on a regional scale, between 5000 and 4500 BCE. It is likely that foragers eventually annihilated the entire initial wave of European farmers, and agriculture did not resume in the region until about a millennium later (Graeber and Wengrow 2021, 260–262).[19]

Finally, agriculture is difficult and fraught with unpleasant side effects.[20] Some populations aware of agriculture explicitly rejected it. One such "anti-agricultural" group was the indigenous peoples of California (Bellwood 2005, 40; Graeber and Wengrow 2021, 165–166, 254).[21] Regarding Jōmon people in the Japanese Islands: "A relatively small number . . . living in a tolerably productive environment would have had no major incentive to engage in agriculture, let alone wet-rice cultivation, which was the most arduous, complex, and labor-intensive form of food procurement of ancient times" (Rhee and Aikens 2021, 49). Similarly, Bellwood (2005, 114) describes Jōmon Japan as "a situation in which affluent foragers showed a decided reluctance to adopt formal grain agriculture, despite its obvious availability" in China and Korea. For similar reasons, even after wet-rice agriculture began to thrive in northern Kyushu, populations in central and northern Japan adopted it slowly and reluctantly. Jōmon societies in the Tohoku region "are known to have tried and rejected" wet-rice agriculture (Rhee and Aikens 2021, 49).

I discuss the question of whether *gusuku*-era Ryukyu was an agricultural society in chapter 7. The point of the above examples is to establish firmly the historical reality that the presence of agriculture in a society did not necessarily lead to it becoming an agricultural society. In other words, the presence of agriculture did not determine the economic destiny of a society.

Consider the common image of premodern states as sedentary communities based primarily on grain cultivation, with elite members of society supported by grain taxes. In such places disease was rampant, the work of tilling was difficult, debilitating, and uninteresting, personal freedom was minimal, and possibilities such as warfare or crop failure made life insecure. Add in the typical high tax rates, and life as a peasant was often a de facto state of servitude. Among the farmers, why would any individual or family seek to live in such conditions? The short answer is that most people did not. Whenever the coercive mechanisms of states slackened and an open frontier became accessible, peasants tended to abscond.[22] The frequent "collapse" of early agrarian states and civilizations often functioned as liberating events for surviving farmers. They often reverted to older patterns of life, which combined multiple modes of obtaining food and resources. We should keep in mind that many premodern people actively sought to avoid living in states. These are some of the arguments that James C. Scott (2017) advances.

Scott makes a useful distinction between agrarian states and the people those states often called "barbarians." From a state's perspective, barbarians were people who lived beyond state borders but who frequently interacted with the state via trading and raiding. Using the term in an ironic sense, Scott refers to a "golden age of barbarians" that lasted until about 1600 and possibly later in some parts of the world. During this golden age, "it was in many ways 'better' to be a barbarian *because* there were states—so long as those states were not too strong. States were juicy sites for plunder and tribute" (Scott 2017, 223). Although states and outlying communities of "barbarians" (in Scott's sense) were competitors, sometimes violently, they also supplied each other with necessary resources.[23] I revisit this matter in chapter 13, but for present purposes it is plausible that many of the agricultural peoples who migrated to the Ryukyu Islands did so at least in part to avoid or free themselves from state institutions.[24] Although they continued to engage in agriculture to augment fishing, hunting boar, gathering nuts, and so forth, they came to the Ryukyu Islands mainly to participate in potentially lucrative trade. As I argue in *Maritime Ryukyu,* trading in this region was always intertwined with raiding. Within the geographical context of the East China Sea, the Ryukyu Islands were an ideal location for "barbarian" communities to prosper vis-à-vis surrounding states.

Japonic Ryukyu began in the eleventh century with the southward expansion of people and commercial activities from the international trading base at Kikaijima. This event represents a major discontinuity in the early history of the Ryukyu Islands, as northern migrants from Japan and, in smaller numbers, possibly from Korea settled the Ryukyu Islands from north to south. In the process the northerners replaced the sparse local population of Jōmon people and introduced a cultural package that included group B pottery, *kamuiyaki,* soapstone cauldrons, iron tools, agriculture, fortresses, and proto-Ryukyuan languages.

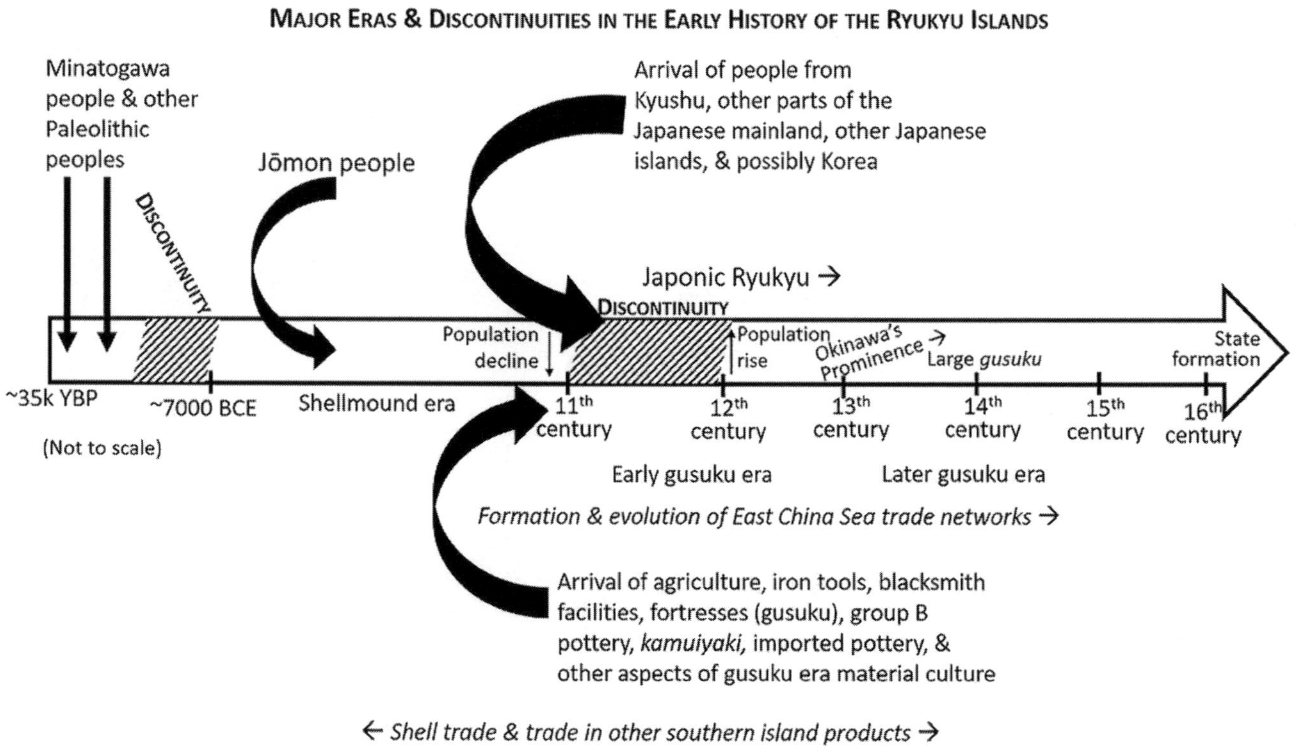

MAJOR ERAS & DISCONTINUITIES IN THE EARLY HISTORY OF THE RYUKYU ISLANDS

Minatogawa people & other Paleolithic peoples

Jōmon people

Arrival of people from Kyushu, other parts of the Japanese mainland, other Japanese islands, & possibly Korea

Japonic Ryukyu →

DISCONTINUITY

DISCONTINUITY

~35k YBP

(Not to scale)

~7000 BCE

Shellmound era

Population decline

Population rise

Okinawa's Prominence →

11th century

12th century

13th century

14th century

15th century

16th century

State formation

Early gusuku era

Large gusuku

Later gusuku era

Arrival of agriculture, iron tools, blacksmith facilities, fortresses (gusuku), group B pottery, kamuiyaki, imported pottery, & other aspects of gusuku era material culture

Formation & evolution of East China Sea trade networks →

← Shell trade & trade in other southern island products →

Figure 4.2. Major eras and discontinuities.

The history of Japonic Ryukyu began in Kikaijima and the nearby northern Ryukyu Islands, which supplied Gusuku with necessary material. As migrants moved southward, the population of the island of Okinawa increased. Eventually, owing to immigration and geographical advantages, Okinawa became the most prosperous and populous of the Ryukyu Islands. By the end of the thirteenth century, large fortresses began to appear on the island of Okinawa, even though the formation of a centralized state was still far in the future.[25]

Although the early *gusuku*-era migrants came from agricultural societies and brought agriculture with them, nothing indicates that they traveled to the Ryukyu Islands in search of new fields to till. Instead, trade in southern island products was the main economic force behind the migrations. Moreover, it is possible that the declining indigenous Jōmon population led to a reduction in the supply of these products at a time of rising demand. This situation, along with the decline of the power of the Heian court, provided an incentive for Japanese to settle into the Ryukyu Islands and conduct trade. Additionally, it is possible that at least some of these early *gusuku*-era settlers actively sought a "barbarian" lifestyle whereby they lived outside of state control but profited via interactions with the region's states.

Figure 4.2 summarizes the major conclusions up to this point regarding the groups of people who came into and dwelled in the Ryukyu Islands. Notice the presence of at least two major discontinuities in which populations died out or were replaced.

CHAPTER FIVE

Spokes and Hubs

Modeling East China Sea Regional Trade

Chapter 4 examined the early *gusuku* era migration into the Ryukyu Islands and noted that immigrants came mainly for trade, not in pursuit of new lands to farm. Relying mainly on archaeological evidence, this chapter examines regional trade during the early *gusuku* era, roughly the eleventh through early thirteenth centuries. I propose a hub-and-spoke model, similar to the mapping of air travel, as the best way of characterizing this trade (figures 5.1 and 5.2). This approach brings a complex geographic situation into relatively clear relief, and it enables easy modification to accommodate important changes when new hubs or spokes come into existence and others fade.

In *Maritime Ryukyu* I introduced the term "Northern Tier islands" to describe the closely interlinked group of Kikaijima, Amami-Ōshima, and Tokunoshima. During the early *gusuku* era, the Northern Tier islands constituted a major trade hub to which all the Ryukyu Islands were connected. In the northern direction, trade routes linked the Northern Tier islands with the southern part of the Satsuma Peninsula near the mouth of the Manose River (Minami-Satsuma City). Here I refer to this area as Mottaimatsu, after the largest of several archaeological sites located there. North from Mottaimatsu, coastal sailing along western Kyushu led to the region's most important port, Hakata (Fukuoka City).

Hakata rose to prominence during the middle to late eleventh century, at about the same time Gusuku began to flourish and Dazaifu began to fade. The Kōrokan at Dazaifu lodged foreign envoys and embassies, and it was in use until approximately the mid-eleventh century. The ascendancy of Hakata marked the beginning of the age when Japanese and foreign maritime traders became especially active. About a century into that era, during the 1150s, Taira-no-Kiyomori seized control of trade and drove Minamoto elements out of Kyushu. The Taira had become involved in Song trade during the time of Kiyomori's father, Tadamori. Tadamori defeated Inland Sea pirates, extended his power westward, and traded with foreign merchants at Hizen Kanzaki no Shō. Kanzaki was a large estate facing the Ariake Sea, and it also held territory in Hakata. It was in the

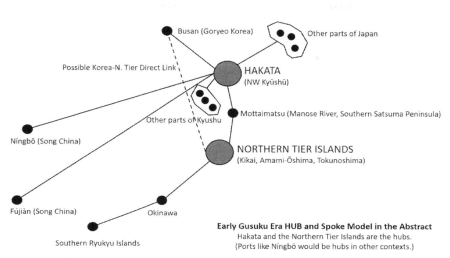

Figure 5.1. Hub-and-spoke relationships, early gusuku era (abstract).

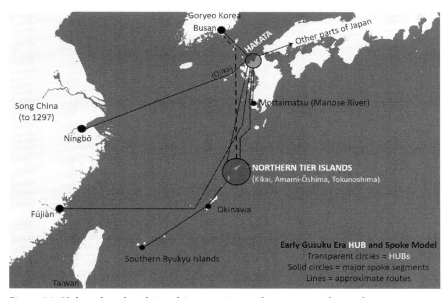

Figure 5.2. Hub-and-spoke relationships superimposed on a map, early gusuku era.

Hakata territory that Song ships anchored and conducted trade (Batten 2006, 120–123; Tanigawa 2008, 18–19).

Chinese merchants came to Hakata and set up shops and trading facilities there during the eleventh century. Major imports from China were incense, brocade, copper coins, writing tools, books, sugar, sappanwood, and porcelain. The major exports sent from Japan to China were gold or silver, sulfur, mercury, pearls, lumber, fine jewelry and crafts, and weapons. Of these items, lumber and sulfur were especially prominent in terms of volume. Among the fine jewelry and crafts were fans, swords, mother-of-pearl desks, and *suzuribako* (writing tool boxes). This situation prevailed from the second half of the eleventh century through the twelfth century. Vast quantities of Song and Goryeo trade porcelain have been excavated from Hakata. It served as a base for trade that extended as far north as the Tōhoku provinces of Mutsu and Dewa and as far south as the Ryukyu Islands (Tanigawa 2008, 19–20, following Kamei Meitoku and Saeki Tomi).

Hakata–Korea Spoke

In *Goryeo History* we find the following items brought by Japanese traders to Korea during the second half of the eleventh century: mother-of-pearl inlaid saddles, swords, writing tool boxes (*suzuribako*), mirror boxes, combs, desks, illustrated folding screens, incense burners, arrow quivers, mercury, mother-of-pearl, pearls, livestock, sulfur, and turbo and spiral (conch) shells (*Goryeo History* 1:48, 50–53). The southern products such as spiral and turbo shells most likely shipped to Korea from Hakata and would have been stored there for transshipment (Tanigawa 2008, 22–23). Korean ceramics have been excavated in large quantities from sites in or near Hakata, but they become much less common moving farther south in Kyushu (Nakamura 2008, 76). Since ancient times, Northwest Kyushu had served as the major point of contact between mainland Japan and the Korean Peninsula. As the pace of East China Sea trade increased during the eleventh century, Hakata, via Iki and Tsushima, became the major conduit for goods flowing between the Korean Peninsula and the Japanese mainland.

Hakata–Song Spoke

During the late Heian and early Kamakura periods, Japanese sailors began to use monsoon winds to sail to China. This and other advances in navigation made the journey from Hakata to Níngbō in China as short as one week (Tanigawa 2008, 19, citing Saeki Tomi). Underwater excavations have recovered many anchor stones from Chinese ships and Chinese trade ceramics from Maegata harbor in the small island of Ojika, one of the Gotō Islands. It is now clear that the island was a pivotal anchorage along a trade route that ran directly across the East China Sea from Níngbō to Ojika and then north to Hakata (Azuma 2008, 30–34; Kurima 2013a, 232, following Saeki Kōji).

In addition to this relatively direct route was the southern islands route discussed in chapter 3. Early in the *gusuku* era, this route ran from Fúzhōu or nearby areas in southern China across to Okinawa, then up through the northern Ryukyu Islands and along western Kyushu to Hakata. Starting in 1995, large quantities of Chinese ceramics were recovered from the seafloor off Uken in Amami-Ōshima (the Kurakizaki Undersea Site at the mouth of Yakiuchi Bay). They date from the twelfth to thirteenth century. Two anchor stones from Chinese ships were also recovered (Azuma 2008, 33). The nearly fourteen hundred pieces of excavated blueware were determined to have come from the Tóng'ān and Lóngquán kilns in southern China. These and other excavated items came from a single Chinese ship bound for Hakata (Nakayama Kiyomi 2008, 196–197). In addition to providing information about one of the routes that Chinese ships traveled, the site provides a snapshot of a merchant vessel's cargo.

Discovery of the Hakata Site Group in 1977 in connection with subway construction turned up large quantities of trade ceramics. During the eleventh century, whiteware predominated, giving way to blueware from the Lóngquán and Tóng'ān kilns during the late twelfth and early thirteenth centuries. Especially striking is black writing pottery (*bokusho tōjiki* or *bokusho doki*), with each item bearing a brushed-on character to indicate the merchant shop to which it belonged. Characters included surnames such as Dīng, Lín, Wáng, Chén, Zhāng, and others. The characters also included names with *-gāng* 綱 (J. *-kō*) as a suffix to indicate specific export associations. The title Hakata *gāngshǒu* (J. *kōshu*) refers to leaders of the merchant associations. Black character pottery is found elsewhere in Kyushu, but the vast majority is in Hakata (Batten 2006, 127–129; Azuma 2008, 37–38).

By the early twelfth century, we find the term "Hakata-tsu Tōbō" 博多津唐房 (or "Hakata-tsu Karabō") or "Hakata harbor Chinese neighborhood" appearing in documents. The Chinese merchant community in Hakata composed Japan's earliest Chinatown. Roughly twenty other coastal locations in western Kyushu are named Tōbō or Karabō, or contain those elements in the name, including the Mottaimatsu area. Chinese trade porcelain has been excavated near most of them (Azuma 2008, 43–48; Tanigawa 2008, 23–24). Despite the presence of Chinese ware at these locations, their pottery profiles differ significantly from that of Hakata. There is no strong evidence that Chinese merchants set up long-term residence at any location in Kyushu other than Hakata. It is more likely that

Chinese ships bound for Hakata periodically stopped at these locations (Shinzato Akito 2018, 141). During the twelfth century, ambitious Japanese merchants occasionally sailed to China directly. One result was improved knowledge of navigation and shipbuilding. These merchants brought new technologies to the Ryukyu Islands early in the *gusuku* era (Shimoji 2008, 330).

Hakata–Northern Tier Spoke

Hakata was the main gateway into Japan for Chinese people and products early in the *gusuku* era. It was also the primary conduit for Chinese and Korean products coming into the Ryukyu Islands. Furthermore, soapstone cauldrons, manufactured mainly in the Nishisonogi Peninsula of Nagasaki, entered the Ryukyu Islands via the Hakata–Northern Tier spoke before some moved southward. The prominence of the Northern Tier islands is indicated by the distribution of imported kitchenware during the late eleventh through mid-twelfth centuries. Of a total of 842 excavated sherds from this time period, 480 came from the Northern Tier islands, 328 from Okinawa and the surrounding islands, and 34 from the southern Ryukyu Islands (Shinzato Akito 2018, 79).

By the late twelfth century, this pattern began to change. The late twelfth century to the mid-thirteenth was the peak of Chinese ceramics in Kyushu, with blueware becoming especially prominent. Ryukyuan sites also reflect this situation, with an increase in both the number of sites in which imported kitchenware was found and the number of sherds (1,260 total as of ca. 2018). The number of sherds increased significantly in Okinawa (902) and the southern Ryukyu Islands (99) but decreased in absolute and relative terms in the Northern Tier islands (259). This shift is one indication that Okinawa had begun to replace the Northern Tier as the center of economic activity in the Ryukyu Islands.

Soapstone cauldrons tell a similar story. The Ryukyu Islands are home to the third-largest concentration of soapstone cauldron fragments. Moreover, because many of these cauldrons were ground up to make powder to mix with clay for soapstone-infused local pottery, the actual quantity of cauldrons imported into the Ryukyu Islands may have been much larger than the sherd count suggests. The vast majority of this ware has been excavated at Gusuku, and very little has been found in the southern Ryukyu Islands (Shinzato Akito 2008, 65; 2018, 55–56). The type of cauldrons found in the Ryukyu Islands feature ear-like lug handles. One way to explain this distribution pattern is as a multitiered delivery system, with the main conduit from Hakata to Gusuku and a secondary distribution zone from Gusuku to other Ryukyu Islands. Because soapstone cauldrons spread at the same time and in the same pattern as Chinese trade ceramics, it is likely that Chinese merchants in Hakata or their agents sent cauldrons to Gusuku in exchange for southern island products (Shinzato Akito 2018, 55–56, 62).[1]

Starting in the late twelfth century, a new type of soapstone cauldron was produced that featured a brim and no lug handles. This new type is extremely rare in the Ryukyu Islands. Therefore, soapstone cauldrons stopped coming into the Ryukyu Islands around the end of the twelfth century (Shinzato Akito 2018, 79–80). The cessation of stoneware imports is probably one indication of the decline of Gusuku, and thus the Northern Tier islands, as a trade hub.

The imported pottery distribution suggests that until the late twelfth century, all the Ryukyu Islands moved in step with Gusuku and the Northern Tier. From the thirteenth century onward, however, trade routes became more complex. It is possible that one or more alternative routes developed to bring Chinese pottery into the Ryukyu Islands, offsetting the decline of the Hakata–Northern Tier spoke. Okinawa began to break away from Gusuku around this time, and communities in Okinawa probably found alternative sources for Chinese ceramics (Yoshinari 2020, 89–91). The invasion of Kikaijima by the forces of Minamoto Yoritomo in 1188 was undoubtedly a major reason for both the decline of imported kitchenware into the Northern Tier and for Okinawa moving away from Gusuku's control (Yoshinari 2020, 92).[2]

In any case, the Hakata–Northern Tier spoke was a vigorous trading conduit during the eleventh and most of the twelfth century. Thereafter, it declined. Replacing this spoke was trade between merchants in a variety of Kyushu locations and the Ryukyu Islands, especially Okinawa. At some point, direct trade between Okinawa and China began, a topic I take up in chapter 10. The southern Ryukyu Islands also developed direct trade ties with southern China, probably earlier than Okinawa did (chapter 2).

Northern Tier-Mottaimatsu Spoke

The excavation of sites near the mouth of the Manose River in the southern Satsuma Peninsula indicates that this area was an active trading center during the eleventh and twelfth centuries. One characteristic of Mottaimatsu, the most prominent of these sites, is the dominance of containers among the excavated pottery. A relatively large proportion of containers indicates trade. Excavations that started in 1997 revealed five sunken pillar buildings, a dugout building, and two earth pit graves. Among these remains were found Japanese *hajiki* and *sue* ware, pottery from every region of Japan, soapstone cauldrons, grindstones, inkstones, and iron goods. Of the approximately 11,200 pieces (fragments) of remains excavated, about half was local pottery. Chinese blueware totaled

17 percent; Chinese whiteware, 11 percent; and Chinese containers, 11 percent. Pottery from other parts of Japan composed 12 percent (Nakamura Kazumi 2008, 80–82). In short, Mottaimatsu was a site at which imported Chinese and Japanese pottery and other valuable items were exchanged.

Small quantities of *kamuiyaki* have also been found at Mottaimatsu, with more excavated at the nearby Shibahara site and other sites in the area. One of the Japanese-made items is revealing: tile ware bowls of the *kuzuha* 楠葉 type from the early twelfth century. They were not trade goods, and their presence indicates that a group of people, probably outsiders with connections to the capital, resided in the area. It is quite possible that this group was overseeing the trade (Nakamura Kazumi 2008, 83–88).[3]

The composition of imported trade pottery found in the Mottaimatsu area roughly matches the items that a Chinese cargo ship's hold would have carried. The port at the old mouth of the Manose River was suitable for conducting direct trade with Chinese ships. The time frame and composition of the Kurakizaki Undersea Site in Amami-Ōshima (discussed previously) closely resembles the Chinese ware in Mottaimatsu and nearby sites. Bōnotsu, just to the south, is usually considered the largest international trade port in the region, but prior to the Kamakura period, the Manose River area was a stopping point for ship traffic (Kurima 2013a, 228–230).

The presence of a significant quantity of Chinese porcelain in the lower Manose River area, as well as the "Chinatown" place-names mentioned previously, indicates a connection with Hakata and the likely possibility that Chinese ships on their way to Hakata sometimes anchored in the area. The extensive presence of *kamuiyaki*, which is rare elsewhere in Kyushu, indicates a significant regional spoke extending from the Northern Tier islands to the Mottaimatsu area for the conduct of trade between the northern Ryukyu Islands, the Tokara Islands, and the Satsuma Peninsula during the early *gusuku* era (Shinzato Akito 2018, 142; Seto 2019, 56). Another indication of this link is the excavation of turbo shells from the Shiraitobaru site in the lower Manose River area (Nakamura Kazumi 2008, 88).

In *Maritime Ryukyu,* following the work of several Japanese scholars, I noted that when paired with Yashiro (Yatsushiro), *Omoro sōshi* references to "Yamato" did not mean Japan as a whole but the southern edge of the Japanese mainland (Smits 2019, 31–32, 258n72). It is possible that this early trade spoke between the northern Ryukyu Islands and the Satsuma Peninsula (the Manose River area and later Bōnotsu) contributed to a sense of geography whereby the southern Satsuma Peninsula functioned as "Yamato" from a Ryukyu Islands perspective.

Northern Tier-Central and Southern Ryukyu Spoke

Early *gusuku* era communities in Okinawa are found mainly along the central and southern coasts. Unlike Shellmound-era communities, these newer settlements featured standardized buildings and pit tombs for the reburial of cremated bones, as well as the usual *gusuku*-era pottery package. These features shared much in common with Gusuku in Kikaijima and also resembled Mottaimatsu (Seto 2019, 46–47, 56). Okinawa had two types of early *gusuku*-era communities. One appears to have functioned mainly as a trading post; the other type was a settlement community. Trade-oriented communities were located in coastal areas, and their buildings were typically haphazard in orientation. There were ditches in these communities, but they did not separate the buildings. Graves of the same type at Gusuku are found close to the buildings and oriented toward them. These sites were probably used as temporary residences by a variety of trading groups with primary bases in the northern Ryukyu Islands (Seto 2019, 47–49). By contrast, the settlement-oriented communities were further inland. They featured buildings with the same orientation and open spaces for agriculture (Seto 2019, 49–51).

The *gusuku* era began during the eleventh century in the northern and central Ryukyu Islands but not until the early twelfth century in the southern Ryukyu Islands. This time difference is another indicator of the north-to-south movement of people and culture characterizing the era. On the island of Miyako, all but one (Sumiya) of the seven known early settlements were located along its northeast coast. At these northeast coast sites, excavated items include two types of Chinese whiteware bowls, several types of blueware bowls, plates from the Tóng'ān kiln, and blue-white ware. However, the quantity of these items is small. By contrast, dark-brown glazed ware and *kamuiyaki* from Tokunoshima were found in greater quantities than Chinese ware. The majority of the dark-brown glazed ware and *kamuiyaki* came into Miyako from points further north. Similarly, the Miyako communities themselves were likely founded by people who came to the island from Okinawa, the northern Ryukyu Islands, or Japan. They were communities of mariners, which persisted until the fourteenth or fifteenth century (Shimoji 2008, 334–336). The twelfth- and thirteenth-century population of Miyako was relatively small, but during the fourteenth century, it grew rapidly (Shimoji 2008, 339–340).

In the Yaeyama Islands between the eleventh to thirteenth centuries, trade was conducted by groups from Japan traveling south. Products included soapstone cauldrons and Chinese whiteware and eating utensils. Later, more varieties of whiteware, several varieties of blueware, dark-brown glazed storage pots, and a variety of *magatama* and other beads or jewels came into the area. Other excavated early *gusuku* (*suku*)-era goods include stone ovens, soapstone cauldrons, broad fibrous leaves (Kuba [*birō*], banana, and others), *kamuiyaki,* and other large earthenware storage containers. These items reflect a major change in material culture for a region that had previously been without any pottery (Ōhama 2008, 355–357).

Origins of Ryukyu describes the Sakibaru grove in Ōhama, Ishigaki Island. It honors two brothers, Hirumakui and Kōchitamagane. Noticing that there were no iron farm tools on the island, the brothers built a ship and sailed with a small crew to Bōtomari, near Bōnotsu in the southern Satsuma Peninsula, to buy these items. There they met a white-haired old man, possibly the deity Hachiman in blacksmith mode, who gave them a box. The box magically guided their ship back home and functioned as a container for transferring a blacksmith deity to Ishigaki (*Origins* [1713] 1988, 600–601). This tale is but one of hundreds of blacksmith-related legends and origin stories in the Ryukyu Islands. It reflects the importance of iron and ironmaking technology, as well as the northern origins of that technology. Tuyeres for small-scale earth bellows have been found at sites throughout the Yaeyama Islands.[4] In other words, during the twelfth and thirteenth centuries, blacksmith facilities spread throughout the southern Ryukyu Islands.

Compared with the fourteenth and fifteenth centuries, the early *gusuku* era appears to have been relatively peaceful. However, one intriguing passage from *History of Song* (*Sòngshǐ*) suggests the Yaeyama Islands served as bases for marauders. It states that the country of Liúqiú is to the east of Quánzhōu. The description of this place indicates that it is Taiwan. The next passage states that next to it—that is, next to Taiwan—is an "evil country, whose people are naked and almost non-human." During the Chúnxī era (1174–1189), the chieftains of this country led hundreds of followers in attacks on villages such as Shuǐàotóu in Quánzhōu, wantonly killing and pillaging. The passage also notes that these marauders were especially fond of iron tools and would actively attack armored cavalry in the hope of killing them and stealing their armor (*Sòngshǐ* 1346, 490-1, 490-2). If the passage is reasonably accurate, these brigands from the southern Ryukyu Islands must have possessed significant military power. In any case both Song and Ming sources mention the strong demand for iron and iron products in the Ryukyu Islands (Uehara 1992, 196). If indeed marauding along the southern coast of China had been fairly common, this situation might explain the lack of a China-southern Ryukyu spoke during the early *gusuku* era.

A major change during the late twelfth century was the relative decline of Gusuku and the rise of Okinawa in prominence. The Northern Tier-southern

Ryukyu Islands spoke did not last long. During the thirteenth century, it was replaced by an Okinawa-southern Ryukyu Islands spoke. During the fourteenth and fifteenth centuries, as we will see, the southern Ryukyu Islands became very active, trading or otherwise interacting directly with Southeast Asia and southern China as well as Okinawa. Indeed, they became a hub much like the Northern Tier islands had been during the eleventh and twelfth centuries.

Possible Korea-Northern Tier Spoke

Maritime routes connected southern Korea, Hakata, and the Ryukyu Islands. As noted previously, it is likely that Koreans resided in Gusuku during phases 1 and 2. Excavations indicate the manufacture of iron goods during the eleventh and twelfth centuries in Kikaijima. The furnaces there were the same model as those found in the Ariake Sea coast of Higo, all of which used technology imported from the Korean Peninsula (Yoshinari 2020, 41–42, following Murakami Yasuyuki).

Given the vast size of the pottery production in Tokunoshima and its use of Korean technology, it is likely that Korean technicians resided there. The northern Ryukyu Islands constituted one of four large pottery regions in the Japanese Islands, and *kamuiyaki* production was on a par with the other great kiln sites in Japan.[5] Assuming that technicians from Korea indeed resided in Tokunoshima, it indicates direct trade with Korea, something otherwise poorly attested to in documents (Kurima 2013a, 238). How Koreans arrived in the Ryukyu Islands is unclear. Many or most probably traveled via the usual segments, such as Busan, Tsushima, Hakata, western Kyushu, Kikaijima, or Tokunoshima. However, a direct route from Korea to the northern Ryukyu Islands is also possible (Naka 1992, 134).

During the early *gusuku* era, the Ryukyu Islands were linked to regional trade networks extending throughout the East China Sea region. The archaeological record not only shows the progress of northern migrants in settling the Ryukyu Islands but also reveals their extensive trading activity. Again, we see people from outside the Ryukyu Islands coming in and transforming culture and economic life—the overall theme of this book.

Within the Ryukyu Islands, the relative vigor and extent of economic activity varied geographically over the course of several centuries. Initially, the northern Ryukyu Islands were especially prominent. Starting at the end of the twelfth century, Okinawa rapidly gained in population and economic activity. Activity in the southern Ryukyu Islands also increased during the twelfth century as merchants from points further north came in to trade in southern island products and possibly to conduct coastal raids in China. In this chapter I have used a hub-and-spoke approach to model trading activity around the region. In chapter 8 I update the model to reflect conditions that prevailed in the fourteenth century.

One point to notice about the early *gusuku* era is that despite the absence of a centralized state anywhere in the Ryukyu Islands, migrations and trade appear to have been relatively orderly during the eleventh and most of the twelfth century. The Northern Tier hub centered at Gusuku at least partially functioned to regulate trade elsewhere in the Ryukyu Islands.

Finally, Korean technology played a major role in the early *gusuku*-era Ryukyu Islands. This technology, part of a larger Korean cultural influence on the Ryukyu Islands, is not widely discussed, or even mentioned, in most surveys of premodern Ryukyuan history. Several cornerstones of classical Ryukyuan culture came from Korea, as chapter 6 explains.

CHAPTER SIX

Sacred Groves, Fortresses, and More
The Korean Impact

Korea, in the form of people, technology, and culture, was one of the major external agents to shape early Ryukyuan history. Technology and culture from Korea typically reached the Ryukyu Islands via intermediaries. We have seen that material culture had moved between the Korean Peninsula and the Ryukyu Islands since the Jōmon era (chapter 2). At times, Korean people, willingly or otherwise, came directly into the Ryukyu Islands. As the first major wave of *wakō* activity began during the thirteenth century and intensified during the fourteenth, Korean people ended up in different parts of East China Sea maritime networks. Some were victims of human trafficking. Others were the *wakō* themselves. Koreans and people of mixed Japanese and Korean ancestry composed a large portion of most *wakō* crews. During the fourteenth century, a group closely connected with the Korean Peninsula controlled the Urasoe area. Its leader, Satto, became the first trade king in Okinawa.

Korean cultural influence on the Ryukyu Islands during the *gusuku* era was deep. Two manifestations of culture, today regarded as distinctively Ryukyuan, are of Korean origin. They are sacred groves (*utaki*) and stone-walled fortresses (*gusuku*). Ryukyu's official histories were written between approximately 1650 and 1750, a time when the kingdom operated within a space defined by its relations with China (mainly the Qing court and the area around Fúzhōu) and Japan (mainly Satsuma and the Tokugawa bakufu in Edo).[1] Therefore, the official histories have little to say about Korea. Because the official histories continue to frame modern and contemporary accounts of Ryukyu's past, the profound Korean presence in early Ryukyu is typically overlooked. This chapter foregrounds that Korean impact on early Ryukyu.

Sacred Groves

Sacred groves known as *utaki* (J. *otake*) are an iconic variety of Ryukyuan culture.[2] *Origins of Ryukyu* lists 772 *utaki*, including the Yabusatsu *utaki,* a sacred grove located at Hyakuna beach in the Tamagusuku area of southeast Okinawa.

Yabusatsu is one of the eight sacred groves that the creator deity Amamiku estab-lished on Okinawa, according to *Reflections on Chūzan*.[3] In appearance it is a typical *utaki,* consisting mainly of a thick, tangled growth of trees and other vegetation. This thick growth of vegetation is a characteristic feature of many sacred groves. For example, an *omoro* highlights the impressive density of the Kanamori grove in Sashiki (southeast Okinawa) as "Kanamori where rain does not penetrate" (*Omoro sōshi* 19–1288).

Like most sacred groves, Yabusatsu *utaki* contains no shrine buildings or other structures. Within it are two sacred spaces. The generic term for these spaces is *ibe* (O. *ibi*), which typically feature or consist of a rock or a tree. The grove is atop a hill approximately sixty meters high, whose slope was once used for open-air burials (Okaya 2019, 8, 12, 126, 128). This hill is in the midst of an area full of other sacred sites.[4]

Sacred groves in the Ryukyu Islands typically enshrine unique deities, which can be divided into two broad, potentially overlapping categories: founders of communities and deities who arrived from across the sea. The majority of groves in Okinawa are of the community founder type, although Yabusatsu and the others founded by Amamiku are of the sea deity type. In the southern Ryukyu Islands and on the various small islands near Okinawa, groves enshrining deities who arrived from across the sea are relatively more common (Miyagi and Taka-miya 1983a, 60–61, 131).

Today's Yabusatsu *utaki* resembles an overgrown jungle.[5] There is no road leading all the way to Yabusatsu *utaki,* and few people visit the site. As is typical for such groves, cutting wood there, or even accidentally breaking a branch, invites a divine curse. According to legend, a ball of fire might rise up from Yabusatsu *utaki* as a sign of divine displeasure, which is also a characteristic of the *yabusa* site at Sashiki, near Yatsushiro in Kyushu (Eguchi 2008, 92–93).

Yanagita Kunio and Orikuchi Shinobu (1887–1953) famously hypothesized that the people who became Japanese migrated into the Japanese Islands from the south through the Ryukyu Islands. In this context both men characterized sacred groves as prototypes of Shinto shrines. However, groves are entirely dif-ferent from mainstream Japanese shrines (*jinja, jingū*). For example, sacred groves have no shrine buildings (*shaden*), *torii* gateways (before the twentieth century), coin boxes, or guardian lion-dogs (*komainu*). Women perform formal rites at sacred groves, whereas men do so at shrines. It is extremely rare for differ-ent sacred groves to venerate the same deity. By contrast, tens of thousands of Japanese shrines exist for each of the most popular deities such as Hachiman or Inari. Each sacred grove is deeply rooted in its specific location. Eight major Shinto shrines are in Okinawa, but they are unconnected with sacred groves.

Two attempts by the modern state to make Ryukyuan groves into shrines, in 1909 and 1943, mostly came to naught, although a few groves were outfitted with shrine gateways (*torii*) as a result. Another problem with Orikuchi and Yanagita's hypothesis is that no sites resembling sacred groves lie anywhere south of the Ryukyu Islands. There are, however, many sacred groves to the north (Okaya 2018, 8–22, 96–102, 108, 110). To state my conclusion in advance, the ultimate ancestor of Ryukyuan sacred groves is a type of sacred grove in Korea known as *dang* 堂.

Distribution of Sacred Groves

The worship of local deities or other divine forces at sacred groves can be found throughout coastal areas of western Japan from Wakasa Bay (Fukui Prefecture) southward through the Ryukyu Islands. Such worship is also found inland from Wakasa Bay, around Lake Biwa, and at a few other Kansai area locations (Lee 2011, 10–50). I call this region the Sacred Grove Zone (figure 6.1). This zone includes the routes connecting Korea and the Ryukyu Islands discussed in chapter 2 plus some additional territory in western Honshu.

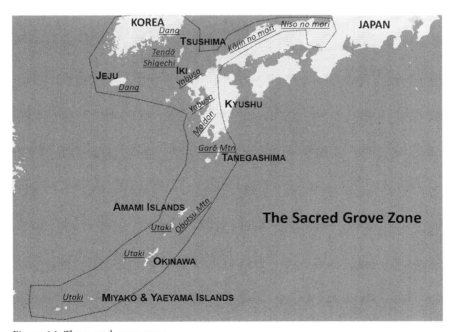

Figure 6.1. The sacred grove zone.

Western Honshu

In the Ōshima area of Wakasa Bay are at least thirty-three sacred groves of a type called *niso no mori*. They feature a simple sacred space, often part of a rock formation amid a dense growth of vegetation. Sacred trees also figure prominently at these sites, which enshrine ancestral spirits. Taboos at *niso no mori* are strict. Not only is cutting vegetation prohibited, but unrelated or unauthorized people are prohibited from entering many locations in and around the groves (Anma [1952] 1995, 80; Okaya 2019, 110).

Similar groves are found in Tottori and Shimane Prefectures, consisting of a small shrine (*hokora*) amid a tangle of trees. These groves are often called *kōjin mori* or *kōjin yabu*. The area is sometimes enclosed by a simple fence or stones, and cutting wood from these sites invites divine punishment (Okimoto [1950] 1995, 108–109).

Moving to the southwest end of Honshu, sacred groves are found in Yamaguchi Prefecture, with an especially good example on the small island of Futaoi, off the coast of Shimonoseki. Writing in 1957, Kokubu Naoichi described the large Futaoi grove, known by the names Yotsu no Yama or Yotsu no Mori. The entire site consists of four contiguous groves located atop hills. Kokubu was struck by the close resemblance of this site complex to similar groves in Korea. He noted that all things in the groves are property of the deities, and for humans to remove anything would invite a divine penalty (Kokubu [1957] 1995, 128, 131). Customs connected with similar groves in Korea and many other locations also prohibit removing anything from them for this reason.

Iki and Tsushima

South of Futaoi is the island of Iki offshore from Hakata Bay, which along with Tsushima was a major conduit between the Japanese Islands and the Korean Peninsula. In Iki a type of sacred grove known as *yabusa* or *yabosa* (and other pronunciation variants) is especially prevalent, a point to which I return. *Yabusa* sites are also found in Tsushima, all the way down the western coast of Kyushu, at Shomi in Izena just north of Okinawa, and in Okinawa as the Yabusatsu *utaki* discussed above (Tanigawa 2010, 76–77).

Another type of grove found in Tsushima is called *tendōchi* and by other names containing *tendō*. The main origin legend of these sites involves a Buddhist priest named Tendō, but there is nothing Buddhist about *tendō* groves other than parts of the origin story. *Tendō* groves consist of densely overgrown primal forest. Cutting trees or branches in them is prohibited, as is the entry of unauthorized people. If, for example, someone inadvertently enters Tsushima's

Hatchōkaku *tendō* site, that person must walk out backwards with footwear humbly placed atop the head to avoid divine penalty (Okaya 2019, 110–111).

In addition to *yabusa* and *tendō* sites, another variety of sacred grove, known as *shigechi* (or *shige*), is widespread in Tsushima. Religious anthropologist Suzuki Tōzō regarded *shigechi* sites as corresponding to Ryukyuan sacred groves. As reasons, he noted that *shigechi* sites were off-limits to entry for most people and that originally they contained no buildings. Like many other sacred groves in the region, *shigechi* sites often feature sacred trees. In Suzuki Tōzō's (1972, 15, 36, 117) analysis, *tendō* sites and *shigechi* sites are nearly synonymous, and *shigechi* sites were the original variety. The *shigechi* groves of Tsushima are related to the *shike* shamanic trances of Tokara Island priestesses and the *shike* spaces in certain *Omoro sōshi* songs describing Ryukyuan priestesses entering shamanic trances (Smits 2019, 32–33).

Sacred groves are found throughout the coastal areas of western Honshu and many islands in the waters between the Japanese Islands and Korea. They are known by diverse names that are sometimes helpful for tracing the spread of these groves (table 6.1). Nevertheless, the overall point is that despite the different names, these groves typically share a set of common-core characteristics (table 6.2).

Higo (Kumamoto Prefecture) and Satsuma (Kagoshima Prefecture)

Moving south along the western coast of Kyushu from Hakata, in addition to *yabusa* sites we find sacred groves that go by a variety of names, typically including -*mori* (stand, grove) or -*san/yama* (mountain). As examples described in the 1950s but using present-day place-names, in the Tomochi neighborhood in the town of Misato in Kumamoto Prefecture, there is a Mori no Moto no Kamisan grove with three stones at its core (reminiscent of many Ryukyuan groves). Nearby, also in Misato, is another sacred grove called Moridon, closely connected with local agriculture and with an old graveyard adjacent to it (Kokubu [1957] 1995, 128–131).

There are ancient connections between sacred groves, Korean technology, Higo (Kumamoto), and the Ryukyu Islands. The *kamuiyaki* kilns in Tokunoshima closely resemble the Mujang-ri kiln site in Seosan, South Korea. Kilns of the same type are also found in Sagariyama, in Kuma-gun, Kumamoto Prefecture. In other words, both the Sagariyama kilns and those in Tokunoshima shared the same Korean-derived technology base (Yotsumoto 2008, 247, 152–153; Shinzato Akito 2017, 133–137, 139).[6] Kuma-gun is also the location of two (formerly five) extant *yabusa* sacred grove sites (Suzuki Tōzō 1972, 181; Eguchi 2008, 108–109). These western Kyushu *yabusa* sites are related to the Yabusatsu *utaki* in Okinawa.

Table 6.1. Locations of sacred groves by name.

Type \ Location	Western Honshu	Iki Island	Tsushima Island	Western Kyushu	Satsunan + Tokara Isl.	Ryukyu Islands	Jeju Island + Korea
Niso no mori	**Main**						
Kōjin no mori/ yabu	**Main**						
Tendō			**Main**				
Shige/ shigechi			**Main**		Yes	Traces	
Yabusa/ yabosa		**Main**	Yes	Yes		Yes	
Moidon				**Main**			
Garō/garan mtn.			Yes		**Main**		
Obotsu mtn.						**Main**	
Utaki						**Main**	
Dang/ dangsan			Traces				**Main**

In both the Satsuma and Ōsumi Peninsulas of Kagoshima Prefecture, over one hundred *moidon* sacred groves have been identified. *Moi* is *mori* (grove) and *don* is the honorific *dono*. Local communities worship at these groves, with some variation in practices and lore. Most *moidon* sites are located alongside graveyards, and sometimes graves are located within the groves. Other than at the time of annual community worship, many local people avoid these sites out of fear of offending the deity within them. Cutting trees or branches, or breaking them, will invite divine wrath, so the sites are thick with vegetation (Okaya 2019, 120–122).

Tanegashima, the Tokara Islands (and Tsushima)

Moving into the southern islands, we find *garō* mountains (*garō-yama* 伽藍山).[7] The name derives from Buddhism, but like *tendō* sites in Tsushima, *garō* mountains lack temples or other obvious Buddhist connections. These sites are sacred

Table 6.2. Characteristics of sacred groves.*

Characteristic\n\nType	Strict deity / no cutting or removal / restricted entry	Typically or often located on high ground	Connected with gravesites	Rites performed by women	Sacred stones or trees	Stone wall or fence enclosure	Spirit of founding human or divine ancestor(s)**
Niso no mori	Yes	Yes	Yes	?	Yes	Sometimes	Yes
Kōjin no mori/yabu	Yes	Yes	Yes	?	Yes	?	Yes
Tendō	Yes	Yes	?	No	Yes	Yes	Yes
Shige/shigechi	Yes	Yes	?	?	Yes	Yes	Yes
Yabusa/yabosa	Yes	Yes	Yes	Sometimes	Yes	?	Yes
Moidon	Yes	?	Yes	Sometimes	Yes	Sometimes	Yes
Garō/garan mtn.	Yes	Yes	Yes	Sometimes	Yes	?	Yes
Obotsu mtn.	?	Yes	Yes	?	Yes	No	?
Utaki	Yes	Yes	Yes	Yes	Yes	Yes	Yes
Dang/dangsan	Yes	Yes	?	Yes	Yes	Yes	Yes

Notes: *All are or originally were stands of trees or other vegetation without major shrine buildings or torii.**May also house other types of spirits or deities in addition to or instead of ancestors.

groves, and their spirits protected the original land cultivator or were deities of rivers and springs. Some *garō* groves feature a sacred tree at the center (Okaya 2019, 122–123). The deities of *garō* sites are partly feared and partly reviled. They are quick to curse anyone entering the groves without good reason. Not surprisingly, cutting wood is strictly prohibited (Shimono [1969] 1995, 483–485). Further south, in the Tokara Islands, *garō* is known as *geerō* or *garan* and tends to be regarded as the name of a deity. For example, in Kuchinoshima, Geerō is a deity of barley. Throughout the Tokara Islands, the deities of *geerō* sites require strict worship, lest they become offended and inflict penalties on local communities (Shimono 2005, 371).

Writing in 1969, Shimono Toshimi stated that *garō* mountain sites are related to Okinawan sacred groves, the *obotsu* mountains of Amami-Ōshima, the sacred mountains of the Tokara Islands, and the *moidon* of Kagoshima. In discussing gravesites and their relationship to the groves, he noted similarities between Tanegashima and Kakeroma, an island just south of Amami-Ōshima. In both places, graves are located adjacent to the sacred mountains (Shimono [1969] 1995, 487, 498, 504).

The island of Tsushima is also home to sacred groves called *garan,* an older name, which became *garō* in Tanegashima (Suzuki Tōzō 1972, 218, 353–354).[8] These Tsushima *garan* groves are of ancient vintage and are similar in appearance and function to *shigechi* and *yabusa* groves. It is significant that Tsushima is home to four types of sacred groves—*tendō, shigechi, yabusa,* and *garan*—that are all similar in appearance and function to each other and to groves in Jeju Island and mainland Korea. Tsushima appears to have been the major point outside Korea from which sacred groves spread to western Japan and the islands of the Ryukyu Arc.

Busan, South Korea, is visible from northern Tsushima. Just north of Busan, in Gyeongju, are approximately twenty extant *dangsan* (*dang* mountain) sacred groves (Lee 2011, 115). Other such groves are scattered throughout South Korea, but these sites have been suppressed or otherwise put under pressure for centuries and have declined as a result.[9] Today, sacred groves called *dang* are the most numerous and vigorous on the Korean island of Jeju, where 392 remain (Okaya 2019, 159). These Jeju *dang* closely resemble Ryukyuan sacred groves, and I compare them in detail below. Before proceeding with that analysis, it is necessary to pause and consider the important matter of dating these sacred groves.

Approximate Dates of Sacred Grove Varieties

Sacred groves are difficult to date, especially because they typically lack formal buildings or associated written records. Although *yabusa* sites were originally

groves without buildings, over the centuries many in Kyushu gradually transformed into shrines, with "Yabusa" or some variant thereof becoming the name
of an enshrined deity or one of several enshrined deities. In his 1941 study of
yabusa sites, Suzuki Tōzō noted that the *yabusa* shrine Kume-son in the Satsuma
Peninsula has a building tag (*munefuda*) dated 1525. Another at Inuzako outside
Kagoshima City has a tag dated 1530 (Suzuki Tōzō 1972, 200). Because these sites
were originally groves without buildings, they would have existed in that state
prior to, and possibly long before, the early sixteenth-century construction of
shrine buildings. In his study of over one hundred *yabosa* sites in Iki Island,
Yamaguchi Matarō includes a list of all historical documents listing or describing the sites. The earliest is dated 1572 (Yamaguchi [1941] 1995, 291). Based on
the distribution of the different terms for sacred groves and other indirect evidence, Shimono ([1969] 1995, 504) estimates that *garan*-named sites date from
"medieval" times and that sacred grove worship itself goes back even further.

The 1471 *Account of East Sea Countries* discusses *tendō* sites in Tsushima (J. *jindō*
神堂; K. sacred *dang*). The account notes that the only people who might dare to
enter such groves are criminals on the run because nobody would willingly pursue
such people into the grove (*East Sea Countries* [1471] 1991, 195). In the Korean context, the mention of *dang* or similar sites in ancient legends and the descriptions of
associated folk practices in documents from the Goryeo and early Joseon eras suggest they existed well before the fourteenth century (Chang 1973, 87–96, 130–141).
Sacred mountains appear in Korean documents as far back as 1106, and the creation
of mountain groves is mentioned as early as 1398 (Lee 2011, 104, 110).

As for Ryukyuan groves (*utaki*), over seven hundred are listed in *Origins of
Ryukyu* and described to varying degrees. Sometimes the description provides
clues to the age of a site. All such instances indicate a time prior to the establishment of a central kingdom, and no groves were created by the royal government
(Okaya 2019, 136). Because most Ryukyuan sacred groves remain active religious
sites, only a few have undergone archaeological excavation. When the Inafuku
Kamiugan *utaki* in southern Okinawa (Ōzato, Nanjō City) was excavated in
1981, Chinese ceramics dating from the late thirteenth to the fourteenth century
were found. At a grove site in Tonaki Island, Chinese ceramics from the twelfth
century and other *gusuku*-era pottery were recovered. Excavations of a grove site
in Miyako and another in Ishigaki revealed imported ceramics from the fourteenth through sixteenth centuries. Based on the available textual and archaeological evidence, Okaya Kōji concludes that Ryukyuan sacred grove sites date
from the *gusuku* era (Okaya 2019, 136–137).

In short, diverse evidence suggests that sacred groves existed in Korea by the
twelfth century. They spread to western Japan and the Ryukyu Islands during

approximately the thirteenth and fourteenth centuries—precisely the time of increased *wakō* activity in the region.

Characteristics of *Utaki, Dang,* and Other Sacred Groves

The extent to which the types of groves we have surveyed retain their original characteristics and remain vibrant religious sites in the present varies. *Utaki* in the Ryukyu Islands and *dang* in Jeju Island constitute the vibrant end of the spectrum. A few Ryukyuan groves have *torii* gateways, erected during the twentieth century, and some have fallen into disuse. Moreover, some *utaki* have recently undergone repurposing as tourist attractions (Rots 2019). Most, however, retain their essential characteristics as groves and continue to function as religious sites. The same can be said for *dang* in Jeju Island but less so for *dang* on the Korean mainland. Many *tendō* sites in Tsushima have acquired *torii* gateways, but most otherwise remain groves. *Moidon* sites in Kagoshima Prefecture similarly have mostly retained their character as groves. By contrast, many *yabusa* sites, especially outside Iki and Tsushima, have lost their original character as groves and exist as conventional Shinto shrines.[10]

Some scholars have regarded the fundamental meaning of *yabusa* as an ancestor's grave, most commonly in the form of an open-air burial site (Nakayama Tarō [1929] 2012, 121–122). This point also applies to some *shigechi* sites in Tsushima. Suzuki agrees, pointing out that *yabusa* never functioned as general burial sites. Instead, they housed the bones of the ancestral founder or founders of a community. Over time, an association of these sites with spirits or deities who could take possession of someone (*yorigami*) overshadowed the gravesite function (Suzuki Tōzō 1972, 196–198). Recall that many *moidon* are also associated with gravesites and that one part of the hill on which Okinawa's Yabusatsu *utaki* is located was an open-air gravesite. Indeed, human bones have been found at almost every Ryukyuan grove, and it is likely that one of their original functions was to act as gravesites (Okaya 2019, 22–24; Inamura 1969, for extensive examples). Similarly, *garō* mountain sites appear originally to have functioned in part as memorial sites for the founders of local communities, and many are connected to graveyards or the sites of small memorial shrines (Shimono [1969] 1995, 498, 504).

It is unclear to what extent, if any, Korean *dang* functioned as gravesites. It is noteworthy that the strong association in the Ryukyu Islands with the bones of important people (*madama*, "true bones/jewels") being capable of bringing forth rain or otherwise influencing the course of nature probably originated in Korea (Smits 2019, 123–124, 130). Another commonality was bone-washing funerals, emblematic of Ryukyuan culture but also widely practiced in island Korea (Chang 1973, 336).

In the Ryukyu Islands, sacred groves are associated with specific deities, often the spirits of the founders of local communities. Most sacred groves are located on hills or other elevated areas. On flat islands, however, sacred groves are usually located near the beach and have a horizontal (*niraikanai*) orientation. These groves typically enshrine deities who arrived from across the sea. Most *utaki* consist of wooded groves, some surrounded by simple stone fences or walls. Ryukyuan groves often contain simple stone altars or dividers but have no buildings of the sort associated with Shinto shrines. In many cases the deities of the groves are thought to be capable of possessing people. Some Ryukyuan groves prohibit men from entering them, or from entering certain areas of them (Lebra [1966] 1985, 50, 52, 98). In any case, it is women who are in charge of performing or leading sacred grove rites.

Ryukyuan sacred groves are rooted in specific places, and some prohibit entry by those unaffiliated with the relevant community or group. Rites at groves are sometimes conducted in secret. (Public village rites and festivities are conducted in built structures called *kami ashiage*.) Cutting or breaking branches is prohibited in groves for fear of divine punishment. *Utaki* often feature one or more sacred stones and, less commonly, a sacred tree (Inamura 1969, 98; Lebra [1966] 1985, 98, 139–140; Okaya 2019, 8–19). As anthropologist William P. Lebra ([1966] 1985, 70) described them, an Okinawan *utaki*, which "consists of a clump of trees with a censer, is simplicity itself." In some Yaeyama groves, deities or the humans created by deities to populate an island can emerge from within the ground. Deities emerging from within the earth are also a characteristic of *dang* deities or ancestor deities in Jeju Island (Chang 1973, 131–132).

Dang in Jeju Island and the mainland of Korea consist mainly of stands of trees. Vegetation and a variety of items accumulate in them because once something is offered to the grove's deity, removing it is inappropriate. *Dang* often feature simple stone altars and contain no buildings. A simple stone fence or wall usually encloses the grove. There are some exceptions to this general pattern. One *dang*, for example, is located in a cave. Significantly, as at Ryukyuan *utaki* and some of the Kyushu groves, women perform rites to the deities at *dang* (Okaya 2019, 157–164). In these and other respects, *utaki* and *dang* closely resemble each other. Moreover, it should be clear that all the varieties of sacred groves from Jeju and Tsushima through the southern Ryukyu Islands have, or once had, a large set of common characteristics. Importantly, other than being religious sites associated with deities, most groves have little or nothing in common with Shinto shrines (figure 6.2).

Figure 6.2 Sacred groves in Okinawa (*left*) and Jeju Island (*right*). *Source: left*, Okinawa Monogatari, https://www.okinawastory.jp/spot/600003564; *right*, Cheju no Tan, blog.livedoor.jp/omtakebe/archives/29928892.html.

The Sacred Grove Zone marks an area that was once an interconnected maritime region. It is nearly the same region of travel described in chapter 2. Although regarded as emblematic of classical Ryukyuan culture, sacred groves are not unique to the Ryukyu Islands, nor did they originate there. They came into the islands from the north and are ultimately Korean in origin. Most of the *gusuku*-era migrants to the Ryukyu Islands came from Kyushu, and western Kyushu had long been influenced by inflows of Korean people and culture. Furthermore, during the fourteenth and fifteenth centuries Korean people came into the Ryukyu Islands owing to the activities of *wakō*.

Korean Mountain Fortresses and *Gusuku*

Sacred groves are an example of transplanted Korean culture flourishing in the Ryukyu Islands. Stone-walled fortresses are another. Although the stone was local, the know-how for building the fortresses came from Korea. It is almost certain that some of the builders did as well, not all of them willingly. The iconic type of Ryukyuan *gusuku,* large castles or fortresses featuring stone walls, were descendants of, and closely resembled, Korean mountain fortresses (*sanseong* 山城). South Korea contains over twenty-four hundred known fortresses, 90 percent of which are located in mountainous areas (Korea Fortress Academy 2008a, 29).

The term *gusuku* in the Ryukyu Islands refers to fortresses, typically located on high ground. There are two major unrelated types. One featured stone walls. Katsuren Gusuku and Nakagusuku Gusuku are typical examples. The other type lacked stone walls and instead relied on trenches and earthworks to thwart attackers. Trench-and-earthworks *gusuku* are of Japanese origin, and Shō Hashi's

Sashiki Gusuku is a good example. All five castles registered on the United Nations Educational, Scientific and Cultural Organization (UNESCO)'s World Heritage List in 2000 are stone-walled *gusuku*.[11] In this chapter, the term *gusuku* refers to stone-walled fortresses. In 2010, seven Korean mountain fortresses joined UNESCO's tentative list of World Heritage Sites.[12]

Throughout the 1960s and 1970s, a *gusuku* debate (*gusuku ronsō*) raged in Ryukyu-related academic circles. These debates continued from the 1980s onward, but they became subsumed within broader scholarship about the nature of the Ryukyu Kingdom in the context of the rise of the internal development model. Simply stated, many participants in the debate sought a single defining quality of Ryukyuan *gusuku*. Noting that *gusuku* were often located near communities but separate from them, some scholars proposed that *gusuku* functioned as emergency shelters to which community members could flee in times of danger. Others rejected the idea that *gusuku* functioned as fortresses, proposing instead, for example, that they were mainly religious sites (chapter 8).

Scholars of Korean mountain fortresses all acknowledge the obvious point that the structures fundamentally served a military purpose. They also note that people did not normally live in the fortresses but instead stored provisions and weapons in such locations in case of warfare (Korea Fortress Academy 2008a, 39).[13] In addition to its military function, each Korean fortress functioned as a sacred space, in some locations with a local hero who became the deity of the fortress (39).[14] In this sense a fortress might function similarly to sacred groves. Some Korean fortresses included altars for the performance of rain rituals during times of drought (Korea Fortress Academy 2008b, 107). According to one study, "In Sangdang [Fortress], there was an altar for rain rituals, so it seems that it was not only a defensive mountain fortress, but also a location where people bowed to nature" (166). As we will see in detail (chapter 8), the same points apply to most Ryukyuan *gusuku*. They were military facilities at their core, but religious power was inextricably interconnected with those military functions.

Korean mountain fortresses are of ancient vintage. The know-how for their construction spread to Japan, especially Kyushu, during the seventh century. The reason was the fall of Baekje, which sent many Korean immigrants to Japan and encouraged the building of fortresses in Kyushu and elsewhere in anticipation of a possible Tang-Silla invasion (Korea Fortress Academy 2007, 21–22; 2008a, 35).[15] These seventh-century fortresses in Japan that were modeled on Korean counterparts had fallen into disuse by the time the *gusuku* era began in the Ryukyu Islands. It is highly unlikely, therefore, that these Japanese versions of Korean fortresses were the source of know-how for *gusuku* construction.

Korea's Goryeo dynasty (918–1392) was a time when many older fortresses were upgraded and newer ones built. Characteristics of Goryeo mountain fortresses include (1) construction in high mountainous areas (figure 6.3); (2) cliffs and steep drop-offs functioning as de facto fortress walls; (3) battlements featured on most walls; and (4) buildings of a larger scale compared with previous

Figure 6.3. Part of the stone wall of the Gyeonghwon Mountain Fortress in Korea. *Source:* Korean Culture and Information Service, Wikipedia.

eras (Korea Fortress Academy 2008a, 37).[16] The same points apply to Okinawan *gusuku,* which appeared during the latter part of Korea's Goryeo era.

Large-walled *gusuku* consisted either of a series of laterally connected enclosures (for example, Nakagusuku or Nakijin) or, in the case of Shuri Castle, a series of concentric walled enclosures (figure 6.4). Importantly, Okinawan *gusuku* predated Japanese stone castles by over a century. From where, therefore, did the know-how for building them come? *Gusuku* scholar Tōma Shiichi (2012, 44–45) states that based on the distinctive structural characteristics of large stone-walled *gusuku,* the technology and know-how for their construction came from China and Korea. I would say Korea, not China. Although some Korean-style fortresses can be found within Northeast China's modern boundaries, typical Chinese castles and city walls were of an entirely different character than *gusuku* or Korean mountain fortresses. Among other characteristics, Chinese fortified cities and castles were located in low-lying areas, and their walls consisted of baked bricks, not stones (Korea Fortress Academy 2008a, 33).[17] It is also important to note that few Chinese people ever settled in the

Figure 6.4. Part of the walls of Nakagusuku Gusuku, Okinawa.

Ryukyu Islands during the *gusuku* era, nor do we find strong Chinese cultural influences apart from the presence of large quantities of trade ceramics and other goods. Korea, not China or Japan, was the source of *gusuku* construction know-how.

One indication is that structures within three of Okinawa's largest castles, Shuri, Urasoe, and Katsuren, featured roof tiles made from Okinawan clay but identical to distinctively Korean tiles. Producing these replica tiles would have required the presence of Korean technicians both to carry out and supervise the tile-making and to supervise roof construction and installation (Okada 2000, 156; Yoshinari 2018, 197).

Most important, large Okinawan *gusuku* look exactly like Korean mountain fortresses. Writing around 1460, Korean castaway Ryang Seong described Shuri Castle as "fairly high, like capital castles in our country." Moreover, its gates "are also like those of our country" and its walls are like a meandering stream (Ikeya, Uchida, and Takase 2005, 144).

The design of battlements, flanking towers (O. *azama*), and eyebrow-like overhanging stones in the walls of *gusuku* closely match the construction found in Korean castles. (Gungnip Munhwajae Yeonguso 2012, 496, 1353; Tōma 2012, 431; Okinawa Kōkogakkai 2018, 157). Especially important is that the three types of wall construction found in Ryukyuan *gusuku* closely correspond to the three types of walls in Korean fortresses. For example, many Korean fortresses are made of uncut naturally occurring stones (e.g., Gungnip Munhwajae Yeonguso 2012, 482, 639, 705–706, 823, 792, 877, 1136). The same construction is found in much of Nakijin Gusuku, Tamagusuku Gusuku, and portions of the first enclosure wall of Nakagusuku Gusuku. Other fortress walls are made from well-fitted cut stones (e.g., Gungnip Munhwajae Yeonguso 2012, 504, 578–579, 702–703). Okinawan examples of the same include portions of the first enclosure of Nakagusuku Gusuku, portions of Itokazu Gusuku, and Katsuren Gusuku. Also common are walls from cut stone of similar shape, tightly stacked (for examples, Gungnip Munhwajae Yeonguso 2012, 711, 840, 1096, 1146, 1274). Okinawan examples include the third enclosure wall of Nakagusuku Gusuku and portions of Zakimi Gusuku.[18]

Ryukyuan stone-walled *gusuku* closely resemble Korean mountain fortresses with respect to the technical details of wall construction, with respect to all the specific characteristics of Goryeo-era fortresses mentioned above, and with respect to their nonmilitary functions. Moreover, the practice of piling up loose stones to use as weapons was the same in both types of places (Tōma 2012, 269). Looking at photographs of walls, it is often impossible to determine whether an example is Korean or Ryukyuan (Tōma 2012, 341). Korean fortresses predate

Ryukyuan *gusuku,* whereas Japanese stone castles appeared over a century later than Ryukyuan *gusuku* and are constructed differently. As noted above, *gusuku* and Korean fortresses are unlike Chinese castles and walled cities in almost every respect.

Finally, large stone-walled *gusuku* appeared in Okinawa precisely at a time of extensive *wakō* activity in Korea. Although *wakō* is conventionally translated as "Japanese pirates," many *wakō,* in some areas even a majority, were not Japanese. Nor did they always behave like pirates. One function of *wakō* was technology transfer (Smits 2019, 39–42). The heavy *wakō* presence in the Ryukyu Islands functioned as a direct and indirect infusion of Korean people (technicians, slaves, *wakō,* others) and know-how.

Flow of Commodities

We have seen that local products and finished goods moved between the Ryukyu Islands and the Korean Peninsula beginning with the Jōmon era. From the late fourteenth through the early seventeenth centuries, we have good written records about the exchange of goods between these places. S. M. Hong-Schunka has compiled a meticulous record of commodities exchange between Korea and Ryukyu for the period 1389–1638 (Hong-Schunka 2005, 135–147, 153–155). Most of the roughly eighty products that made their way into the Ryukyu Islands from Korea during this period fit into the categories of fabrics, handicrafts, local products, stationery, furs, and Buddhist books (Hong-Schunka 2005, 135). Conversely, the eighty-nine commodities that reached Korea via the Ryukyu Islands mostly fit into the categories of medicinal products; plants; fabrics; local products and handicrafts; and raw materials such as horns (rhinoceros, buffalo, others), skins, and minerals. Many of these items originated in Southeast Asia, or even as far away as Africa in some cases (Hong-Schunka 2005, 141).

This trade had faded away by the early seventeenth century, soon before the appearance of the first of Ryukyu's official histories. The rich history of exchanges between Korea and the Ryukyu Islands is largely absent in the official histories. Because of the tremendous influence of these works, modern survey histories of Ryukyu similarly tend to overlook the Korean impact.

Korean People and Culture in the Ryukyu Islands

China played a crucially important role in early Ryukyuan history, but it was mainly in the economic realm. Chinese people, culture, and technology had only a small impact on the early Ryukyu Islands. Like China, Japan and Korea were important economically for the Ryukyu Islands. In addition, Japan and Korea provided the main sources of Ryukyuan people, classical culture, and technology. The typical narrative of early Ryukyuan state formation sets up a China-Japan binary, with little or no mention of Korea. This binary makes sense for the early modern era, starting in the seventeenth century. From the eleventh through the early sixteenth centuries, however, Korea played a prominent role in shaping the development of the Ryukyu Islands.

Shō Taikyū's 1458 Bridge to the Many Countries Bell began by boasting that his kingdom had gathered together the excellence of Korea. The precise term on the bell for Korea is "Three Han" (三韓 K. Samhan, J. Sankan, Ch. Sānhán), possibly a reference to the three states of Goguryeo, Baekje, and Silla. It is probable, although we cannot be certain, that these three Korean kingdoms later served as a general inspiration for the official histories' portrayal of Okinawa's Sanzan era. Chūzan's alleged military victories over Sanhoku and Sannan corresponded to Silla's victories over Goguryeo in the north and Baekje in the south (Yoshinari 2015, 153–154).[19] In any case, the Korean Peninsula supplied several key technologies to Ryukyu, including the Buddhist sutras of which Shō Taikyū was much enamored.

Outside of Buddhism, the prominent role of women in official and unofficial religious life in the Ryukyu Islands is another Korean legacy. For example, the king-sister Kikoe-ōgimi institution that Shō Shin established was almost identical to a comparable institution in Silla (Yoshinari 2018, 199, following Ōbayashi Taryō). In both the Ryukyu Islands and in Korea, ideologies that we could loosely call "Confucian" eventually circumscribed the role of women in both official and private rites (regarding Ryukyu, see Smits 1999, 55–57, 113–117). However, this change made fewer inroads into Ryukyuan society compared with Korea. Today, women still dominate religious life in the Ryukyu Islands. The historical practice found in Okinawa and the northern Ryukyu Islands of placing corpses in baskets or cages and leaving them in the treetops or atop poles to decompose is probably of continental origin, and it came into western Kyushu and the Ryukyu Islands via the Korean Peninsula (Smits 2019, 28–29, following Ōbayashi Taryō and others).

The direct and indirect presence of Korean technology in the Ryukyu Islands is evident from the start of the *gusuku* era. *Kamuiyaki* was made in Korean-style kilns using Korean technology and, like the roof tiles discussed above, almost certainly required the presence of Korean technicians in Tokunoshima, at least initially. We have also seen that iron furnaces of the early *gusuku* era were based on Korean technology and that Korean merchants resided at Gusuku. As chapter 2 demonstrated, the transmission of material culture between the Korean Peninsula and the Ryukyu Islands took place throughout the Shellmound era.

The first person in Okinawa to hold the title "king"—that is, the first trade king—was Satto, whose group originated in and maintained ties with Korea. At least two members of the Satto group resided in Korea while the group was active in Okinawa, and the last members of the group died in Korea after fleeing there from Okinawa (*JVRR-r* 2005, 31–32, 34–35; Yoshinari 2020, 158–160). Moreover, although there are several hypotheses regarding the origin of the name Satto, the most persuasive one (based on a close reading of Korean records) is that Satto is a generic name. It comes from the Korean *sado* 使道, a term for local officials (Smits 2019, 83; Yoshinari 2020, 161). A variety of circumstantial evidence indicates that Satto and his group settled in Urasoe amid the tensions in Korea between anti-Yuan (Mongol) and pro-Yuan factions. Moreover, they began formal trade and diplomacy with Korea as soon as the Goryeo dynasty fell (Yoshinari 2020, 158–160). Interestingly, in Jeju Island there is a legend in the oral tradition about a "Ryukyuan prince" who died there. Sūn Wěi argues that this prince was Shōsatto of Sannan (Sūn 2005, 94–95).[20]

The oldest extant map of Okinawa is Korean, and it appears in *East Sea Countries* ([1471] 1991). Many of the place-names on the map are the same as those in *Omoro sōshi* songs (*East Sea Countries* [1471] 1991, 390–391; Robinson 2001, 121). Although direct voyages between Okinawa or other Ryukyu Islands and Korea were comparatively rare, sea lanes kept the two places connected.

The early or first-wave *wakō,* those active from the thirteenth through the late fifteenth centuries, included large numbers of Koreans or people of mixed Japanese and Korean ancestry among their crews. In other words, many of the *wakō* who passed through or ended up residing in the Ryukyu Islands were Korean. These *wakō* participated in human trafficking, and Naha was a major hub. Korean captives often passed through the Ryukyu Islands. Some stayed for terms as unfree laborers, although eventually many returned to Korea. Almost every official voyage from Okinawa to Korea during this era included Korean people for repatriation.

Although its origin is unclear, we have good evidence that a Korean community resided in Kumemura during the fifteenth century. In 1456, Korean castaway Ryang Seong noted that all the households in Kumemura consisted of people from "my country" (Korea) or from China (*JVRR-r* 2005, 140). In other words, there was a significant resident Korean presence in Naha harbor at this time, almost certainly to assist with overseas trade (Yoshinari 2015, 115; Murai 2019, 114, 179). Although Ryang happened to make this observation during Shō Taikyū's reign, the presence of a resident Korean population may have extended as far back as Satto's era.[21] Korean people frequently came into the Ryukyu Islands in different capacities and circumstances. Many of them resided there for varying lengths of time, and a few lived out the rest of their lives in Okinawa.

Some Ryukyuan sacred songs mention the offering of hallowed wine to deities in red bowls (*akawan* and similar terms). Sometimes red bowls are paired with black bowls, and sometimes white bowls are mentioned. Regardless of their color, the bowls are ritual objects to bring about social renewal (O. *yunoushi* and other terms, J. *yonaoshi*). In many songs the bowls are described as having come from Yamato or from Yamato-Yashiro (Yatsushiro), a pairing common in the *Omoro*.[22] So the basic format would be "the rectification caused by the red bowl (or red and black bowls), which came down from Yamato (or from Satsuma and Yatsushiro)." These bowls "come down from" (*kudaritaru* and similar terms) northern locations (for examples, Hokama and Tamaki 1980, 252, 293, 482, 487, 539, 659). In one sacred song from Kudakajima, the social-renewing red and black bowls have come from Seoul (Yoshinari 2018, 198, following Hokama Shuzen).

This genre of sacred songs is a good illustration of a broader point about the flow of people and culture into the Ryukyu Islands. Most of it came from Japan, especially from western Kyushu. However, western Kyushu was also the part of Japan that had received the largest quantity of people and culture from Korea. Mixed into that flow via western Kyushu, or in some cases more directly, was a substantial influx of Korean people, culture, and technology that made its way into the Ryukyu Islands. Its impact was profound, and it is likely that focused research will reveal more details in the future. The history of early Ryukyu cannot be told well without recognizing its Korean components.

CHAPTER SEVEN

Agriculture

There is widespread agreement among scholars that agriculture has existed within the Ryukyu Islands since the ninth or tenth centuries.[1] In other words, agriculture began in some locations slightly before the start of the *gusuku* era.[2] During the first two centuries of the *gusuku* era, agriculture spread throughout the Ryukyu Islands. Given that the *gusuku*-era settlers came from well-established agricultural societies, it is hardly surprising that many of them practiced agriculture after arriving in the Ryukyu Islands.[3] In this context, agriculture refers to both the cultivation of edible or useful plants and the raising of livestock. This chapter focuses on cereal grains, the usual foundation of taxation in premodern agricultural societies. Agriculture was a hallmark of the *gusuku* era, but were the *gusuku*-era Ryukyu Islands agricultural societies? This question is the topic of this chapter.[4]

Nearly all scholars of early Ryukyu would answer the question affirmatively. Indeed, it is commonplace to assume that the presence of agriculture inevitably leads to the development of an agricultural society. Recall from chapter 4, however, the examples from around the world in which the presence of or proximity to agriculture did not lead to agricultural societies. Relevant factors include whether other sources of food are abundant, whether other economic activities are more profitable, and/or whether the conditions for agriculture are suboptimal. All three of these factors were present in the early Ryukyu Islands.

In academic literature, the term "agricultural society" (J. *nōkō shakai*) is typically juxtaposed against "hunter-gatherer society" (J. *shuryō saishū shakai*). Moreover, a common assumption is that social progress means transformation from the latter into the former. Movement from hunter-gatherer to agricultural societies is associated with social stratification, systematic taxation, bureaucrats, and the emergence of urban centers—among much else. Social stratification, systematic taxation, bureaucrats, and urban centers all existed in Okinawa by circa 1530. Before the sixteenth century they did not.

In recent years I have become convinced that understanding the status of agriculture in the Ryukyu Islands is crucial for understanding Ryukyuan history

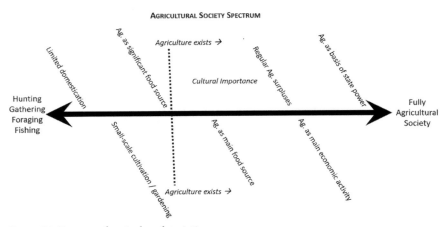

Figure 7.1. Degrees of agricultural societies.

and social dynamics not only during the *gusuku* era but all the way into modern times. For this reason I explore agriculture in detail. As a starting point, I note that the agricultural society versus hunter-gatherer society distinction need not be an either-or status. There is a spectrum of possibilities between the two poles of a full hunter-gatherer society and a full agricultural society (figure 7.1).[5]

Starting with a society whose food supply is based entirely on some combination of hunting, gathering, foraging, and fishing, the partial domestication of plants and animals on a small scale is a possible strategy for increasing food quantity and variety. For example, members of a mobile community might raise a few stray wolf puppies or strategically broadcast the seeds of edible plants in anticipation of their increase the following spring and summer. The small-scale cultivation of plants and animals—gardening—would be a further step in the direction of agriculture. Systematic cultivation on a scale in which the products of agriculture provide a significant proportion of the overall food supply would be a reasonable point at which to say that agriculture exists within a society. Moving further along the spectrum, the products of agriculture might become the predominant source of food without, however, leading to a significant or regular surplus. When a society's farmers produce a regular, significant surplus or, similarly, when agriculture becomes the main or foundational economic activity of a society, it would be reasonable to apply the label "agricultural society." If a state regularly extracts most or all of that agricultural surplus through taxation, then depending on specific circumstances, agriculture may become the economic foundation of state power.

Recall that in both the ancient branch model and the internal development model, agricultural surpluses constituted the driving force for social stratification and ultimately the creation of a centralized monarchy. In this view the Ryukyu Islands were a late-developing, small-scale version of the Japanese mainland, and they became a fully agricultural society. Obviously, historians writing in both of these models discuss the trade that developed during the *gusuku* era. The typical approach is to assume that social stratification and state formation were the result mainly of agricultural surpluses. These surpluses produced locally powerful rulers (*aji*), many of whom were in a position to initiate trade. Agricultural surpluses made trade possible, and trade supplemented agriculture as a source of wealth.

In this chapter I argue that this understanding is flawed. Certainly, agriculture existed throughout all the Ryukyu Islands by the twelfth century. Agriculture, however, did not lead to the creation of a fully agricultural society. Instead, agriculture became the main food source in some areas and a significant supplement to the food supply in most areas.[6] However, agriculture did not develop to the point of generating surpluses leading to the development of local principalities and eventually a centralized state. It was trade, or trading and raiding, not agriculture, that provided the wealth that drove state formation. In this context, in addition to supplementing the food supply, agriculture became culturally important. Many of the newly created state rituals of the 1530s, for example, were connected with agriculture.

Claims about Agriculture

My argument is that *gusuku*-era Okinawa did not constitute a full agricultural society and that agricultural surpluses did not drive state formation. I support this argument using a multidisciplinary approach. Before discussing the relevant details, in the paragraphs below I establish a context by surveying typical assessments of agriculture among historians and archaeologists, starting with Iha Fuyū and ending with several examples of recent work.

In both the ancient branch and internal development models, agricultural surpluses enabled the rise of local warlords (*aji*). The struggle for supremacy among these warlords led to the development of states, initially three principalities in Okinawa, then to a centralized kingdom based in Shuri, and finally to a state that encompassed all the Ryukyu Islands. It is a neat, linear model of state formation, first outlined by Iha. For example, in "Ko-Ryūkyū no seiji" (Government in Old Ryukyu) he stated that the people of southern Okinawa made their living by fishing; those in the middle, by agriculture; and those in the north, by hunting in the mountains. Therefore, it is not surprising that the agriculturalists of central Okinawa led the way in state formation (Iha 1974a, 428).

Writing in the late 1960s, Inamura Kenpu provided a more rigorous and nuanced hypothesis. Stated very briefly, the earliest social units in the Ryukyu Islands were consanguine communities of Japanese settlers, called *makyo* or *kyoda*. Although many of these communities engaged in agriculture, they lacked iron tools and therefore supported themselves mainly by hunting and fishing. A lack of agricultural surpluses as buffers against disaster kept population levels low. During the thirteenth century, powerful local rulers known as *aji* established iron foundries at their fortresses, manufactured weapons and agricultural tools, distributed the tools to local communities, and created power centers based on agricultural surpluses. It was a significant new level of social organization, which included the relocation of communities for ideal agricultural production. Inamura called this era the agricultural age (*nōkō jidai*) or the medieval agricultural society (*chūsei nōkō shakai*). Eiso, the earliest known ruler to appear in *Omoro sōshi* songs, was probably a typical example of these new agriculture-based local lords. One variety of evidence Inamura adduced is the ruins of seven iron forges known at the time of his writing. He also reasoned that insofar as *aji* existed, only agricultural societies could have supported them and their fortresses (Inamura 1969, 64–65, 72–73, 80, 84, 116–117, 165–166, 243–244, 254–272, 470–472).

When Inamura was writing, there was no awareness of the *gusuku* era as a time of major transition. His estimate of the start of the agricultural era, the thirteenth century, was based on the approximate time when fortress-based local lords began to appear. Inamura was well aware that agriculture in Okinawa could not be viable on a large scale without the widespread use of iron tools. Therefore, it was the establishment of iron forges that made agriculture viable, and these facilities were associated with fortresses. How was it that these local lords were able to establish large fortresses and manufacture iron tools as a prelude to agriculture? Inamura did not raise this question, and obviously, agriculture could not be the answer.

Similar to Inamura's account but with an important difference, a local history of Gushikami (Gushichan) in southeastern Okinawa, today part of the town of Yaese, begins by noting the absence of iron tools until well into the *gusuku* era. Because most of the soil in the area is *Shimajiri-maaji,* such land could be brought under cultivation with stone and wooden tools. When local powers began to engage in large-scale trade, they were able to import iron and establish forges to manufacture agricultural tools. These iron tools enabled local farmers to begin cultivating areas of *jaagaru* soil, which does require iron tools (*Gushikami-son shi daishikan sonraku hen* 1993, 201–202). Notice that in this account agriculture did not produce local powers (*aji*). Instead, the regional and international trade that these local powers conducted permitted improvements in agriculture.

The official histories claim a divine origin for agriculture, from the North, eliding the matter of precisely identifying the early human agriculturalists. In the typical narrative associated with the internal development model, some room is necessary for positing trade with visiting Japanese ships as the source of the iron tools necessary for large-scale agriculture. The general assumption, however, is that once established, agriculture soon became the economic basis of increasingly complex societies in Okinawa. This social complexity eventually permitted Okinawan kings to enter into formal tribute trade relations with China during the 1370s. In this view, trade later supplemented the agricultural base, thereby contributing to a golden age, which began around the end of the fifteenth century.

Looking at more recent scholarship, Shinzato Akito points out that based on the dates of carbonized grains at specific sites, a transformation from hunter-gatherer societies to agricultural societies took place in a north-to-south direction. Moreover, there was a close connection between pottery and agriculture, with group B pottery reflecting large-scale grain farming (Shinzato Akito 2018, 19, 41–42, 116, citing Asato Susumu and Takamiya Hiroto). In the aggregate, however, Shinzato's data do not support this claim.

At the conclusion of his monograph on Ryukyuan prehistory through the lens of pottery, Shinzato notes that in an "ideal" model of a stratified agricultural society, the distribution of different types of pottery would be represented as a pyramid (figure 7.2). Ordinary earthenware would be most numerous, forming the base. More sophisticated locally produced pottery, especially *kamuiyaki*, would be less common but still widely distributed, like the middle of a pyramid. Imported Chinese or Korean ceramics, the most expensive kitchenware, would mainly be in the hands of elites and therefore occupy the tip. The actual evidence, however, is nearly the reverse, with Chinese and Korean ceramics overwhelmingly more numerous than *kamuiyaki* and ordinary earthenware combined. According to the data, the quantity of locally produced pottery resembles the stem of a wine glass (Shinzato Akito 2018, 162).

Convinced that the *gusuku*-era Ryukyu Islands must have been home to agricultural societies, Shinzato is not able to explain this apparent anomaly. I would say that the actual distribution of pottery types does not look anything like the "ideal" agricultural model because the Ryukyu Islands were not home to full agricultural societies. Instead, they were home to trading societies, broadly defined to include the full range of activities in which *wakō* engaged. The pottery distribution Shinzato observed fits such a trading society perfectly (cf. Yoshinari 2022, 79–80, citing Smits).

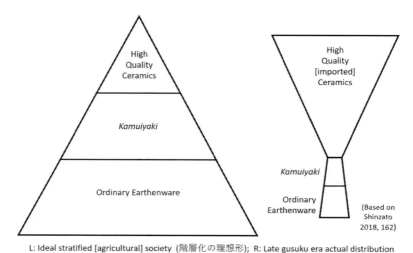

L: Ideal stratified [agricultural] society (階層化の理想形); R: Late gusuku era actual distribution

Figure 7.2.   Expected pottery distribution (*left*) versus actual distribution (*right*).

To take another example, soil scientist Hokama Kazuo published a four-article series on the relationship between soil and the *gusuku* era in Okinawa. The articles are rich in information and insights, but in places Hokama's analysis is burdened by the unassessed assumption that Okinawa became an agricultural society during the *gusuku* era.

Toward the beginning of the first article, Hokama (2015a, 57) states his foundational premise that Okinawa became an agricultural society during the *gusuku* era and that agricultural surpluses enabled local rulers (*aji*) to emerge. The rest of the article is a detailed analysis of soil metrics. The second article restates the premise of Okinawa having become an agricultural society. It notes that the concentration of *gusuku* in the south of Okinawa correlates with the prevalence of agriculture there (Hokama 2015b, 76). Hokama then examines the distribution of Okinawa's population in 1611 (including other Ryukyu Islands), in 1872 (Okinawa only), and in 2011 (Okinawa Prefecture). He notes that the basic population distribution has not changed for four hundred years. Up to this point, Hokama has sketched the population geography accurately, but his reason for it is problematic. It is soil quality, says Hokama, not topography, that accounts for the disproportionately large population in the South. Similarly, Okinawa, a "society with no way of obtaining food other than agriculture, is a society dependent on soil" (Hokama 2015b, 76). In Hokama's view, Okinawa was not only an agricultural society but one entirely dependent on agriculture. I disagree for reasons that will be made clear below. Moreover, topography is sufficient to explain the population distribution. Stated simply, tall, rugged mountains, the terrain in most of northern Okinawa, are not conducive to a dense human population.

Hokama (2018, 35, citing Asato Susumu) reminds us toward the start of the third article that "as agricultural productivity increased, settlements became denser, and [agriculture] became the basis of political power." However, problems soon appear with Hokama's assertion. We have excellent carbonized grain data, and many iron items have been excavated from archaeological sites. However, the only agricultural tools among these excavated items have been small hoes and spades (*hera*). Such tools are better regarded as gardening implements than equipment for large-scale farming. Large farming tools would have been necessary for a major expansion of agricultural lands, but none have ever been excavated. Similarly, fifteenth-century Korean records indicate only the use of spades, not plow-hoes (*sukikuwa*). Indeed, plow-hoes were not known in Okinawa until the early modern era (Hokama 2018, 35). The observations of Korean visitor Ryang Seong note the lack of large agricultural tools. Writing around 1460, Ryang stated that farmers tilling dry or wet fields use spades (Ch. *chā* 鍤), not plows (Ikeya, Uchida, and Takase 2005, 143.)

While acknowledging the lack of large agricultural tools, Hokama notes that the official histories tell stories of kings Satto and Shō Hashi obtaining iron by trade. Hokama appears to take these tales at face value. He then states that villages increased rapidly during the thirteenth and fourteenth centuries and asserts that because these villages were supported by agriculture (an unassessed assumption), iron tools must have increased as well. Otherwise, agricultural expansion would not have been possible (Hokama 2018, 35–36). My view, contra Hokama, is that agricultural expansion was severely limited, not only by poor soil but also by the lack of iron tools.

The lack of excavated agricultural tools is problematic, and Hokama discusses the matter at some length. The only two types of tools that have been found in *gusuku*-era sites are spades for cultivation and small harvest sickles, with blades a few centimeters long. Hokama speculates that small iron tools like hatchets and knives could have been used to fashion wooden plows and other agricultural tools. A combination of small iron tools and wooden or bone tools would have been sufficient to cultivate *Shimajiri-maaji* soils. However, such tools would not have been effective in *jaagaru* soil (nutrient-rich but with poor drainage and containing heavy clay) or for use in wet-rice agriculture. Wooden tools have been used in Ryukyuan agriculture until recently. When combined with cow and horse treading cultivation, certain types of farming were possible. However, Hokama acknowledges that opening new fields or creating irrigation systems requires surveying and the use of large iron farm tools, axes, and other such equipment, none of which have been excavated. Adapting *Shimajiri-maaji* agricultural tools and techniques to *jaagaru* soil would have been extremely difficult (Hokama 2018, 36). Seto Tetsuya (2019, 57) notes that archaeological evidence of wet-rice fields in Okinawa is very sparse, and he mentions only the Aragusuku Shichabaru 2 Site in Ginowan as an example. To his credit Hokama does not ignore this problematic gap in the archeological evidence. In my view his analysis indicates a problem with the premise that *gusuku*-era Okinawa was an agricultural society. This premise needs to be examined.

The Dissenters

To my knowledge only four historians have hitherto argued that *gusuku*-era Okinawa was not an agricultural society. The first is Asato Susumu, the scholar Hokama cites in support of the premise that *gusuku*-era Okinawa was an agricultural society. However, well before Hokama published his first article, Asato had reassessed his position and changed his mind. According to Asato, *gusuku*-era agriculture was conducted with spades made from bone, wet fields were trampled by oxen, and harvesting was accomplished with small iron sickles. There is no evidence of iron hoes or plows, and this situation persisted into the fifteenth century (Asato 2010, 18–19). The economic basis of local rulers and the early kingdom "was not agricultural harvests, but an accumulation of wealth from maritime trade." Moreover, "We should not use the agricultural society that was Japan as a standard by which to measure Okinawa, a society powered by trade" (Asato 2010, 19).[7]

Tomiyama Kazuyuki argues that the Ryukyu Kingdom became an agricultural society for the first time only during the early modern era, as a result of the 1609 war with Satsuma. He calls this change "agriculturalization from the top down" (*ue kara no nōgyōka*). Out of necessity the royal government appointed agricultural officials and established policies and institutions to promote farming (Tomiyama 2003, 77–81).

Kurima Yasuo, an agricultural historian by training, agrees with Tomiyama that Okinawa was not an agricultural society prior to the early modern era. However, Kurima disagrees that Okinawa became a viable agricultural society during the seventeenth century as a result of top-down policies. He notes that agricultural productivity was so low that even Okinawa Prefecture in the early twentieth century could not have qualified as a genuine agricultural society—much less the Okinawa of earlier eras. Kurima's argument that at no point in the past was Okinawa an agricultural society is based mainly on a close reading of early modern and modern documents. If Okinawa was not an agricultural society during the seventeenth or eighteenth century, Kurima argues, it could not have been an agricultural society during the *gusuku* era (Kurima 2013b, 235–249).

Yoshinari Naoki finds Kurima's arguments convincing. Yoshinari incorporates them into an even more extensive argument that the Ryukyu Islands of the *gusuku* era possessed agriculture but were not home to agricultural societies (Yoshinari 2020, 49–72).

I agree with all four of these historians that the driving force behind social stratification in the *gusuku*-era Ryukyu Islands was trade—or trading and raiding—not agriculture. Building on the work of Yoshinari and Kurima, my view is the following:

1. I agree with the academic consensus that agriculture began in the Ryukyu Islands around the tenth century and spread widely during the early *gusuku* era.
2. Agriculture not only existed but was an important source of food. Furthermore, in some locations there is good evidence that agriculture became the main source of food.
3. While it is possible that local surpluses occasionally accrued, there is no evidence of regular agricultural surpluses during the *gusuku* era nor any evidence of agricultural taxation.
4. During the *gusuku* era, and even later, the foundational economic activity in the Ryukyu Islands was trading and raiding, not agriculture. Okinawa became a trade society, and agriculture was of secondary importance.
5. I agree with Tomiyama that during the seventeenth century, the royal government attempted to create a fully agricultural society, and I agree with Kurima that this attempt was largely a failure.

Points one and two above are widely accepted, so I do not discuss them further. In the rest of this chapter, I provide evidence to support point three and, indirectly, point four. In chapter 8 I describe trading activity in detail, thereby providing further support for point four. Point five is outside the scope of this book, but I address it briefly because of its importance in the larger scheme of Ryukyuan history.

In the sections below, I examine the main topics by which I support points three, four, and five: the soil itself, agricultural tools, documentary evidence from within Okinawa, the observations of Chinese investiture envoys, malaria, and the absence of a state.

Soil

Although some small pockets of soil are well suited for cereal agriculture, most of the soil of Okinawa and the other Ryukyu Islands is either unsuitable or requires significant inputs of labor and fertilizer to be productive. To state my conclusion in advance, the soil of the Ryukyu Islands was a major obstacle to agricultural productivity.

In chapter 3 I introduced the three main soil varieties in the Ryukyu Islands, the two reddish soils *Kunigami-maaji* and *Shimajiri-maaji* and the gray soil called *jaagaru*. There are several small patches of other soil types, including alluvial soil (*kaniku*), which is good for agriculture and is mostly found in coastal areas. The majority of the pockets of alluvial soil are in central and northern Okinawa, an area otherwise dominated by *Kunigami-maaji*.[8]

In south and central Okinawa, *Shimajiri-maaji* and *jaagaru* predominate. Both types require significant intervention for use in agriculture. *Shimajiri-maaji* is the less difficult of the two types to work, and wooden tools can produce productive dry fields. *Shimajiri-maaji* quickly loses its nutrients, however, so they must be replenished frequently with fertilizer or by letting land lay fallow. This soil type drains well but requires irrigation. *Jaagaru* is the most fertile soil, but its physical qualities make it especially difficult to work. Large iron plows, for example, would be required to cut through it.

Surveying the distribution of soil types for all the Ryukyu Islands requires greater specificity than what we have seen thus far in Okinawa. In the following paragraphs, I rely on the Japan Soil Inventory (Nihon Dojō Inbentorii, online). The inventory lists ten broad categories of soil, labeled A through J, with each having as many as six subtypes. The soil in the Ryukyu Islands consists of types E (dark-red soil), F (lowland soil or alluvial soil), G (red-yellow soil), and J (immature soil).[9]

G1 (clay-accumulation red-yellow soil; *Kunigami-maaji*), the main soil in northern Okinawa, can be used for wet-rice agriculture today because of modern fertilizer. However, the natural fertility of this soil is very low, it is strongly acidic, and it drains very poorly (Japan Soil Inventory; Okazaki et al. 2010, 15–16). Other than for use as pastureland or for growing certain fruit trees, it would have been unsuitable for agriculture in premodern times. Nearly all the soil of Amami-Ōshima is G1. Furthermore, G1 predominates in Tokunoshima, Kumejima, Ishigaki, and Yonaguni. Iriomote is approximately half G1 and half G2, a closely related type. The widespread distribution of G1 and G2 soils limits cereal agriculture, but these soils also occur mainly in mountainous areas, so unsuitable topography overlaps significantly with the G1 and G2 soil types (Japan Soil Inventory).

The soil type in areas that have traditionally produced good rice yields in the Ryukyu Islands is E1 (limestone dark-red soil). Today E1 is mainly used for dry fields, and although fairly common in the Ryukyu Islands, it accounts for only 0.5 percent of Japan's soil. E1 soil predominates in low islands. It is the main soil in Kikaijima and the part of the Kasari Peninsula in Amami-Ōshima facing Kikaijima. It is also the main soil of the fringing lowlands around Tokunoshima and Okino-erabu. E1 is the dominant soil type in the Miyako Islands, and significant pockets of it are found in southern Ishigaki and Yonaguni. E1 is susceptible to drought damage, and its pH varies widely from base to acidic (Japan Soil Inventory). Documentary records suggest that many of the areas with significant E1 were valuable for grain production. However, E1 is not ideally suited to wet-rice agriculture (for reference, Okazaki et al. 2010, 20). All indications are that rice produced in E1 soil was naturally irrigated and enhanced by treading cultivation (cf. chapter 3).

Lowland soils (types F2 [gley], F3, F4, and F5) are located in coastal and riverine areas of Okinawa. Such soil is suitable for wet-rice cultivation, and 70 percent of Japan's irrigated rice fields are of type F. Although distributed throughout Okinawa, F soils compose a larger proportion of central and southern Okinawa (Japan Soil Inventory). Some of the soil Hokama calls *jaagaru* appears in the Japan Soil Inventory as type F (Hokama 2018, 38–42).[10] It is these type F soils that have the potential to become productive irrigated wet-rice fields, given sufficient tools, labor, and know-how (Hokama 2018, 42). It is important to keep in mind the sparse distribution of the F soils. As Richard Pearson (2013, 27) notes, only about 3 percent of Okinawan soil is suitable for irrigated crops.

The fortress of Guraru Magohachi at Goran in Okinoerabu is located in a small gap between two areas of F3 soil. Magohachi was a *wakō* chief and associate of Shō Hashi. Guraru (today, Goran) is an example of what I call Gaara group place-names, which overlapped with areas of wet-rice agriculture (Smits 2019, 102). Interestingly, both Sashiki in Kyushu, the land of Shō Hashi's origin, and a band of land surrounding Baten harbor just below Sashiki Castle, his base in Okinawa, are both predominantly F3 soil (Japan Soil Inventory; Hokama 2018, 38–42). In other words, Shō Hashi's group settled into a pocket of land in Okinawa whose soil was nearly identical to that of their former home in Kyushu.

On the whole, most of the soil of the Ryukyu Islands would have been ill-suited to cereal agriculture in the premodern era.[11] Of the soil suitable for cereal agriculture, most of it would have been viable only for dry field crops, not wet-rice agriculture. Japan and Korea were agricultural societies based mainly on rice grown in irrigated fields. It would have been physically impossible for Okinawa and the other Ryukyu Islands to replicate this type of agriculture except in a very few isolated locations. Literary scholar Nagafuji Yasushi points out that although rice was the overwhelmingly dominant grain in mainland Japan, it is but one of several grains in myths and legends from the Ryukyu Islands. In some accounts of the origin of grain, rice is not even mentioned (Nagafuji 2000, 69–84). Insofar as rice was cultivated in the Ryukyu Islands, most was probably Indica (Champa) rice that came into the islands from southern China, not Japonica rice from Kyushu. Indica rice can be cultivated on dry fields by simply broadcasting the seeds without ploughing (Kurima 2013a, 123, 125–126).[12]

Agricultural Tools

We have no evidence of iron agricultural tools during the *gusuku* era other than items similar to modern garden spades and small cutting or pruning tools. Ōshiro Kei, writing around 1983 about iron in *gusuku*-era excavations, noted that "actual iron agricultural tools have not yet been found," other than two or three small sickles for harvesting the ears of plants (Ōshiro Kei 1983, 285). As mentioned above, writing around 2015, Hokama noted that nothing other than spades and small sickles have been found in excavations. Based on soil indentations in excavated areas that were probably dry fields, it is likely that wooden poles were used in cultivation (Seto 2019, 56–57).

This lack of iron agricultural tools persisted. Even as late as the middle of the eighteenth century, it appears that nothing more than small iron hand tools was available to farmers. Moreover, they were in very short supply. In 1745 the official Kanagusuku Chikudun-peichin Wasai inspected agriculture in Okinawa's five most productive districts, Mawshi, Haebaru, Ōzato, Kochinda, and Tomigusuku in the south. He noticed that in preparing the ground the peasants did not use spades (*hera*) or grass-cutting scythes. He inquired, discovered that the peasants lacked such tools, and petitioned the government to buy and distribute spades. As Kurima Yasuo points out, it is astonishing not only that the peasants in the most productive districts lacked metal tools but that the best the royal government could provide in 1745 were simple spades (Kurima 2013b, 239–240). It appears that Okinawa may not have been a fully agricultural society even in the middle of the eighteenth century.

Early Modern and Shōwa-Era Documents

No relevant documents from the *gusuku* era itself exist other than reports from Korean observers. Kurima makes the reasonable assumption that agricultural technology and productivity did not decline during the early modern and modern eras relative to the *gusuku* era. Therefore, if Okinawa was not an agricultural society in, for example, the seventeenth century, it would not have been one during the fourteenth century.

In 1613, in connection with defeat in the 1609 war with Satsuma, the domain sent the document "List of Regulations" (*O-okite no jōjō*) to the government in Shuri. One item decrees that agriculture has hitherto been pursued mainly by women and that henceforth men are to engage in agriculture vigorously. The likely context is that men customarily engaged in fishing and hunting, and women supplemented the food supply by cultivation. Agriculture, in other words, does not appear to have been an energetic sector of the economy at the start of the seventeenth century (Kurima 2013b, 235–236).

In *Haneji shioki* ([1673] 1981, 46–47) Shō Shōken stated that agriculture had improved to the point that Okinawa could now pay its rice tax in full. However, this statement was bragging or wishful thinking on his part, and no evidence supports it. Only under Shō Shōken did the royal government begin to take agriculture seriously, or at least appear to do so. It seems odd for Okinawan agriculture to play only a supporting role until the 1660s and then suddenly, by 1673, to surge in productivity (Kurima 2013b 236–237). In this connection it is significant that measured agricultural productivity declined between 1634 and 1726. According to a cadastral survey in 1634, Ryukyu's total productivity was 123,742 koku, but that figure dropped to 94,230 koku according to a survey in 1726 (Tamura [1927] 1977, 179).

Leaving out the details here, Kurima cites a variety of agriculture-related directives and policy statements from the late seventeenth and early eighteenth centuries, noting that agriculture still appears to have been disorganized. He argues, contra Tomiyama, that the existence of government policies and pronouncements does not mean that an actual agricultural society had developed (Kurima 2013b, 238–239). Despite the royal government's frequent pronouncements about agriculture being the foundation of society, official documents abound with statements like this one from 1856: "The peasants were negligent in agriculture, and we were not able to collect taxes" (Kurima 2013b, 241).

An extended discussion of the early modern era is beyond the scope of this book, but a quick answer to the question of what people ate includes tubers, which grow well in *Shimajiri-maaji* soil and appear to have been in good supply. During the 1930s sweet potatoes made up about 50 percent of cultivated land and *satoimo* tubers, 25 percent. Only 10 percent of land under cultivation was devoted to rice fields (Kurima 2013b, 243, 244). Significantly, according to a 1935 report based on observations in the field, "the crops of this prefecture are not actively produced, but only come about naturally" (quoted in Kurima 2013b, 247).

From the 1660s onward, the royal government began to claim that Ryukyu was an agricultural society, and it made occasional attempts to bring about that situation. Nevertheless, the government does not seem to have succeeded in creating a society supported mainly by agriculture (setting aside sugarcane, which became a major cash crop around the turn of the eighteenth century). The key point for our purposes is that if early modern Ryukyu was not fully an agricultural society, it is difficult to imagine that the situation was significantly different during the *gusuku* era.

Observations by Chinese Investiture Envoys

One source that Kurima and others did not consult was the detailed reports of Chinese investiture envoys. Although many early Ryukyuan kings and trade kings received formal recognition from the Chinese court, Shō Sei appears to have been the first king to participate in the complete investiture process. That process included documentary verification, formal rituals, and a lengthy stay in Okinawa by a Chinese investiture envoy and his entourage. One result was the publication in 1534 of a book-length record of conditions in Ryukyu by the envoy Chén Kǎn. Subsequent envoys published similar accounts, often copying material from their predecessors while sometimes adding new original observations.

Chén observed, and many subsequent envoys repeated, that Ryukyuans valued iron and cotton cloth, not fancier decorative items.[13] Work in the kitchen was usually accomplished using implements made from conch shells, and most weaving was done using hemp or banana plant fibers. Those who wanted to use knives or pots for boiling, or who wanted to use iron agricultural tools, had to purchase them from the royal government, and evading this rule was a punishable crime (*Shi Ryūkyū roku* 1534, 75). Chén's point resonates with the experience of the official in 1745, discussed above, who had to petition the government to obtain simple agricultural tools.

Guō Rǔlín was the envoy for Shō Gen's investiture. He observed that rocks and sand were numerous in the countryside and the soil was impoverished. Although people raised cows, sheep, chickens, and pigs, the animals were so thin as to be of little benefit. The people were inept at agriculture, and they rarely cultivated using fertilizer. People's meagre grain consumption put them on the verge of starvation, and they rarely ate fish or meat (*Jūhen shi Ryūkyū roku* 1561, 166). Shō Ei's investiture envoys, Xiāo Chóngyè and Xiè Jié, made nearly the same observation. They also reported being told that taxes were not levied on such poor people "in accordance with reason" (*Shi Ryūkyū roku* 1579, 177–178).

None of the envoys thus far have described a society supported mainly by agriculture.

Wáng Jí served as investiture envoy for Shō Tei. He observed that the peasants ate only sweet potatoes and appeared unable to obtain rice (*Sakuhō Ryūkyū shiroku sanpen* [1684] 1997, 72). In the early eighteenth century, envoy Xú Bǎoguāng noted significant environmental constraints on Okinawan agriculture. He pointed out that farmers sowed seeds in the ninth and tenth lunar months and harvested in the fifth.[14] This unusual cycle resulted from the severe wind- and rainstorms that regularly occur during the sixth month and damage crops. Limited rainfall at other times of the year also dictated this pattern. Importantly, these constraints prevented double-cropping even though the temperature would otherwise allow it (*Denshinroku* [1721] 1982, 294). Discussing agricultural tools, Xú pointed out that spades were small and that mountain fields were irrigated only by rainwater. Otherwise, wet fields had to be located under a spring because rivers and ponds are subject to saltwater intrusion and thus cannot be used for irrigation (*Denshinroku* [1721] 1982, 340).

Chinese investiture envoys were not in positions to make detailed agricultural surveys. Nevertheless, their stays in Okinawa typically lasted months, and one of their duties was to report on local conditions. All indications from their accounts are that agriculture was poorly developed in Okinawa. Especially important is Xú's discussion of fundamental environmental constraints on agricultural productivity.

Malaria

Malaria is detrimental to agriculture because of its impact on labor. As late as 1900, malaria could be found in the Japanese Islands from the Kansai area of Honshu southward throughout all the Ryukyu Islands (Hay et al. 2004, 328, fig. 1). Malaria afflicted the Ryukyu Islands until the early 1960s. It was known by a variety of names in premodern texts, and determining their precise correspondence to the four *Plasmodium* parasites now known to infect humans is difficult.[15] We can divide historic malaria in the Japanese and Ryukyu Islands into two major varieties. The first is tropical malaria, the most severe type, which mainly infected people in the southern Ryukyu Islands. This type almost certainly corresponds to infection by *Plasmodium falciparum* and was associated with the southern Ryukyu Islands.[16] Tropical malaria typically flares up on a daily basis and was often fatal. The second type is indigenous malaria, of which there are two subtypes. One features occasional flare-ups that last for up to three days. In the other, flare-ups of malarial fever can persist for up to four days. Although rarely fatal, those infected with indigenous malaria usually suffer periodic repeat outbreaks (Inafuku 1995, 455, 457, 460–461; Ōtsuru 1998, 151). In the past, three-day malaria was known by names such as *okori* 瘧, *warawayami* 和良波夜美, and *eyami* 衣夜美. These names appeared in Japanese texts such as *Wanashō* (early tenth century), *Genji monogatari* (early eleventh century), *Ujishūi monogatari* (early thirteenth century), *Meigetsuki* (early thirteenth century), and *Azuma kagami* (late thirteenth century). Considering the timing of its appearance in the mainland, trade network dates, and mitochondrial DNA evidence, malaria most likely had become established in Okinawa by the early *gusuku* era, arriving along with the groups of immigrants who brought agriculture (Yoshinari 2020, 55–56). In the southern Ryukyu Islands, tropical malaria came from points further south.

Malaria in Okinawa correlates closely with one environmental variable: forestation. In past eras, malaria increased as one went north, with the heavily forested areas of Kunigami the most infested. In exact proportion to deforestation during the modern era, malaria has decreased. Forest pools were the main sources of malaria in Okinawa, and the disease lingered in the Kunigami region well into the twentieth century (Yoshinari 2020, 58–59, citing Nakamatsu Yashū).[17] With respect to this point, clearing land for dry field cereal agriculture may have reduced the incidence of malaria insofar as it eliminated mosquito-breeding areas. Nevertheless, malaria would have been a constant presence throughout the *gusuku* era. In that sense it had a negative impact on agriculture, although the extent is impossible to measure.

Lack of a State

In considering the majority claim that *gusuku*-era Okinawa became an agricultural society and the counterclaim that it was not, it is important to consider some broader points. First, there was no central state during the *gusuku* era. As explained in detail in the next two chapters, the main political unit until the sixteenth century consisted of a harbor or other anchorage paired with a fortress located on higher ground overlooking the harbor. These units were primarily trading and raiding centers, even though some inhabitants engaged in agriculture. There is no evidence that any of these harbor-fortress units employed a bureaucracy, created written documents for domestic recordkeeping, or systematically levied taxes.[18] In other words, they did not employ the coercive mechanisms of agrarian states or resemble agrarian states in any other significant way. Most *gusuku*-era immigrants came from Japan during times when agricultural estates (*shōen*) were widespread. Importantly, there is no indication that any such estates developed in Okinawa or the other Ryukyu Islands.

It is also important to bear in mind the distinction between states and "barbarians" advanced by James C. Scott (chapter 4). Until the sixteenth century, the Ryukyu Islands were not home to states. They were home to "barbarian" groups, several of which I identify and discuss in later chapters. These groups both preyed upon and traded with states in the region. As a barbarian zone (in Scott's sense), the Ryukyu Islands were a frontier region. It is likely that many immigrants to the islands during the *gusuku* era moved there specifically to avoid state control, whether in Japan or elsewhere in the region. With these points in mind, it should not be surprising that state-directed attempts to create an agricultural society in the Ryukyu Islands did not begin until well into the seventeenth century.

The Ryukyu Islands are unusual in world prehistory in at least two ways. First, although it was rare for small islands to be settled prior to agriculture, the Ryukyu Islands have a long history of continuous occupation by hunter-gatherers. Second, the arrival of agriculture in the islands was "one of the latest primary farming dispersals in Eurasia" (Jarosz et al. 2022, 1–2). One likely contributing factor to the very late dispersal of farming was simply that the Ryukyu Islands are poorly suited to agriculture.

Kurima estimates that before the cultivation of sweet potatoes began during the early seventeenth century, agriculture of any kind took up roughly 5 percent of the land in the islands. With this point in the background, he denies that the emergence of a Ryukyu Kingdom was the result of agricultural expansion. He also denies the claim that formal social stratification developed as a result of agriculture, or indeed that it developed at all during the *gusuku* era. Furthermore, Kurima makes the important point that the Ryukyu Kingdom was mainly the creation of an outside agent, the Ming court (Kurima 2013b, 248–249). In subsequent chapters I discuss in detail the role of Chinese wealth in creating trade kings in the Ryukyu Islands.

In a recent book, archaeologist Takamiya Hiroto argues against Kurima and Yoshinari Naoki, in support of the consensus view that *gusuku*-era Okinawa and Amami-Ōshima became agricultural societies. Takamiya begins by stating that the relevant evidence is archaeological data revealing what people were eating. However, he also notes that much of the data about cultivated plants depend on chance (Takamiya 2021, 197). Takamiya's first point is that although both cultivated grain and gathered nuts have been found at *gusuku*-era sites, grain is much more numerous. Because nuts were a minor source of food, *gusuku*-era Okinawa was "agriculture-centric" (*nōkō chūshin*) with respect to people's diets. Further support for this point is a decrease in seafood consumption during the *gusuku* era, suggesting a turn from the sea to the land (Takamiya 2021, 197–198).

Takamiya also points out that archaeologists have unearthed wet and dry fields, as well as the bones of likely draft animals. They have also reported evidence of agricultural rituals. In connection with arguing that a tax system was possible despite the absence of writing, Takamiya cites the case of an excavated wet-rice field at the Maeatari site in Tokunoshima. The site contains very few carbonized rice grains. Takamiya speculates that this lack of rice indicates that perhaps people ate all of it or that it was shipped off as tax. He also notes that the majority of grain excavated from Akagina Gusuku in Amami-Ōshima was rice. Therefore, it is possible that the rulers of this fortress levied taxes on farmers. In summary, although rice was rare there is good evidence that people consumed a variety of grains and that grains from cultivated crops were more numerous in the diet than foraged food during the *gusuku* era (Takamiya 2021, 198–200).

I find Takamiya's claim that a tax system might have existed to be unconvincing. Certainly, it is likely that grains grown near fortresses contributed to the diet of those connected with those fortresses. However, such a situation hardly constitutes evidence of either a tax system or agricultural surpluses capable of driving state formation. Otherwise, Takamiya's refutation of Kurima and Yoshinari boils down to an assertion that (1) agriculture existed during the *gusuku* era and (2) that it constituted an important part of people's diets. These points, however, are not in dispute. Moreover, Takamiya does not address Kurima's document-based arguments or any of the major impediments to agriculture discussed above, such as soil type, tools, environmental constraints, and malaria.

World history demonstrates many instances of premodern societies that practiced agriculture but did not become agricultural societies (chapter 4). Poor soil, a limited number of small iron tools, seasonal severe weather, saltwater intrusion, and the presence of malaria all worked against agricultural productivity in the Ryukyu Islands. Abundant wild tubers, nuts, food from the sea, and a population of feral pigs and wild boars meant that agriculture could function to supplement other food sources. One other point to bear in mind is that intensive wet-rice agriculture as practiced in Japan and Korea was extremely rare in the Ryukyu Islands. The majority of rice in the islands was of the Indica variety, grown in dry fields and fields prepared by treading cultivation. The majority of grain was millet, barley, wheat, and other dry field crops.

The physical environment, the infrastructure, and a political geography based on harbor-fortress units worked against the development of widespread, intensive agriculture. Takamiya's counterargument notwithstanding, I see no strong evidence in support of the claims that *gusuku*-era Ryukyu was home to fully agricultural societies or that agricultural surpluses drove increasing social complexity and state formation. While it is possible to argue about the precise definition of an agricultural society, the crucial question is whether agriculture was a driver of social complexity and, especially, state formation. I am confident that it was not.

As a final point, consider agriculture during the early modern era. We have seen extensive documentary evidence that agriculture in the Ryukyu Islands at that time was poorly developed. Although a topic for a future book, there is good evidence that early modern reformers such as Shō Shōken and Sai On attempted to make the Ryukyu Kingdom into an agricultural society centered on cereal crops. Abundant evidence also suggests that, over the long run, these attempts failed in the face of the severe environmental constraints discussed previously. In this connection it is noteworthy that crops such as rice and other staple grains compose less than 1 percent of the agricultural output of Okinawa Prefecture today.[19] Understanding that the Ryukyu Islands are poorly suited for cereal agriculture is an important context for explaining the heavy taxation and grinding poverty that became especially problematic during the nineteenth century and later. The question of whether and to what extent the Ryukyu Kingdom was an agricultural state is crucial for understanding the course of early modern Ryukyuan history and the ultimate collapse of the kingdom.

CHAPTER EIGHT

Trading and Raiding Intensify

The Late *Gusuku* Era

This chapter, as well as chapter 9, concentrates on the Ryukyu Islands as home to trading-and-raiding societies. The temporal focus here is the end of the twelfth century to the late fourteenth. Three major arguments are discussed. The first, covered in much more detail in *Maritime Ryukyu*, is that *wakō*, in the context of frequent warfare and intensified competition, were the main drivers of Ryukyuan history at this time.

The second is that major political upheavals around the region had an impact on the Ryukyu Islands, and they contributed to new inflows of people. The earliest relevant event was the Sambyeolcho 三別抄 Rebellion in mainland Korea and Jeju Island (1270–1273). Next was the deterioration of the Southern Song dynasty and the rise of the Mongol Yuan dynasty (ca. 1260s–1270s). Even more important was the deterioration of the Yuan dynasty and the rise of the Ming dynasty (ca. 1340s–1370s). At roughly the same time, ca. 1350s–1392, the Goryeo dynasty in Korea entered an especially tumultuous period as it collapsed. In Japan, the Kamakura bakufu fell in 1333, and civil war soon enveloped the Japanese Islands until 1392 or later.

Finally, the third argument is that the traditional story whereby direct trade between the Ryukyu Islands and China began during the 1370s with the start of tribute trade is clearly inaccurate. An abundance of archaeological evidence indicates that direct trade between entities in China and entities in the Ryukyu Islands began well before the establishment of the Ming dynasty.

Warfare

During the thirteenth century, fortresses (*gusuku*) became more numerous and more militarily formidable, especially in Okinawa. The frequency of warfare increased during the latter half of the *gusuku* era,[1] and the Archaeological Society of Okinawa explains this trend as follows:

> The number of arrowheads excavated from twelfth century settlement sites is very small. During the second half of the thirteenth century, the

number increases. From the fourteenth century onward, many have been excavated from large *gusuku*. Accordingly, as *gusuku* became larger during the last half of the fourteenth century, the introduction of planar construction featuring overhanging extensions on walls to protect against arrows took place. Owing to the widespread use of arrows, slingshots, and other projectile weapons in battle, the construction of stone walls became more tightly packed for maximum effectiveness. (Okinawa Kōkogakkai 2018, 157)

Similarly, Seto Tetsuya points out that in Okinawa, the quantity of excavated arrowheads increased during the latter half of the *gusuku* era, peaking in the early fifteenth century. According to Seto (2019, 65):

Among the local powers who emerged from the early gusuku era economy—whose foundation was commerce and agriculture—their military struggles appear to have intensified in pursuit of trade and profit during the late fourteenth to early fifteenth centuries. Moreover, these military struggles were not only between domestic combatants. It is also essential to bear in mind that they occurred within the context of interactions with outside groups.

The warfare in and around Okinawa was in part a reflection of political and military upheaval throughout the region.

Gusuku (Fortresses)

The term *gusuku* can be confusing. The iconic Okinawa *gusuku* are large fortresses, or castles, with multiple enclosures of stone walls such as those located at Nakijin, Katsuren, Nakagusuku, Urasoe, Naha, and Shuri. In addition to the large stone-walled *gusuku* are many smaller fortresses with stone walls. These stone-walled *gusuku* closely resemble Korean mountain fortresses (chapter 6). Importantly, there is another type of *gusuku* in the Ryukyu Islands, which is of Japanese origin: trench-and-earthworks fortresses. Typically dug into narrow valleys and ridges, they feature trenches (*horikiri*) and earthworks, sometimes augmented with stones and wooden palisades (Tōma 2012, 44).[2] Examples include Sashiki Gusuku (Sashiki Ui Gusuku) in southern Okinawa, Nago Gusuku in northern Okinawa, and Akagina Gusuku in Amami-Ōshima. Today, these *gusuku* sites typically feature a raised area that affords a commanding view of the surrounding scenery. Although they lack the impressive walls that attract modern tourists, trench-and-earthworks *gusuku* were highly effective as defensive structures in warfare. That both types of structures are called *gusuku* is a potential source of confusion, as is the use of *gusuku* to refer to a general time period (ca. the eleventh through fifteenth centuries) and its frequent appearance in place-names (including Gusuku in Amami-Ōshima).[3]

The stone-walled type of *gusuku* is found in the islands of Okinoerabu, Yoron, and especially Okinawa and surrounding islands. There are also a few in the southern Ryukyu Islands. Regarding the stone walls of *gusuku,* construction using small, uncut, or unprocessed stones is known as "field stone stacking" (*nozurazumi*). Piling up rectangular stone in a horizontal orientation is known as "cloth stacking" (*nunozumi*). Walls made with stone of various sizes, typically with the large stones cut into five- or six-sided shapes and forming a random pattern, are constructed with "fitted stacking" (*aikatazumi*). Some *gusuku* walls consist of more than one type (for comparative photos, see UNESCO World Heritage Convention 2001, 36). These three types of Ryukyuan *gusuku* walls resemble counterparts among the walls of Goryeo- and Joseon-era Korean fortresses.[4]

The trench-and-earthworks type of fortress is the main variety found in the northern Ryukyu Islands. Takanashi Osamu has proposed that the ruins of this type of fortress be referred to by the term *jōkaku iseki* (fortress sites), not *gusuku*.[5] Nevertheless, I use the conventional term *gusuku* for all fortifications, distinguishing between the types when necessary.

During the late *gusuku* era, the geopolitical landscape of the Ryukyu Islands was characterized by local powers based at paired harbor-fortress units. Moreover, in this context there were significant differences between the east and west coasts of Okinawa. For example, along the east coast of Okinawa, large *gusuku* developed from preexisting communities. By contrast, on the west coast, in areas like Urasoe or Naha, large *gusuku* appeared in locations with no preexisting community (Seto 2019, 63–64).

Arguments about the Meaning of *Gusuku*

Many of the hypotheses about the origin of the term *gusuku* are plausible, and none have garnered a consensus.[6] During the modern era, *gusuku* have provoked much argumentation among scholars. In work published in 1938, Toba Masao classified *gusuku* into five types and noted that the majority of Okinawan *gusuku* functioned as the residences of local warlords (*aji*). Implied in this characterization is that *gusuku* were the castles. Higa Shunchō reiterated Toba's classification in his *History of Okinawa* (*Okinawa no rekishi,* 1959). In a 1961 article, "Gusuku kō" (Thoughts on *gusuku*), Nakamatsu Yashū argued that *gusuku* were originally sacred sites, and only later, during the age of local rulers, did some evolve into castles. With the publication of Nakamatsu's article, the so-called *gusuku* debate (*gusuku ronsō*) began. At issue was the "true" function or significance of *gusuku*. The debate raged throughout the 1960s and 1970s and did not produce a consensus (Naka 1992, 130–133, 145–146; Tōma 2012, 65–70). By the 1980s the debate was still underway, but it became absorbed into a larger debate about the nature of the Ryukyu Kingdom (Takanashi 2015, 246–247). In the paragraphs below, I list the major hypotheses, point out some problems, and summarize my view on the matter.

The *gusuku* debate has tended to assume that there was a single fundamental function of *gusuku,* some kind of genuine essence of *gusuku*-ness. In this context, scholars have argued that *gusuku* fundamentally were the dwelling places of local warlords, sacred places (functionally, a type of sacred grove), communities (*shūraku*), and walled fortresses or military bases.[7] Within this latter category, *gusuku* might also function as places of refuge for local populations—for example, to prevent them being carried away by outside raiders (Ikuta 1992, 266). In this sense *gusuku* fulfilled the same function as Korean mountain fortresses (chapter 6). Some scholars have proposed variations and combinations of these basic functions. For example, Ōhira Satoshi suggests that larger *gusuku* functioned less as military installations than as a means to show off the aesthetic sensibilities (including nice landscape views) and advanced engineering capabilities of those who dwelled in them (Kurima 2013b, 156).

Ōhira's view is one variation on a recurring idea that persists despite extensive evidence to the contrary: the Ryukyu Islands were an inherently peaceful place. In 1963, for example, Yamazato Eikichi (1963, 239) argued that most *gusuku* were built "for purposes other than warfare."[8] He claimed that "Ryukyuans [*Ryūkyūjin*] are an ethnos [*minzoku*] that fundamentally adores peace. Even the overturning of royal lines was, in most cases, accomplished without warfare." Yamazato (1963, 240–241) acknowledged some of the conflict in Ryukyuan history, but he minimized it as something akin to internal family squabbles. Therefore, "Why would it have been necessary for *aji,* large or small, actively to compete to build walled castles?" Yamazato constitutes a typical postwar example of attempts by scholars or journalists to minimize the obvious military function of *gusuku* because of a perceived need to portray the Ryukyu Islands as a place devoid of warfare.[9] Notice also in Yamazato's take on *gusuku* the underlying assumption that "Ryukyuans" constituted a stable, definable group during the *gusuku* era, about which it is possible to ascribe fundamental cultural or psychological characteristics. I do not agree, and I revisit this point in chapter 13.

A general problem with the *gusuku* debate literature is a tendency to assume that there was a single fundamental essence that all spaces called "*gusuku*" shared, at least "originally." That said, some scholars have acknowledged the futility of trying to find such an essence. In this view *gusuku* were multifaceted structures whose uses evolved over time (Naka 1992, 134 discussing Takemoto Masahide and Nakamatsu Moto). My view is the same.

Scholars of Korean mountain fortresses, the ancestors of stone-walled *gusuku* (chapter 6), readily acknowledge that the fortresses functioned for more than one purpose. Importantly, several major hypothesized functions of *gusuku* in the *gusuku* debate were also functions that Korean mountain fortresses performed. Mountain fortresses were military facilities first and foremost. A derivative function was as locations to which the nearby population could flee during times of outside attack. Korean mountain fortresses also functioned as sacred and ritual spaces (Korea Fortress Academy 2008a, 39; 2008b, 107, 166).

One issue that frequently arises in modern and contemporary discussions of *gusuku* is the question of whether they were castles. This question is often complicated by the lack of a clear or informed definition of castles. For example, scholars arguing that *gusuku* were something other than military bases often assume that castles were military bases and assert, therefore, that *gusuku* were not castles. However, castles in Europe and around the world often functioned as much more than military facilities. Castles were also administrative, commercial, and religious centers, to name a few possibilities. Moreover, there is no exact conceptual or functional boundary between castles and structures like fortified manner houses. The same terminological slipperiness also applies to places called *gusuku*, which varied in terms of their structures and functions. Large castles were multiuse structures, and the same can be said for large *gusuku*. Large *gusuku* were residences of locally powerful people (and some or all of their soldiers), storehouses, and administrative centers. They contained sacred groves. The common practice today of calling some large *gusuku* "castles" (J. -jō), although somewhat inconsistently applied, is reasonable.

Whatever the range of functions that large *gusuku* served, that they were military installations is undeniable. During the fifteenth century, two- and three-barreled hand cannon from China became commonplace in Ryukyuan warfare. The walls of Agena Gusuku in Uruma and Nakagusuku Gusuku show wear from hand cannon fire, and battlements in the walls of large *gusuku* facilitated the use of this weapon. Parts of swords and other striking weapons have been excavated from sites dating to the fourteenth and fifteenth centuries, the majority from the sites of large *gusuku* (Okinawa Kōkogakkai 2018, 158). Significantly, one of the distinctive functions of Okinawan stone-walled *gusuku* is as excavation sites for large quantities of military items such as pieces of armor and helmets, iron arrowheads, and arrowheads made from dugong bones. By contrast, discoveries of military gear are extremely rare in the majority of castle sites in mainland Japan (Tōma 2012, 45).

Naka Shōhachirō points out that classifying *gusuku* according to topography and design features results in four types.[10] Regarding their function, the only reasonable conclusion, says Naka, is that *gusuku* were primarily defensive structures, not religious sites. If religion had been the primary purpose, there would have been no need to build *gusuku* at high points, build multiple walls, or dig trenches. Some served as emergency facilities and were not regularly occupied, and some were inhabited year-round. Military and religious functions were intertwined. For example, priestesses were in the forefront of both armies during Shuri's 1500 invasion of Yaeyama (*Kyūyō* [1743–1876] 1974, 1978, 147–148 [#160]), and sorcery skirmishes between priestesses had a long history in Ryukyuan warfare. *Magatama* (jewels worn by priestesses) have been excavated from most *gusuku* sites, where priestesses would offer prayers for success on the battlefield. This point is key to the arguments of Nakamatsu and others who asserted that *gusuku* were originally sacred sites. Gusuku were originally *military* sites, but a crucial part of the military system was the presence of religious facilities and personnel (Naka 1992, 148–151; Yonami 2005, 13–14; Gi 2007, 87). According to Ikeda Yoshifumi, *gusuku* were a product of "the process of social strain" (Ikeda 2012b, 340). In other words, they embody the social conflict of the late *gusuku* era.[11]

Wakō

The early history of the Ryukyu Islands is inextricably connected with *wakō*, seafaring raiders and traders. Based on archaeological evidence, Shirakihara Kazumi has pointed out that the overall pace of activity in the Ryukyu Islands corresponded closely with an upsurge in *wakō* activity in the region. Moreover, at the same time, legends derived from Japan's Genpei Wars spread throughout the region, the most important being that of Chinzei Hachirō (Minamoto) Tametomo (Shirakihara 1992, 126). Similarly, drawing on evidence from a variety of academic fields, I argue in *Maritime Ryukyu* that the main drivers of Ryukyuan history from the late thirteenth century onward were *wakō* (Smits 2019).

Overall, Okinawa was an especially favorable location for *wakō* groups if for no other reason than its location. Okinawa was connected with Japan, Korea, and northern China via relatively easy-to-navigate island hopping and coastal sailing. For larger ships with skilled crews, the wealthy areas of the lower Yangzi

(Yangtze) River and coastal southern China were approximately a week's voyage away with decent weather. It is also important to note that during the Yuan dynasty, and continuing into the Ming, the demand for sulfur in China increased as gunpowder weapons became prominent in warfare. *Wakō* groups were closely connected with the sulfur trade (Smits 2019, 64, 70–72).[12] Okinawa possessed good harbors, especially the deepwater harbor at Naha, and it was well outside the range of the military forces of established states in the region. It was, in other words, perfectly suited to functioning as a barbarian zone (chapter 4).

I have examined *wakō* and the Ryukyu Islands in *Maritime Ryukyu* (Smits 2019, especially 36–59). Here I briefly summarize a few of the main points. The term *wakō* (K. *waegu*) first appeared in *Goryeo History* in an entry dated 1223 (1, 19–20, 56). The common translation "Japanese pirates" is misleading because many *wakō* were not Japanese. During the time covered in this book, most *wakō* were either Japanese, Korean, or people of mixed Japanese and Korean ancestry. Outside the Ryukyu Islands, their bases were often located in Japanese territory, especially the Inland Sea, western Kyushu, Iki, and Tsushima.

Wakō of this era often engaged in piratical activities such as marauding, human trafficking, and smuggling. They were dangerous and destructive. However, depending on circumstances, *wakō* also engaged in trade and diplomacy and provided security. They maintained horse pastures in several locations, in part to provide for their own cavalry and in part to profit from selling horses.[13] The dividing line between maritime merchants, who operated with armed crews, and *wakō* was often unclear.

Attacks by *wakō* on coastal areas of southern Korea were especially common during the fourteenth century. Attacks on coastal China were comparatively less frequent, but they became a grave concern for the Ming dynasty. In their raids, *wakō* carried off food, livestock, other valuables, people, and even boats and ships. Captives were especially valuable. Many were sold into servitude, although often for limited periods of time. Brokers from Korea sought to repatriate victims of *wakō* raids, and Korean captives might also be of diplomatic value. For example, nearly every voyage to Korea authorized by Okinawan trade kings included "rescued" Koreans. In this context Naha functioned as a major center for human trafficking (Uehara 1992, 199). Koreans captured by one *wakō* group, for example, might end up in Naha. From Naha, there were several possibilities, including that another *wakō* group would profit from sending them back to Korea. I examine human trafficking in more detail below.

Like pirates the world over, *wakō* mainly pursued profit. They switched modes accordingly, sometimes marauding, sometimes acting like conventional merchants, and sometimes engaging in other pursuits, even fishing or agriculture if conditions were favorable. They could be bought off, which was the preferred approach of the early Ming dynasty.

In the context of late *gusuku*-era Ryukyuan history, it is common to speak of local warlords (*aji*) and, from the 1370s onward, "kings" (trade kings). As I discuss in *Maritime Ryukyu,* many of these people were also *wakō* or worked closely with *wakō* groups. That almost every official voyage from Naha to Korea included repatriated captives necessarily meant that Ryukyuan powers worked closely with *wakō.* This and subsequent chapters provide additional insights into this situation.

Large Gusuku and Outside Groups

Large stone-walled fortresses capable of functioning as bases for powerful maritime traders, typically *wakō* powers, started to appear in the early fourteenth century (Tōma 2012, 44). Although settlements or simpler fortifications existed at some large *gusuku* sites before the fourteenth century, the large, complex stone walls did not go up until after 1300. Katsuren, for example, has a long history, with a community dwelling in the location of the fortress since the twelfth century. However, Katsuren's stone walls date from the early fourteenth century (Ikeda 2019, 29–31). As Ikeda Yoshifumi points out, large *gusuku* "did not take their mature form until the fourteenth century. In the case of Okinawa, it was during the fourteenth century that society developed to the point where stone-walled *gusuku* became necessary" (quoted in Yoshinari 2020, 273). Examples include the castles at Shuri, Nakijin, and Urasoe. Such large *gusuku* were a new phenomenon, and in southwest Okinawa, they did not develop from preexisting communities. These structures attest to the arrival of new, powerful groups.

The stone enclosure walls at Nakijin were built in the early fourteenth century atop a mountain plateau. Katsuren reached a comparable state of completion later in the century. There is no indication that a community existed at the site of Urasoe Castle prior to its construction in the 1300s. One distinctive feature of Katsuren, Urasoe, and Shuri Castles was their use of Korean-style roof tiles. Both the Japanese-style and Korean-style tiles during this era were made using clay from an area just northwest of Nago. It is likely that the tilesmiths for both types came from abroad (Yoshinari 2020, 104–105).

It is also important to note that during the end of the Goryeo era, large quantities of Korean blue ceramics came into Okinawa's major *gusuku.* The surge in trade that began around 1300 among Okinawa-based powers took place not only with Japan and China but also with Korea. Although formal tribute relations with China in the 1370s increased trade volume even further, powers in the Ryukyu Islands had been trading with Chinese entities well before then. For example, during the tumultuous years of the late Yuan, sulfur would have been in great demand by both pro- and anti-Yuan forces (Yoshinari 2020, 105–106).

Korean-Style Roof Tiles

The Korean-style roof tiles mentioned above are all inscribed with a date from the sexagenary cycle, the tenth heavenly stem and the tenth earthly branch (癸酉年). This sexagenary date almost certainly refers either to 1273 or 1333. Among archaeologists and historians with an interest in early Ryukyu, there has been considerable debate regarding these two years. The arguments are typically based on which date is closer to when the tiles were manufactured.[14] However, the castles at Urasoe, Katsuren, and Shuri (ca. 1405–1406) were all built at different times. For this basic reason, it does not seem likely that the date on the tiles is connected with or reflects the time when the tiles, castles, or the buildings within them bearing the tiles were constructed.

The debate over the specific year referenced by the sexagenary date on the tiles is relatively unimportant because we know that the buildings bearing those tiles were built during the fourteenth and early fifteenth centuries. Nevertheless, I would say that 1273 is the more likely reference date of the tiles. Although speculative, it is possible that the tiles commemorate the anti-Goryeo and anti-Mongol Sambyeolcho Rebellion, which played out along the coast of Korea from 1270 to 1273. The rebellion went through several stages, but it ended in Jeju Island with Goryeo and Yuan forces crushing the rebels, who were seafarers. Did rebel remnants flee to Okinawa? It is possible, and several scholars have hypothesized that they did (Heo 2012, 302, citing Ikeda Yoshifumi). We have seen that there was extensive contact between the Korean Peninsula, including Jeju Island, and the Ryukyu Islands (chapters 2 and 6). The year 1273 would have been significant to Sambyeolcho Rebellion remnants refugees in Jeju Island and possibly Okinawa. If indeed 1273 is the correct date, its appearance on the tiles may indicate that some memory of the rebellion persisted in Okinawa well into the fourteenth century.

Iron Tools

Ryukyuan origin tales about *aji* and *noro* (priestesses) come in several different motifs, but in all cases, *aji* and *noro* arrive in island communities from the outside, typically Japan, either vertically (from the heavens) or horizontally across the sea. Origin tales of kings developed later, as early modern adaptations of the origin tales of *aji* and *noro* (Tonaki 1992, 159–160, 169–172). In the legendary royal biographies, Shunten, Satto, Shō Hashi, and Shō En managed to obtain the throne after considerable adversity. They did so in large part because of iron and assistance from blacksmiths (Tonaki 1992, 175–176; Smits 2019, 124–125). Satto, Shō Hashi, and Shō En were all outsiders who came into Okinawa from points north. In royal biographies the motif of iron provided by outsiders from Japan functions to identify the protagonist as an outsider himself (Yoshinari 2020, 156). Tales of blacksmiths and iron, in connection with figures like Satto, coincide with the start of large stone-walled *gusuku* construction. An increase in iron tools would almost certainly have been necessary for that construction (Yoshinari 2020, 83–84).

One *omoro* tells of the Serikaku priestess making a stone wall using an *ishihetsu* and/or (they are paired terms) a *kanahetsu*. The latter term could mean a metal hammer or a "strong" hammer. The former is a stone tool (*Omoro sōshi* 17–1204). Because this song is in the middle of a series of Nakijin *omoro* (Nakijin was the base of the Serikaku priestesses), the stone wall is likely a reference to the construction of Nakijin Castle. Similarly, another song tells of the stonemason Machiyayo working in southern Okinawa with a stone ax/metal ax (*Omoro sōshi* 20–1348). The pairing of stone and iron tools for cutting stone occurs in three other *omoro* (*Omoro sōshi* 9–496, 10–527, 10–538).

Recall the severe shortage of iron agricultural tools during the *gusuku* era and even much later. From the start of the *gusuku* era and through the fourteenth century, stone tools filled in for a lack of iron ones. Similarly, large quantities of stone cannon balls have been excavated from Shuri Castle. Stone cannon balls, and other stone weapons such as arrowheads, can do as much damage as iron, or more. Compared with stone, iron tools would have been much more efficient for castle wall construction (Yoshinari 2020, 82–85). Nevertheless, relatively inefficient stone tools would have been economically viable when labor was plentiful and cheap.

The Slave Trade

The era of large *gusuku* in Okinawa substantially overlaps with a time of vigorous *wakō* marauding along the coasts of Korea, and to a lesser extent China, during the fourteenth and fifteenth centuries. During this same time, Naha became a regional center for human trafficking. As Akamine Mamoru explains:

> Once Ryukyu had embarked upon tributary exchanges with China, it became a gathering place for pirates in search of Chinese merchandise.

Furthermore, Chinese smugglers . . . appeared in the Ryukyu archipelago, sailing from island to island conducting their clandestine business. People taken in pirate raids were offered for sale at a slave market in Naha. . . .

Ryukyu was involved in the pirates' trade in human beings. It was the Ming court's plan that Naha should become a rich trade market that would attract pirates and encourage them to sell their captives there. (Akamine 2017, 30–31)

Large *gusuku* required large labor forces to quarry stone, haul it up to high locations, and build the high stone walls with simple tools. Given the prevalence of unfree labor in the region and the prevalence of *wakō* in Okinawa, it is almost certain that unfree labor built, or substantially contributed to building, Okinawa's large *gusuku*.

The discussion of the slave trade in this section is slightly later than the temporal focus of the chapter. Archaeology cannot provide the details we need for this topic, and it is not until the fifteenth century that we have any relevant documentary sources.

Information in the *Joseon Veritable Royal Records* provides much evidence of human trafficking in general, but one entry from 1453 is especially valuable for revealing important details of human trafficking networks in the Ryukyu Islands and the role of Naha and Okinawan trade kings in the process. It is a lengthy account in which Ryukyuan envoy Dōan (a Japanese priest and merchant from Hakata) explained to a Korean official that in 1450 four Koreans drifted into the Gaja 臥蛇 (K. Wasa; i.e., Tokara) Islands (*JVRR-r* 2005, 93). Thus began a saga that affords a glimpse at the local trade in people.

Over the years, many scholars have commented on this entry, and to my knowledge, the most insightful analysis comes from Takahashi Ichirō. If read in its superficial meaning and in terms of modern geography, Dōan stated that the four Koreans drifted into Gajajima, a tiny island in the Tokara chain that is uninhabited today. Moreover, he stated that Gajajima was half under the control of Ryukyu and half under the control of Satsuma. This literal reading, which I have used in earlier work, does not make good sense. Here "Gajajima" means the Wasa Islands—that is, the Korean term for the Tokara Islands. Moreover, as Takahashi points out, the term "half belonging" does not appear to mean that some islands were under Satsuma control and some were under the control of a Ryukyuan entity. Instead, it means that the Tokara Islands as a whole were a border region where the influence of Ryukyu and Satsuma overlapped. The Tokara Islands had no overlord. They functioned as a maritime commons in which, among other things, the business of buying and selling people took place (Takahashi Ichirō 2008, 172–173).

Dōan explained that these shipwrecked Koreans were divided up. Two of them went to "people from Satsuma." The other two, Mannyeon 萬年 and Jeonglu 丁祿, ended up being taken to Kasari in Amami-Ōshima, just across from Kikaijima. After about ten days, a "Kasari-ōyako" official, or agent, arrived from "Ryukyu" (Okinawa) and purchased Mannyeon, using fine cloth as payment. The agent took Mannyeon to Okinawa and gave him to the (trade) king, Shō Kinpuku. Mannyeon and two other people were assigned to learn how to use a "torch" (Ch. huǒtǒng), possibly here meaning a blowpipe.

One day Mannyeon observed one of the others stealing ramie from a storehouse, and Mannyeon reported the theft. Impressed, the king put Mannyeon in charge of watching over a royal storehouse. After three months, another Okinawan agent with the title wan-okite (harbor chief) went to Kasari and purchased Jeonglu with copper cash. This wan-okite was working in some capacity other than as Shō Kinpuku's agent because the king did not initially know of the purchase. When Mannyeon found out about Jeonglu's arrival, he told the king. Shō Kinpuku ordered Mannyeon to ride to the house where Jeonglu was residing and exchange another slave for him. Mannyeon and Jeonglu worked for the king for three years, after which time he sent them back to Korea with Dōan. He told Dōan that if Korean officials were pleased with the return of Mannyeon and Jeonglu, there were other Koreans who could be returned as well (JVRR-r 2005, 93–94; Gi 2007, 87–88).

We can see from the details of this encounter that agents of the king in Shuri, or other Okinawan agents, sometimes procured slaves in Amami-Ōshima. The passage also indicates that slaves were often exchanged. For example, a new one would come into the king's service and free one up to be repatriated. Also, even if the person one did business with was the king, he had to pay or compensate others appropriately. In other words, there was a fundamental equality among the Ryukyuan agents (Takahashi Ichirō 2008, 174–176). Notice as well that kings at this time appear to have functioned more like wakō chiefs than as heads of centralized bureaucracies.

The case of the four Koreans illuminates some important details about human trafficking networks. It also indicates that circa 1450, agents of the Shuri king and other Okinawans were active in the northern Ryukyu Islands, as were military forces from Okinawa. The passage mentions, for example, that the king's brother was preparing to invade Kikaijima. Nevertheless, the Kasari Peninsula (northern Amami-Ōshima)-Kikaijima region does not appear to have been under Shuri's firm control. As I explain below, excavations of *gusuku* sites in northern Amami-Ōshima indicate the presence of significant local powers in this area well into the fifteenth century.

The powerful lord Gosamaru (d. 1458), who eventually resided in Nakagusuku Gusuku, previously built Zakimi Gusuku. It "was built by local people and by laborers brought in from places like Kikaijima and [Amami-]Ōshima" according to an early modern biography (quoted in Kamei 1993, 33, from *Mō-uji genso yuraiden*).[15] Unfortunately, we have no further details. As we will see in chapters 9 and 10, Nakagusuku Gusuku and Katsuren Gusuku maintained close ties with the northern Ryukyu Islands—and in the case of Katsuren at least, also with Korea.

One final point to make about human trafficking is perhaps obvious. Owing to fortune and perhaps other factors, the circumstances of Koreans and others who found themselves in the Ryukyu Islands as unfree people varied significantly. Mannyeon may well have suffered privation, including poor compensation for his labor. Nevertheless, as an overseer of a storehouse his situation was much better than, for example, that of a laborer quarrying, hauling, or cutting rocks to build the steep walls of a large *gusuku*.

Hub-and-Spoke Changes

Dividing the Ryukyu Islands into three groups—the Northern Tier, Okinawa and nearby islands, and the southern Ryukyu Islands (the Miyako and Yaeyama groups)—the general pattern from the late thirteenth century to the early fifteenth is vigorous activity in Okinawa and the southern Ryukyu Islands. At this time, the Northern Tier islands became more closely connected with Satsuma and less closely tied to the other Ryukyu Islands. However, around the start of the fifteenth century the Northern Tier islands again became closely connected with Okinawa, as the discussion of the slave trade above illustrates.

The overall quantity of Chinese ceramics in the Ryukyu Islands rose starting in the late thirteenth century. This increase became especially noticeable from the middle of the fourteenth century onward in both Okinawa and the southern Ryukyu Islands. However, interpreting this increase includes difficulties. The main question is whether certain powers in Okinawa traded directly with counterparts in China or whether they continued to obtain Chinese goods via intermediates at Hakata or elsewhere. Similarly, did the southern Ryukyu Islands obtain Chinese goods from Okinawa, direct trade with China, or a combination? Moreover, when did direct trade with China begin?

Moving forward in time to about 1350, the existence of direct trade with China in both Okinawa and the southern Ryukyu Islands is nearly certain.

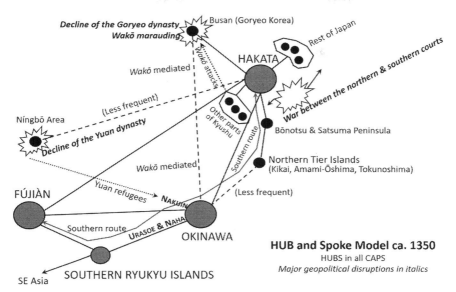

Figure 8.1. Hub-and-spoke model, ca. 1350.

Seafarers in the southern Ryukyu Islands also had access to products from Southeast Asia, at least occasionally. Notice that, in any case, direct trade between parts of the Ryukyu Islands and China took place before the formal entry of certain Okinawan powers into the Ming tribute system during the 1370s.

Hakata remained a major regional hub,[16] but significant changes to the trade networks occurred during the late *gusuku* era (figure 8.1). Many of these changes were the result of, or partially the result of, political and military turmoil around the East China Sea region. In the sections below, I survey topics relevant to these changes.

Northern Ryukyu Islands

The thirteenth and early fourteenth centuries were a time of significantly less exchange between the Northern Tier and the rest of the Ryukyu Islands. This is mainly because these islands came under the control of Japanese officials based in Satsuma. The document *Chikama* (or *Chigama*) *monjo* 千竃文書, dated 1306.04.14, provides a glimpse of the situation. *Chikama monjo* was an asset-disposal document pertaining to the property of Chikama Tokiie, a *jitō-daikan* official in Kawanabe-gun, Satsuma. Kawanabe-gun was one of the Hōjō patrimonial holdings during the Kamakura era, and the Amami Islands were part of that territory. The document awarded islands and certain Satsuma ports to family members in the following way:

> Oldest son Sadayasu: Kuchi gotō (Takeshima, Iōjima, Kuroshima, Kuchinoerabushima, and possibly Yakushima), Wasa-no-shima (one or more islands in the Tokara group), Kikaika[ga]shima (Kikaijima), Ōshima (Amami-Ōshima), and Yaunotsu (Bōnotsu)
>
> Second son Tsuneie: Erabunoshima (Okinoerabu)
>
> Third son Kumayamatamaru: Shichitō (Tokara Islands) and Ōtomarinotsu
>
> Oldest daughter Himekuma: Tokunoshima
>
> Second daughter Yakuma: Yakunoshima no shimanokōri (Yakushima or part of it). (Gi 2007, 61–62; Yoshinari 2018, 97; Murai 2019, 85–89)

Notice the ports. This territory was a maritime zone with economic value. There is a well-known half of a map of Japan from the early fourteenth century in Kanazawa Bunko. A snakelike dragon surrounds the main islands of Japan. Outside of the dragon's body is territory labeled "Ryūkyū-koku Ushima [Okinawa] . . . Amemi [Amami], private territory" (Yoshinari 2018, 97–98). In other words, during the early fourteenth century the northern Ryukyu Islands were the territory of the Chikama family.

Control of the northern Ryukyu Islands by the Chikama at this time was surely one reason why those islands interacted much less often with Okinawa and the southern Ryukyu Islands. The 1333 fall of the Hōjō greatly weakened the Chikama, as did the rise of the Shimazu family. A 1363 deed granted Shimazu Sadahisa "Kawanabe-gun, its eleven islands, and its outer five islands." The outer five were probably the northern Ryukyu Islands down to and including Yoron (Murai 2019, 80–84; Yoshinari 2020, 118–119, 124).

At no precise point in time did the northern Ryukyu Islands suddenly increase their exchanges with the rest of the Ryukyu Islands, but their coming under at least nominal Shimazu control was one important reason for the rise in contact. Another was the deterioration of the Yuan dynasty starting in the 1340s. This deterioration made the voyage from Hakata to Níngbō increasingly perilous, and more ships began using the southern islands route, from Hakata to Fujian via western Kyushu and islands of the Ryukyu Arc. Maritime traffic thereby reconnected the northern Ryukyu Islands to Okinawa and points south.

Resource rich Amami-Ōshima was home to several prominent castle and *gusuku* sites. For example, a castle at the Toguchi site in Tatsugō imported, among other things, Southern Song blueware. The castle caught fire in the mid-thirteenth century but was rebuilt. In the mid-fifteenth century it caught fire a second time, was destroyed, and was not rebuilt. In other words, locally powerful people occupied this site into the fifteenth century (Takahashi Ichirō 2008, 176).

Similarly, Akagina Gusuku, in an elevated location in the Kasari Peninsula, faces Gusuku in Kikaijima.[17] Items excavated from Akagina from the eleventh and twelfth centuries, at the peak of Gusuku's prosperity, overlap considerably with those found at Gusuku. Akagina's trade declined during the early fourteenth century, but by the fifteenth century, its trade had revived. Chinese trade ceramics from that era were among the excavated items (Nakayama Kiyomi 2008, 188–193; Takanashi 2015, 261).[18]

The Southern Ryukyu Islands

Given their location, it is not surprising that entities in the southern Ryukyu Islands began trading directly with counterparts in China. According to many scholars, such trade began in the thirteenth or early fourteenth centuries. For example, in a recent monograph on *gusuku*-era pottery, Shinzato Akito argues for a mid-thirteenth century start to trade between the southern Ryukyu Islands and Fújiàn, which brought whiteware manufactured in Fújiàn into the Ryukyu Islands. One result was a new and improved variety of *kamuiyaki* (larger items, smaller variety, new production techniques), possibly to compete with the new imported ware. Ultimately, *kamuiyaki* was not able to compete, and it faded away in the fourteenth century. In other words, changed conditions in the southern Ryukyu Islands reverberated all the way to Tokunoshima (Shinzato Akito 2018, 131, 156). This narrative makes good sense, but the evidence is inconclusive.[19] Stronger evidence is the case of traders from Bora in Miyako who were blown into China in 1317 (chapter 2). Given the details of that incident, it is entirely possible that traders from Miyako had been sailing to Southeast Asia and China even before the fourteenth century.

As was the case with Okinawa, during the fourteenth century the southern Ryukyu Islands became more populous and active. During the twelfth and thirteenth centuries, all but one of the eight known settlements on the island of Miyako were located along the northeast coast. The number of settlement sites increased rapidly during the fourteenth century, totaling more than thirty around Miyako and in nearby islands. Clearly, the population increased, and the only explanation is that outside people arrived and established settlements. There are legends describing the origins of many of these settlements. In them, the settlers came from Okinawa or Japan. In some cases the founder or putative founder of a settlement became the deity of a local sacred grove (Shimoji 2008, 339–340).

During the 1370s, the Ming court banned international private trade. However, smuggling and illicit trade flourished in the Fújiàn area, and a flood of Chinese ceramics came into all parts of the southern Ryukyu Islands. From the late fourteenth century onward, Chinese goods poured into the southern Ryukyu Islands in relatively larger quantities than was the case in Okinawa or the Japanese mainland. Items exchanged for Chinese goods included the usual lineup of maritime products such as seashells and turtle shells. In addition, local residents traded sea cucumbers, shark fins, dugongs, cowhide, ramie, banana fiber cloth (*bashōfu*), and medicinal plants. Nagura Bay on the west side of Ishigaki was a major site of this trade. Several thousand pieces of fifteenth- and sixteenth-century Chinese whiteware and blueware have been excavated from the bottom of the bay (the Shitadaru Seafloor Site). These items came from a sunken Chinese trade ship and are indicative of the large scale of private trade. Moreover, tribute trade ships from Okinawa would occasionally have put in at local ports (to avoid storms, for example), so the situation in the region would have been known to both Shuri and Chinese authorities (Ōhama 2008, 366–368).

It is important to note that in relative terms, the late fourteenth century through the fifteenth century was the time of maximum maritime activity in the southern Ryukyu Islands. Most of this activity was illegal, at least in the eyes of the Ming court. In *Maritime Ryukyu* I noted a 1452 order from the Chinese Ministry of Justice to residents of the Fújiàn coast in the context of a local uprising. Among other things, the order prohibited "any dealings with Ryukyuans by ship and serving as guides for pirates" (Smits 2019, 68). In this context, pirates and Ryukyuans were synonymous.

The surge in southern Ryukyu-southern China illicit trade is also an important consideration with respect to the largest military campaign Shuri ever undertook, the 1500 invasion of Yaeyama (also known as Honkawara no ran). As I argue in *Maritime Ryukyu,* this war was in part a conflict between rival *wakō* groups (Smits 2019, 167–168). In the background of this rivalry was a vigorous illicit trade with southern China. It is possible that official Chinese pressure on Shuri to curtail this trade was another factor in the invasion. It is noteworthy that soon after Shuri's conquest of Yaeyama, tribute trade frequency briefly (1507–1522) increased from once every two years to once a year (Smits 2019, 136, 171). This increased frequency was a sign that the Ming court regarded Shuri favorably circa 1507.

Reverberations of the Yuan Dynasty's Decline

The Yuan dynasty (1271–1368) established pastoralists, known as *mùhú,* to raise horses on Jeju Island. When the Goryeo king Gongmin (r. 1351–1374) decided to assert independence from the Yuan, the *mùhú* pastoralists and part of the island's regular population rebelled in 1367 (*Goryeo History* 2005, 1:229). These local rebels joined with *wakō,* who prized Jeju horses. Gongmin sent a military force, but it was unable to pacify the island until 1372 (*Goryeo History* 2005, 1:236–237). Some *wakō* and Mongol pastoralists married and started families. In 1376 large-scale *wakō* attacks took place in locations throughout southern Korea, including Jeju Island. In addition to the usual seeking of plunder, an additional factor in these attacks was a desire to rescue wives and children (*Goryeo History* 2005, 2:226–230; Okaya 2019, 154).

Pirates are typically detrimental to some areas but beneficial to their home base. That Jeju Island was a *wakō* base and horse pasture is well known, but the presence of Mongol remnants in close association with *wakō* is what is important for our purposes. When *wakō* pursued by Goryeo forces fled to Jeju in 1367, the Mongols in Jeju fought alongside the *wakō*. When *wakō* landed in Jeju in 1372, the local people went into hiding and would not help suppress them. Joseon founder Yi Seonggye fought a young fifteen- or sixteen-year-old *wakō* commander, whose nickname was Akibatsu 阿只拔[拔]都. After defeating Akibatsu, Yi took sixteen hundred head of horses from the island. Jeju was home to Mongol remnants closely connected with *wakō,* and they were active during the late Yuan and early Ming eras (Seyock 2005, 95–96; Yoshinari 2020, 130).

In this context it is almost certain that Ryukyuan powers were obtaining sulfur from Iōtorishima (and possibly elsewhere) and selling or trading it to military forces in and around China during the Yuan-Ming transition era and even after the establishment of the Ming. This was also the time of the Seiseifu (Southern Court government) in Kyushu, a source of sulfur and of *wakō*. Both arrived in China via the Ryukyu Islands. The Lín Xián and Hú Wéiyōng Incident of 1380 is an example of the smuggling of militarily useful goods from Japan (Smits 2019, 64; Yoshinari 2020, 131–132). Zhū Yuánzhāng, as the Hóngwǔ emperor (r. 1368–1398), actively combatted piracy and smuggling. His antipiracy policies had a powerful impact on the history of the Ryukyu Islands (Smits 2019, 60–76).

The Yuan dynasty deteriorated noticeably with the Red Turban revolts of 1351 and 1368, but the trouble started earlier, in the 1340s, with Fāng Guózhēn. Fāng established a separatist area based in Táizhōu (near Níngbō), closely connected with pirates. Fāng surrendered to the future Ming founder Zhū Yuánzhāng at the end of 1367. It was from the 1340s that the Níngbō–Hakata route became unstable, and maritime traffic increasingly used the southern route through the Ryukyu Islands. After the establishment of the Ming, the remnants of the military forces of coastal rebels like Fāng remained active, this time as pirates. Inland, fighting continued against various Mongol powers in the North.

Pockets of Mongols and their allies remained within China (Yoshinari 2020, 126–127). Some of them crossed over to northern Okinawa.

Yuan Dynasty Remnants in Nakijin

Uema Atsushi argues that during the late fourteenth century, refugees from the Yuan dynasty took up residence in Nakijin. A large portion of these refugees consisted of ethnic Alans who had served the Yuan court. Moreover, the San-hoku ruler Han'anchi came from these people. Uema's evidence is extensive, and in the paragraphs below I present a highly condensed summary.[20]

Alans were widely distributed across the Eurasian continent. In the mid-thirteenth century, while living at the foot of the Caucusus Mountains, a group of Alans adopted Greek Orthodoxy and started writing their language in the Greek script. When Kublai put together an army comprising units from central Asia, an Alan cavalry unit served as an advanced guard.[21] Later, when pressing his invasion of the lower Yangzi delta, Kublai deployed Alan cavalry as part of his forces. There is a 1330 record of a Christian force on the outskirts of Yángzhōu. It is plausible that an Alan squadron was posted there to keep guard over recently pacified Southern Song territory (Uema 2018, 63–66).

Alan-specific items excavated from Nakijin include left turning, Greco-Roman style grooved portable stone grain mills. (Stone mills for grinding grain in East Asia were right turning.) Wheat and barley compose a very large quantity of exca-vated carbonized grain at Nakijin. The Nakijin mills are small, commensurate with cavalry use, and they existed approximately two centuries before grain mills spread throughout Japan (Uema 2018, 14–18). Items associated with the mantic arts have been excavated, such as white ceramic bowls stamped with swastikas to form a convex impression. In Mongolian culture, these swastikas were amulets that protected horses (among other protective functions). It was common, for example, to brand such images onto a horse's back thigh (Uema 2018, 19–32).

Han'anchi ruled Nakijin from about 1401 to 1406.[22] According to the account of Han'anchi's defeat in *Genealogy of Chūzan,* when the situation turned hope-less, he carved a cross (*jūji*) in the sacred stone of Kanahiyabu with his sword Chiyoganemaru before killing himself (*Chūzan seifu* [1725] 1988, 53). Was Han'anchi or some members of his group of Christian background? Items exca-vated from the center of Nakijin Castle included two blueware bowls with solid bodies and Greek-style crosses stamped into them and a blue flower bowl deco-rated with a Greek cross on the bottom (Uema 2018, 51–54).

A winged-horse pattern adorns some of the ceramics. Such flying horses are associated with central Asian legends among pastoral nomads of Eurasia, specifically the blood-sweating horses of the Ferghana Valley. Legends of heavenly horses that dwell in the mountains are associated with the Ossetians, people of the Caucusus who descended from the Alan (Uema 2018, 88–91; 111–114). Nard is a Persian game similar to backgammon. Nard dice and stone playing pieces were excavated at Nakijin (Uema 2018, 155–156, 172–173).

Military gear excavated from Nakijin includes portable rasps in the manner of those used by Mongolian cavalry, flat and chisel-headed arrowheads, and small swords and daggers. The triangular flat arrowheads from Nakijin resemble those of Mongol cavalry, as do the arrowheads in the shape of chisel heads, which also differ greatly from any arrowheads used in medieval Japan. Arrowheads made from bone were also excavated. There are no such examples in Japan, even as far back as the Jōmon era, but they are characteristic of Mongolian arrowheads. Excavated small swords are of the same design as those used by peoples of the Eurasian plains (Uema 2018, 184–198).

Why and how did these Mongols and Alans end up in northern Okinawa? During both the Song and Yuan eras, Persian, Arab, Jewish, and Armenian merchants resided in the Jiāngnán trading cities and formed foreign enclaves along the coast. However, at the end of the Yuan and the start of the Ming rebels like Fāng Guózhēn and Zhāng Shìchéng, as well as Zhū Yuánzhāng, expelled these enclaves as part of a general antiforeign sentiment. This foreign exclusion policy continued after the founding of the Ming (Uema 2018, 37–44). In other words, Uema argues that the distinctive items found at Nakijin were not the result of trade but of refugees from the collapsing Yuan dynasty crossing over to northern Okinawa.

Although extant sources do not allow us to corroborate Uema's argument directly, Yoshinari Naoki has pointed out the large body of supporting circumstantial evidence. First, the Alan served the Yuan court as cavalry and frontline soldiers, but they were not the only foreign force. Those who may have ended up in Nakijin from the continent were not limited to the Alan people but probably constituted a broad spectrum of Mongol remnants. In Jeju Island, anti-Ming Mongol remnants aligned with *wakō*. The same thing may have happened in northern Okinawa (Yoshinari 2020, 151). It is also worth noting that Nakijin was the earliest of Okinawan's large *gusuku* sites to engage in international trade.

According to a 1388.07.06 entry in *Ming Veritable Records,* Dìbǎonú 地保奴, brother of the Northern Yuan emperor, was exiled to "Ryukyu" (*MVR* 2001, 1:13, 76). However, there is no reliable record of this person ever arriving in Okinawa, so it is possible that the place of exile was Taiwan (*MVR* 2001, 1:76n108). The broader point, however, is that exiles and refugees connected with the Yuan dynasty dispersed across the region. Recall the recent discovery of the three sets of human remains dating to the fifteenth or sixteenth century in Okinawa, one of which had a Japonic maternal ancestor, another a maternal ancestor of central Asian or European origins, and a third with a maternal ancestor from the Korean Peninsula (see the introduction). Regional disruptions sometimes propelled people into Okinawa and other Ryukyu Islands.

Direct Trade with China

A variety of whiteware mass produced in Fújiàn began to be consumed in the Ryukyu Islands starting in the middle or late thirteenth century. The majority of it was excavated at Nakijin, so it is called "Nakijin type." Later varieties of this whiteware are called *birōsuku,* named after the Birōsuku site in Ishigaki. This ware is especially common in the southern and central Ryukyu Islands (Shinzao Akito, 2008. 69, 69; Yamazato Jun'ichi 2012, 183–184). Several scholars have speculated that this Fújiàn whiteware indicates the likely opening of a direct trade route between Fújiàn and the southern Ryukyu Islands around 1300 (e.g., Shinzato Akito 2018, 81–83). Although possible, there are other plausible explanations for the distribution of this whiteware.[23] One prominent question among archaeologists and historians is when and where did direct trade between entities in China and Okinawa began?

Survey histories commonly assume that no such trade existed before the start of formal tribute relations with the Ming dynasty in the 1370s. For example, Mamoru Akamine (2017, 22) states that prior to 1372, "there had been no intercourse with China." All indications, however, are that direct trade between Ryukyuan powers and Chinese merchants became well established during the Yuan dynasty, although we cannot say exactly when (Tōma 2012, 205). That horses and sulfur were tribute goods from the beginning of the tribute trade, and that Chinese agents came to Okinawa to buy horses in 1376, strongly suggests that a trade in these items had already been well established (Yoshinari 2020, 126).

Significantly, the Chinese merchant Chéng Fù (J. Tei Fuku 程復) began assisting Satto and his group in conducting trade with China, most likely starting in the 1350s. An entry in *Ming Veritable Records* dated 1411 states that Chéng Fù had been in Okinawa assisting Satto for over forty years (*MVR* 2001, 1:21 [#45]). The official date of Satto's death is 1397. Assuming this date and the stated period of service are roughly accurate, Satto's group began trading with entities in China during the 1350s (Yoshinari 2020, 155). The basic framework for what, in the 1370s, would become tribute trade was already in place some two decades earlier. Given that Chéng Fù was in Okinawa from the 1350s or 1360s helping with trade, clearly Satto's group carried out private trade from approximately that time. Urasoe Gusuku, Satto's base, did not become a large *gusuku* until after the arrival of the Satto group around 1350 (Yoshinari 2020, 155–156).

The time line of Chéng Fù is compelling evidence of direct trade with China before 1372. Other evidence points to a surge in trade with China circa 1350, when the Yuan dynasty was in serious decline. Consider the powerful Katsuren Gusuku on Okinawa's east coast. It did not accumulate much Chinese ceramic ware before the mid-fourteenth century, nor was it ever formally a player in the tribute trade after 1372. However, from the mid-fourteenth century onward the quality and quantity of Chinese pottery at Katsuren exploded. Prior to Amawari (d. 1458), the lord of Katsuren was someone called Mochizuki, almost certainly a newcomer from Japan. The rapid wealth of Katsuren must have come from private trade with China (Yoshinari 2020, 133–134). In the southern Ryukyu Islands, we have seen that direct exchanges with entities in China probably began in the early fourteenth century or possibly earlier (chapter 2).

Regional Political and Military Disruptions

During the first half of the fourteenth century, Okinawa filled up with powerful traders who could function as pirates or smugglers depending on the circumstances. What caused this increase in *wakō* activity both in the Ryukyu Islands and throughout the region? One factor is regional political and social dislocation. Consider the year 1350. The Yuan dynasty in China was beginning to break up as different native Chinese generals fought with Yuan forces and with each other for supremacy. Even after Zhū Yuánzhāng established the Ming dynasty in 1368, he faced continued hostility from the remnants of the Yuan dynasty and from powers in southern China. In 1350, Japan was in the midst of civil war between the northern and southern courts, a situation especially conducive to *wakō* activity (Smits 2019, 46–49). Strife in Korea was also intensifying at the same time. One likely result was the arrival in Okinawa of Satto and his group. Moreover, the port of Naha had become a major center for human trafficking by the late fourteenth century (Akamine 2017, 30–31; Smits 2019, 49–51).

Unrest in China caused the southern islands route to become especially active, thus increasing the volume of shipping passing through the Ryukyu Islands from about the 1340s onward. Conditions in Korea, Japan, and China all had direct and indirect impacts on the Ryukyu Islands. That Okinawa, especially, became home to powerful maritime merchants or *wakō* makes sense given these circumstances. Moreover, as I discuss in *Maritime Ryukyu*, concentrating *wakō* in the Ryukyu Islands became official Ming policy during the 1370s,

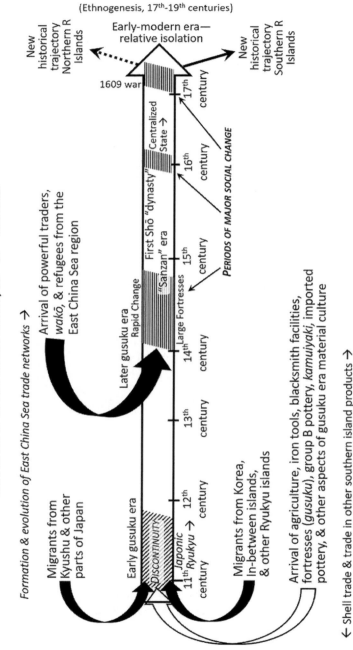

Figure 8.2. Major developments and discontinuities in premodern Ryukyuan history.

following an unsuccessful attempt to entice Prince Kaneyoshi into suppressing *wakō* activity (Akamine 2017, 30–31; Smits 2019, 62–66). This situation set the stage for several decades of intense warfare in Okinawa, which the official histories later portrayed as a military struggle between three small kingdoms. In fact, as we will see in chapter 10, the struggle was much more complex.

Political disruptions around the East China Sea region caused dislocations of people, trade routes, and trade dynamics. These dislocations resulted in an increase in *wakō* activity, and they pushed new waves of people of diverse ethnic backgrounds into the Ryukyu Islands. Some arrived willingly; others as a result of human trafficking. The most striking physical manifestation of this situation was the creation of large *gusuku*. During the fourteenth century, prior to the start of formal tribute trade in the 1370s, local powers in Okinawa and the southern Ryukyu Islands began trading directly with their Chinese counterparts.

Zooming out to consider the big picture, the early history of the Ryukyu Islands includes a major discontinuity, the *gusuku* era, and three major eras of change (figure 8.2). The discontinuity is that Japanese and other northern immigrants began replacing the previous indigenous populations in approximately the eleventh century (chapters 3 and 4). This change in population was the start of Japonic Ryukyu, featuring the establishment and growth of societies in the Ryukyu Islands based on trade and supplemented by agriculture. The fourteenth century was a time of major change within the broad framework of Japonic Ryukyu as the entire East China Sea region experienced political turmoil. New powers emerged within the Ryukyu Islands, and the competition for profit became more violent and intense. The other two periods of major social change in the Ryukyu Islands were the formation of a centralized state early in the sixteenth century (chapter 12) and defeat in the war with Satsuma in 1609 (covered in *Maritime Ryukyu*).

To reiterate a major argument of this book, notice that the Ryukyu Islands were not isolated at any time during the *gusuku* era. In *Maritime Ryukyu* I characterize the *gusuku*-era Ryukyu Islands as a frontier region of Japan. From what we have seen thus far, that description needs modification. Japan was by far the most influential place in terms of cultural influence and a source of people for the Ryukyu Islands. Nevertheless, the Ryukyu Islands potentially functioned as a frontier region for the entire East China Sea region.

Finally, notice also that, at least as of the end of the fourteenth century, a distinct ethnic group we could reasonably call "Ryukyuans" had yet to emerge. I address the topic of ethnogenesis in chapter 13.

CHAPTER NINE

The Geopolitical Landscape

Fundamental inaccuracies have been built into the typical terminology used to describe early Ryukyu. The outsized influence of the official histories is one reason for this. These texts describe a teleological movement toward a centralized state, and they identify that state as having existed as early as the thirteenth century in the case of "King" Eiso. The official histories arrange diverse warlords into a dynasty of kings, the First Shō dynasty, and they impose order and centralizing tendencies on what was a chaotic and dispersed political landscape. It was perfectly reasonable for the seventeenth- and eighteenth-century authors of these histories to portray Ryukyu's past as they did. Ryukyu's official histories reflect the circumstances and values of when they were written.

Modern and contemporary historians have rejected or modified some of the claims of the official histories. To take an obvious example, few if any think that deities created the island of Okinawa. Moreover, very few modern historians regard Eiso as having ruled over the entire island of Okinawa. In the majority view, Eiso was a local warlord in the Urasoe area. Nevertheless, most modern and contemporary survey histories, and even many specialized monographs, adopt the framing and many background assumptions of the official histories. Historians writing in both the ancient branch model and the internal development model would generally agree that Okinawan society developed along the path of local chieftains (*aji*) → three small territorial states (the Three Principalities) → a centralized kingdom (Shō Hashi onward). Moreover, they would agree that agricultural surpluses powered this sociopolitical consolidation. Such a portrayal mischaracterizes early Okinawan and Ryukyuan society and locates a centralized state approximately one century too early in time.

Chapter 7 advanced the argument that *gusuku*-era Ryukyu possessed agriculture but that agricultural productivity was insufficient to drive state formation. Instead, the islands were home to trading and raiding societies in which agriculture augmented the food supply. This chapter argues that understanding the political geography of the Ryukyu Islands circa the fourteenth and early fifteenth centuries requires setting aside the idea of agriculture-powered territorial states. Instead, the main political unit at this time was the harbor-fortress pair. These units resembled small city-states, but they were maritime city-states. Most of these maritime city-states were linked to other harbor-fortress pairs in other islands and to trading centers within the East China Sea region.

Here I examine this political geography using a representative sample of harbor-fortress pairs, most outside the Shuri-Naha area. Using archaeological and textual evidence, I show that major harbor-fortress units had much in common. The textual evidence comes not from the official histories but from the *Omoro sōshi*.

The Geopolitical Landscape according to the *Omoro sōshi*

Omoro sōshi (or "the *Omoro*") refers to a collection of 1,553 old Ryukyuan songs (owing to repetition, 1,144 are unique). Some of the songs may be as old as the early *gusuku* era, but most cannot be dated. The individual songs (*omoro* with a lowercase *o*) are arranged in twenty-two volumes, the first compiled circa 1531, the second in 1613, and the rest in 1623. There is a general topical logic to many of the volumes, but the version of the *Omoro* we have today was reconstructed from parts of the text in the possession of elite households following the destruction of all complete copies in a 1710 palace fire. The repetition or partial repetition of some songs, and the appearance of others seemingly out of place, may have been the result of this 1710 reconstruction. It is also possible that other reasons lie behind the repetition and the occasional peculiar placement of songs. Linguists Leon Serafim and Rumiko Shinzato have recently published a thorough and technically rigorous analysis of the *Omoro sōshi* (Serafim and Shinzato 2021). Using *omoro* as historical sources presents several difficulties, which I have discussed elsewhere (Smits 2019, 2–4). Nevertheless, *omoro* can provide valuable clues not found in conventional documents.

Songs in the *Omoro* occasionally mention *ne no shima*, always in the context of the priestesses (*noro*) residing there. Here, *ne* means something like root or central location, so *ne no shima* are islands at which priestesses are based. Although the term *shima* can refer to communities of any kind, in this specific context it means "island." Moreover, all of the "base islands" are north of Okinawa. In Okinawa itself, a similar term, *nekuni*, refers to the bases of powerful local rulers. Some *omoro* refer to specific territory as *nekuni*, an honorific term that literally means "root country" or "central country." In this case, however, *kuni* refers to territory under a ruler's control, that ruler's base. I will therefore render *nekuni* as "base."

The term *nekuni* is an honorific, and *omoro* tend to project praise widely. Nevertheless, the number of places called *nekuni* is relatively small, and most of these places are described with similar qualities. Specifically, places called *nekuni* tend to

1. accumulate or pile up wealth, often acquired from far and wide;
2. pacify and/or rule over a wide area;
3. possess soldiers and impressive weapons;
4. possess impressive infrastructure or resources, often connected with water.

Ne no shima were bases for priestesses and therefore were powerful locations. *Nekuni* were bases in trade networks, with "trade" broadly defined to encompass the full range of *wakō* activities. Let us take a closer look at specific bases (plus Katsuren), all of which are in central or southern Okinawa (figure 9.1).

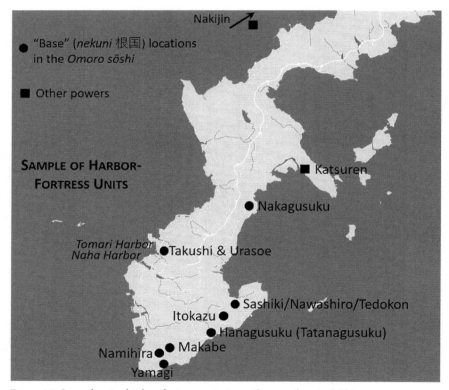

Figure 9.1. Several major harbor-fortress units in southern and central Okinawa.

When translating *omoro*, it is sometimes necessary to reverse the order of some lines to fit English syntax. This song is about Nakagusuku, a powerful castle overlooking the east coast of central Okinawa (Ginowan City):

Nakagusuku, the base [*nekuni*]
The ship Falcon at the base
Pulls in and controls
Tokunoshima and Amami-Ōshima
Resounding base of the territory
Base of the territory wherein the ship Falcon [weighs anchor].
(*Omoro sōshi* 2–53)

This song connects the ships of Nakagusuku with territory in Tokunoshima and Amami-Ōshima. Recall that the most prominent lord of Nakagusuku, Gosamaru, probably used laborers from the northern Ryukyu Islands to build his previous castle, Zakimi Gusuku (chapter 8). Nakagusuku was a power center well before Gosamaru's time.

Next is Takushi, which is today a neighborhood in Urasoe. It is located just inland from Tomari harbor (just above Naha harbor), an anchorage that connected Okinawa and the other Ryukyu Islands. It is mentioned as a base in two songs, but they do not provide details (*Omoro sōshi* 8–471, 472). Urasoe, in roughly the same location, is "the base" that "constantly piles up gold." Moreover, it also possesses pure spring water, a relatively scarce resource (*Omoro sōshi* 15–1079, 1080).

Sashiki, in southeastern Okinawa, was the base of Shō Hashi, who figures prominently in chapter 11. Sashiki is described as a base in seven different songs—eight, counting a repetition. Just below Sashiki Castle was the harbor Yamato Banta (Yamato cliffs). In the *Omoro*, Sashiki is often referred to as Nawashiro, a likely reference to the Nawa lineage in the Yatsushiro area of Kyushu, the original home of Shō Hashi's family (Eguchi 2008, 94–95; Smits 2019, 107–110). One *omoro* praises the water control infrastructure at base Sashiki and its Oyahigaa spring, followed by a song lauding its "admirable man who conquers the many villages" (*Omoro sōshi* 14–1012, 1013). Following two more songs mentioning base Sashiki is another referring to the lord of Tedokon (part of Sashiki) as having "opened the route to China" and "resounding throughout Japan," which is called "Nihon" only in this song (*Omoro sōshi* 14–1018).[1] The water resources of Sashiki result in rice that is as white as snow. Sashiki is also home to a powerful eagle (*oni-washi*), which keeps watch over the fortress, the Tsukishiro shrine, and the drum that symbolizes the power to rule (*Omoro sōshi* 19–1287, 1291, 1292, 12–95 [repeated 22–1532]). Clearly, Sashiki was a powerful base connected to distant locations, at least according to the *Omoro*.

Nearby, Itokazu Gusuku in Tamagusuku is a base with a splendid fortress, and it receives envoys from Ōgusuku (Ōshiro), whose lord commands a splendid military force and rules over a wide area (*Omoro sōshi* 17–1223, 1224, 18–1279, 1280). Namihira Gusuku at the southern edge of Okinawa is a base blessed with wealth, a stone bridge, and an impressive sword. The lord of Namihira rules over "wealthy land" beyond Namihira (*Omoro sōshi* 20–1335, 1336; Okinawa-ken 1983, 146).

The base at Yamagi Gusuku, also at the southern edge of Okinawa, takes in tribute goods from the East and from the West (*Omoro sōshi* 20–1345). The ruler of Makabe Gusuku, a base located nearby, pacifies the myriad villages, selects people from his territory as officials, and crosses bridges to reach Naha (*Omoro sōshi* 20–1354).

Katsuren is not called a base in the *Omoro*. However, it is described very much like nearby Nakagusuku and in terms similar to the locations mentioned above:

The sailors of Katsuren
Are a bridge to Ukeshima and Yoroshima
Tokunoshima and Okinoerabu
Are relatives [of]
[Katsuren] sailor Mashifuri.
(*Omoro sōshi* 13–938)

The sailors of Katsuren
Gain wealth when they sail
[From] Kikaijima and Amami-Ōshima
With which they are connected
[Katsuren] sailor Mashifuri.
(*Omoro sōshi* 13–939)

Ukeshima and Yoroshima are small islands forming the southernmost part of Amami-Ōshima and adjacent small islands. They likely functioned as navigational markers for ships sailing northward to Kikaijima. Katsuren was closely connected with Kikaijima and may have controlled all or part of the island prior to 1458 (Takeuchi [1933] 1960, 77, 79).

In the following *omoro*, Kenachi grove refers to the Keraji grove at the southern edge of Kikaijima. This song may have been sung prior to or during a northward voyage to Kikaijima (Iha 1974c, 455):

Setting sail for the sea off Yoroshima
Praise to Takamaru
Protecting us

As we cross through the sea off [Yoroshima]
Setting sail for the sea off [Yoroshima]
Praise to the Kenachi grove.
(*Omoro sōshi* 13–945)

Finally, Katsuren was closely allied with nearby Ezu Gusuku, a matter I discuss
in chapter 11 in connection with Shō Taikyū's conquest of Katsuren and Nakagusuku.

The above locations, plus Hanagusuku (Tatanagusuku), constitute a good
sample of communities centered on harbor-and-fortress pairs, mostly in southern Okinawa, possessing wealth and military power.[2] Importantly, these locations connect to other sites, many of which are outside Okinawa, in a manner
similar to the hub-and-spoke model introduced in previous chapters (figure 9.2).

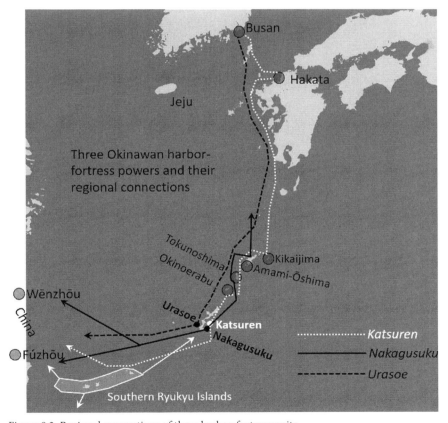

Figure 9.2. Regional connections of three harbor-fortress units.

Having gathered this set of local powers from the *Omoro,* I turn to a brief discussion of each to reveal the political geography of Okinawa during the fourteenth and fifteenth centuries.

Select Harbor-Fortress Pairs

Katsuren and Katsuren in Comparison

"With what might we compare Katsuren," begins one short *omoro.* "It compares with Kamakura in Yamato" (*Omoro sōshi* 16–1145). From the middle of the fourteenth century, Katsuren rapidly accumulated wealth. According to legendary accounts, the ruler of Katsuren at this time was Mochizuki, one of the many local strongmen from this era whose names suggest *wakō* origins (Yoshinari 2020, 135–135).[3]

Katsuren Gusuku features impressive fortifications, including four different walled enclosures and dugout trenches in strategic locations. Of the Chinese ceramics excavated from Katsuren, a large quantity consists of Yuan dynasty blue-flower ware, which indicates active international trade (Okinawa Kōkogakkai 2018, 170–172). Some structures in Katsuren feature roof tiles made in imitation of Korean tiles. The other locations whose buildings included the Korean-style tiles were Shuri and Urasoe Castles. Both Katsuren and Urasoe had close ties with Korea, which I discuss in subsequent chapters.

Richard Pearson has pulled together data from site reports to compare and contrast a selection of (1) unfortified sites (villages), (2) fortified sites outside of areas ever regarded as capitals, and (3) fortified sites in areas regarded as capitals (including Nakijin, as capital of Sanhoku). The data are cumulative and extend into the sixteenth century, so there is skewing with respect to the influx from the tribute trade. Moreover, some of these locations were in business longer than others. Nevertheless, total sherds from the category "major Chinese wares" provide a useful rough comparison. Goeku was a large *gusuku* in central Okinawa:

Goeku = 318
Itokazu = 4,484
Katsuren (enclosures one and two combined) = 5,769
Urasoe = 23,774
Nakijin (Shigemajō, the castle town below the fortress) = more than 11,190.[4]
(Pearson 2013, 223–231)

The main point for our purposes is that during the late fourteenth century, Itokazu, Katsuren, and Urasoe were large, powerful, fortified bases, connected with areas outside Okinawa. The large quantities of trade ceramics are one indication of their wealth and power.

Nakagusuku

Nakagusuku Gusuku is a large fortress consisting of six adjacent stone-wall enclosures arranged northeast to southwest. The core of the fortress consists of three enclosures along the edge of a cliff. The largest and highest is the first enclosure, with the adjacent second and third located to the northeast of the first. Nakagusuku is located atop a limestone rise that is 150–160 meters high. The walls of the fortress closely follow the contours of the land. The east side of the fortress overlooks Nakagusuku Bay and makes use of a cliff to create a defensive wall nearly 20 meters high (figure 9.3). The walls on other sides range from 8 to 10 meters in height. The north, south, and west walls feature parapets, troop passageways (*musha-bashiri*), and infoldings such that attacking soldiers would face defenders both head-on and on their flanks (*aiyokoya* in castle terminology). Key strategic locations, such as the area surrounding the entrance, were equipped with battlements for firearms (Tōma 2012, 15–17, 219, 225; Okinawa Kōkogakkai 2018, 172). Recently, a large-scale water drainage system has been discovered in the northern enclosure, and the earth foundation for the first enclosure has been dated to the early fourteenth century (Okinawa Kōkogakkai 2018, 172).

Figure 9.3. Part of the walls of Nakagusuku Gusuku, Okinawa.

In addition to its connections with locations in the northern Ryukyu Islands, the *Omoro* portrays Nakagusuku as a powerful military center:

> Acclaimed Nakagusuku
> Should the southern powers think to come up our way
> And attack
> With [our] metal and stone [weapons]
> We will push them back
> Acclaimed Nakagusuku.
> (*Omoro sōshi* 2–47)[5]

Okinawan warlords adopted firearms in the early fifteenth century, slightly before their Japanese counterparts did. Tōma Shiichi (2012, 52, 219) points out that the early adoption of firearms and advanced military architecture in fortresses like Nakagusuku indicates a technology transfer resulting from trade between these places and China and Korea. I have already discussed in detail the resemblance of Nakagusuku and other stone-walled *gusuku* to Korean mountain fortresses (chapter 6).

A closer look at Nakagusuku reveals two major time periods, at least two different groups of occupants, and trade with Japan. The fortress itself is located on high ground overlooking but removed from the coast. Yagi (today a neighborhood in Nakagusuku Village) was a coastal location about two kilometers away that functioned as a port (figure 9.4). The *Omoro* mentions Yagi immediately after the

Figure 9.4. Harbor area as seen from the walls of Nakagusuku Gusuku.

songs describing Nakagusuku's connections with the northern Ryukyu Islands. One song describes a magnificent folding screen (*byōbu*) that has arrived at Yagi (*Omoro sōshi* 2–59). As Inamura Kenpu (1969, 49) points out, this screen was almost certainly a trade item obtained from Japan and ultimately bound for China.

The next song describes the splendid military gear that has arrived from Japan:

Up from Yagi [to Nakagusuku]
Warrior clothing and armor [from Japan]
Who should wear such things?
Rulers and lords
Should wear such things
Up from Higa [=Yagi].
(*Omoro sōshi* 2–60)

In these songs we see Yagi receiving valuable trade items from Japan, which were stored at the Nakagusuku fortress.

Inamura notes that the manner in which the first and second enclosures of Nakagusuku were constructed differs from that of the third enclosure (called Miigusuku, "Third Gusuku"). Therefore, these two parts of the fortress were constructed at different times. In local legends the ruler of Nakagusuku before Gosamaru, who arrived there in the middle of the fifteenth century, is called saki Nakagusuku aji (previous Nakagusuku ruler). Most likely, the group associated with this local ruler built the first and second enclosures, whereas Gosamaru and his group built the third. I call the group connected with saki Nakagusuku aji the Original Nakagusuku Group, and Inamura estimates that they were active in the Nakagusuku area during the late fourteenth century. Moreover, it is likely they abandoned Nakagusuku prior to the arrival of Gosamaru. Inamura speculates that the Original Nakagusuku Group, as well as other powerful rulers in central Okinawa, came to know of the profitable tribute trade with China and allied themselves with Satto, based in Urasoe (Inamura 1969, 50–51). That is one possibility, but it may also be possible that this group carried on independent trade or conducted trade under the banner of the Sannan principality—as I explain in chapter 10.

Inamura, who did pioneering work on *wakō* in the Ryukyu Islands, makes an important point in connection with the Original Nakagusuku Group. Occupants of Nakagusuku and other fortresses were seafarers, and they often relocated. Although we cannot be certain where this group resided after leaving Nakagusuku, Hanagusuku along the coast of southwest Okinawa is a likely location. According to local tradition, a group of seafarers from Nakagusuku Bay came to the area around the late fourteenth century and built Hanagusuku Gusuku, also called Tatanagusuku or Tadanagusuku (Inamura 1969, 51–52).

Hanagusuku (Tatanagusuku)

Whichever group operated from Hanagusuku, everything indicates that it was a powerful location with the same characteristics of the other base locations. The *Omoro* refers to it as *kuni no ne* (base of the region; *Omoro sōshi* 19–1330). Hanagusuku was a large three-enclosure stone fortress thirty-three thousand square meters in area, and its walls featured outcroppings. It appears to have been built to fit the contours of the harbor just below its walls. Excavated items include a large quantity of imported blueware ceramics (Shinjō 1982, 307–308; Okinawa-ken 1983, 127–128; *Gushikami-son shi dainikan tsūshi hen* 1991, 56, 60–62).

Numerous *omoro* describe the wealth of Hanagusuku. In one, it is a portal through which a variety of riches (likened to wine) enter. It is a site of many large umbrellas and priestesses (images of power and prosperity), and it rules nearby communities (*Omoro sōshi* 14–1050). The umbrellas are repeated in several other songs. Especially significant, Hanagusuku is the site of beautiful eagles and drums, which enable it to rule. Eagles appear in the *Omoro* as militarily and spiritually powerful animals closely associated with powerful people (Fuku 2021, 144–185). The drum symbolizes political authority, which the *Omoro* typically describes in sonic terms (Smits 2019, 85–86, 126). The many songs describing Hanagusuku portray it as a location into which wealth flowed from the outside world and from which political, military, and spiritual power radiated (*Omoro sōshi* 19–1318 through 1330).

Urasoe

One matter that bears brief review is the chronology of large *gusuku*. Because several of the sites of large *gusuku* were the location of prior settlements, there is a tendency to assume that large, walled *gusuku* existed as early as the thirteenth century. For example, the site of Katsuren Castle was a settlement area during the twelfth century or possibly earlier. The walled fortress there, however, did not come into existence until the fourteenth century. Buildings supported by pillars appeared at Nakijin as early as the end of the thirteenth century, but walls and buildings with foundations did not appear until the fourteenth. The walls at Urasoe went up during the fourteenth century, and the Korean-tiled buildings are products of the fourteenth and fifteenth centuries (Ikeda 2019, 29–33). In other words, most large *gusuku* that served as bases for powerful local rulers began to take that form within a decade or two after 1300. Recall from chapter 8 that the number of arrowheads and other excavated weapons began to increase from this same time and that changes to the walls themselves, to better counteract or accommodate arrows and hand cannon, also took place during the fourteenth and fifteenth centuries.

Urasoe Castle may be the most misunderstood of the large *gusuku*. Richard Pearson's (2013, 170) statement that it "was the residence of the rulers Shunten, Eiso, and Satto" is typical of most Japanese-language surveys and even specialized literature. These claims all derive from accepting the chronology in the official histories at face value. However, Shunten almost certainly did not exist. Eiso probably existed, but the likelihood that he resided in Urasoe Castle or was interred in Urasoe Yōdore is extremely small. Satto (r. 1355–1397) was the first occupant of Urasoe Castle in its iteration as an Okinawan power center.

Connected with the idea that Urasoe Castle was Eiso's base is the assumption that Urasoe Yōdore, a nearby mausoleum, houses Eiso's remains (for the conventional view, Pearson 2013, 173–177). The earliest extant statement of this idea is found in a 1620 monument, Yōtore no Hi no Mon, that Shō Nei had erected about one month before his death. Like many monuments of the era, the text on the front is classical Chinese, and the text on the back is Japanese, written mainly in hiragana. The monument states that Urasoe Yōdore is the tomb of Eiso, the fourth king of Ryukyu, and that it shall be refurbished to house the remains of Shō Nei, his father, and a grandfather (Tsukuda 1970, 119–122). Either Shō Nei created the idea that Eiso was entombed in Urasoe Yōdore, or it was already in circulation prior to 1620. According to the 1725 version of *Genealogy of Chūzan*, Eiso's first specific act after taking the throne was to have his tomb constructed at Urasoe, and it was called Paradise Mountain (Ch. Jíleshān; *Chūzan seifu* [1725] 1988, 34). Earlier official histories, however, do not mention the tomb.

Yoshinari Naoki has long been a critic of the assumption that Eiso (r. 1260–1299) built Urasoe Yōdore and is entombed there. He convincingly argues that the dates of the construction of Urasoe Castle and Eiso's lifetime do not align. Assuming that Eiso built Urasoe Yōdore in the thirteenth century, he would have to have resided somewhere other than Urasoe Castle. The main reason is that both the Korean-tiled structures in Urasoe Castle and the castle's construction as a walled fortress are of fourteenth-century vintage (Yoshinari 2020, 182–183).

The walls of Urasoe Castle feature cloth-stacking construction similar to that of Itokazu Gusuku, and both sets of walls were probably completed during the latter half of the fourteenth century (Okada 2000, 152). From about 1350 onward, during the time of the Satto group, Urasoe Castle became powerful and wealthy. Its riches came in part from direct trade with China, which, as we have seen, had been ongoing for at least several decades before the start of formal tribute trade in the 1370s (chapter 8). Although Eiso probably did not reside at Urasoe Castle, there is reason to think that some of his descendants were major players during the era of the Three Principalities. As we will see, however, they were located farther south and east, in the territory that later came to be associated with Sannan.

Itokazu

Itokazu Gusuku in today's Nanjō City in southern Okinawa was excavated between 2006 and 2013. The large, extensively fortified site was built atop a 183-meter limestone ridge during the fourteenth century (Okinawa-ken 1983, 123; Nanjō-shi 2017, 130). The ridge plus the walls makes Itokazu Gusuku the highest fortress on the island of Okinawa (Okada 2000, 136).[6] The fortress is well equipped for warfare. The west side makes use of a natural cliff. The east side features a dugout trench to enhance the protective function of the walls. This side is also where the entrance is located. The north and south sides feature extensions that protrude from the walls (*azama*), functioning much like towers in European castles. The walls consist of cut stones and were equipped with stairways to facilitate the rapid movement of defenders (*musha-bashiri*) (Okada 2000, 136; Tōma 2012, 430–431; Nanjō-shi 2017, 130–131).

Excavations of Itokazu have recovered 2,956 sherds of *gusuku*-era earthenware, 97 of *kamuiyaki,* 7,580 of Chinese and Korean trade ceramics, and 41 of Southeast Asian ceramics. Moreover, 52 iron goods, 305 fragments of iron goods, and 26 iron nails have been excavated (Nanjō-shi 2017, 132). Weapons and military gear were among the items excavated from Itokazu, and it was clearly a base for foreign trade (Okada 2000, 137; Tōma 2012, 302). The *azama* of Itokazu closely resemble similar structures in Goryeo mountain fortresses in terms of shape, function, and construction (Tōma 2012, 431). In short, Itokazu was a large fortress, a base of commerce, and it was connected with areas outside Okinawa.

Namihira, Makabe, and Yamagi

Namihira Gusuku in Itoman is built into the flat top of a fifty-meter limestone ridge. Items found there include fragments of Chinese ceramics and iron goods (Okinawa-ken 1983, 145–146). Makabe Gusuku consists of two enclosures and sits atop a limestone ridge that is eighty-two meters high. The fortress is associated with a temple bell from 1394, now lost. Sherds of Chinese ceramics are among the items found in its ruins (Okinawa-ken 1983, 149–150). There are local legends connected with most of the fortresses in Okinawa, and Makabe is no exception. One legend tells of a war fought over the rare white horses associated with Makabe Gusuku.[7] Also located atop a limestone ridge, Yamagi Gusuku is relatively small in area, but its walls were ten meters in height. Nearby is the Kaniman sacred site (Okinawa-ken 1983, 143).

SASHIKI

Of all the locations called *nekuni,* Sashiki is mentioned most often. Little remains of Sashiki Gusuku today. It is located atop a 150-meter hill overlooking a harbor in the south of Nakagusuku Bay (figure 9.5). Sashiki was a small fortress with a simple design: four levels dug into the hillside. The first level is nine meters high (not counting the slope of the hillside), and the top level is forty-nine meters from the base. The fortress is built into the landscape very effectively for military defense. According to legend, it once had stone walls, but all the stones were carted away to build Shuri Castle. However, nothing indicates that Sashiki ever had stone walls in the manner of walled Okinawan fortresses. Instead, its defensive bulwarks consisted of piled-up stone and earth. Excavated items include *kamuiyaki,* fourteenth-century Chinese trade ceramics, tea items, coins, iron nails, carbonized grain, and iron arrowheads and other military gear (Okinawa-ken 1983, 112; Tōma 2012, 298–300).

After noting the extensive scholarship supporting the view that Shō Hashi (1372–1439) and his family (the Samekawa) migrated to Okinawa from Sashiki (near Yatsu-shiro) in Kyushu, Hokama Kazuo points out that similar alluvial soil, suitable for wet-rice agriculture, is found in both the Sashiki in Kyushu and the Sashiki in Okinawa. Although no longer the case today, in Shō Hashi's time there were abundant water resources in the Sashiki area in the form of streams and rivers flowing into

Figure 9.5. Harbor area as seen from the ruins of Sashiki Gusuku, southern Okinawa.

Nakagusuku Bay. Making this area suitable for wet-rice agriculture would have required several tens of people with engineering and agricultural know-how using iron tools. Sashiki Castle itself attests to the skill of Shō Hashi's group in landscaping. Later in his career, Shō Hashi at least nominally presided over the landscaping around Shuri Castle. Given the strife during this era in Kyushu and around the East China Sea region, Hokama concludes that a displaced group probably island-hopped down from Japan and established wet-rice agriculture in southern Okinawa (Hokama 2018, 38–46). The previously mentioned *Omoro* praise for the water-control infrastructure in Sashiki and its snow-white rice likely reflects such a situation.

Sashiki Gusuku was a trench-and-earthwork fortress of a design common in Kyushu and the northern Ryukyu Islands. During the fourteenth century, these Japanese-style fortresses also appeared in the northern part of Okinawa and were numerous.[8] One northern Okinawa example is Oyagawa Gusuku. Similar to Sashiki, Oyagawa features three levels built into a hillside, protected by earthworks and trenches. Piled-up rocks above one of the trenches on the north side functioned as a defense mechanism. Trade ceramics from the fourteenth and fifteenth centuries have been excavated from the site (Tōma 2012, 272–275).

Out of the nearly two hundred *gusuku* in Okinawa, here I focused on a small sample, those the *Omoro* calls bases (*nekuni*), plus Katsuren. We know relatively little about Makabe, Namihira, and Yamagi, although they may well have been prominent during the fourteenth or fifteenth century. The others have much in common. They were militarily and economically powerful, they were the locations of significant infrastructure, and they were enmeshed in trade networks extending outside Okinawa. The excavation of trade ceramics dating from the fourteenth and fifteenth centuries, often in large quantities, indicates that most or all of these sites conducted independent international trade. Pearson (2013, 230), for example, refers to this commerce as "unofficial trade"—that is, activity outside the tributary trade with China.

There are many other examples of harbor-fortress political units in addition to those discussed here (figure 9.6). The key takeaway point is that even while "kings" (trade kings) were operating in Okinawa, the basic political unit was not small territorial states. It was seafaring groups conducting trade at harbor-fortress locations. Although many such communities practiced agriculture, trading and raiding was the basis of their wealth. Agriculture provided food but not the surplus wealth that powered state formation. The Ryukyu Islands at this time were home to maritime groups, not territorial states.

The official histories focus exclusively on tribute trade and the trade kings who conducted or presided over it. Recall that the English term "king" (and the Japanese ō)

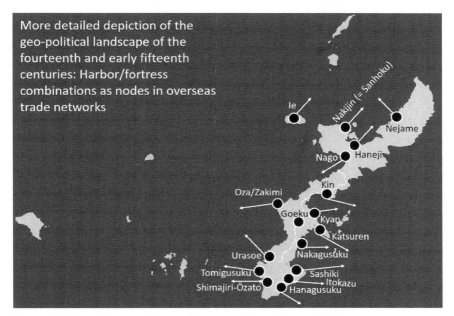

Figure 9.6. Many of the major harbor-fortress units in and around Okinawa.

is misleading in this context. The kings of the Three Principalities era were the names of real or fictitious people under whose auspices Ming authorities accepted tribute trade. These names appeared only in official documents. It is highly unlikely that "king" (Ch. wáng), a Chinese title, was a term used within Okinawa during the fourteenth or fifteenth century. A similar Japanese term was *yononushi,* which the Muromachi shōguns used in correspondence with trade kings based at Shuri. The trade kings of Okinawa were local warlords who enjoyed a favorable economic position. Although being a trade king was potentially lucrative, it was also dangerous. Local warfare in connection with the tribute trade was constant and severe.

Okinawa's large walled fortresses were one manifestation of Korean influence in the Ryukyu Islands (chapter 6). The proliferation of trench-and-earthworks fortresses in northern Okinawa and a few other places, especially Sashiki, indicates the arrival of *wakō* or warrior groups from the Japanese mainland.[9] During most of the fourteenth century, Japan was in a state of civil war, and disruptive warfare there continued throughout the fifteenth century. Groups from Japan and Korea, as well as remnants of the collapsing Yuan dynasty in China, made their way into the Ryukyu Islands during the fourteenth century. Most arrived as seafarers. Those who were not seafarers would have been forced to adapt to the circumstances of maritime Ryukyu described in this chapter.

CHAPTER TEN

Many More than Three

The Tumultuous Sanzan Era in Okinawa

The names of Okinawa's Three Principalities (Sanzan), Sanhoku, Chūzan, and Sannan,[1] appear in official Chinese records connected with trade, along with the names of people representing those entities bearing titles such as king, royal uncle, royal brother, or envoy. *Omoro sōshi* songs mention none of the principalities, none of the kings except Shō Shisho and Shō Hashi, and only a single envoy. In *Maritime Ryukyu* I argue that these document-based principalities did not correspond to land-based territorial states and that they functioned as brand names or dummy corporations. Evidence that the Three Principalities were not territorial states includes a lack of boundaries or any indication of principality-level government administration and the fact that they all made shipments to China via the port of Naha on Chinese ships. Often more than one principality's tribute goods and entourage sailed on the same ship, and sometimes the same envoys represented both Chūzan and Sannan (Smits 2019, 77–87). I was not the first to call the conventional view of the Three Principalities into question. For example, historian Ikuta Shigeru (1992, 286) convincingly argued against the standard narrative that Okinawa became divided into three territorial states during the fourteenth century, which Shō Hashi united in the 1420s. Nevertheless, the idea of the Three Principalities as territorial states remains tenacious among historians and in Okinawan popular historical memory.

During the fourteenth and fifteenth centuries, the main geopolitical units in Okinawa and the other Ryukyu Islands were harbor-fortress pairs (chapter 9). Although these units sometimes fought each other, they were maritime entities. In other words, their main "territorial" orientation was out to sea, to harbors in other islands and in other countries. Why have most historians, whether working in the ancient branch model or the internal development model, assumed the existence of three small states whose territory encompassed all the land of Okinawa? While inertia is certainly a factor, there are at least three deeper reasons. One is that the official histories discuss the Three Principalities, albeit providing differing accounts regarding their details. Another is that the basic story fits in perfectly with a developmental model based on agriculture that tends to regard

Ryukyuan history as a late-developing version of Japanese history (Yoshinari 2020, 177). The basic outline is that agricultural surpluses first gave rise to local warlords (*aji*). As these warlords grew in power and ambition, they coalesced into three confederations. Because agriculture was the economic foundation of society, these confederations occupied and controlled as much land as they could. The three confederations or principalities constituted a natural intermediate stage in the development of the Ryukyu Kingdom.[2] The third related reason is a general reluctance to acknowledge that the early local powers in the Ryukyu Islands were *wakō*.

This chapter is a close examination of Okinawa's Three Principalities. In it I expand the argument in *Maritime Ryukyu* that the Three Principalities were not territorial states. I also take a close, critical look at the trade kings who purportedly headed these principalities. I argue that they should be regarded first and foremost as names under which trade took place, not as specific individuals. For example, instead of "King Satto" it usually makes more sense to speak of "the Satto group"—that is, the people conducting trade under the Satto name. In the process I propose a new model for understanding the Three Principalities era that includes Okinawa's major harbor-fortress pairs. This era was a time of constant warfare. It is also a misnomer because many more entities than three participated in those conflicts.

This chapter begins with background, moves to an examination of eastern versus western Okinawa, and then closely examines the "kings" and royal lines of the era. Next, I read the Chinese records closely to reveal key details about the Three Principalities. With this information in mind, I present a new model of the era. The chapter ends with two follow-on topics, a close look at the Satto group, and a recharacterization of the era's warfare.

Background

Although the traditional dates of the Three Principalities era are 1314–1429, there is no basis for so early a start.[3] The Three Principalities were the result of Ming tribute trade. The first one, Chūzan, appeared in a 1377 entry in *Ming Veritable Records* (*MVR* 2001, 1:12 [#9]). Sannan first appeared in 1380 (*MVR* 2001, 1:12 [#12]), and Sanhoku first appeared in 1383 (*MVR* 2001, 1:12 [#15]). Therefore, let us define the Three Principalities era as the time when the tribute trade with China, operating through the port of Naha, took place under the auspices of more than one trade king. The dates for this era would be approximately 1377 until 1429, the last time Tarumi of Sannan appears in Ming records. Incidentally, the phenomenon of sprouting new local kings soon after establishing tribute trade with the Ming court was not unique to Okinawa. It also took place in the sultanate of Sulu and on the island of Java (Murai 2019, 106; Smits 2019, 62).

Instead of thinking of the political geography as consisting of three territorial states encompassing the island of Okinawa, we should think of it consisting of dozens of harbor-fortress units of varying size and power (figure 9.6). These units traded with counterparts in other islands, and many of them traded, directly or indirectly, with ports in Japan, Korea, and/or China. I refer to the personnel associated with each of these harbor-fortress units as "groups." Group members also included allied harbor-fortress units and associated personnel elsewhere in Okinawa or other Ryukyu Islands. For example, the personnel working under the auspices of the trade king Satto would be the Satto group. Similarly, personnel working under the auspices of the trade king Han'anchi would be the Han'anchi group. Such terminology does not necessarily mean that specific people named Satto or Han'anchi existed or that they existed whenever a trade ship departed Naha with cargo and envoys bearing their names.

The official histories make claims about the Three Principalities that are clearly incorrect. For example, *Reflections on Chūzan* states that Shō Hashi of Chūzan conquered the other two principalities to end the suffering of the common people. It then claims that Hashi notified the Ming court of this unification in 1423. In fact, nobody from Okinawa notified the Ming court of such a thing, whether in 1423 or at any other time (Smits 2019, 77–85). Indeed, the official histories are not even in agreement regarding when the Three Principalities came to an end, with *Reflections* claiming that Hashi completed the process in 1422 and *Genealogy* putting the year of purported unification at 1429 (*Reflections* [1650] 2011, 92n23; *Chūzan seifu* [1725] 1988, 57–58). Similarly, the precise start of the Sanzan era is unclear, taking place sometime during the reign of Tamagusuku (r. 1314–1336) in both of these official histories.

The Okinawans who sent tribute to the Ming court were those *wakō* groups who prevailed, at least for a time, in ongoing struggles to position themselves for maximum profit. Some participants in this struggle had resided in Okinawa for several generations, whereas others, like Satto and Shō Hashi, were newcomers. During the Sanzan era their struggle turned especially violent (Yoshinari 2020, 178).

In *Maritime Ryukyu* I argue that the concentration of *wakō* in the Ryukyu Islands was official Ming policy, enacted as a de facto plan B after Ming attempts to gain the cooperation of Japanese southern court prince Kaneyoshi (?–1388). The Ming policy was to channel *wakō* powers into tribute trade and gradually regulate and tame them (Akamine 2017, 28–32; Smits 2019, 62–66; Yoshinari 2020, 176–177). According to Yoshinari (2015, 93), "Upon the stage of Ryukyu, the unlawful behavior of *wakō* was fundamentally transformed via the framework of the tribute system." The Three Principalities functioned as channels whereby certain groups based in Okinawan harbors could participate in tribute trade under highly favorable and profitable terms.[4] One result of these lucrative terms was constant warfare in Okinawa, even after Shō Hashi's rise to prominence in the early 1400s (Smits 2019, 121).

The most intense period of competition was approximately 1380–1430. Several events from around the East China Sea region fueled this struggle. The first was the collapse of the Yuan dynasty. The dynasty did not fully collapse in 1368, however, and the Ming court remained at war with Mongol Yuan remnants throughout Okinawa's Three Principalities era. The turbulent decline of the Goryeo state in Korea eventually resulted in the rise of the Joseon dynasty in 1392. In the background of the Korean situation were frequent attacks on the Korean coast, and even inland areas, by *wakō* based in Tsushima, Iki, and western Kyushu. Many of these *wakō* were affiliated with the northern or southern courts in Japan's civil war. Civil war had been raging throughout Japan since 1335, and during the 1380s the position of the southern court in Kyushu declined precipitously. Many southern court *wakō* in search of new bases came into the Ryukyu Islands (Smits 2019, 46–49). In the southern Ryukyu Islands, these arrivals became the "heroes" of the so-called age of heroes (*eiyū jidai,* ca. the 1400s) in that region (Smits 2019, 53–59). In the midst of this turmoil, the Ming court attempted to make tribute trade more profitable than marauding and smuggling for *wakō* groups in Okinawa.

Eastern Okinawa and Western Okinawa

One of the Ming court's incentives was to "give" old naval vessels to Ryukyuan kings for use in shipping tribute. Ryukyuans were among the crews of these ships, some as official envoys and their entourage (who also conducted private trade in China). Nevertheless, the "Ryukyuan" ships sailed with Chinese captains and officers. In other words, the ships were nominally Ryukyuan but actually under the control of Chinese officers and merchant officials. This arrangement had several benefits, including that Chinese merchants could legally circumvent the Maritime Prohibitions by using ostensibly "Ryukyuan" ships (Ikuta 1992, 269–270; Smits 2019, 66, 171–172). Administrative efficiency may have played a role too. A single large Chinese ship could accommodate "tribute" items from a variety of sources. In the longer term, the use of Chinese ships made Ryukyuan powers dependent on them. Creating dependency was a long-term goal of this Ming policy, and it gradually worked as intended.

Many harbors in Okinawa and the other Ryukyu Islands are suitable as anchorages for ships. However, the deepwater port of Naha was one of the few Ryukyuan locations where large Chinese ships could safely dock. It was after the start of the tribute trade in the 1370s that Naha began to eclipse other ports and harbors in the volume and importance of shipping. In the previous discussion of harbor-fortress units that the *Omoro* called bases, most were located along the east or southeast coast of Okinawa. The oldest extant map of Okinawa is Korean, and it appears in Sin Sugju's *Account of East Sea Countries* (1471).[5] One noteworthy feature of the map is that many of its Okinawan place-names are identical to those found in the *Omoro*. Another is that both in terms of its visual lines and nomenclature, Sin's map divides Okinawa into an eastern section, from Kunigami in the north through Shimajiri in the south, and a western section centered on the "Ryukyu capital" (Shuri). The western section extends from Nago and Nakijin in the north, southward to Naha harbor.

Most of the harbor-fortress units in the eastern section are called -*gusuku* castle (*gusuku jō*), although some are only "castle." From north to south, they are Kunigami Gusuku Castle, Ike Gusuku Castle, Katsuren Castle, Goeku Castle, Naka Gusuku Castle, Oni Gusuku Castle, Ō Gusuku Castle, Tama Gusuku Castle, and Shimajiri Castle. The -*gusuku* element is not found in any of the western locations, although some are called castles (*East Sea Countries* [1471] 1991, 44–46, 390; Robinson 2001, 121–122). Therefore, even as late as 1471 we find the perception that the eastern and western parts of Okinawa differed to some degree.[6] With respect to this point, Ikuta Shigeru has argued that the major power centers in the east, such as Katsuren, developed earliest as trading centers with foreign powers. The Naha-Shuri-Urasoe area developed later, and it was this late-developing territory that became the core of Chūzan (Ikuta 1992, 287–288). Seto Tetsuya also notes a fundamental difference between *gusuku* on the east and west coasts, with those on the east coast, like Katsuren and Nakagusuku, evolving from previously existing communities in the same location. He agrees with Ikuta that whatever Chūzan may have been, it pertained only to Okinawa's west coast (Seto 2019, 63–64).

It is impossible to pin down the exact geopolitical map of Okinawa or other Ryukyu Islands during the fourteenth century or even most of the fifteenth. This is partly because the situation was dynamic, with powers ebbing and flowing in various locations. This ebb and flow included the frequent movement of people, including arrivals from outside the Ryukyu Islands. From the Sanzan era to the sixteenth century, the Ryukyu Islands in general, and Okinawa specifically, were unstable.

Mysterious Trade Kings

The term "king" is especially problematic during the Sanzan era. Nearly all the kings have peculiar names, at least several of which are generic. Many kings have extremely long life spans, sometimes punctuated by as much as a decade of inactivity before coming back to life—at least as names in documents. Just because a king exists as a name in Chinese records does not necessarily mean that this name corresponded to an actual person or to the same person over the course of that name's appearance in documents. Moreover, some kings are so obscure that they may have been entirely fictitious. Significantly, with one possible exception, none of the trade kings of the Sanzan era are mentioned in the *Omoro* except Shō Shishō and Shō Hashi.[7]

At least four criteria can assess whether the name of a trade king that appeared in Chinese records corresponded to a specific individual living in the island of Okinawa. First, does the person's name appear in the *Omoro?* Second, is there a tomb somewhere in Okinawa purporting to be the grave of that person?[8] Third, is the king's name generic, based on a place-name, or in some other way peculiar? Fourth, are there local legends about the trade king? Finally, although not necessarily a criterion for whether a trade king existed in the flesh, it is worth noting kings with extremely long life spans, especially those who experienced an afterlife. In several cases a trade king's name reappears in Chinese records after a dormant period of up to a decade. In such instances, even if that trade king once existed in the flesh, the reappearance was almost certainly a case of using a deceased person's name for trade purposes.

These items do not necessarily carry identical weight. Especially difficult to assess are legends, many of which appear to be of early modern vintage. Similarly, the names of all these trade kings appear in certain family genealogies and mortuary tablets, which are also of early modern (often nineteenth century) vintage.[9] In other words, legends and purported genealogies coalesced after the official versions of the Three Principalities had become firmly entrenched in Okinawan culture and lore. In my view the strongest reason to doubt the personal existence of some or many of these trade kings is their absence from the *Omoro.*

Based on these criteria, I would say there is a strong likelihood that Bunei, Haniji, and Bin were names, not individuals. Similarly, it is quite possible that Satto and Shōsatto did not exist in the flesh. There is a greater likelihood that the names Onsado (if different from Shōsatto), Ōeijishi, Ōoso, Tarumi, and Han'anchi did correspond to living individuals, but we cannot be certain. However, I want to emphasize that the question of whether a specific trade king actually existed in the flesh is relatively unimportant. The larger point is that, whether or not they were living individuals, these trade kings' main function was to provide names under which tribute trade took place.

Trade Groups

Whether specific trade kings existed as individuals or only as names in documents, trade took place in the context of groups of Okinawans working with Chinese merchant-officials. These Okinawans probably had contacts with traders in the northern Ryukyu Islands and points farther north. They may have cooperated with each other in some cases, and it will become clear that they definitely competed with each other at times. We now begin the process of identifying some of the major groups, starting with the most complex one, a group descended from Eiso.

TRACING EISO'S LINE AND GROUP

The traditional account of Eiso indicates that he was a sage king who ruled Okinawa from 1260 to 1299. Urasoe Castle was his base, and he is buried in Urasoe Yōdore near the castle. Modern academic historians typically assume Eiso was a local ruler, not the ruler of all Okinawa, but they otherwise tend to accept the narrative derived from the official histories. Most elements of the traditional narrative, however, range from impossible (that Eiso ruled all of Okinawa) to unlikely (that he was a sage king based at Urasoe Castle). Nevertheless, Eiso and his probable line of descendants are vital for understanding the Sanzan era. Here I present the framework for a more plausible account, informed by the recent work of Yoshinari Naoki.

First, did Eiso or a ruler with a similar name exist during the late thirteenth century? There is no firm proof. Nevertheless, given his widespread mention in the official histories, early sixteenth-century monuments, and in the *Omoro*, Eiso likely was a real person. It is not the case, however, that these sources all agree about the details of his life and reign. Let us start with the official histories.

Looking briefly at three of the official histories in chronological order, we see that *Reflections* states that King Gihon (r. 1204–1260) abdicated the throne to Eiso, whose glorious reign was on a par with those of legendary Chinese sage kings Yáo and Shùn and even featured a revival of scholarship in Okinawa (*Reflections* [1650] 2011, 18–19). Eiso was the son of Lord Eso, or his grandson (the text is inconsistent). Eiso was born miraculously, when his mother dreamed of the heavenly emperor (J. Jōtei; Ch. Shàngdì). "The various ministers" selected Eiso to succeed Gihon after Eiso had been serving as prime minister (*sessei*, an anachronism) for seven years. Eiso's good government was so potent that the islands around Okinawa submitted tribute to him in 1264, and the "northern barbarians" of [Amami-]Ōshima happily did so in 1266, albeit via the mediation of interpreters (*Reflections* [1650] 2011, 57–62).

Sai Taku's *Genealogy* states that Eiso was the son of Lord Eso and that his mother, although "unknown," became pregnant after seeing the sun in a dream. The skies were purple at the time of Eiso's birth, a good omen, and an indescribably lovely aroma filled the house. Thereupon people realized that a son of the sun had been born. Otherwise, the account of Eiso's reign is similar to that of *Reflections* (*Chūzan seifu* [1701] 1998, 60–61). The account in Sai On's *Genealogy* is substantially the same, with additional details about creating the port of Tomari to receive tribute from the northern Ryukyu Islands and Eiso's directive to build a tomb (*Chūzan seifu* [1725] 1988, 34–35). Modern scholars have typically interpreted the tomb to mean Urasoe Yōdore.

These accounts reflect the issues and ideologies of the seventeenth and eighteenth centuries, not events of the thirteenth century. For example, the empire (Okinawa, the surrounding islands, and the northern Ryukyu Islands) attributed to Eiso's virtue came into being much later, during the early sixteenth century, and by military conquest (Smits 2019, 87–89, 161–177). Indeed, there is almost nothing in the official history accounts of Eiso upon which we can rely, even the suggestion in Sai On's *Genealogy* that Eiso was interred in Urasoe Yōdore. The only conclusion I will draw from the official histories is that Eiso lived in the thirteenth century and was a local ruler in the Urasoe area.

In the *Omoro,* Eiso appears as Iizu (spelled "Iso" 伊祖; Izu is also a possible pronunciation) or, more often, as Iizu-niya 伊祖にや (person of Iizu).[10] This name is significant. Eiso's likely base was not Urasoe Castle, which did not exist as a walled fortress during the thirteenth century. Instead, nearby Iizu Gusuku (Iso Gusuku in modern pronunciation) was Eiso's home base. In other words, the *Omoro* refers to Eiso by his place of origin, Iizu Gusuku.

In one repeated song, Iizu is described as a capable warrior who drinks different types of wine in both the summer and winter. In other words, Iizu was so prosperous and wealthy that he drank wine year-round. The second instance of the same song is immediately preceded by three *omoro* praising Iizu Gusuku, another indication that Iizu Gusuku, not Urasoe Castle, was Eiso/Iizu's base (*Omoro sōshi* 12–671, 15–1066, 1067, 1068, 1069).[11] Significantly, the place-name Urasoe appears often in the *Omoro,* especially in chapter 15, but it never occurs in connection with Iizu-niya or any other iteration of Eiso's name.

Omoro songs place Eiso in Iizu Gusuku. According to legends in the Urasoe area, Eiso's father and other forbears were also based at Iizu Gusuku, and Eiso was born there (Higashionna 1980, 568; Okinawa-ken 1983, 85; Yoshinari 2020, 163). The construction of Urasoe Castle began in the early or mid-fourteenth century, around the time the Satto group arrived in Okinawa, well after Eiso's time. It is highly unlikely that Eiso ever resided in the space that became Urasoe Castle, and his purported entombment in Urasoe Yōdore is contingent on highly improbable conditions.[12] As with so many other "facts" about early Ryukyuan history, the widespread acceptance of Urasoe Castle as Eiso's base and Urasoe Yōdore as his tomb reflects a tendency to assume that the official histories are basically accurate records of what actually happened. These documents may indeed provide clues, if read critically, but the official histories mainly reflect the issues and ideologies of the time they were written. For example, placing Eiso at Urasoe Castle helped give the impression that disparate lines of "kings" were connected (Smits 2019, 151).

In a series of *Omoro* songs about Itokazu Gusuku, described in chapter 9, one song mentions "the lord of Iizu"—that is, the lord of Iizu (Iso) Gusuku. This lord is apparently on very good terms with the lord of Itokazu, and the two walk together to nearby Yakabe (*Omoro sōshi* 17-1245, 18-1275). Itokazu Gusuku is very close to Tamagusuku Gusuku. This point is significant for tracing Eiso's line (figure 10.1).

According to the official histories, Eiso's line consisted of Taisei (r. 1300–1308), Eiji (r. 1309–1313), Tamagusuku (r. 1314–1336), and Seii (r. 1337–1354). Notice the "-ei" element in each name except Tamagusuku, which stands out. Like Iizu, Tamagusuku is a place-name. The official histories have very little to say about any of these purported kings. Using Sai Taku *Genealogy* as a guide, Taisei gets one long sentence explaining that he was a good ruler, as does Eiji. However, for Eiji we are told cryptically that he uncovered "a quiet scheme." Otherwise, there is no further explanation (*Chūzan seifu* [1701] 1998, 64–65). Tamagusuku's description is slightly longer. It starts with a standard trope from the Chinese classics about neglecting his duties due to indulging in lust and hunting. Tamagusuku's deficiencies as a ruler caused the breakup of a unified kingdom into the Three Principalities. Although Tamagusuku tried to reunite the country by military force, the other principalities were well governed and thus resisted effectively. Warfare, however, continued (*Chūzan seifu* [1701] 1998, 65–66). Seii came to the throne at age ten and was unable to govern. His unnamed mother tried to seize the reins of power, but society declined further. Wise people went into hiding and inferior people prospered (a standard Chinese trope). The people revolted and installed the virtuous Satto as king (*Chūzan seifu* [1701] 1998, 67).

Here we see classic Chinese historiography shaping the narrative into a morality play. Nevertheless, we can extract some likely points. Eiso was a

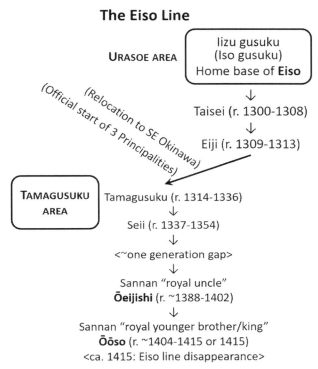

The Eiso Line

URASOE AREA — Iizu gusuku (Iso gusuku) Home base of **Eiso**

↓

Taisei (r. 1300-1308)

↓

Eiji (r. 1309-1313)

(Official start of 3 Principalities)

(Relocation to SE Okinawa)

TAMAGUSUKU AREA — Tamagusuku (r. 1314-1336)

↓

Seii (r. 1337-1354)

↓

<~one generation gap>

↓

Sannan "royal uncle" **Ōeijishi** (r. ~1388-1402)

↓

Sannan "royal younger brother/king" **Ōōso** (r. ~1404-1415 or 1415)

<ca. 1415: Eiso line disappearance>

Figure 10.1. The Eiso line.

powerful local ruler in the Urasoe area, and for a decade or two after his death, his descendants held onto Eiso's fortress. Sometime between roughly 1315 and 1336, however, the Eiso group was pushed out of their home base amid widespread warfare. They managed to relocate to Tamagusuku Gusuku, a major fortress in southeastern Okinawa near Itokazu Gusuku. There is another source for this scenario besides the official histories. According to genealogical records in the Tamagusuku area, "Tamagusuku, fourth child of Eiji, a descendant of Eiso, acquired the territory of Tamagusuku, inheriting it from Tobutono" (quoted in Tamura [1927] 1977, 84).[13]

With Tamagusuku, the Eiso line relocated to southern Okinawa—that is, the region the official histories describe as Sannan. The line eventually came to a sudden end, but not in circa 1350 with the rise of Satto. Eiso's line most likely carried forward, first as Ōeijishi 汪英紫氏 (r. ~1388–1402), known in Chinese records as the "royal uncle" of the king of Sannan.[14] Next is Ōōso 汪應[応]祖 (r. ~1404–1414 or 1415). In 1403 Ōōso appears as "royal younger brother" of the

Sannan king in Chinese records. In 1404 he appears as king. Although the names Ōeijishi and Ōōso look quite different in typical Japanese pronunciation, in Chinese they are Wāngyīngzǐshì and Wāngyīngzǔ, respectively. In other words, in the Chinese records their names are similar. Ōōso, and with him the Eiso line, vanished around 1414 or 1415.

It is also noteworthy that local legends regard Ōeijishi and Ōōso as having been lords (*aji*) of Yaese (O. Eiji) in southern Okinawa. Shōsatto and Onsado, by contrast, were lords of nearby Ōzato (Murai 2019, 100–103). Although we cannot date such lore, it is consonant with the point that the Eiso line of Sannan "royalty" and the Satto group or line were two distinct "royal" groups in southern Okinawa.

THE SATTO/SATO/SADO GROUP

Given the unstable demographics of the Ryukyu Islands during the thirteenth and fourteenth centuries, it is often difficult to make distinctions between insiders (second-generation or longer residents) and outsiders (first-generation arrivals from outside the Ryukyu Islands). The biographies of Satto, Shō Shishō, Shō Hashi, and Kanemaru (Shō En) all prominently feature iron brought into the Ryukyu Islands by Japanese ships. Although Satto and his group were Korean in origin (chapter 6), his biography in the official histories locates his birth in Okinawa, and he rose to power as a result of obtaining iron by trading with Japanese ships (Smits 2019, 151). Recall that in official biographies the motif of iron acquired from outsiders during a person's formative years identifies that person himself as an outsider (Yoshinari 2020, 156).

In the official story, Satto was born a farmer in the village of Jana, in the Urasoe area. Hard work, sagacity, help from his wife, and good luck enabled Satto to purchase iron from Japanese ships, distribute iron agricultural tools to the peasants, enable agriculture to flourish, and otherwise play the role of a Confucian sage ruler of an agricultural society. In fact, however, Satto was mostly likely the head of a group of seafarers who left the turmoil of late Goryeo Korea and ended up in Urasoe, probably in the 1330s. The official date of his becoming "king" of Chūzan, 1355, marks the approximate point at which he and his group had built up Urasoe Castle and developed a significant maritime trade network. This is also the approximate time that direct trade between the Urasoe area and China began (chapter 8).

If Satto was a real person, his name is enigmatic. Satto or Sato were generic names,[15] most likely based on the Korean term *sado,* which meant local officials (Yoshinari 2018, 196–197; Smits 2019, 83, chap. 6). The name Satto is found only in Chinese and Korean records. For convenience, I sometimes write about Satto as if he was a single local ruler, but it is likely that different people conducted

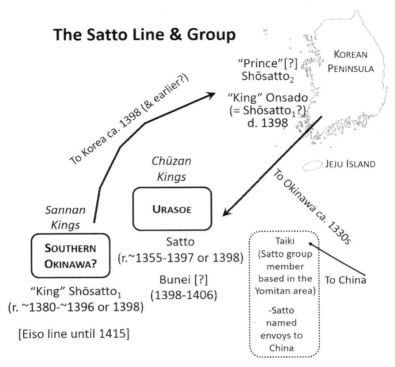

Figure 10.2. Satto line and group.

business under the Satto name, especially after 1397. Satto vanished without a trace, leaving behind not even a putative tomb.[16] The same goes for all of his group (figure 10.2).

The last recorded member of the group, Onsado 温沙道, appears in *Joseon Veritable Royal Records* in an entry dated 1398. According to the account, Onsado was the Sannan king, but he and fifteen others fled to Korea under pressure from the Chūzan king. They received support from the Korean government, but Onsado died in the tenth month of that year in Jinju in southern Korea (*JVRR-r* 2005, 34–35; Murai 2019, 98–99; Yoshinari 2020, 158).

Scholars have speculated on the identity of Onsado, with many regarding this name as a variation of Shōsatto.[17] However, for reasons that will become clear below, it makes better sense to regard Onsado simply as one of the members of the Satto/Sato/Sado group of mariners. The key points to note include this group's close connection with Korea (chapter 6) and their disappearance from Okinawa by 1398.

Zooming out for a broader perspective, large walled fortresses emerged in Okinawa as regional power centers. Their rapid appearance after 1300 indicates an influx of outside arrivals. These powers conducted maritime trade, as well as piratical activities such as smuggling, marauding, and human trafficking. The fourteenth century was a time of increasingly vigorous *wakō* activity in the East China Sea region and political instability in China, Korea, and Japan. The *wakō* activity was both a reason for the instability, especially in Goryeo Korea, and a reflection of it. *Wakō* of this era consisted mainly of Korean and Japanese people, as well as those of mixed origins. Another related point is that regional instability caused many merchants in the region to use the southern islands route, the route that ran through the Ryukyu Islands, to and from China.

With this situation in mind, consider the emergence of Urasoe Castle in the fourteenth century. In addition to walled fortifications, it featured buildings with roof tiles made in the Korean manner. This Urasoe group almost certainly included Korean technicians because the tiles' production and use in roof construction would not have been possible without the supervision of specialists. Most likely, the core of the Urasoe group were Koreans who left the peninsula owing to political tensions (Yoshinari 2018, 194–197; 2020, 160). It is also probable that some Japanese and hybrid Japanese were part of their original group or joined it after its relocation to Okinawa. The group probably also came to include people already in Okinawa by the early 1330s.

Circumstantial evidence indicates that this group was anti-Goryeo or at least had come under pressure from the Goryeo state. Although he had been trading with entities in China since the 1350s, Satto did not initiate any contact with Korea until 1389. Although Goryeo formally ended in 1392, Yi Seonggye had been de facto ruler since 1388. The following year, Satto dispatched an envoy to the Korean court, repatriating Koreans who had been captured by *wakō* and bearing gifts of sulfur, sappanwood, black pepper, and twenty shells, probably turtle shells (Ikeya, Uchida, and Takase 2005, 141–142; Yoshinari 2020, 157). In other words, Satto sent an embassy to Korea soon after the political tide turned definitively against the Goryeo regime. Moreover, the list of products is significant. The repatriated Koreans indicate *wakō* connections; the sulfur would have come from Japan or possibly Iōtorishima (west of Tokunoshima). The tropical wood and pepper would have been obtained in trade with Chinese or Southeast Asian merchants, most likely via the southern Ryukyu Islands. The shells probably came from the Ryukyu Islands. In 1394, Satto of Chūzan asked the Korean court to send Shōsatto 承察度, son of the Sannan king, back to Okinawa (*JVRR-r* 2005, 31–32). Whoever this Shōsatto was (there was also a Sannan king called Shōsatto, same characters), the point is simply to note the close political connection between the Satto group in Okinawa and post-Goryeo Korea (Yoshinari 2020, 157–158).

BUNEI

A mysterious figure called Bunei was king of Chūzan from 1398 to 1406, at least for documentary purposes. His name was the same as that of King Muryeong of Baekje (r. 462–523). *Reflections* states that Bunei was Satto's heir but provides no other family details (*Reflections* [1650] 2011, 84). Both versions of *Genealogy* state that Bunei's mother was a daughter of the ruler of Katsuren (*Chūzan seifu* [1701] 1998, 80; *Chūzan seifu* [1725] 1988, 45). None of the official histories list a queen or any progeny for Bunei, who is described as having been immersed in debauchery throughout a short, miserable reign that ended around 1405 or 1406.

There is no place purporting to be Bunei's tomb. All that we can say for sure is that "Bunei" functioned as a name under which tribute embassies were dispatched. If Bunei really did exist, he probably took over from Satto forcefully rather than succeeding him as an heir (Yoshinari 2020, 191). The appearance of Bunei in documents may reflect someone having created a Korean-sounding name to appear as a plausible successor to Satto. Assuming Bunei was not a member (much more likely, I think), the Satto group vanished in Korea upon the death of the mysterious "Sannan king" Onsado in late 1398. If Bunei was a member of the group, then the date would be 1405 or 1406.

The Three Principalities in Chinese

We can learn much about the Three Principalities, and about Okinawan society during the Sanzan era, through a careful reading of official Ming records. One key point is that merchant-officials from China managed the trade for all three of the principalities. Additionally, the details about Ryukyu and Ryukyuans appearing in Ming records resulted from self-reporting by Ryukyuans and their Naha-based Chinese handlers. In this way, the same royal envoy might appear, for example, as a "niece" of three different, unrelated kings. Similarly, kings who had almost certainly been long dead sometimes reappeared—in name—to sponsor tribute shipments. There is no indication in Ming records that the Three Principalities were territorial states at war with each other, but they sometimes suggest a more general state of conflict. Various kings, envoys, and princes often appear as relatives of each other, even though they could not have been. Such things were possible because of very loose verification practices, one aspect of the especially favorable trade terms during this era. Finally, Ming records reveal tensions and conflict as Ryukyuans in China aggressively pursued profits.

Merchant-Officials in Naha

The existence of three principalities, at least on paper, probably facilitated the work of the Chinese merchant-officials residing in Naha.[18] That several of these merchants had official status is clear from Chinese records. For example, Chéng Fù, the merchant-official who assisted Satto for over forty years, formally petitioned the Ming court to be permitted to return to China (*MVR* 2001, 1:21 [#45]). "Minister" Yà Lánpáo first appears as an envoy of Satto of Chūzan in 1383 (*MVR* 2001, 1:12 [#14]), and he frequently appears as an envoy thereafter. In 1394, Yà is listed as an envoy of both Satto of Chūzan and Shōsatto of Sannan (*MVR* 2001, 1:15, [#48]), and while in China later that year, the Ming court bestowed court rank and other honors on "the Prime Minister of Ryukyu" Yà Lánpáo (*MVR* 2001, 1:15 [#50]). At least some of the Chinese residing in the Naha area had official status in the eyes of the Ming court and were therefore likely positioned to exert significant influence within Okinawa. It was people like Chéng and Yà who made sure that the documents were in order and that the situation in Okinawa appeared orderly enough to satisfy officials in China. Undoubtedly, their job was very difficult at times.

Ryukyuan Envoys and Self-Reporting

Many of the listed envoys were from Okinawa. Their names typically appear "spelled" with four or five characters, often with minor inconsistencies such as an extra character or a different character with the same or similar pronunciation. To illustrate, let us take the example of someone important and interesting. As background, Chūzan and Sannan, but not Sanhoku, sent a few people to China to receive higher education at Chinese government expense. Some of these official students (*guānshēng*; J. *kanshō*) were clearly the sons of resident Chinese merchant-officials (*MVR* 2001, 1:21 [#40]). Others appear to have been Okinawans not connected with China, from the Naha area. Permission to send official students to China was a typical benefit of tributary countries.

In 1392.12.14, Ming records indicate that a niece of Sannan's Shōsatto arrived along with a tribute embassy to become an official student. Her name was Sangurumii. Two others, both children of local Okinawan warlords (*zhàiguān*; J. *saikan*), accompanied Sangurumii. It is possible that, initially, things did not go well for Sangurumii because she arrived in China again in 1396, as an official student (*MVR* 2001, 1:16 [#59]). It is also possible that Sangurumii prospered in 1392 and that she or others believed she would benefit from a second course of study. In 1398, Ming records noted that "a female official Sangurumii" or "a female official student Gurumii" (there are two ways to read the phrase) was studying in the capital (*MVR* 2001, 1:17 [#71]; Murai 2019, 200). The vast majority of official students were men, and it would be fascinating to know the details of Sangurumii's biography. We know from the account of Korean Ryang Seong, who was at Shuri Castle in 1456, that soldiers did not reside inside the king's quarters. While in his residence, a retinue of armed women served as the king's (Shō Taikyū) bodyguard (Murai 2019, 140; Smits 2019, 93). There is also evidence that women other than Sangurumii occupied official positions in Ryukyuan embassies (Murai 2019, 120).

When Sangurumii appeared as a student in 1392.12.14, her name was glossed Sānwǔlángwěi 三五郎尾 (*MVR* 2001, 1:14 [#40]). In 1396 the spelling was Sānwǔlángmén 三五郎亹, and in 1498 it was Shēnggūlǔmèi 生姑魯妹. In 1403, Sangurumii, glossed as Sānwúliángdié 三吾良疊, appeared as Satto's niece and envoy (*MVR* 2001, 1:18 [#2]). In 1404, glossed as Sānwúliángmén 三吾良亹, Sangurumii was back in China as Bunei's niece and envoy to announce the death of Satto (*MVR* 2001, 1:18 [#6]). Sangurumii served as an envoy many times—for example, in 1406 representing both Chūzan's Bunei and Sannan's Ōōso (*MVR* 2001, 1:20 [#26]). When [Shō] Shishō of Chūzan burst onto the scene in 1407, claiming to be the son of Bunei, Sangurumii became his niece and envoy (*MVR* 2001, 1:20 [#30]). Sangurumii was especially active as an envoy under Shishō. Her final appearance in Chinese records was in 1416, when she went to China on a difficult mission. The previous year, Chūzan envoy Choku Karo (Zhí Jiālǔ) and others had gone on a violent spree, which included the murder of a Chinese official. The incident generated an angry rebuke of the Chūzan king by Chinese officials (*MVR* 2001, 1:23 [#67]; Murai 2019, 199; Smits 2019, 67).

Looking more closely at some details, Chinese officials do not appear to have been familiar with Ryukyuan names. This point may be obvious and trivial, but more important is that officials in China probably knew little or nothing of conditions in Okinawa. That was one reason someone like Sangurumii could appear as the "niece" of several unrelated trade kings. The information that harbor officials in China received was self-reporting, transmitted via Chinese merchant-officials working in Naha. If we think of those merchant-officials as translators, much was lost or altered in the interest of sustaining a profitable trade. Although Sangurumii stands out both for frequency of travel and her gender, other Okinawans in the records saw repeated service as envoys, many of whom represented more than one principality.[19]

What Sangurumii learned as an official student, we cannot know. Ming-era records are sparse and perfunctory in this realm. At a minimum she must have learned spoken Chinese and been literate to some degree, all the more so after spending two full terms in China as an official student. Such people would have been in high demand as royal agents, and they typically served more than one trade king. The whole system of official students during the Ming era functioned to facilitate the tribute trade (Yoshinari 2015, 88).

CONFLICT AND WARFARE IN OKINAWA

Despite official history accounts stating that the Three Principalities were at war, we find no evidence in the Ming records that Sannan and Chūzan were significantly different entities or that, as different states, they were in conflict. Sanhoku was distinct in that its envoys never overlapped with those of Chūzan or Sannan. However, Sanhoku tribute embassies frequently arrived in China on the same ships as embassies from Chūzan or Sannan. In other words, none of the principalities seem to have corresponded to enemy groups.

Although the Three Principalities do not appear to have been three different territorial states at war with each other, indirect evidence of conflict in Okinawa is abundant. Unlike other tributaries of the Ming court, whose embassies were typically limited to one every three years, entities in the Ryukyu Islands operating under the banners of Chūzan, Sannan, and Sanhoku were permitted to send tribute as often as they wanted. And send it they did. In 1405, for example, four different tribute embassies arrived in China, one under the name of Han'anchi of Sanhoku, one under the name of Ōōso of Sannan, and two under the name of Bunei of Chūzan. The two from Bunei arrived only a month apart (*MVR* 2001, 1:19–20). Recall that with the death of Onsado in Korea in late 1398, the Satto group disappeared. Ming records show tribute activity in 1398 under the name of Chūzan's Satto. In 1398.3.16, by way of an envoy, Satto received a royal crown and belt from the Ming court (*MVR* 2001, 1:17–18 [#73]). If Satto had been an actual person, however, he was almost certainly dead by then. If so, somebody else used the Satto name to receive prestige goods from the Ming court.

What follows the disappearance of the Satto group in 1398 is remarkable. Chinese records indicate no tribute or other activity connected with Ryukyu from 1398.4.13 to 1403.2.22, a gap of nearly five years. Whatever caused the Satto group to disappear in 1398 (the use of Satto's name again in 1403 notwithstanding) was so disruptive that it stopped tribute shipments for years. Nothing like this had happened in the past or would happen again until the aftermath of Ryukyu's 1609 war with Satsuma. Higa Chōshin (2006, 60–61) hypothesizes that Sannan was without a king for five years because of an intrafamily dispute until Ōōso took the throne in 1404. The disruption and lengthy cessation of tribute shipments, however, affected more than only those Okinawans operating under the Sannan banner.

Disappearing and Reappearing Kings

The name Bunei refers to a person or group who replaced or superseded the Satto group and operated as trade king of Chūzan. From 1391, Bunei sent envoys twice as Satto's crown prince and agent. In 1396.11, he sent tribute as crown prince (*MVR* 2001, 1:14 [#33], 16 [#64]). If we assume that Satto died in 1395, the date given in the official histories, Bunei did not report it at the time of the 1396 tribute. In 1397 and 1398, Bunei sent a total of five tribute embassies under the Satto name (*MVR* 2001, 1:16–17). After the five-year gap described above were two tribute embassies in Satto's name in 1403. It was not until 1404.2.21 that Bunei reported Satto's death, most likely about nine years after the fact (*MVR* 2001, 1:18 [#6]). Yoshinari's interpretation is that this extended use of Satto's name reflects intense conflict between competing *wakō* groups in Okinawa during these years, and I agree (Yoshinari 2020, 188–189).

Bunei's group did not last much longer. In 1405.3, King Bunei sent an envoy to thank the Ming emperor for his investiture, in 1405.4 he sent a congratulatory envoy for the emperor's birthday, and in the twelfth month, he sent a new-year envoy (*MVR* 2001, 1:19–20). In 1406.3 Bunei sent tribute along with the Sannan king, after which Bunei disappeared from the stage entirely. This disappearance occurred soon after an incident on 1406.1.11 in which several castrated men arrived from Ryukyu to potentially serve as eunuchs, causing an angry response from the Yǒnglè emperor (*MVR* 2001, 1:20 [#25]; Sūn 2016, 171–175; Smits 2019, 111). The incident may have been in part a miscalculation, and it may also have been a reflection of ongoing conflict in Okinawa.

Han'anchi of Sanhoku also disappeared at about the same time (figure 10.3). Tribute sent in Han'anchi's name occurred fairly often, up to the dispatch of a new-year tribute envoy in early 1406 (*MVR* 2001, 1:20 [#23]). Almost a decade passed with no mention of Sanhoku or Han'anchi until 1415.6.6, when Han'anchi appeared in a terse entry as having sent an envoy along with Shishō. However, the demise of the Bunei group and Han'anchi took place in approximately 1406, most likely at the hands of Shō Hashi and possibly with local Chinese encouragement or assistance (Smits 2019, 111–113). The Han'anchi of 1415 was a phantom of the trade documents.

In addition to the brief appearance of the phantom Han'anchi in 1415, the Eiso line vanished that year. In an entry dated 1415.3.19, Tarumi 他魯海 suddenly appeared as "the late Ōōso's crown prince," dispatching tribute under the Sannan banner (*MVR* 2001, 1:22 [#68]). There had been no previous announcement of Ōōso's death. Tarumi, whose name in modern Japanese would be Tarō-sama (Yoshinari 2018, 204), sent tribute three times between 1415 and 1417 as "crown prince." A seven-year gap in Sannan tribute then ensued, indicating a

Sanzan Era 三山時代 Trade Kings
& Reigns
Sanhoku 山北 Kings
Haniji 怕尼芝 (ca. 1322-1395)

Bin (or Min) 珉 (ca. 1396-1400)

Han'anchi 攀安知 (ca. 1401-1406 [1415*])

Chūzan 中山 Kings
Satto 察度 (ca. 1355-1395 [1403*])

Bunei 武寧 (ca. 1398-1405 or 1406)

Shō Shishō 尚思紹 (1406-1421)

Shō Hashi 尚巴志 (1422-1439)

Sannan 山南 Kings
Shōsatto 承察度 (ca. 1380-1398)

Ōeijishi 汪英紫氏 (ca. 1398-1402**)

Ōōso 汪応祖 (ca. 1404-1414 or 1415)

Tarumi 他魯海 (1415-1429)

*reappearances **royal uncle

Figure 10.3. Three Principalities–era trade kings.

major disruption. From 1424.6 to 1429.10, Tarumi sent tribute six times, as "king" from 1424.12 onward (Yoshinari 2020, 188–189). It is entirely possible that one group contributed to tribute missions under Tarumi's name circa 1415–1417, and a different one did so later, circa 1424–1429. The period in between may have been a time of warfare among those operating, or aspiring to operate, under the Sannan banner.

Based on *Ming Veritable Records,* therefore, we can identify four likely points of change resulting from conflict in Okinawa. The most prominent is 1398, when the Satto group vanished, and all tribute ceased for nearly five years. Next is 1406, when both the Bunei and Han'anchi groups vanished. In 1415, Tarumi, or a group using that name, replaced the latter Eiso line of Ōeijishi and Ōōso. As noted above, the period between 1417 and 1424 may also have been a time of armed conflict, with a new group emerging in 1424, using the name Tarumi. Because Tarumi made his last appearance in documents in 1429.10.20, the standard narrative concludes that he and the army of Sannan went down in defeat at the hands of Shō Hashi and his Chūzan army. Significantly, the Ming records make no mention of such an event or of the downfall of either Sannan or Sanhoku. In any case, after 1429 Shō Hashi was the only person in Okinawa holding the title of (trade) king.

IMPOSSIBLE RELATIVES AND THE PURSUIT OF PROFIT

Some other details in the Ming records are revealing. We have seen that in 1407, Shishō suddenly appeared as "Crown Prince of Chūzan." Who was Shishō's purported father? King Bunei, the one who disappeared in 1406.3 without a trace. In 1405.11, however, someone posing as Bunei's crown prince was honored at an imperial banquet along with a Jurchen leader (*MVR* 2001, 1:19–20 [#22]). His name would be read in Chinese as Wánníng-sījié 完寧斯結, and the last part of the appellation was the title *utchi* (J. *okite*). I will call him Kane-utchi. How was Kane-utchi able to pose as a crown prince, and how were unrelated people able to posit plausible father-son relationships? Such machinations were possible because although investiture by the Ming court in Korea and many other tributary countries was strict and applied to crown princes and queens as well as kings, in Ryukyu it applied only to kings (Yoshinari 2018, 187). Therefore, completely unrelated people could pose as fathers and sons, and a "son" might be older than his "father." The Ming court did eventually tighten its verification process, but not until the reign of Shō Sei (r. 1527–1555).

Ming records typically list only one or two envoys, followed by "others" or "et cetera" (*děng*). Therefore, we cannot usually know how large of a group typically made the voyage from Naha to Fúzhōu. However, a 1403 entry appears to have specified the size of the full party. Satto of Chūzan and the "royal younger brother" Ōōso of Sannan sent two envoys accompanied by a party of sixty-five (*MVR* 2001, 1:18, [#4]). Each of these sixty-five arrivals from Naha would have had the chance to engage in private trade. This point is important. The official part of the tribute trade was mildly profitable in that Ryukyuan envoys received generous gifts from the Ming court in return for the "tribute" they sent. However, the main opportunity for profit, both for the Okinawans and the Chinese merchants, was private trade while the envoys were in residence. In general, the larger the entourage accompanying the tribute envoys, the greater the total profit potential.

Apparently, there were some restrictions on private trade. In 1404.5.4, the Board of Rites weighed in on an incident that arose in connection with a

1404.4.12 Sannan tribute embassy. Some members of the party unlawfully traveled to purchase ceramics, but the board stated that "people from afar know only the pursuit of profit, so how could they have known that they acted illegally? . . . The matter does not rise to the level of a crime" (*MVR* 2001, 1:19 [#10]). This incident is an early and mild example of a host of problems that Ryukyuans in China would cause during the fifteenth century, including illegal commerce, abuses of official hospitality, disorderly conduct, illicit military activity, arson, and murder (Smits 2019, 60–61, 67–69, 134–136). The lenient and generous terms the Ming court extended to Okinawans during the Sanzan era was not an indication of endearment. On the contrary, the Ming plan was to cause Okinawa-based *wakō* to become reliant on tribute trade as a way of taming and controlling them.

One final aspect of apparently lax or indulgent treatment on the part of the Ming court was accepting tribute sent by people other than kings. It was common not only for "crown princes" in Okinawa to send tribute but also for a younger brother and an uncle of a king to send tribute, in the case of Sannan. Tribute from people other than kings was not normal procedure for the Ming court. In 1383 the emperor bestowed a royal seal on both the Chūzan and Sannan kings (*MVR* 2001, 1:12 [#15]. However, two years later there is an entry stating that the emperor bestowed royal seals on the Sannan and Sanhoku kings (*MVR* 2001, 1:13 [#21]). In other words, it appears to have been Ming policy to recognize *two* de facto Sannan kings, those of the Satto group and those of the Eiso line. Each line operated at about the same time and sent approximately the same number of tribute embassies (Sūn 2016, 53–57; Yoshinari 2020, 165–166). Chūzan and Sannan both accommodated multiple royal lines, with two lines in Sannan operating simultaneously until about 1396.

A New Model of the Three Principalities

From a Chinese perspective, the main point of Sanhoku appears to have been to cordon off potentially dangerous *wakō* and Yuan remnants and channel them into tribute trade. The Sanhoku kings before Han'anchi are completely obscure. Haniji appears to have been the place-name Haneji (also a possibility for Han'anchi), and this "king" reigned for an improbably long seventy-three years, starting in 1322. I suspect that pushing his reign back to 1322 in Ryukyuan official histories was a necessary move to make Haniji's reign begin during the time of Tamagusuku of Chūzan. Bin is even more obscure, and he or his group appear to have been operating sometime in the 1390s. Whatever Sanhoku may have been, it was based at Nakijin, in the western part of northern Okinawa. Recall that northern Okinawa at this time also featured many Japanese-style fortresses.

The relationship between Nakijin and other powers in northern Okinawa during the Sanzan era is unclear, and there may have been no relationship. Higa Chōshin (2006, 150) points out that even after the fall of Nakijin, Nago Gusuku, twelve kilometers away as the crow flies, does not appear to have undergone any change.

The main point of Chūzan and Sannan was probably similar to that of Sanhoku, although there is more we can say about them. Given that, at least in some cases, the same envoys represented Chūzan and Sannan and both of these entities sent official students to China, they appear to have enjoyed a more privileged status vis-à-vis the Ming court. I propose that Chūzan and Sannan should be regarded as banners under which tribute missions were dispatched, or perhaps as brand names. Importantly, multiple groups of local Okinawan powers operated under these two banners (figure 10.4). One, the Satto group, regularly operated under both the Chūzan and the Sannan banners, and in the next section I identify a few members of this group. The point of these banners seems to have been flexibility in accommodating diverse, fluid, and sometimes conflicting *wakō* powers and channeling as many as possible into the tribute trade.

Crucial to this process were the resident Chinese merchant-officials, some of whom also appear in the Ming records as envoys. They were the ones who translated the multifaceted Okinawan reality into a form that, sometimes just barely, met the formal requirements of the tribute trade. These requirements were relatively loose in the Ryukyuan case. Nevertheless, as the eunuch incident and instances of illegal activities indicate, managing Ryukyuan seafarers at this time was a challenge. In any case, it was the merchant-officials in Naha who dispatched all the tribute missions from all the groups and under all the banners—all on de facto Chinese ships.

It is difficult to say how much power these merchant-officials wielded and in which realms. Given the extensive conflict of the era, especially the large post-1398 gap in tribute, the merchant-officials were obviously unable to keep the peace. The conflict during the era of the Three Principalities does not appear to have been warfare between the armies of different territorial states. It makes more sense to think in terms of conflict between groups of maritime traders, some of which we can identify. Similarly, we should be careful when it comes to the names of kings, as some are generic or highly peculiar, and some reigned for suspiciously long periods. If the generic-named Satto, for example, was indeed born in 1321 (*Chūzan seifu* [1701] 1998, 68) and died according to what is written in the Ming records, he would have been eighty-three. Because we have no reliable accounts of the domestic activities of any king prior to Shō Hashi, it is best

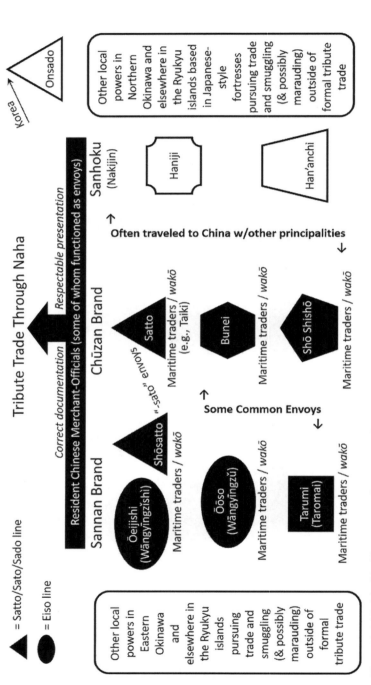

Figure 10.4. Model of the Three Principalities era in Okinawa.

to regard those kings as *names* under which tribute was sent. Most likely, multiple maritime traders or *wakō* groups contributed to the tribute shipments sent under those royal names.

A Closer Look at the Satto Group

People operating under the royal name Satto sent tribute under the Chūzan banner during the last three decades of the fourteenth century. Moreover, the Satto group had been conducting private trade with entities in China since as early as the 1350s. Besides Satto of Chūzan and Shōsatto of Sannan, we have also encountered a "Prince" Shōsatto in exile in Korea and the Sannan royal refugee Onsado in Korea in 1398 as part of a group of fifteen refugees from Okinawa. Additionally, two envoys appear in Ming records with "-sato" in their names. One was Sato 察都, who was an envoy from Satto of Chūzan in 1392 (*MVR* 2001, 1:14 [#39]). Another with "-satto" in his name appears as an envoy of Satto of Chūzan in 1395 (*MVR* 2001, 1:16 [#56]). A similarly named envoy also appears in 1398 (*MVR* 2001, 1:17 [#71]). After 1398, "-satto"-named envoys no longer appear, with one possible exception.[20] This point is further evidence that the Satto group vanished from Okinawa in 1398.

Particularly noteworthy is someone named Taiki 泰期. According to Ming records, Taiki was King Satto's younger brother. Satto dispatched him as an envoy in 1372, on the first official tribute mission, and again in 1376 and 1377 (*MVR* 2001, 1:11–12). Unlike other names from the Chinese records, Taiki also appears in the *Omoro,* as Taichi:

Taichi of Oza
Made trade with China flourish
This lord is beloved
The magnificent Taichi!
(*Omoro sōshi* 15–1117)

Taichi of Oza
Set out on the sea
Gazed upon Chinese palaces and returned
The magnificent Taichi!
(*Omoro sōshi* 15–1118)

Oza is a location in Yomitan, on the western coast of central Okinawa. Yomitan is approximately halfway between Naha and Nakijin. Here we have a rare overlap between official records and the *Omoro.*

Whether Taiki was actually the younger brother of Satto, as the Ming records state, or simply posed as such does not really matter. He was almost certainly a local strongman based in Yomitan, and he was part of, or allied with, the Satto group. Insofar as Taiki sent tribute to China or contributed to tribute shipments, he did so under the Chūzan and Satto banners. This situation whereby local maritime powers in different parts of western Okinawa sent tribute to the Ming court under the name of one or another trade king and under the banner of one or another principality was probably the norm during the Three Principalities era. People like Taiki would have been the main workhorses of the tribute trade. It is likely that some of the other envoys who appear in Ming records were local Okinawan strongmen who sought profit by trading in China. The Original Nakagusuku Group, mentioned in chapter 9, may have participated in tribute trade in a similar manner.

Taiki and most others who arrived via the tribute trade were conducting legal trade in China, at least most of the time. Other powers in Okinawa and in other Ryukyu Islands continued trading with Chinese entities even after the Ming Maritime Prohibitions. Indeed, throughout most of the fifteenth century the Ming court considered the Ryukyu Islands to be the abode of pirates (Smits 2019, 67–68). Some of those pirates entered the tribute system, eventually became dependent on it, and became less of a threat to China in the process. Others continued to pursue private trade, which by official Ming definition was smuggling. Opportunistic marauding was also a possibility. In some areas this situation probably persisted until Shō Shin's wars of conquest from approximately 1500 through the 1520s.

Wakō Melee (Not Sanzan Tōitsu)

One of the most common terms in early Ryukyuan history is sanzan tōitsu (unification of the Three Principalities). It is a misnomer. As should be clear from this chapter, the emergence of Shō Hashi in 1429 as Okinawa's only king was neither a case of three territorial states becoming unified though a clash of armies nor a case of Shō Hashi unifying all of Okinawa. First, many more entities than three struggled for power and profit between the 1370s and the 1420s.[21] Second, those entities were harbor-based wakō powers, not territorial states. Chūzan, Sannan, and Sanhoku were banners or brand names under which numerous local entities, like Taiki in Yomitan, traded with China by sending "tribute" and voyaging there as part of the entourages on tribute ships. Once in China, these Okinawans pursued private trade under the cover of the tribute system.

As I explain more thoroughly in chapter 11, the emergence of Shō Hashi as the only king—that is, as the only person who could authorize legitimate trade with China—was an important development. However, it was not the unification of Okinawa under a single ruler, much less all the Ryukyu Islands. All the harbor-fortress powers we examined in eastern Okinawa still operated, acquiring power and wealth. Seafarers in the southern Ryukyu Islands continued their far-reaching trade. The unification of Okinawa under a single political center was about a century in the future at the time of Shō Hashi's reign.

CHAPTER ELEVEN

Era of the First Shō "Dynasty"

In retrospect, the Three Principalities era came to an end in 1429. Despite the narrative in *Genealogy of Chūzan,* there is no evidence that the era ended with a final battle between the armies of Chūzan and Sannan. No other obvious event brought the era to a close. Instead, multiple trade kings stopped appearing in Chinese records. After 1429, Shō Hashi, and those who came after him using the Shō surname, were the sole trade kings. The authors of the official histories gathered seven trade kings together into a single lineage, which we conventionally call the First Shō dynasty.

Despite the streamlining of trade kings, the total volume of tribute trade did not drop off during the 1420s or 1430s. It must have been the case, therefore, that Shō Hashi continued working with many of the same local powers who had contributed to the tribute trade earlier in the Three Principalities era. Hashi came to power with Chinese assistance, and Chinese "ministers" probably ran the day-to-day aspects of his operation (Smits 2019, 85, 111–113). Otherwise, the geopolitical and economic situation continued much as it had during the Three Principalities era, and the main economic and political unit remained harbor-fortress pairs. This chapter argues that Shō Hashi did not unify or rule all of Okinawa and that during his time on the throne, the Ryukyu Islands were substantially the same as they had been during the Three Principalities era. An important change, however, took place in 1458. That year, Shō Taikyū consolidated his conquests of Katsuren and Nakagusuku, thus bringing into his hands trade both with northern locations and with China. As important as Shō Taikyū's conquests were, they did not result in a centralized state or in Taikyū's ruling all of Okinawa.

At no time during the First Shō dynasty did any of the trade kings rule over the entire island of Okinawa. Moreover, until Shō Taikyū (r. 1454–1460), the domestic power of most trade kings extended no farther than the Shuri-Naha-Urasoe area and possibly also Nakijin. Taikyū was different, both in that he was unrelated to his predecessors or successor and that he was militarily ambitious. Shō Hashi and Shō Taikyū were the two most important figures of this era. Many of the other trade kings are so obscure that we cannot say anything about them.

In this chapter I review some basic information about the nature of Ryukyuan society and the First Shō dynasty before presenting a model for this era. After briefly describing the model, we take a close look at the important trade kings Shō Hashi, Shō Taikyū, and Shō Toku. Finally, moving beyond Okinawa, I examine the Tomoi group in the northern Ryukyu Islands, Guraru Magohachi and his group in Okinoerabu, and locally powerful figures in the southern Ryukyu Islands.

Trade Networks, Not Agricultural Fields

"There is no more important work throughout the country than the peasants' cultivation." "There is no greater joy than tilling the soil and harvesting the crops." "Agriculture is the foundation of the country. To love the peasants is to love the country." These are but a few typical statements about agriculture made by Sai On, powerful politician and author of the 1725 *Genealogy* (*Sai On zenshū* 1984, 18, 25, 137). Sai On and the other authors of Ryukyu's official histories faced a fundamental difficulty. They were writing at a time when the Ryukyu Kingdom formally claimed to be an agricultural society. Recall, however, that even during the eighteenth century, Ryukyuan agriculture was poorly developed (chapter 7). The authors of the official histories imagined that Ryukyu had always been an agricultural society, but they had difficulty finding it.

During the Three Principalities era and the First Shō dynasty era, institutions and practices associated with agricultural societies were lacking, even in the pages of the official histories. Fictionalized biographies might laud Satto or Shō Hashi for advancing agriculture, but no written source mentions specific agricultural policies for that era. Insofar as the official histories discuss the activities of early kings, the vast majority of space is devoted to the trade with the Ming court that took place during their reigns.

Consider the task of ruling all of Okinawa, especially Okinawa as an agricultural society. It would require at least a basic network of inland roadways, a centralized bureaucracy maintaining written records of land holdings, tax payments, and more, and a system of local officials. There is no evidence that any of these things existed during the early fifteenth century. The only extant written documents pertain to trade and trade-related diplomacy. We find no evidence of well-organized domestic governance and no formal social structure.[1] There is no indication that any king until Shō Shin was literate. Chinese merchant-officials or their immediate descendants handled the documentation connected with the tribute trade, and Buddhist priests from Japan produced any other required documents pertaining to trade and diplomacy. Eventually, Shuri became the center of a maritime empire that did adopt many of the institutions and practices associated with agricultural societies, but that did not happen until the sixteenth century.

The First Shō "Dynasty"

As I explain in *Maritime Ryukyu,* the term "dynasty" is a misnomer in the case of the First Shō dynasty because not all the kings were relatives. Several were outsiders who took over by force and then adopted the Shō surname to pursue the tribute trade (Smits 2019, 113–119). Some of these trade kings are completely obscure, having left no traces other than names in Chinese documents and purported tombs in diverse locations around Okinawa. Most appear to have been passive figures, but a few, especially Shō Taikyū, made significant changes to the geopolitical landscape.

By the end of 1429, Shō Hashi, whose family had recently settled in Okinawa after leaving the Yatsushiro area of Kyushu, was the only trade king remaining in Okinawa. Many survey histories misconstrue the meaning of this point, in part because they conceive of the Three Principalities as having been small agricultural kingdoms whose territories encompassed all of Okinawa. If Shō Hashi unified them through conquest (*sanzan tōitsu*), then Hashi must have ruled all of Okinawa. As noted in chapter 10, however, this view is problematic for several reasons. Certainly, Hashi's military victories during the early fifteenth century were significant. In other words, his military prowess was surely a major contributor to his becoming the sole trade king. What that meant, however, was that Hashi became the sole king of the tribute trade, not the ruler of Okinawa.

The Trade Kingdom at Shuri and Naha

What did it mean to be king of the tribute trade? We cannot know in detail, but simply because of the volume of trade and the number of envoys and others mentioned in Chinese records, managing that trade would have been a major undertaking. Moreover, although the main trade took place between Naha and Fúzhōu in southern China, after reaching Fúzhōu many of the tribute ships sailed on to Southeast Asia to conduct trade there. The ships themselves were former Chinese naval vessels commanded by Chinese officers and manned by Chinese sailors. Nominally, however, they belonged to Ryukyuan kings, and they carried Okinawan envoys (Smits 2019, 66). In this way, favored Chinese merchants were legally able to circumvent the Maritime Prohibitions (Hashimoto 2008, 295, following Murai Shōsuke).[2] Slightly later, a similar situation prevailed vis-à-vis Ryukyu and Korea, with Japanese ships and Japanese sailors and traders as the crucial intermediaries.[3]

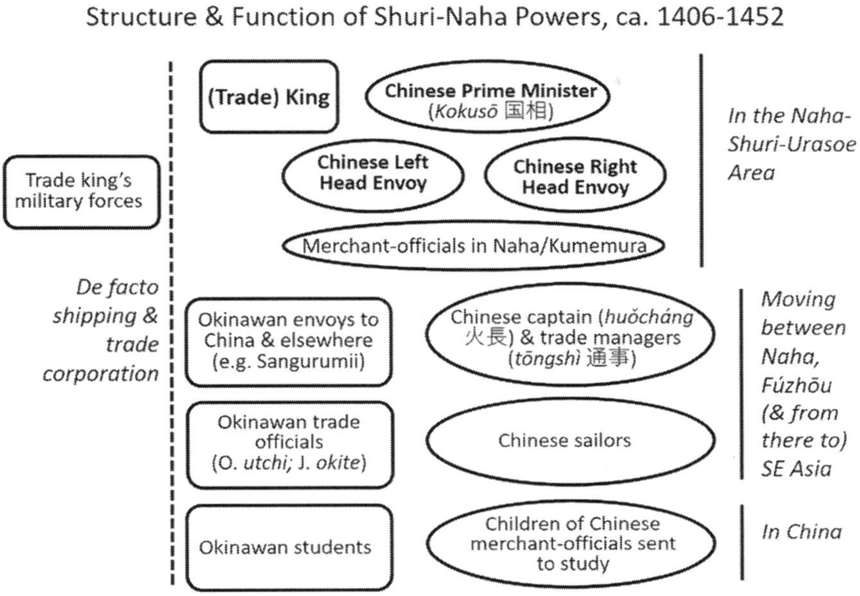

Structure & Function of Shuri-Naha Powers, ca. 1406-1452

(Trade) King — Chinese Prime Minister (*Kokusō* 国相)   *In the Naha-Shuri-Urasoe Area*

Trade king's military forces

Chinese Left Head Envoy — Chinese Right Head Envoy

Merchant-officials in Naha/Kumemura

De facto shipping & trade corporation

Okinawan envoys to China & elsewhere (e.g. Sangurumii) — Chinese captain (*huǒcháng* 火長) & trade managers (*tōngshì* 通事)   *Moving between Naha, Fúzhōu (& from there to) SE Asia*

Okinawan trade officials (O. *utchi*; J. *okite*) — Chinese sailors

Okinawan students — Children of Chinese merchant-officials sent to study   *In China*

Figure 11.1. Powers and stakeholders in the Shuri-Naha area ca. 1406–1452. Chinese entities indicated by oval shapes.

Figure 11.1 illustrates the situation that prevailed up to Shō Taikyū's reign. Nominally, the trade king was the ruler of "Ryukyu," meaning Okinawa, but particularly the Shuri-Naha-Urasoe area in this case. However, the Chinese prime minister appears to have been the genuine locus of power in Shō Hashi's government. The trade king would have been able to draw on local military forces, but it is not clear how they fit into the trading system, if at all. Below the prime minister were two Chinese head envoys, distinguished by left and right designations. They were assisted by other merchant-officials residing in the area of Naha harbor that later came to be called Kumemura. If there was a native Okinawan hierarchy of court officials under the king during the first half of the fifteenth century, we do not know anything about it.

Moving to the personnel who actually conducted the trade, there was a dual structure consisting of Okinawans and Chinese. The Chinese term for ship's captain, *huǒcháng*, literally meant "fire chief." It appears that these ship captains formed peer networks throughout the Asian ports frequented by Chinese vessels and that they had substantial autonomy (Murai 2019, 238). The other major Chinese officials on board trade vessels were *tōngshì*, a term that can mean "interpreter" in many contexts. However, we know that some ship captains were promoted to *tōngshi,* so something like "trade manager" would be a better rendering of the term (Murai 2019, 204–205). With a few exceptions, most of the trade king's envoys to China and to Southeast Asian countries were Okinawans, and we have seen the example of Sangurumii.

Tribute ships sailed with several tens of Okinawan traders, who typically appear in records with the title *-utchi* (J. *okite*). The relatively elaborate hierarchy of government officials found during the sixteenth century and later did not seem to have existed yet, and any Okinawan formally in charge of something in the early fifteenth century was typically an *utchi* of that realm. The ships also sailed with a crew of Chinese sailors, and ship captains sometimes came from their ranks. Finally, tribute vessels often carried students to China, who were sometimes the children of Chinese merchant-officials or of local Okinawan background.

A Model for First Shō Dynasty Okinawa

Although clearly a capable warrior and lord of the newly built Shuri Castle, Shō Hashi appears to have ended up much like his predecessors—as a *name* under which tribute trade with China took place. Iha Fuyū (1974a, 93) noted that Shō Hashi's inability to control Katsuren shows that his was not a centralized government with widespread authority. Iha was correct about the limited extent of Hashi's control. I would add that we have no indication that Hashi even sought control over Katsuren or any other territory outside of the Shuri-Naha area, with the possible exception of Nakijin.

Hashi became sole trade king with Chinese backing, and it also appears that Chinese merchant officials directed Hashi's government, such as it was. Indeed, the change to a single trade king may have been mainly the merchant-officials' attempt to gain better control over the tribute trade. Whatever the degree of local Chinese political control may have been during Hashi's reign, Shō Taikyū's seizure of the throne in 1454 ended or greatly reduced it.

The best model for the political geography of Okinawa during the first half of the fifteenth century, and possibly later, is a modified version of that presented in chapter 10 (figure 11.2). Chūzan had become the only banner under which tribute trade to China took place. Another important change was the Muromachi bakufu reaching the peak of its power during the early and mid-fifteenth century. Trade between Ryukyuans and Japanese merchants flourished, and Ashikaga Yoshimitsu established the Ryūkyū bugyō, an office to deal with Ryukyuan ships (Inamura 1969, 234–235, 243).

Like the Sanzan era, the fifteenth century was a time of frequent warfare, especially during the 1450s and 1460s. Warfare is a major theme in the *Omoro sōshi.*

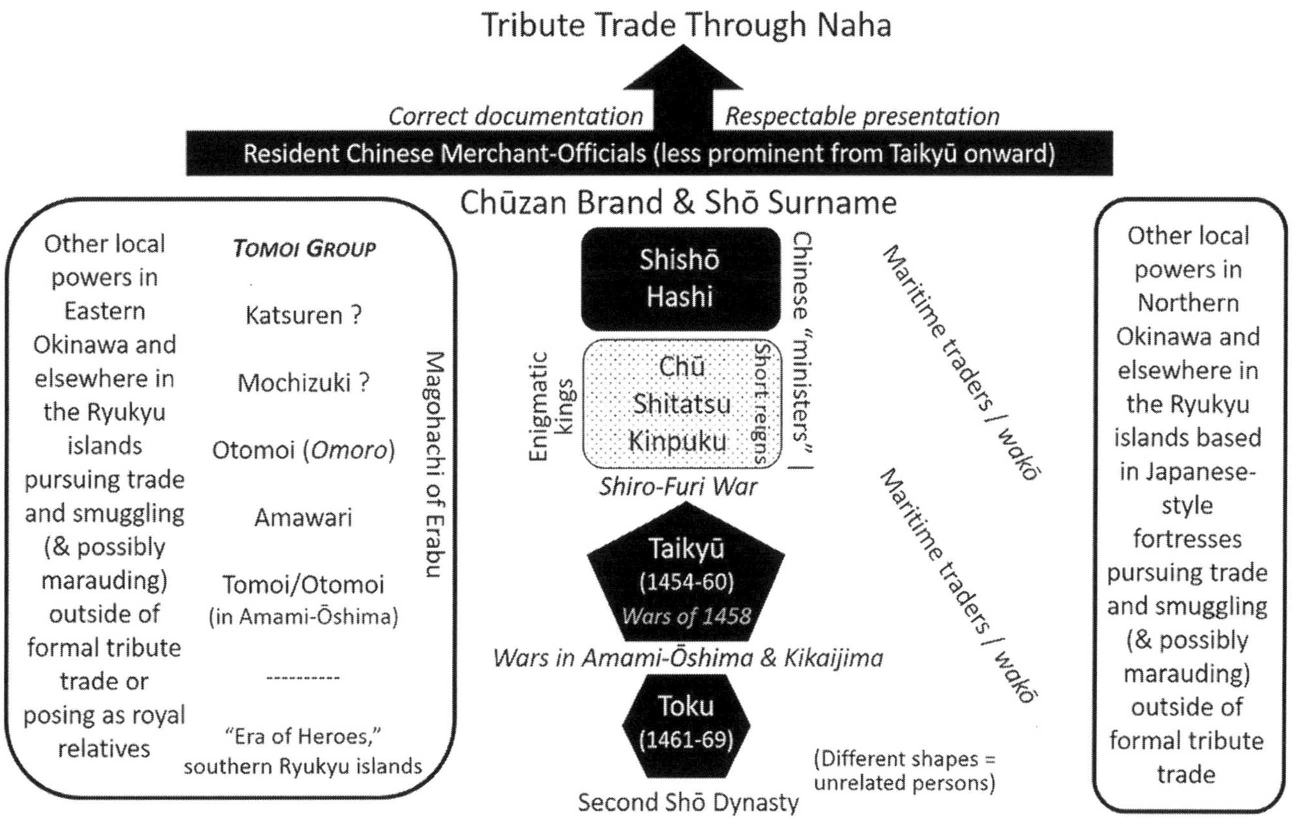

Tribute Trade Through Naha

Correct documentation / *Respectable presentation*

Resident Chinese Merchant-Officials (less prominent from Taikyū onward)

Chūzan Brand & Shō Surname

Other local powers in Northern Okinawa and elsewhere in the Ryukyu islands based in Japanese-style fortresses pursuing trade and smuggling (& possibly marauding) outside of formal tribute trade

Maritime traders / *wakō*

Maritime traders / *wakō*

Chinese "ministers" |

Short reigns

Shishō Hashi

Chū Shitatsu Kinpuku

Enigmatic kings

Shiro-Furi War

Taikyū (1454–60)

Wars of 1458

Toku (1461–69)

Wars in Amami-Ōshima & Kikaijima

Second Shō Dynasty

(Different shapes = unrelated persons)

Magohachi of Erabu

TOMOI GROUP

Katsuren ?

Mochizuki ?

Otomoi (*Omoro*)

Amawari

Tomoi/Otomoi (in Amami-Ōshima)

"Era of Heroes," southern Ryukyu islands

Other local powers in Eastern Okinawa and elsewhere in the Ryukyu islands pursuing trade and smuggling (& possibly marauding) outside of formal tribute trade or posing as royal relatives

Figure 11.2. Model for the era of the First Shō "dynasty".

As one example, the term "island smashing" (*shima-utchi*), with "island" meaning "community," occurs at least once in twenty-eight different songs by my count. Piratical activity comes up in the *Omoro* as well, with one song placing the "king of Okinawa" amid a celebration of a successful raid that has obtained "splendid goods" by "stealth" and "pilfering" (*Omoro sōshi* 10–546; Smits 2019, 90–92). In another, a local power in the island of Kumejima "grabs the valuable goods of other people's harbors" (*Omoro sōshi* 11–597; Smits 2019, 100). I discuss some of the relevant warfare during the era of the First Shō dynasty later in the chapter.

Other conditions carried over from the Three Principalities era. Okinawa and the rest of the Ryukyu Islands were home to local rulers based at fortress-harbor units. These local rulers conducted trade and maintained military forces. Other than the replacement of Urasoe Castle with Shuri Castle as the administrative center of the Naha area, little changed in terms of the geopolitical landscape we examined in previous chapters. The Ryukyu Islands remained the abode of *wakō*, and the Ming dynasty continued its policy of taming these *wakō* groups via generous tribute trade conditions. Outside of the tribute trade, *wakō* powers became especially prominent in the southern Ryukyu Islands during the fifteenth century (Smits 2019, 54–59). Also outside the tribute system was the Tomoi group, discussed in detail later in this chapter. Guraru Magohachi in Okinoerabu appears to have been an ally of Shō Hashi and probably helped Hashi obtain horses for warfare, tribute shipments, or other purposes.

Whatever its origins, Shō Hashi began using the Shō 尚 surname around 1415 while still technically crown prince (*MVR* 2001, 1:23 [#73]; Higa Chōshin 2006, 79).[4] Thereafter, all subsequent kings did so, whether biologically related to their predecessor or not. The origin of the notion that the Ming emperor bestowed the Shō surname on Shō Hashi comes from *Genealogy,* although the dates and details differ in the two versions of that text (*Chūzan seifu* [1701] 1998, 93, 96n8; *Chūzan seifu* [1725] 1988, 58–59). There is no mention of such a bestowal in any Chinese record, nor was bestowing surnames a customary practice. Because George Kerr ([1958] 2000, 89) repeated this claim, it has become well established in Anglophone literature.

Looking at the trade kings of the First Shō dynasty, the most important were Shō Hashi and Shō Taikyū, followed by Shō Toku. Shō Hashi's father, Shishō 思紹, is an enigmatic figure. *Reflections,* for example, mentions him only once in the context of listing Hashi's father (*Reflections* [1650] 2011, 87). The brief paragraph on Shishō in the 1701 *Genealogy* is mostly about Hashi and the envoys sent to China during Shishō's reign (*Chūzan seifu* [1701] 1998, 83–87). Although the

1725 *Genealogy* contains a chapter on Shishō, it says very little about Shishō himself. It identifies Shishō's father as Lord Samekawa but otherwise fills in from the Ming records regarding tribute embassies and details about the various other kings of that era, as well as Hashi's activities (*Chūzan seifu* [1725] 1988, 49–53). In other words, Shō Shishō functioned much as other trade kings, as a name or banner under which Okinawan entities conducted tribute trade.

Likewise, trade kings Shō Chū, Shō Shitatsu, and Shō Kinpuku are enigmatic figures with short reigns. The official histories list only sparse biographical information for them, filled in with material from Chinese records about tribute embassies and their formal recognition as kings. There is no mention of significant domestic activities except that Shō Chū served as overseer of Sanhoku and was based in Nakijin.[5] The *Omoro* is of little help regarding any of these figures. There is no mention of Shō Shitatsu. Two passages mention a Lord Kimishi, and Kimishi was the posthumous divine name of both Shishō and Kinpuku. So the reference is unclear. One passage describes religious rites involving the solar deity at Shuri Castle, and the other passage likens Kimishi's rule to the spiritual power of eagles (*Omoro sōshi* 7–370, 15–1078). In short, like so many of their predecessors, Shō Chū, Shō Shitatsu, and Shō Kinpuku functioned mainly as names under which tribute trade took place. There is nothing we can say about them as people or with respect to any kind of domestic political impact or program.

Shō Hashi

The official histories appear unsure of the origins of Shō Hashi and Shō Shishō. In *Reflections,* Hashi's father was Shishō, lord of Sashiki, and no other family information is provided (*Reflections* [1650] 2011, 87). In the 1701 *Genealogy,* it is the same. Shō Shishō's father, mother, queen, and date of birth are all listed as unknown (*Chūzan seifu* [1701] 1998, 83, 90). The information in the 1725 *Genealogy* for Shishō is the same; however, a parenthetical note cites a collection of official legends (*Irōsetsuden*) that Shishō's father was Lord Samekawa, who came from Iheya Island (*Chūzan seifu* [1725] 1988, 49). Samekawa (O. Samega or Samegaa) was also the father of the Baten priestess, based at the Yamato Banta harbor near Sashiki (*Origins* [1713] 1988, 320; Tanigawa and Orikuchi 2012, 35).

If his official birth date of 1372 is correct, then Shō Hashi was probably born in or near Sashiki in Kyushu, near Yatsushiro. In other words, Shō Hashi was not born in Iheya, Okinawa, or any other Ryukyu island. Following a long line of scholars, I argued in *Maritime Ryukyu* that the Samekawa group were seafarers or *wakō* associated with the Southern Court in Kyushu who migrated to Okinawa in the late fourteenth century (Smits 2019, 107–110; Tanigawa and Orikuchi 2012).[6] The Nawashiro shrine at Sashiki Gusuku in Okinawa indicates that the Samekawa group was a subset of the Nawa of Yatsushiro. Similarly, the "-shō" 紹 in Shishō's name is the same character used in all the posthumous Buddhist names of the heads of the Yatsushiro Nawa (Tanigawa and Orikuchi 2012, 43). *Genealogy*'s placement of Samekawa's birth at Iheya served several purposes, which I have discussed elsewhere (Smits 2019, 151–153). Here I simply note that Iheya situates Samekawa as someone who came into Okinawa from the north. One indication of the close connections between Okinawa and the Yatsushiro area is the frequent mention of "Yashiro" in the *Omoro*, which, following other scholars, I argue is Yatsushiro (Smits 2019, 31–32, 53, 73–74, 108, 258n72).

Like Satto, Shō Hashi was an outsider in terms of his origins. Not surprisingly, the official biographies of Shō Hashi and Jana (Satto) are similar. Both men obtained iron from Japanese ships, used it to make agricultural tools, distributed these tools to the peasants, and thereby improved the peasants' lives (Higa Chōshin 2006, 73). As noted in previous chapters, even though the official biographies claim birth in Okinawa or a nearby island, this motif almost always identifies someone who came into Okinawa from outside the Ryukyu Islands.

Shō Hashi seems to have excelled as a warrior, although he rose to power with some degree of support from Naha's Chinese merchant officials. According to *Kyūyō*, while based at Sashiki, Shō Hashi drilled cavalry forces (*Kyūyō* [1743–1876] 1974, 1978, 117 [#74]; Inamura 1969, 236). The *Omoro* makes a similar point:

At Nawashiro in Sashiki castle
The soldiers are spirited
They compete to display their power
At splendid Nawashiro in Sashiki castle
The troops shout "Sare, sare!" [before their commander]
The troops shout, "Doke, doke!"
Competing to display their power.
(*Omoro sōshi* 19–1297)

Inamura Kenpu has pointed out that this song preserves medieval Japanese military language. *Sare* was a greeting, said to one's commander or superior, and *doke* was a term shouted to disperse civilians who might be in the way, meaning something like "Out of the way!" (Inamura 1969, 236).

By 1430, Shō Hashi, the powerful warlord, had become king of the tribute trade. However, the extent to which he administered that trade is unclear, nor were there any domestic policies associated with Hashi. During the reigns of Shishō and Hashi, Chinese "ministers" (e.g., Yà Lánpáo; see chapter 10) and merchant-officials took care of administering trade, erecting monuments, and even maintaining the elaborate landscaping around Shuri Castle (Smits 2019, 84, 93, 111–113). Among these ministers, the standout figure was Prime Minister (*kokusō*) Kaiki (Ch. Huái Jī, dates unclear), who appears to have been the de facto ruler of the Naha area during the reigns of Shō Hashi through Shō Kinpuku. The relative domestic calm during this era may have been the result of Kaiki's firm control.

Several scholars have noted that one reason for Shō Hashi's success was that he traded Chinese porcelain and other goods for weapons from Japan (e.g., Inamura 1969, 235; Higa Chōshin 2006, 77). This surmise is reasonable based on the archaeological evidence, but weapons, many of Japanese origin or design, have been excavated at many *gusuku* sites. In other words, Shō Hashi was not unique or distinctive in his day because he obtained weapons from Japan via trade.

Shō Hashi's major accomplishment was prevailing in the maelstrom of warfare during the late Sanzan era and thereby becoming the sole Okinawan under whose name tribute trade with China could proceed. He was also, at least nominally, the one who built the first version of Shuri Castle. That he purportedly founded a dynasty and gained political control over all of Okinawa are accomplishments ascribed to him much later, in vastly different circumstances than those of the early fifteenth century.

Shō Taikyū

By conquering several major centers in eastern Okinawa, Shō Taikyū made strides in the direction of unifying Okinawa under a single ruler. Trade with Japan had become highly profitable by the 1450s, and these two centers had well-developed trade networks that extended north. It made economic sense, therefore, that Taikyū sought to conquer these locations. Whether Taikyū planned further conquest is unknown.

Taikyū was a local ruler in Goeku who took the throne in Shuri in the wake of, and likely as a result of, warfare that destroyed parts of Shuri Castle (Smits 2019, 113–116). The traditional date of Shō Kinpuku's death is 1453. An entry in the Ming records for 1454.2 explains that an envoy arrived from Shō Taikyū, younger brother of the recently deceased king Shō Kinpuku. The envoy explained to Ming officials that warfare had recently broken out between Kinpuku's next youngest brother, Furi 布里, and Kinpuku's son, Shiro 志魯. In the process the royal storehouse had caught fire, melting the royal seal. Furi and Shiro had both died of their wounds. The envoy reported that Taikyū had taken over the reins of government and requested a new seal (*MVR* 2003, 2:19 [#70]). Archaeological excavations at the most likely site of the 1453 fire have unearthed extensive fragments of military gear (Yoshinari 2015, 125).

Kaiki, likely the de facto ruler of the Naha area during Shō Hashi's lifetime, continued to "serve" Shō Chū, Shitatsu, and Kinpuku. According to *Kyūyō*, during Kinpuku's reign Kaiki made major improvements to the port of Naha, including construction of a long levee and bridge (*chōkōtei*) in 1451 or 1452 to facilitate travel between Shuri and Naha (*Kyūyō* [1743–1876] 1974, 1978, 124–125 [#98]). All evidence indicates that Kaiki died sometime during Shō Kinpuku's reign. I agree with Murai Shōsuke (2019, 124) that Kaiki's death likely ushered in a period of warfare and instability, starting with the Shiro-Furi war.

Warfare of some kind broke out in 1453, causing damage to Shuri Castle. Taikyū emerged from this warfare in control of Shuri Castle and its surroundings. Nothing else in the official account is certain. According to the *Omoro*, Taikyū was born in Goeku, and his father was the ruler of Goeku (*Omoro sōshi* 2–78). The official histories disagree with each other regarding basic biographical information. According to *Reflections* and the 1701 *Genealogy*, Taikyū was Kinpuku's son (*Reflections* [1650] 2011, 112; *Chūzan seifu* [1701] 1998, 105). According to the 1725 *Genealogy*, Taikyū was the son of Shō Hashi—that is, Kinpuku's brother (*Chūzan seifu* [1725] 1988, 68). Most secondary sources accept the 1725 *Genealogy* account uncritically. As for Shiro and Furi, although they appear in the official histories, their status cannot otherwise be verified. One possible scenario is that Shiro and Furi, whoever they were, went to war in an effort to gain the throne and killed or weakened each other. Then Taikyū of Goeku moved in and took over. Another scenario is that it was a three-way contest from the start. Interestingly, although the official histories state that both Shiro and Furi died from wounds, local legends assert that Furi survived and went into hiding. Furi has a tomb in Fusato (southern Okinawa), but any possible locus of Shiro's remains is unknown (Higa Chōshin 2006, 31, 47, 81).

The major accomplishment of Shō Taikyū was to expand significantly the scope of his control beyond the tribute trade with China and beyond the west coast of Okinawa. *Omoro sōshi* 13–939 describes the wealth Katsuren accumulated from its ships. In the last line, someone named Mashifuri controls the ships, although his precise capacity is unclear. Omitting the technical details, some scholars have proposed that this Mashifuri refers to Furi of the Shiro-Furi war (Naze-shi 1996 [Ōyama Ringorō], 250; Takahashi Ichirō 2008, 165–166). Although this point about Mashifuri is speculative, coming from Goeku in central Okinawa, Taikyū would have been familiar with the wealth and power of nearby Katsuren Gusuku and the newer Nakagusuku Gusuku. As we have seen, both of these places were enmeshed in networks of trade with the northern Ryukyu Islands and points farther north.

Ezu Gusuku and Katsuren Gusuku, both located near each other, shared a close connection. According to one legend, Furi once dwelled in Ezu 江州 Gusuku (modern Esu, at the head of the Katsuren Peninsula). After losing out in the war, Furi went into hiding, and Taikyū sent one of his sons to rule Ezu (Higa Chōshin 2006, 112). In the 1725 *Genealogy,* Sai On added a note about this matter, concluding that it is impossible to know which of Taikyū's sons was lord of Ezu (*Chūzan seifu* [1725] 1988, 68). In any case it is likely that a relative of Taikyū took control of Ezu Gusuku during Taikyū's reign. Later, Taikyū's daughter, Momotofumiagari 百度踏揚, married Amawari of Katsuren. Although the details are obscure, it appears that from the start of his reign Taikyū laid the groundwork for connecting himself with Katsuren (Takahashi Ichirō 2008, 170).

There is much we do not know about Taikyū's conquest of Katsuren. The chapter on Taikyū in *Reflections* is extremely brief. Other than mentioning his formal recognition by the Ming emperor, it states that Taikyū was active in establishing Buddhist temples and installing large bells in them (*Reflections* [1650] 2011, 112–113). It is almost as if the author of *Reflections,* Shō Shōken, did not want to dwell on this awkward member of the line. Similarly, the 1701 *Genealogy* has little to say about Taikyū, but it provides an outline of the conquest story. Amawari of Katsuren convinced Taikyū that Gosamaru of Nakagusuku was plotting against the king. Taikyū ordered Amawari to destroy Gosamaru. Soon thereafter, Amamwari plotted to seize the throne, but the loyalty of his daughter Momotofumiagari and her soon-to-be-new-husband Oni-Ōgusuku saved the day for Taikyū (*Chūzan seifu* [1701] 1998, 105–106). Sai On's *Genealogy* and *Kyūyō* contain the same story in a more detailed and dramatic version. Notice that the official histories assume an Okinawa united under one king from as far back as Eiso's time. Therefore, in their pages local warfare had to be framed in terms of loyalty or disloyalty to the throne.

The accounts in the official histories resemble classic war stories, with Gosamaru as the typical Japanese tragic hero. They are not believable in their particulars. By the end of 1458, Taikyū or his allies such as Ōni-Ōgusuku controlled Goeku, Nakagusuku, Ezu, and Katsuren. It would be fascinating to know exactly how he pulled it off. Prior to Taikyū, to be "king" of Chūzan meant being the person under whose name the tribute trade with China and trade with the

Korean court took place. It was a lucrative position, and the kings in Shuri of this era were potential targets of ambitious outsiders such as Taikyū (and possibly Furi and/or Shiro). Taikyū's significance was that he added northern trade routes and territory within Okinawa to the royal portfolio. Taikyū took significant steps in the direction of creating a unified Okinawa, but he died in 1460 in his midforties. No cause of death is stated, but given that Taikyū's allies went into hiding when Shō Toku took the throne, Taikyū's death may not have been a natural one.

With his conquest of Katsuren, Taikyū wrested control of the two major centers in Okinawa that traded with Korea. In a very concrete sense, therefore, Taikyū had "gathered the excellence of Korea," to quote from his Sea Bridge to the Many Countries Bell inscription discussed previously. An additional important point to make about this bell is that no king before Taikyū would plausibly have been able to make the claims stated in the bell's inscription. After seizing control of at least some of the northern trade routes previously maintained by Nakagusuku and Katsuren, Taikyū's Shuri became the center of trade with Korea, China, and Japan, although still not the exclusive center. Notice also that in the context of its time, and contrary to modern claims, this bell inscription was anything but an indication of a peaceful Ryukyu Kingdom.

Taikyū was probably a devout Buddhist personally. Nevertheless, his establishment of temples and the casting of bells for them (by Japanese technicians) also functioned as symbolic legitimation of his rule. Moreover, Taikyū was one of only three Ryukyuan kings who minted coins bearing their divine names. The others were Shō Toku and Shō En (Kanemaru). This minting of coins was of no importance economically. It, too, functioned to bolster the legitimacy of three men who took the throne by force (Smits 2019, 117).

The extensive warfare in and around the Ryukyu Islands deserves a book of its own. Here I briefly mention that both Shō Taikyū and Shō Toku conducted military operations in the Kasari Peninsula of Amami-Ōshima and sought to conquer Kikaijima. In the official histories, Shō Toku is the one credited with the final conquest of Kikaijima, but a variety of sources make clear that military forces connected with Shuri had been attempting to conquer the island since the 1450s (Smits 2019, 117–120). Recall that Katsuren either controlled Kikaijima or was at least closely connected with the island. It makes sense, therefore, that after Taikyū conquered Katsuren he and his successor would try to bring Kikaijima firmly into their portfolios of valuable harbors and trading centers.

Shō Taikyū's reign marked a significant turning point for several reasons. First, the days of high-ranking Chinese "ministers" ended with Taikyū, never to return. Offsetting the former influence of powerful Chinese was an influx of

Buddhist priests from Japan.[7] Indeed, from Shō Taikyū's time onward, Japanese cultural and technical influence had been increasing at Shuri. Taikyū's kingdom still resembled a shipping corporation, but a significantly expanded and more powerful one. For the first time, an Okinawan king could plausibly claim that his operation was a "bridge to the many countries."

Korean observers during the reigns of Shō Taikyū and Toku describe a complex society in the Naha area, one rooted in significant royal military and judicial powers. Although they mention social hierarchies, they do not describe formal ranks or offices demarcated by, for example, different colors of caps or any kind of organization resembling the *hiki* system, both of which we find in the sixteenth century. The king presided personally over disputes or criminal accusations instead of relying on a judicial system, and there is no mention of written documents for administrative purposes. Although the Korean observers described food and agriculture in detail, nobody described anything resembling a tax system.[8] Finally, Taikyū's power, while more extensive than his predecessors, did not encompass all of Okinawa. In short, Shō Taikyū more closely resembled a powerful chieftain than the ruler of a bureaucratic state. Nevertheless, his significantly expanded trading operation set the stage for the potential emergence of a centralized state.

Shō Toku

Like so many early trade kings, Shō Toku is a mysterious figure. According to *Reflections,* he was either the third son of Taikyū or the seventh (*Reflections* [1650] 2011, 21, 114, 116n2). Also, his "rule was more violent than that of Jié and Zhòu," making reference to two classical Chinese bête noire rulers, the last kings of the Xia and Zhou dynasties, respectively (*Reflections* [1650] 2011, 21). The relatively short chapter on Shō Toku emphasizes his flawed and violent personality and goes into detail about his leading an army of two thousand to conquer Kikaijima. It describes the violence of the Okinawan force in detail, including the burning of civilian houses and, after their surrender, the killing of the Kikaijima leaders "one by one."[9] After the description of the campaign comes a quotation from Mencius about governing by means of benevolence, wisdom, and respect, followed by a lament that if only Shō Toku had operated this way, the people of Kikaijima would have willingly submitted tribute, and the brutal war would have been avoided (*Chūzan seikan* 1650, 114–116). Based on this passage, it would appear that the conquest of Kikaijima was extremely violent and costly in terms of lives and good relations, and *Reflections* seeks to make the allegedly depraved king into a scapegoat.

Interestingly, the 1701 *Genealogy* presents a more compact, clinical account of the conquest and leaves out the passage from Mencius and other classical Chinese moralizing. Without specifically arguing a causal relationship, it states that after returning from the campaign, Shō Toku grew ever more depraved and "killed blameless people capriciously." Perhaps referring to Taikyū's allies, the text explains that "good ministers hid in the forests and mountains" (*Chūzan seifu* [1701] 1998, 108–109). The 1725 *Genealogy*, in addition to including information from Ming records about tribute embassies that went to China under Shō Toku's name, includes details about Toku's behavior during the conquest of Kikai that are *wakō* specific (*Chūzan seifu* [1725] 1988, 73–74). These details include a bird shot out of the sky as a good omen, the miracle of a large temple bell floating on the waves, and the establishment of a shrine to Hachiman upon his return (Smits 2019, 118–119).

There is no cause listed for Shō Toku's death after a reign of about eight years, but the official histories note that his surviving family were slaughtered while hiding in one of Shuri Castle's sacred groves. This area of the castle later became known as Kundagusuku, and the remains became the focus of a popular cult of the power of royal bones, possibly a version of older Korean bone cults (Smits 2019, 122–124). According to the official histories, the coup d'état that brought Kanemaru to the throne as Shō En took place after Shō Toku died (cause of death not mentioned). However, according to one legend, Shō Toku became enamored of an eighteen-year-old priestess while visiting Kudakajima to perform religious rites. He lingered on the island with the priestess after the rites ended. In his absence, Kanemaru and his partisans seized the throne. Hearing of the coup from a fishing boat while returning to Shuri from Kudakajima, Shō Toku threw himself into the sea to drown (Takeuchi [1933] 1960, 82). While the Kudakajima material is probably anachronistic, it is entirely likely that Shō Toku did not die naturally.

Few sources about Shō Toku are available other than official trade records and the official histories. He appears to have indeed been a *wakō* whose group managed to seize power from Shō Taikyū and enjoy the benefits of the tribute trade for a while. He also likely engaged in warfare in Kikaijima. In general, however, Shō Toku's reign is a blank space. A probable backlash from remnants of Taikyū's group led to the violent end of Toku's group and the ascent to the throne of yet another outsider, Kanemaru, who may have been an associate of Taikyū.

The Tomoi Group

In chapter 10, we examined the Eiso line and the Satto group in as much detail as the limited sources currently permit. In this section I introduce the Tomoi group, assisted to a substantial degree by the historical detective work of Takahashi Ichirō (2008).

In Korean records there are nine instances of someone posing as a younger brother of the Ryukyuan king and calling himself Tomoi 等悶意 or Otomoi 弟閔意.[10] In each case, Tomoi or Otomoi dispatched an envoy and presented tribute to the Korean court, ostensibly on behalf of the Ryukyu court. The dates of each occurrence are 1468, 1470, 1480, 1509, 1519, 1523, 1525, 1527, and 1533. In many of these instances, Tomoi/Otomoi titles himself 琉球国中平田大島平州守 等悶意, which, for reasons explained below, I render as "Otomoi, Lord of Ezu in Heda, Ōshima, Ryukyu" (*JVRR-r* 2005, 180).

This Tomoi group was probably based in Amami-Ōshima, at least loosely. Most likely it was a mobile group of seafarers who opposed the Ryukyuan court at Shuri (Takahashi Ichirō 2008, 162–164). The origins of the Tomoi group, however, were probably at Katsuren and the nearby Japanese-style trench-and-earth-works fortress of Ezu.

Recall the *Omoro* songs describing the ships and sailors of Katsuren functioning as a bridge to Amami-Ōshima and Kikaijima. Now consider the following *omoro,* which makes a similar point:

The people of Katsuren take to the sea
Take to the sea and reap profits
From Tokunoshima and Amami-Ōshima
And connect to the mainland
Otomoi takes to the sea.
(*Omoro sōshi* 13–867)

The "mainland" in the fourth line may refer to Japan, Korea, or both places. The final line is especially important. It mentions someone like Taiki, someone (or several people using that name) whose name is also found in official sources. If we take the usual variation in "spelling" (glossing the names of Ryukyuan people using Chinese characters) that we have previously seen into account, the name of this person or group is Tomoi or Otomoi.

According to Takahashi, this *omoro* dates to the early fifteenth century because it is in close proximity to an *omoro* (*Omoro sōshi* 13–862) about the Baten priestess (Takahashi Ichirō 2008, 166). Baten is a place in Sashiki, closely connected with the Samekawa family and Shō Hashi. Indeed, the Baten priestess was active during the early and middle fifteenth century. We also know from archaeological evidence that Katsuren was especially active in international trade between about 1350 and the late 1450s. Therefore, the early fifteenth century is entirely possible, although we cannot date *omoro* 13–867 with precision.

Looking more closely at Katsuren, Amawari was its lord in 1458 when Shō Taikyū conquered it. We do not know when Amawari became the ruler of Katsuren, but according to legend, Amawari killed Katsuren's previous lord, Mochizuki (Iha 1974a, 94–96). If so, then Mochizuki was a local ruler based in Katsuren sometime in the early fifteenth century. Several *omoro* mention a shamanic female dancer and priestess, Agaru-mochizuki. One of them, situated in a series of *omoro* about Katsuren and Amawari, mentions an Agaru-mochizuki who Hokama and Saigō state was Amawari's first wife (*Omoro sōshi* 16–1132; Hokama and Saigō 1972, 373).

Recall that the Tomoi and Otomoi of the late fifteenth and early sixteenth centuries posed as the younger brother of the Ryukyuan king. Such posturing vis-à-vis Korea is recorded as early as 1418. In that year, someone calling himself Katsuren 賀通連 (*JVRR-r* 2005, 48) or Katsuren-Gusuku 賀通連寓鎖 (*East Sea Countries* [1471] 1991, 233) and stating that he was the second son of the king of Chūzan sent an envoy to Korea bearing a letter and a variety of gifts. In *Maritime Ryukyu* I stated that this person was probably Shō Hashi (Smits 2019, 110). However, after further work I think a better interpretation is that this person was the ruler of Katsuren, possibly Mochizuki, or his representative. In other words, this person had no family connection to any king. He was conducting trade and diplomacy with Korea under the legitimizing cover of the tribute trade. This 1418 Katsuren may also have been the earliest manifestation of the Tomoi group.

Omoro sōshi 16–1163 sings of the close relationship between Katsuren and adjacent Ezu Gusuku, discussed previously. *Omoro sōshi* 16–1132 describes the shamanic figure Agaru-mochizuki and her magnificent dwelling in Katsuren Castle (Hokama and Saigō 1972, 373), or possibly the sacred stone located in the main enclosure (Inamura 1969, 101–102).[11] The men of Ezu visit Katsuren and are impressed. In the final line of the song, these men of Ezu are characterized as "followers of our father, the ruler." Whether this ruler was Mochizuki or Amawari we cannot know, but the key point here is that Ezu and Katsuren were part of the same organization.

Ezu was a Japanese-style trench-and-earthworks fortress, of the type common in Amami-Ōshima. It was also the site of a large storehouse, which may have functioned as a marketplace (*Omoro sōshi* 16–1160). If the 平州 in Otomoi's title is Hezu, then it probably indicated Ezu (Takahashi Ichirō 2008, 168–169). Moreover, it appears that Ezu in Okinawa had connections with Amami-Ōshima. A sacred song describes the priestess of Ezu village as "Amamiwainoro" (Amami parent priestess; Hokama and Tamaki 1980, 384 [#148]; Takahashi Ichirō 2008, 169).

BASIC LINEAGE OF THE TOMOI GROUP

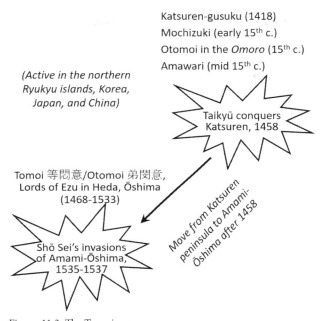

Katsuren-gusuku (1418)
Mochizuki (early 15th c.)
Otomoi in the *Omoro* (15th c.)
Amawari (mid 15th c.)

(Active in the northern Ryukyu islands, Korea, Japan, and China)

Taikyū conquers Katsuren, 1458

Tomoi 等悶意/Otomoi 弟悶意, Lords of Ezu in Heda, Ōshima (1468-1533)

Move from Katsuren peninsula to Amami-Ōshima after 1458

Shō Sei's invasions of Amami-Ōshima, 1535-1537

Figure 11.3. The Tomoi group.

Therefore, early in the fifteenth century Katsuren and its associated fortress Ezu constituted a wealthy, powerful, politically independent naval and trade base occupying the Katsuren Peninsula in eastern Okinawa. This base had close ties to the northern Ryukyu Islands, Korea, Japan, and China (figure 11.3). The *Omoro* portrays its ruler in the 1450s, Amawari, as a person of immense power and far-reaching influence:

Amawari of Katsuren
With the jeweled ladle
As far as Kyō[to] and Kamakura
Your voice resounds and reverberates
Powerful Amawari.
(*Omoro sōshi* 16–1134)

Recall from an earlier discussion that the *Omoro* also likened Katsuren to "Kamakura in Yamato."

We have established a rough lineage of key Katsuren/Ezu personnel: Katsuren-Gusuku (1418)—Mochizuki (early fifteenth century)—Otomoi of the *Omoro* (fifteenth century)—Amawari (middle fifteenth century)—Tomoi/Oto-moi, lords of Ezu in Heda, Ōshima (1468–1533). In 1458, Shō Taikyū, the trade king in Shuri, conquered Katsuren. Like all the harbor-fortress pairs we have examined, Katsuren was part of a larger network. Typically, networks are not hierarchical. Taikyū's conquest of Katsuren, therefore, was not a conquest of the entire network. Most likely, the survivors of what for them was a military disaster in 1458 relocated to Amami-Ōshima, where they continued to pursue trade with Japan and Korea (Takahashi Ichirō 2008, 171). For obvious reasons they were not inclined to cooperate with Shuri. These Katsuren remnants in Amami-Ōshima were the Tomoi group. The date of their last recorded activity, 1533, is probably significant. Faced with growing opposition by local powers in Amami-Ōshima, King Shō Sei launched invasions of the island in 1535, fully pacifying it by 1537 (Smits 2019, 184–185). In addition to gaining firmer control over Amami-Ōshima, Shō Sei's invasions probably put the Tomoi group out of business.

Magohachi of Okinoerabu

Guraru (or Goran) Magohachi 後蘭孫八, known in the *Omoro* as Magohatsu, was a *wakō* chief based on the island of Okinoerabu. We do not know his terminal dates, but he was a rough contemporary of Shō Hashi, appears to have been on good terms with Hashi, and was possibly a close ally. Like Taiki and the Tomoi group, Magohachi and his group were maritime traders. They specialized in horses, valuable animals throughout the region (Smits 2019, 71–72).

One *omoro* describes the ships of the ruler of Okinoerabu (Magohachi or someone similarly placed) functioning as a bridge, a description similar to that of Katsuren or Nakagusuku. The next song describes the herd of splendid horses at his disposal. The subsequent song invokes the deity of a local sacred grove to protect a large ship based in Okinoerabu. We have already seen the next two songs in the sequence. They describe the ships of Katsuren functioning as a bridge to various northern Ryukyu Islands, including Okinoerabu (*Omoro sōshi* 13–935, 936, 937, 938, 939). *Omoro* songs in close proximity are often related geographically or topically. In this sequence we see the ruler of Okinoerabu linked to a maritime trade network connected with Katsuren.

"Heroes" of the Southern Ryukyu Islands

Contemporary Japanese writings about the Three Principalities and First Shō dynasty eras in Okinawa, especially pieces written for general audiences, often refer to the kings and combatants as "heroes" (*eiyū*). Likewise, in the southern Ryukyu Islands the fifteenth century is often known as the "era of heroes." In this case the heroes were locally powerful people who, at least according to legend, often waged war against each other. As Inamura Kenpu (1957) demonstrated in the late 1950s, most or all of these local powers were *wakō* groups. I have summarized some of this legendary material in *Maritime Ryukyu,* making the point that many of the narratives tie into Shuri's invasion of Yaeyama in 1500, the so-called Akahachi or Honkawara "revolt" (Smits 2019, 53–59).

As we have seen, trade networks in the Ryukyu Islands were based at harbors. These harbors were not the capitals of land-based territorial states but hubs connected to other harbors by sea lanes. With this arrangement in mind, it is possible that Nakasone, the most powerful figure in Miyako and a brief ally of Shuri in 1500, controlled parts of the Yaeyama island of Iriomote prior to 1500. The economic dynamic was that Miyako was a center for trade, but as a low island, Miyako lacked timber. The nearest timber suitable for shipbuilding was in Iriomote, Kuroshima, and other locations in Yaeyama. Therefore, powers in Miyako obtained lumber or actual ships (*komibune* were ships built in Komi, Iriomote) from Yaeyama (Shimamura 2008, 306–309, 319–321). Our sources for this era are songs, legends, and various *yuraiki* (collections of origin tales) written in the early modern era, and they are not in agreement. Nevertheless, the general image of the southern Ryukyu Islands during the fifteenth century is one of local warlords competing for resources. Moreover, Miyako appears to have been the most powerful location.

Recall that settlements in Miyako increased dramatically during the fourteenth century. Recall also that people based at Bora (Boranomotojima) in Miyako traded with entities in China and in Southeast Asia (chapters 2 and 8). The image of Ryukyuans boldly sailing to Southeast Asia to trade probably applies to parts of the southern Ryukyu Islands and to the era before 1500. This trade took place in Uruka ships and other vessels made in the southern Ryukyu Islands, as opposed to Shuri's tribute trade, which took place in Chinese ships with Chinese captains and officers.

During the fourteenth century, Chinese ceramics began to accumulate at a number of sites in Miyako, and during the fifteenth century, nearly every harbor or settlement in the southern Ryukyu Islands saw a vast increase in Chinese trade ceramics. For example, Nagura Bay on the west side of Ishigaki was a major location for this trade. Several thousand pieces of fifteenth- and sixteenth-century Chinese whiteware and blueware have been excavated from the bottom of the bay at the Shitadaru Seafloor site. These goods must have come from a sunken Chinese trade ship, and they indicate the extensive trade in the southern Ryukyu Islands (Ōhama 2008, 368). Incidentally, at least according to the *Kyūyō* account, Nagura Bay (Arakawa and Tōnoshiro on the southern side) was where Shuri's forces attacked in 1500 (*Kyūyō* [1743–1867] 1974, 1978, 148 [#160]). Trade with Okinawa is one possible source of Chinese goods in the southern Ryukyu Islands, but it cannot account for the large quantities that have been excavated. Significantly, the origin of many of the fifteenth-century Chinese ceramics in the southern Ryukyu Islands was Fújiàn (Shimoji 2008, 343). Clearly, some Chinese vessels sailed to the southern Ryukyu Islands, and some southern Ryukyuan vessels sailed to the Fújiàn area. This fifteenth-century trade would have been illegal, at least from an official Ming perspective.

According to *Kyūyō*, "tribute" coming from the southern Ryukyu Islands made Chūzan strong (*Kyūyō* [1743–1876] 1974, 1978, 105 [#43]). What this statement means is that the traders operating in Naha received valuable tropical products from the southern Ryukyu Islands, which originated in Southeast Asia. Traders operating under the Chūzan banner (and probably Sannan as well) could then ship these items to China and Korea. In 1390, for the first time, pepper and sappanwood were listed as tribute items from Ryukyu, in addition to the usual horses and sulfur (*MVR* 2001 1:13–14 [#31]). Most likely, contact with Miyako enabled Chūzan to send those tropical products, which were much valued in China.[12] Moreover, the first official trade with Korea was in 1389. Pepper and sappanwood were listed in the items Chūzan sent to Korea along with Koreans who had been captured by *wakō* (Ikeya, Uchida, and Takase 2005, 141–142). It is also possible that *wakō* in the southern Ryukyu Islands captured or transported those Koreans to Naha (Shimoji 2008, 342, citing Sunagawa Akifusa).

The southern Ryukyu Islands were not under the control of Shuri until the sixteenth century. Additional military action was needed after the Yaeyama invasion of 1500 to eliminate Nakasone in Miyako and to conquer Yonaguni (Shimamura 2008, 323; Smits 2019, 167–171). The official histories imply that the southern Ryukyu Islands had been subordinate to Shuri before the "revolt" of 1500, but that inference is part of the general trend of these works to push state and empire formation back far earlier than the evidence available today warrants. Although not part of a relationship of political subordination, we have indirect evidence of trade between Miyako and Naha as early as the 1380s. There is also good evidence for trade between Miyako, China, and Southeast Asia from the early fourteenth century. The southern Ryukyu Islands were probably a significant source of tropical products that powers in the Naha area used in tribute trade and in trade with Korea and Japan.

The scale of illegal trade with China in the southern Ryukyu Islands during the fifteenth century was vast. Although many details and motivations of Okinawan military campaigns in the area between 1500 and circa the 1520s remain obscure, it is likely that the Ming court looked favorably upon Shuri's move to conquer the region.

Spurious Envoys

In *Maritime Ryukyu* I briefly discussed the phenomenon of *wakō* based in Tsushima or Hakata falsely posing as Ryukyuan envoys to the Korean court. This phenomenon appears to have started in 1423, at the end of the era of the Three Principalities, and false envoys posing as Ryukyuans remained a problem for Korean officials into the sixteenth century.[13] In some cases the envoys purported to represent kings who had died some years earlier (Smits 2019, 72–73).[14] Hakata merchants posing as Ryukyuans even created a system of tallies (*wariin*), completely independent of any Ryukyuan trade king, to authenticate their spurious embassies to Korea (Hashimoto 2005, 99–102, 109–110).

The activities of Dōan in 1453 (chapter 8) opened the doors to spurious envoys. Dōan himself was a legitimate envoy, but he was based in Hakata. Soon after Dōan, other Hakata- and Tsushima-based merchants tried their hands at passing for envoys of Ryukyuan trade kings (Murai 2019, 296–299).[15] The phenomenon of spurious envoys was another manifestation of the fact that the main function of trade kings was as names under which official trade took place. Those royal names took on a life of their own in Hakata and Tsushima during the fifteenth century.

Consider the typical case of a group of *wakō* showing up in Korea with forged documents purportedly issued by an Okinawan king who in fact was deceased at the time the documents were made. Such actions were essentially the same as Okinawans sending embassies to China under the name of Satto or Han'anchi years after these men died (assuming they were ever living individuals).

Similarly, ambitious merchants in Japan used shogunal names for the same purpose. During the late fifteenth and early sixteenth centuries, Japanese merchants posed as representatives of the Muromachi bakufu, or as major bakufu retainers, in an attempt to conduct foreign trade (Hashimoto 2008, 301–302, 306–307; Smits 2019, 144–145). Many spurious embassies to Korea, whether posing as representatives of an Okinawan king or the bakufu, succeeded in their quest for trade because of Korean ignorance of conditions in Japan or the Ryukyu Islands (Hashimoto 2008, 302, 306, 310). Taking the logic of spurious names, people, and places to its extreme, around 1478 a group of Japanese merchants arrived in Korea representing a spurious country they called Jiǔbiān 久邊 (reading the name as Chinese). Among other things, when questioned by Korean officials the merchants claimed that the spoken language of Jiǔbiān was a mixture of Chinese and Ryukyuan (Robinson 1997, 62–68; Smits 2019, 73).[16]

The phenomenon of conducting official trade with Korea or China under a royal or shogunal name that may or may not have corresponded to a living person was not limited to Okinawa and Japan. Owing to the logic of Ming tribute relations, during the fourteenth and fifteenth centuries hundreds of spurious embassies from central Asia and some maritime locations presented themselves to the Ming court (Robinson 1997, 60–62). Hashimoto Yū (2008, 311) notes that the problem of spurious envoys appears to have been common throughout East and Southeast Asian states during the fifteenth and sixteenth centuries. Seen in the larger context of Ming-centered diplomatic and trading networks, that Okinawan trade kings functioned mainly as names under which to conduct official trade was not unique or unusual. This phenomenon was mainly a reflection of the logic inherent in Ming foreign relations.

Between roughly 1429 and 1458, geopolitical and economic conditions in the Ryukyu Islands changed little compared with the previous Three Principalities era. The volume of tribute trade with China remained high, although it took place under the auspices of a single trade king, not multiple kings. Harbor-fortress pairs remained the main geopolitical unit. Trade between entities in the Ryukyu Islands and counterparts in Japan and Korea remained vigorous, and the Muromachi bakufu established an office specifically to handle Ryukyuan trade early in the century. Shō Hashi did not unite all Okinawa under his rulership, nor did he seem interested in doing so. He was king of the tribute trade, not king of Okinawa.

The rise of Shō Taikyū in the wake of the Shiro-Furi war changed the geopolitical landscape to some extent. Taikyū and his allies conquered Nakagusuku and Katsuren, two powerful harbor-fortress pairs with close ties to harbors in the northern Ryukyu Islands and ultimately to Japan and Korea. Although not the ruler of all Okinawa, Shō Taikyū became by far the most powerful warlord in Okinawa, at least briefly.[17] The extent to which Shō Toku inherited Taikyū's territory and networks is unclear. In any event, both Shō Taikyū and Shō Toku sought to conquer Kikaijima, an island with close ties to Katsuren. Their difficulty in doing so, despite Toku's ultimate success, suggests ongoing resistance even after Katsuren itself fell in 1458. The activity of the Tomoi group also helps bring the geopolitical situation into sharper relief. After Taikyū's conquest of Katsuren and nearby Ezu Gusuku, the Tomoi group relocated to Amami-Ōshima and continued trading, or attempting to trade, with Korea. They probably also traded with entities in Japan, but the Korean trade is documented. In addition to the Tomoi group, local powers such as Guraru Magohachi in Okinoerabu and *wakō* groups operating in the southern Ryukyu Islands pursued trade and warfare independent of Shuri until the sixteenth century.

CHAPTER TWELVE

The Second Shō Dynasty and the Creation of a Centralized State

According to the official biography, a farmer named Kanemaru from the island of Izena fled to northern Okinawa with his brother after angering his neighbors in a water dispute. Despite his humble origins, Kanemaru ended up working as Shō Taikyū's harbor chief in Naha. After Shō Toku's rise to power, Kanemaru went into hiding. Soon after Shō Toku died, "the various officials" appointed the virtuous Kanemaru as king. Taking the throne as Shō En, Kanemaru established the Second Shō dynasty. It is unlikely that any of these official claims are accurate, and *Maritime Ryukyu* provides a detailed, critical account of this era (Smits 2019, 122–147). This chapter extends the discussion in *Maritime Ryukyu* by examining Kanemaru's origins and the cultural policies of Shō Shin and Shō Sei. Like Shō Hashi, Kanemaru was another example of an outsider who came into Okinawa and captured the lucrative tribute trade. Over the course of several decades, Kanemaru's son, Shō Shin, managed to conquer all of Okinawa and most of the other Ryukyu Islands. To administer this territory, Shō Shin established a centralized government in Shuri, and his successor, Shō Sei, built up its physical, ritual, and cultural infrastructure. By the 1530s, the Ryukyu Kingdom had become a reality in both name and substance.

Kanemaru and the Kawara *Wakō*

According to the official histories, Kanemaru (金丸, also pronounced Kanamaru and Kanimaru), a former official of Shō Taikyū, became king almost against his will. After Shō Toku's death in 1469, a vaguely defined group of "officials" met and decided to offer the throne to Kanemaru, who at the time was in hiding in Uchima in central Okinawa. According to this far-fetched tale, Kanemaru declined the throne twice before finally accepting. His first order as king was the killing of Shō Toku's wife and child (Smits 2019, 122–123).

In the *Omoro* are two names for Kanemaru: Kanemaru and Onisanko. As king, he is known as Shō En, founder of the Second Shō dynasty. We have seen that the founders of the First Sho dynasty came from Sashiki in Kyushu, near Yatsushiro. Kanemaru was also an outsider from the North, but tracing his roots has proven to be more difficult. One problem is that we have no idea who his father was. Nevertheless, by bringing several lines of evidence together, it is possible to draw some conclusions about the likely geographic origins of the Second Shō dynasty.

Throughout the Ryukyu and Tokara Islands, and extending to northwest Kyushu, we find place-names that were closely associated with *wakō*. In *Maritime Ryukyu*, my general term for them was "Gaara group names." Examples include Gara, Gaara, Goriya, Guraru, and Gura. They originally meant "head," as in the leader or chief of a group. Importantly, the name Kawara is one of the Gaara group names, and the term "Honkawara" means "main or big leader." Groups with the Kawara name settled mainly in Kumejima, an island to the west of Naha, and in the southern Ryukyu Islands (Smits 2019, 101–103).

Kumejima and Its Connections

Kumejima is a small island about ninety-four kilometers west of the port of Naha. The island was of great importance to the origins of the Second Shō dynasty. There were close connections between key institutions of the Second Shō dynasty and Kumejima. The *hiki* system, which organized personnel who functioned as soldiers, sailors, and general-purpose laborers, emerged in connection with Shuri's conquest of Kumejima. Moreover, Shuri's high priestess (Kikoe-ōgimi), several Nakijin priestesses, and the (Oni-)Kimihae priestess of Kumejima were all closely connected with each other. Indeed, there is a rich web of interconnections between Kumejima and its deities, the religious hierarchy that Shō Shin created, the royal rituals created during the reign of Shō Sei, important *ibe* names in sacred groves, and the *Omoro*. Makishi Yōko has explored these connections thoroughly in a recent book examining the origin and nature of royal rituals and institutions during the first half of the sixteenth century (Makishi 2023; also Smits 2019, 175–177). Kumejima, also known as Kaneshima (metal island) in the *Omoro*, was a valuable source of iron. Furnaces there produced iron from iron sand, and the island itself was a natural fortress ideally located for control of sea lanes between the Ryukyu Islands and China (Smits 2019, 100–101; Makishi 2023, 243).

Several of the deities of sacred groves in the southern Ryukyu Islands came from Kumejima, which indicates the movement of people (figure 12.1). Especially important is the legend of the three sister deities of Kumejima. The sisters came from Japan and resided for a while at Kumejima. Later, one of them

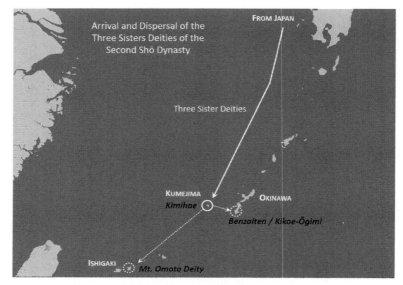

Figure 12.1. Arrival and dispersal of the three sister deities.

went to Okinawa and took up residence at the Ben[zai]ten grove in Shuri, becoming the deity of the Kikoe-ōgimi. One remained in Kumejima as Kimi-hae, and another moved to Ishigaki to reside at Mount Omoto (Smits 2019, 167–168, 198–199). According to legend, therefore, a family of deities arrived from Japan, landed in Kumejima, and soon thereafter settled in Okinawa and Ishigaki.

The Ryukyuan legend does not specify from where in Japan these three female deities came, nor does any other source. Although speculative, one possible connection is the Munakata Shrine in Fukuoka Prefecture, just north of Hakata. The main shrine is located near the coast, in Munakata City. A straight line drawn from Munakata to Busan, South Korea, intersects the island of Ōshima, 11 kilometers offshore, and then the island of Okinoshima, about 49 kilometers from Ōshima. Busan is 145 kilometers west of Okinoshima. The line from Munakata to Busan passes just to the north of Tsushima. Each location enshrines a female deity, and the home shrine for all of them is the Munakata Shrine. These three female deities are sisters, born of Amaterasu and Susanoo. Amaterasu's charge to them was to protect the sea route between Kyushu and Korea.[1]

In addition to the three sisters who came from Japan to Kumejima, there is another migratory deity, or set of deities, who sheds light on Kanemaru's

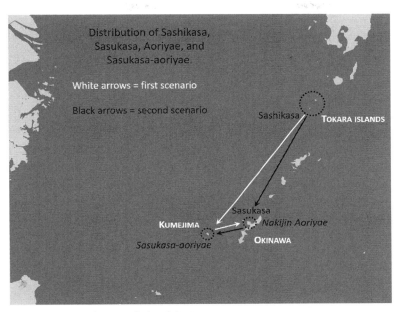

Figure 12.2. Distribution of related deities.

origins (figure 12.2). These deities link Kumejima, Nakijin, and the Tokara Islands. A female deity in the Tokara Islands known as Sashikasa became Sasukasa in the Ryukyu Islands. Sasukasa, a military deity, is closely related to the storm deity, Aoriyae of Nakijin. In other words, the same or similar deities are located in the Tokara Islands, Nakijin, and Kumejima. Moreover, according to Makishi's (2023, 255, 295) analysis, Kumejima is the geographic origin of Aoriyae.

Based on the distribution of these deities, one scenario is that the Tokara Sashikasa migrated to Kumejima, where Sasukasa and Aoriyae are a single deity (Aoriyae-sasukasa). Later this paired deity traveled to Nakijin and elsewhere in northern Okinawa, where they resided as separate deities (they appear separately in the *Omoro*). Sasukasa then migrated to Shuri, along with Kanemaru and his group, where she changed character (compared with Kumejima's Aoriyae-sasukasa), becoming a powerful deity of war.[2] A second possible though less likely scenario is that the Tokara Sashikasa went first to Nakijin and then later to Kumejima, where it became linked with Aoriyae before they both went to Okinawa (Smits 2019, 97–98).

KANEMARU OF THE NORTH

Kumejima was a powerful and prosperous place, closely connected with China, Japan, and the rest of the Ryukyu Islands. Here is one example from the *Omoro:*

> Gushikawa gusuku [in Kumejima]
> Is magnificently built. . . .
> The *gusuku* that accumulates
> Wine and treasure from Chinese ships
> Is magnificently built
> The *gusuku* that accumulates
> Wine and treasure from Japanese ships.
> (*Omoro sōshi* 11–852)

This song indicates that in addition to being valuable territory in its own right, Kumejima was a nexus. It possessed a commanding view of the sea lanes connecting Japan, China, the port of Naha, and the southern Ryukyu Islands.

In *Maritime Ryukyu,* I argue that despite the official histories claiming that Kanemaru was born on the tiny island of Izena, the homeland of the Second Shō dynasty was Nakijin in Okinawa. This argument is based mainly on a close reading of passages from the *Omoro sōshi* (Smits 2019, 97, 125–126). Here is an additional *Omoro* example of Kanemaru's northern Okinawan roots:

> In Kunikasa [in Kunigami, northern Okinawa]
> The priestess is revered
> The conquering
> Lord is celebrated
> In Yakabi grove [in Kunigami, northern Okinawa]
> Kanemaru is revered. . . .
> (*Omoro sōshi* 13–927)

Importantly, the *Omoro* also links Kanemaru with Kumejima:

> Chiefs of Kadekawa [in Kumejima]
> Kanemaru of the north
> Heralds the future [political] order
> Shō Shin is here
> The wind now blowing from the north
> Is Kanemaru of the north

The wind now blowing from the north
Is Kanemaru of the north.
(*Omoro sōshi* 11–618)

Kanemaru's location in "the north" might refer to northern Okinawa, or it might refer to somewhere farther north, or both. Also important is the image of a wind blowing from the north ushering in a new political order. Both the Aoriyae and Sasukasa deities typically manifest their power as wind and storms. The reference to Shō Shin in this song may indicate that it was composed after his conquest of Kumejima, which is traditionally dated as 1506.

KANEMARU'S ORIGINS

In light of this anthropological evidence and *Omoro* songs, I propose the following description of Kanemaru's origins. First, like the three sister deities, Kanemaru came from Japan. We cannot say where, but given his *wakō* roots and the three sister deities enshrined at the Munakata Shrines, western Kyushu is a likely possibility.

Kanemaru and his group came south, through the Tokara Islands and the northern Ryukyu Islands. At this point there are two possible scenarios. The entire group may have sailed first to Kumejima and then later split off into one subgroup who settled in Nakijin (and eventually Shuri) and another who settled in Ishigaki and possibly other locations in the southern Ryukyu Islands. That pattern would fit the three sister deities narrative.

Another possibility is that from the start, part of the group settled in Nakijin and part settled in Kumejima. Later, some of the group migrated to Ishigaki and possibly other locations in the southern Ryukyu Islands. For example, several blacksmith deities in Miyako and Irabu Islands arrived there from Kumejima (Inamura 1969, 320). In either case, early kings of the Second Shō dynasty had close ties to Kumejima (figure 12.3).

OKUMA BLACKSMITH LEGENDS

There is a group of legends linking the Okuma blacksmith in Kunigami with Kanemaru and Satto. The legends resemble the biography of Shō En found in the official histories. Briefly, the Okuma blacksmith gave Kanemaru shelter after he was forced to flee Izena owing to accusations of water theft. After he became king, Shō En bestowed favors on the Okuma blacksmith and appointed his eldest daughter as Okuma priestess. Every seven years, in her palace, the Okuma priestess paid ritual homage to Urasoe, Ōjana (Satto's official birthplace), and Nishimori (where Satto's divine mother came down from the heavens). Moreover,

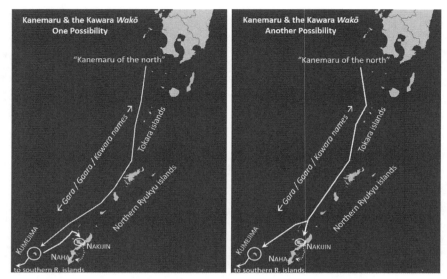

Figure 12.3. Two scenarios for the arrival and settlement of Kanemaru and the Kawara group.

every seven years a representative of the Ie *aji* family, descended from Shō En, paid homage to Okuma in Kunigami, Ōjana, and Okuma in Uchima (Inamura 1969, 312–313).

Why the ritual link between Satto and Kanemaru/Shō En? These legends and traditions reflect the official seventeenth- and eighteenth-century version of events. Most likely, they functioned to link the Second Shō dynasty to Satto, the first king of Chūzan. At the same time, these legends and practices obscure the close ties between the Satto group and the Korean Peninsula. Other maneuvers whereby early modern historians linked unrelated groups of kings are also found in the official histories (Smits 2019, 149–153).

The Kawara *Wakō* Battles

In *Kyūyō* and other accounts of Shuri's 1500 invasion of Ishigaki, a priestess led troops along with a general. Typically, Ryukyuan priestesses participated in battle by way of cursing the enemy and marshaling the power of the deities. In the 1500 invasion, the priestess was Kumejima's Kimihae. When the defenders saw the sister priestess of Ishigaki's Mount Omoto deity in the vanguard, they lost the will to fight (*Kyūyō* [1743–1876] 1974, 1978, 147–148 [#160]; Yonami 2005, 13–14). The *Kyūyō* passage, of course, presents Shuri's victory as a natural restoration of the proper order of things. Several official sources cast the 1500 invasion of Ishigaki as the "Honkawara revolt," led by Oyake Akahachi, who is a hero in Ishigaki to this day. Soon after conquering Ishigaki, the Okinawan forces invaded Kumejima, another Kawara location.[3] Naturally, the official sources have nothing to say about Kimihae in the context of Shuri's invading her home territory.

What was going on? In general terms, Shō Shin was busy forging an empire. Focusing only on the invasions of Ishigaki and Kumejima, note that the conquered group in both places was known generally as Kawara. Given that Shō Shin's forces conquered two Kawara groups in fairly quick succession, in *Maritime Ryukyu* I proposed that "the war that eliminated Akahachi's Kawara group in 1500 and the 1506 invasion of Kumejima were probably connected" (Smits 2019, 103). Furthermore, these wars appear to have been a battle for supremacy over the extended Kawara group. In other words, Shō Shin's father had been a Kawara closely connected with Kumejima. The group that Shuri defeated in 1506 (or possibly earlier) was the Ishikinawa. According to the account in *Gushikawa kyūki*, the Ishikinawa group arrived in Kumejima as outsiders (Higa Chōshin 2006, 173). Quite possibly, they were the original Kawara group in the Ryukyu Islands or their immediate descendants. It was not the case that Akahachi of Ishigaki and his people, or the Ishikinawa of Kumejima, were local rulers rebelling against the state. More likely, these were two Kawara *wakō* groups who asserted their independence from the branch of the Kawara (Kanemaru and Shō Shin) who ended up in Shuri.

Of course, the situation was probably more complex than simply an extended-family feud. For example, both Shō En and Shō Shin struggled to maintain good relations with the Ming court. It is likely that any moves they made to gain control of the southern Ryukyu Islands and stem the tide of smuggling there helped curry favor with Ming officials. It may simply have been a coincidence, but the frequency of tribute missions, which the Ming court reduced to once every two years during Shō En's reign as punishment for abuses of the system and criminal behavior, was restored to once per year in 1507 (Smits 2019, 171). Similarly, by 1500 considerable wealth had accumulated in the southern Ryukyu Islands, and Shō Shin surely wanted some of it. In that sense, Shō Shin was like Shō Taikyū a half century earlier, who fought to gain the wealth of Katsuren and parts of the northern Ryukyu Islands. One big difference was that Shō Shin's conquests, for the most part, held together. By the end of Shō Shin's long reign, Ryukyu had become a genuine state and empire with a central government and vast territory under its control.

Unification of Okinawa and Creation of an Empire

As Richard Pearson notes, "The Second Shō Dynasty could be seen to be the threshold of true state organization." By comparison, prior polities had been "well-developed chiefdoms" (Pearson 2013, 237). My view is the same. The state that began to emerge at the end of Shō Shin's reign marks the first time that the entire island of Okinawa came under the rule of a single center. Moreover, at almost the same time Shō Shin's wars brought the rest of the Ryukyu Islands, from Kikaijima to Yonaguni, under Shuri's control, at least nominally. Reconquest of some areas took place under some of Shō Shin's successors. By circa 1530, Shuri had become the center of a far-flung oceanic empire.

The entire *Omoro sōshi* functions as a glorification and celebration of Shō Shin's accomplishments. Importantly, although many local songs made their way into the *Omoro,* there is no variation in their language. The entire collection reflects the language of the center, the Shuri-Naha area. The effect of diverse songs, many praising powerful local rulers, is to portray Shō Shin as having received spiritual power from all past lineages of powerful rulers and harbor-fortress locations around Okinawa, nearby islands, and the northern Ryukyu Islands. One result, of course, is for the *Omoro* as a whole to exalt and legitimize his rule. Praise for great lords of the past functioned as praise for Shō Shin and the world he created (Yoshinari 2018, 213–217).

Shō Shin's endeavor might have failed at many points in the process. When he was twelve, his partisans, led by his mother, seized the throne and killed his uncle, Shō Sen'i (Shō En's younger brother). That was in 1477. For the next twenty years, tribute embassies set sail and trade specialists in Kumemura compiled diplomatic correspondence. Otherwise, however, there is almost complete silence on the domestic front. Even the official histories have almost nothing to say about this era. Then, starting at the end of the 1490s, Shō Shin burst forth, establishing temples, setting up monuments, setting up a royal mausoleum, undertaking massive landscaping and gardening projects, and of course, waging war.

What happened during those twenty years of official silence? Given the violent nature of Shō Shin's coming to the throne and the dispersed branches of the Kawara, the most likely answer is intrafamily warfare. Local legends lend support to this scenario.[4] Indeed, the Kawara wars of 1500 and circa 1506 may have been the culmination of strife that had been ongoing for years. If so, it makes sense that the official histories would remain silent. Indeed, *Reflections* does not even include a chapter on Shō Shin, despite his being arguably the most important of all the Ryukyuan kings.

Although speculative, if indeed intrafamily warfare had been taking place constantly or intermittently between about 1477 and 1497, whatever happened seems ultimately to have contributed to Shō Shin's military strength. The claim in the official histories that his 1500 invasion force consisted of three thousand soldiers is surely an exaggeration. Moreover, Shō Shin almost certainly used the military forces of Miyako's Nakasone as a force multiplier. Nevertheless, the ability to project significant military force as far away as Yaeyama suggests that Shō Shin and his partisans came out of the twenty-year consolidation phase having amassed great power.

Another feature of Shō Shin's administration was the government in Shuri's use of written documents for domestic matters, the oldest extant examples of which date from the 1520s. Only a small percentage of these documents have survived, but one especially useful example from 1574 indicates that officials in Shuri maintained detailed records of all productive land throughout the Ryukyu Islands and extracted wealth from it (Smits 2019, 186–187). In addition, by the 1520s a formal system of central government and provincial officials began to take shape (Smits 2019, 179–182).

By the end of Shō Shin's reign in 1526, Ryukyu had become a state in the sense that it was ruled by an organized, bureaucratic central government backed by military power. It had also become an empire in the sense that Shuri's military forces conquered other islands and began to extract resources from them in a systematic manner. In *Maritime Ryukyu* I discuss Shuri's post-Shō Shin empire over the course of two chapters. Here I note that the National Museum of Japanese History (Kokuritsu Rekishi Minzoku Hakubutsukan 2021) created a special exhibition, *Umi no teikoku Ryūkyū: Yaeyama, Miyako, Amami kara no chūsei* (Maritime empire Ryukyu: The Middle Ages from the standpoint of Yaeyama, Miyako, and Amami), which ran from March 16, 2021, to May 9, 2021.[5] This exhibition represents an important step in examining Ryukyuan history critically and from perspectives other than that of the royal court in Shuri.

Culture and Royal Rituals

Conquest, resource extraction, and the creation of a bureaucracy was the core of state creation, but cultural matters also played an important role. I conclude this chapter with a few brief points about officially sponsored culture and rites during the era of Shō Shin and his successor Shō Sei.

Chinese and Southeast Asian goods and material culture poured into the Ryukyu Islands during the fifteenth century as a result of private trade and the tribute trade. So, too, did certain aspects of nonmaterial culture. It is important to note, however, that the major wave of Sinicization of elite Ryukyuan culture took place much later, starting at the end of the seventeenth century. Starting at approximately the point of Shō Shin's emergence from the shadows at the end of the 1490s, Shuri Castle began to take on its Chinese-style appearance. There was a genuine Chinese cultural influence on the Ryukyuan court, but it was minor compared to Japanese cultural influences. As Ikuta Shigeru (1992, 292) has pointed out, the establishment of temples staffed with Japanese priests and the use of hiragana to write Okinawan on public monuments are indications of a major wave of Japanese cultural influence.

There is also the important realm of formal state rituals. Shō Shin and Shō Sei initiated agricultural rites, thus formalizing for the first time the idea of Ryukyu as an agricultural society. These rites, known generically as *shikyoma* or *mishikyoma,* included events like the Rice Ear Festival (Ine-no-ho Matsuri) and the Barley Ear Festival (Mugi-ho Matsuri). The most important rite, Kimitezuri, celebrated the arrival of an outside deity, Benzaiten, who linked the Aoriyae of Nakijin with the Aoriyae-sasukasa deity in Kumejima (Smits 2019, 165–167). Notice again the central importance of Kumejima and Nakijin as the local geographic foundation of the Second Shō dynasty.

These rituals were specific to the circumstances of Shō Shin's court, but they were not created from scratch. They more closely resemble Japanese agricultural rites than agricultural rites of the Ming court. The prominence of female religious officials in official Ryukyuan rites would not have been found at any other royal court in the region and probably reflects Korean folk culture.

Court agricultural rites also became connected with solar worship during the time of Shō Shin and Shō Sei. It was then that the island of Kudakajima began to take on its sacred status, and legends developed about the arrival of grain there. Also during the reigns of Shō Shin and Shō Sei, royal worship of the rising sun began at the Bengatake (Benzaiten) Shrine about a kilometer northeast of Shuri Castle. The sun rising in the east became associated with the renewal of royal power. Furthermore, starting in Shō Shin's time, Shuri began to promote a standardized version of *niraikanai* belief, the idea of power coming in from across the sea. In this standardized version, *niraikanai* corresponded to the eastern direction and the rising sun. The merging of rising-sun worship with an official version of *niraikanai* appears to have been the reason for the elevation of Seifaa *utaki,* located on the coast directly across from Kudakajima, as Ryukyu's holiest site (Yoshinari 2018, 243–268).

Throughout the era of the First Shō dynasty, a series of warlords seized power in the Shuri-Naha area, took the Shō surname, and profited from the tribute trade with China. Shō Hashi's origins were in western Kyushu. The deeper geographic roots of Shō Taikyū and Shō Toku are unknown, and all the other trade kings of the era are obscure. The arrival of Kanemaru and the Kawara *wakō* from somewhere in Japan followed a similar pattern. Kanemaru was a trade king in the manner of his predecessors, and his ill-fated younger brother, Shō Sen'i, was the victim of an intragroup power struggle.

Shō Shin, however, ended up changing the previous pattern. His arrival to the throne at a young age afforded him the time to prevail in a series of power struggles and military campaigns and to create the foundations of a centralized state. Over the course of several decades, Shō Shin became a king in the full sense of the term. He put an end to the era of trade kings, and all subsequent monarchs ruled over a bureaucratic state, wielding considerable power.

Korean cultural influence had been strong during the Three Principalities era and during the era of the First Shō dynasty. It interacted or coexisted with the Japonic base culture. From Shō Shin's reign onward, Korean influences faded. During the sixteenth century, certain aspects of Chinese culture, especially Chinese material culture, became increasingly prominent in the Shuri-Naha area. At the same time, however, Japanese cultural influences became even more prominent. Buddhist priests from Japan or trained in Japan began to play prominent roles in government and culture. It was priests, for example, who recorded and compiled the *Omoro sōshi*. They also created the many monuments that began to appear in and around the capital. In the case of most stone monuments, one side was engraved in Okinawan using the hiragana syllabary, and the other side was engraved in classical Chinese. Shō Shin's religious hierarchy drew on Japanese models, as did Shō Sei's agricultural rituals. The many written records that the bureaucracy in Shuri produced were written in Okinawan, using mainly hiragana. The prominent role of women in religious matters, both in official circles and popular culture, may have been the main continuation of Korean cultural influences during the sixteenth century.

We have seen that throughout the history of early Ryukyu, people from outside the Ryukyu Islands were the main drivers of Ryukyuan history. Similarly, over the centuries and millennia, the Ryukyu Islands were home to a variety of people and cultures, including some of Stone Age vintage that we cannot identify with precision. The deep cultural roots of the modern Ryukyu Islands lie in the *gusuku* era, when northern migrants swamped the indigenous populations and made the islands culturally Japonic. Despite the Japonic cultural base, the Ryukyu Islands did not follow the same historical trajectory as the main Japanese Islands. The radically different environment resulted in significant social differences, the most important of which was that the Ryukyu Islands were home to trading-and-raiding societies. They functioned as a "barbarian" zone vis-à-vis the major states in the region. Agriculture supplemented trade, and it was trade profits, not agricultural surpluses, that powered state formation.

Once a centralized state came into existence, it took on many of the outward forms of an agricultural state. In reality, however, the Ryukyu Islands were and are poorly suited to cereal grain agriculture. The state that Shō Shin and Shō Sei created on the basis of trade wealth was already starting to decline economically by Shō Sei's reign. This was because changing world and regional conditions no longer afforded the Ryukyu Islands the favorable position for trade enjoyed since the Three Principalities era or earlier. During the early modern era, some figures like Shō Shōken, and especially Sai On, strove mightily to make Ryukyu into a viable agricultural society, at the cost of considerable misery among ordinary people.[6] Although a topic for a different book, government attempts to make agriculture the economic basis of society functioned as the main force shaping Ryukyuan society during the early modern era.

CHAPTER THIRTEEN

Early Ryukyu in Regional History

The previous chapters presented a new model of the early history of the Ryukyu Islands. In this model, external agents—people who came into the Ryukyu Islands from elsewhere in the region—were the main drivers of the islands' history. In addition to human agents, the physical environment shaped the early history of the Ryukyu Islands. The result was a distinctive trajectory of historical development quite different from that of the main Japanese Islands. In this concluding chapter, I reiterate some of the main points and arguments in the previous chapters from two points of view: the regional impact on the Ryukyu Islands and the impact of the Ryukyu Islands on the East China Sea region. Next, I comment on the powerful role of geography in shaping early Ryukyuan history. Finally, I briefly discuss the matter of ethnogenesis.

Regional Impact on the Ryukyu Islands

People, culture, technology, and goods came into the Ryukyu Islands from different parts of the East China Sea region and even places farther afield, such as Southeast Asia (figure 13.1). We begin with people.

People

Perhaps the most obvious regional impact on the Ryukyu Islands was the arrival of people. From as far back as roughly thirty-five thousand years ago, the Ryukyu Islands have been home to different human populations. Paleolithic and Neolithic human remains have been excavated from sites in Okinawa, Miyako, and Ishigaki. The most famous of these Stone Age people are the Minatogawa skeletons from Okinawa. Several different Stone Age peoples dwelled in parts of the southern Ryukyu Islands. Owing to an absence of artifact assemblages in connection with Stone Age human remains, we know little about these people other than their approximate dates. It was once common to imagine the human history of Okinawa, or the Ryukyu Islands, as an unbroken line from the Stone Age. In that view the Minatogawa skeletons were deep

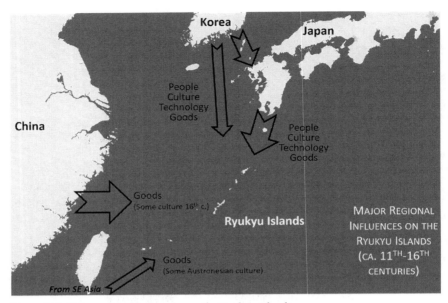

Figure 13.1. Major regional influences on the Ryukyu Islands.

ancestors of modern Ryukyuans or Okinawans. However, it is clear now that they were not.

Hunter-gatherer populations dwelled in Okinawa from about nine thousand years ago and in the southern Ryukyu Islands from about five thousand years ago (with a gap in human habitation from about 1500–800 BCE). We now know that all or most of these populations were Jōmon people. However, there is morphological evidence—for example, at the Hirota site in Tanegashima—suggesting that small populations of other groups, possibly Austronesians, may have dwelled in a few locations within the Ryukyu Arc. Jōmon people came into the Ryukyu Islands from the Japanese Islands and settled at least as far south as the island of Miyako. In short, the main prehistoric population of the Ryukyu Islands, the Shellmound-era population, consisted wholly or mainly of people who were genetically Jōmon.

A vigorous trade in shells and other southern island products from the late Yayoi period brought Yayoi people from Japan to the Ryukyu Islands as traders. Owing to these exchanges, Yayoi material culture, especially pottery, entered the Ryukyu Islands. During the ninth and tenth centuries, the indigenous Jōmon population of Okinawa was in significant decline. Starting in the eleventh century, migrants from Japan and possibly also Korea began to spread southward from the trading center at Gusuku in Kikaijima. By the late twelfth century, these mainly Japonic migrants had settled in all the Ryukyu Islands, and they absorbed or displaced the previous population. These new arrivals became the new base population of the Ryukyu Islands. The *gusuku*-era migrations are the main reason why Hanihara Kazuro's well-known dual structure hypothesis is inaccurate insofar as it claims that the modern population of the Ryukyu Islands derived mainly or exclusively from Jōmon people. As is the case with populations in mainland Japan, recent genetic evidence indicates a small Jōmon genetic component in Ryukyu Island populations and a large Yayoi (Japonic) component.

Within the context of this Japonic population base, other groups of people came into the Ryukyu Islands, often as a result of political disruptions within the East China Sea region. In addition to new arrivals from Japan, the most important group was people from the Korean Peninsula. It is almost certain that Koreans resided at Kikaijima's Gusuku Site Complex as early as the ninth or tenth century. During the late *gusuku* era, many Koreans arrived in the Ryukyu Islands against their will, the result of human trafficking. Some of these people returned to Korea and others remained. Other Koreans were themselves members of *wakō* bands. These Koreans had a profound impact on certain forms of culture and technology. Moreover, Satto, the first person to hold the Chinese title "king" in Okinawa, and many members of his group, were almost certainly Korean.

When the Yuan dynasty went into decline in the middle of the fourteenth century, Alans, Mongols, and possibly other continental refugees settled in Nakijin. That maternal ancestors from Europe or central Asia and Korea were part of the genetic heritage of two of the three skeletons recently found in an ossuary in southern Okinawa should not be surprising given what we know of the movement of people into the islands during the fourteenth and fifteenth centuries.

A small number of Chinese merchant officials resided in Naha from the fourteenth century. Although many of them returned to China, some of their descendants remained in Okinawa. China tends to loom large in modern and contemporary impressions of Ryukyu's past, and there is no doubt that China's economic wealth shaped early Ryukyuan history profoundly. However, compared to other countries in the region, very few Chinese people emigrated to the Ryukyu Islands.

CULTURE, TECHNOLOGY, AND GOODS

Along with the people, of course, came culture, know-how, and goods. Indeed, it is mainly the excavated durable material culture that has enabled scholars to piece together a fairly detailed description of the human history of the early Ryukyu Islands. Even before the *gusuku* era, Jōmon and Yayoi pottery and pottery knowledge came into the Ryukyu Islands from Japan. Some of these wares, such as comb-pattern pottery, were ultimately of Korean origin. Prior to the *gusuku* era, no single type of pottery was found throughout the Ryukyu Islands. As the *gusuku*-era migrants made their way south through the Ryukyu Islands, they brought with them *kamuiyaki* and soapstone cauldrons (or ware containing recycled soapstone cauldron material).

The *kamuiyaki* kilns on Tokunoshima are an example of Korean technology in the Ryukyu Islands. Tokunoshima, Amami-Ōshima (especially the Kasari Peninsula), and the Gusuku Site Complex in Kikaijima were closely linked during the eleventh century. It is from these northern Ryukyu Islands that a common material culture spread southward all the way through the Yaeyama Islands. Similarly, Japonic languages spread throughout the Ryukyu Arc, and it is possible that Kikaijima was the homeland of proto-Ryukyuan. Kikaijima received people, culture, and technologies from Japan and Korea and served as a base for their southward dispersal.

Although not the main source of people for the Ryukyu Islands, Korea was a source of important culture and technology. Sacred groves, a foundation of traditional Ryukyuan religion, are of Korean origin. Moreover, these groves are found throughout a zone extending from southern Korea to western Honshu, to western Kyushu, and all through the islands of the Ryukyu Arc. As discussed at length in *Maritime Ryukyu,* this geographic zone is home to several forms of distinctive culture transmitted by seafarers and migrating populations.

Another Korean contribution to Ryukyuan culture and technology were stone-walled *gusuku,* whose construction closely resembles Korean mountain fortresses. The appearance of large walled *gusuku* in the fourteenth century coincides with the peak of *wakō* activity in the region, and many of the laborers who built these fortresses were likely unfree Koreans and people from islands outside Okinawa.

Along with stone-walled *gusuku* was a surge in the importation of Chinese ceramics and valuable trade goods from Southeast Asia. The local powers in Okinawa, typically based at harbor-fortress units, engaged in intermediary trade between points in Korea, Japan, and China. It is difficult to distinguish clearly between the trade and piratical activities during the fourteenth and fifteenth centuries. The same groups often engaged in a range of potentially profitable licit and illicit activities.

Another important technology to enter the Ryukyu Islands from the broader region was agriculture. There is evidence of agriculture in a few locations during the century or so prior to the *gusuku* era, and agriculture spread throughout the Ryukyu Islands along with the *gusuku*-era migrants. While the islands can accommodate certain forms of animal husbandry, for the most part their soil and other environmental conditions are poorly suited for cereal grain agriculture. As

I have discussed in detail, while agriculture became an important source of food, it did not generate surpluses sufficient to drive state formation. The *gusuku*-era Ryukyu Islands are a relatively rare, but by no means unique, case whereby the existence of agriculture did not lead to the development of full agricultural societies. The various harbor-fortress units in Okinawa and the other Ryukyu Islands were primarily trading-and-raiding centers. When a centralized state emerged in Okinawa in the early 1500s, its economic power derived mainly from trade. The gradual curtailment of trade opportunities throughout the sixteenth century greatly weakened the Ryukyuan state (Smits 2019, 206–207).

Impact of the Ryukyu Islands on the East China Sea Region

Although this book has emphasized the impact of outside agents on the Ryukyu Islands, it is instructive to reverse the perspective (figure 13.2). More than anything else, the geographic location of the Ryukyu Islands shaped their impact on the East China Sea region. First, the islands were the only location in the region where turbo shells were present. Many other valuable shells and southern island products were found most abundantly in the Ryukyu Islands, even if present in other locations. Southern island products stimulated regional trade as early as

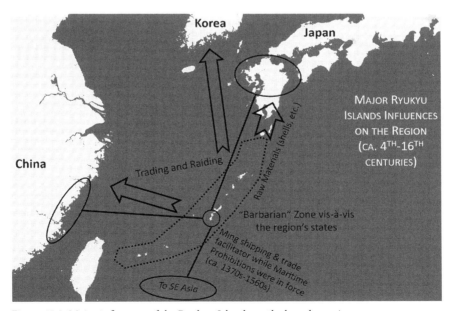

Figure 13.2. Major influences of the Ryukyu Islands on the broader region.

the Jōmon era, and as we have seen, some Ryukyuan shell products made their way as far north as Korea and Hokkaidō. During the seventh and eighth centuries, trade connections between the Japanese court and the "southern islands" began to flourish.

In addition to providing a variety of raw materials, people in the Ryukyu Islands consumed outside products, especially pottery. During the Shellmound era, most of this pottery came from Kyushu. During the *gusuku* era, a wide variety of Chinese, Japanese, and Korean ware came into the Ryukyu Islands via trade. Moreover, kilns in Tokunoshima produced *kamuiyaki*. Although mainly for local consumption, some *kamuiyaki* found its way to southern and western Kyushu, reflecting movements of people between the Ryukyu Islands and western Kyushu.

During the eighth century, albeit passively, the Ryukyu Islands helped facilitate relations between the Japanese court and Tang China. Owing to tension with the Korean state of Silla, between 702 and 752 five Japanese embassies to China used a route through the Ryukyu Islands to get to China.

All indications are that trade relations between the Japanese court, its Dazaifu branch, and the southern islanders were mainly cordial. By the end of the tenth century, however, the northern Ryukyu Islands appear to have been involved in a series of raids on coastal areas of western Kyushu beginning in 996, with occasional flare-ups until as late as 1054. While the documentary evidence is not clear about precisely who participated in these raids, indirect evidence suggests they were at least in part connected with disputes involving an international group of traders based in Amami-Ōshima or elsewhere in the northern Ryukyu Islands.

The first two centuries of the *gusuku* era appear to have been relatively peaceful. During the fourteenth century, however, the Ryukyu Islands increasingly became the abode of *wakō,* a term that covers a wide variety of seafarers, not only pirates of Japanese origin. Based at harbors throughout the Ryukyu Islands and western Kyushu, these *wakō* raided the coasts of China and especially Korea. This resulted in the deepwater port of Naha becoming a regional center for human trafficking. In this connection many Korean people came into the Ryukyu Islands, involuntarily or as *wakō* themselves.

It is difficult to make a clear distinction between seafaring merchants and *wakō* during the fourteenth and fifteenth centuries. In addition to actual or potential piratical activities, many Ryukyuan seafarers engaged in commerce. During the fourteenth century, the Ryukyu Islands facilitated the exchange of goods and technology throughout the East China Sea region. In this connection the port of Naha served the important function of permitting Chinese merchants to conduct far-reaching international trade legally, or legally enough, despite the

Ming court's imposition of the Maritime Prohibitions in the 1370s. Especially during the Three Principalities and early First Shō dynasty eras, Chinese-made ships with Chinese officers and sailors, plus Okinawan envoys and merchants, sailed under the auspices of Ryukyuan trade kings. Their core function was to present "tribute" to the Ming court, which actually meant conveying Ryukyuans to China to conduct trade. Often these ships sailed on to locations in Southeast Asia for further trade after conducting their business in China.

What ties many of the above points together is James C. Scott's idea of a "barbarian" region, discussed in chapter 4. In *Maritime Ryukyu* I argued that the early Ryukyu Islands were a frontier region, and they were. However, Scott's conception is a more precise characterization. Into the sixteenth century, the Ryukyu Islands were the abode of diverse stateless people who paid no grain or other taxes to a central government. The seafarers based in the Ryukyu Islands interacted with the region's states in a variety of ways. Insofar as they transmitted goods, people, and technologies, they performed a generally beneficial function vis-à-vis the established states. On the other hand, their piratical activities were harmful to coastal communities around the region and sometimes even put states at risk, the best example being Goryeo Korea in the late fourteenth century.[1] *Wakō* marauding and smuggling also gave rise to the Maritime Prohibitions, which in turn helped shape trade throughout the region. The Maritime Prohibitions and Ming trade policies vis-à-vis Naha also gave rise to the concept of the Ryukyuan state (in three iterations). Eventually, that concept became reality.

The Ming dynasty's generous tribute trade terms were an attempt to tame the region's maritime barbarians, and over time they worked. Shō Shin's wars of conquest ultimately created a new state out of the barbarian zone that was the Ryukyu Islands. Although Shō Shin and his successors often experienced difficulty holding the edges of their far-flung empire together, from about 1530 onward Ryukyu transformed from a barbarian zone into a state (and empire) centered at Shuri. The systematic extraction of "tribute" (taxes) from the other Ryukyu Islands began at about this time. During the seventeenth century, the state implemented systematic grain taxes throughout Okinawa and the southern Ryukyu Islands in an effort to create a viable agricultural society. By this time almost all vestiges of Ryukyu's former status as a barbarian zone were gone, and so, too, was the era when external agents were the drivers of Ryukyuan history.

New Conceptions of Early Ryukyu

The external agents model zeroes in on the core unit of early Ryukyuan political geography, harbor-fortress pairs, and on the core social unit, groups of traders networked together via sea lanes. In this context I have proposed a hub-and-spoke model to illustrate the major maritime trade routes in which the Ryukyu Islands were embedded. This approach helps clarify the routes by which people, cultures, goods, and technology traveled and interacted. The model can also illustrate major changes over time, and it is scalable in terms of geography. Zooming in on Katsuren, for example, reveals an intricate web of connections throughout the northern Ryukyu Islands and all the way to Japan and Korea. It also brings into focus hitherto unknown groups of traders such as the Tomoi group. The hub-and-spoke model in this book is broadly applicable to other parts of maritime Asia and the world.

Throughout this book I have discussed the ancient branch model, the internal development model, and my proposed external agents model in detail. An obvious challenge for the ancient branch model was creating a plausible theory of early Ryukyuan development amid a severe dearth of evidence, both of conventional documents and the results of archaeology. Taking the premise that the people of the Ryukyu Islands came from Japan to a logical extreme, scholars working in this framework tended to assume the Ryukyu Islands developed in a manner very similar to the ancient Japanese Islands. In this view, agricultural surpluses and warfare drove state formation in approximately the following pattern: local warlords → confederations of warlords (e.g., the Three Principalities) → a centralized kingdom. Scholars associated with this model often acknowledged that Ryukyu's maritime environment influenced its historical development. Nevertheless, they generally viewed the history of the Ryukyu Islands as a late-developing, small-scale recapitulation of the development of the Japanese Islands. As such, there was little about early Ryukyuan history that was truly distinctive beyond the specific details.

The internal development model shines a spotlight on Ryukyuan distinctiveness in the form of the existence of a kingdom. Scholars writing in this framework tend to assume that the physical environment in and around the islands helped shape Ryukyuan distinctiveness. However, few historians working in this model concern themselves in any detail with that physical environment. Favoring the framework laid out in the official histories, most internal development model writing assumes that Ryukyuan history started in Okinawa. Scholars working in this model have had difficulty incorporating the Gusuku Site Complex excavations, the population turnover of the early *gusuku* era, and other findings from archeology into their narratives. Moreover, these scholars have difficulty explaining agriculture adequately.

If local warlords arose because of agriculture, then those warlords must have manufactured or imported iron tools. How did they acquire the necessary resources to obtain the tools? Trade is the obvious possibility, but the dominant narrative is that agriculture, not trade, created the Ryukyu Kingdom. Only after it was in place did the kingdom become wealthy and prosperous by supplementing its agricultural base with trade. The insistence on agriculture as the basis of society and the early kingdom tends to portray Okinawa and the Ryukyu Islands as small-scale, late-developing replicas of the Japanese Islands. These problems caused one prominent scholar, Asato Susumu (2010, 18–19), to abandon the claim that the *gusuku*-era Ryukyu Islands were agricultural societies and argue that they were trade societies. In short, the internal development model has difficulty fitting together assumptions about agriculture, social development and complexity, the archaeology of Gusuku in Kikaijima, the archaeology of the *gusuku* era, and the vast accumulation of other archaeological data.

Incidentally, I should point out that the internal development model works very well for the early modern era. During that time the Ryukyu Kingdom really was isolated, and it had to rely mainly on its internal resources. My external agents model, therefore, applies only to early Ryukyuan history—that is, until roughly 1530.

The external agents model requires setting aside the deep-seated ideas about early Ryukyu that have come down from the official histories, their modern reiterations, and modern and contemporary Romanticism. Obviously, a conceptual change of such magnitude can be psychologically difficult. Moreover, the external agents model results in a much more complex historical narrative than that framed by the official histories. Nonetheless, advantages of the new model include a better understanding of regional maritime networks, the incorporation of all the Ryukyu Islands into Ryukyuan history, and a much better fit to the findings from archaeology and other academic disciplines. Finally, at least in my view, the external agents model results in a much more interesting and nuanced understanding of both the Ryukyu Islands and the region to which they were interconnected.

Power of Geography

A focus on external agents as the drivers of early Ryukyuan history is the obvious feature of the external agents model. Equally important for understanding the distinctive history of the Ryukyu Islands is an appreciation of the power of geography and the physical environment. The islands were ideally located, close enough to the region's states to sail to them but far enough removed to be outside the range of their military power (until 1609). The land was poorly suited for agriculture, but harbors and limestone caves were ideal for raiding and trading.

Okinawa, especially the Naha area, was especially well situated to prosper in the context of the Maritime Prohibitions. That the Ryukyu Islands were a chain facilitated the development of maritime networks, illustrated especially well by the case of the Tomoi group. In short, the location and physical characteristics of the Ryukyu Islands were ideally suited to their function as a maritime barbarian zone. Scott's (2017, 248) observation about central Eurasian nomads and Mediterranean seafarers would also apply to *gusuku*-era Ryukyuans. They were "by virtue of their mobility and dispersion across several ecological zones, the connective tissue between various sedentary cereal-intensive states."

The ancient branch model assumed that the Ryukyu Islands were a late-developing version of the Japanese Islands. The main reason for this assumption was because Japanese people were the ones who settled the Ryukyu Islands. Historians working in the internal development model would agree that Japanese people settled the Ryukyu Islands, but they place greater emphasis on Ryukyuan distinctiveness. The reason for this distinctiveness, however, is often unclear. In many cases the simple fact that the Ryukyu Islands were not part of the Japanese state until 1609 (or 1879) constitutes the distinctiveness, along, of course, with the existence of the kingdom.

In my proposed model, it is essential to acknowledge not only the crucial role of external human agents but also the physical environment's power to encourage certain modes of economic activity and discourage others. As Scott (2017, 128–137) points out, grain has a unique set of qualities that made it the ideal tax crop for early states.[2] The soil, weather patterns, hydrology, and other factors significantly constrained grain production in the Ryukyu Islands. It was mainly for this reason, plus the location of the islands and the presence of harbors, that local power centers developed as trading entities even though the people themselves came from agricultural societies. The base culture of the Ryukyu Islands was Japonic, but the historical development of the early Ryukyu Islands was distinct from that of the Japanese Islands.

The early Ryukyu Islands are also an interesting case of the presence of agriculture not leading to full agricultural societies. As we have seen using examples from around the world (chapter 4), agriculture was not so powerful that it took over wherever it spread. Some societies rejected or curtailed it. Indeed, Scott (2017, 219–256) points out that life as a barbarian held many advantages for individuals and groups. The early Ryukyu Islands were a perfect fit for the barbarian lifestyle in Scott's sense, and it is likely that at least some migrants to the islands sought to escape state control.[3] The basic political unit in the Ryukyu Islands, the harbor-fortress pair, is another development that geographic circumstances encouraged. The prevalence of harbor-fortress pairs, each a nexus in wider trade networks, was one reason for the relatively late development of a centralized state.

Ethnogenesis

This book has mainly used evidence from archaeology to determine the major groups of people who settled in the Ryukyu Islands. In the case of Stone Age groups, there is little that we can say about them beyond their existence. Denizens of the Ryukyu Islands during the Shellmound era were mostly or entirely Jōmon people, and their material culture differed from place to place within the islands. In the realm of pottery, for example, we find a variety of group A types in the central and northern Ryukyu Islands during a time that no pottery existed in the southern Ryukyu Islands (figure 13.3).

The diffusion of *kamuiyaki* and other group B pottery during the eleventh century meant that, for the first time, a common material culture existed throughout the Ryukyu Islands. Archaeologists and others routinely note a common Ryukyu-wide culture and state or imply that it was an important stage along the path eventually leading to the Ryukyu Kingdom. Some even

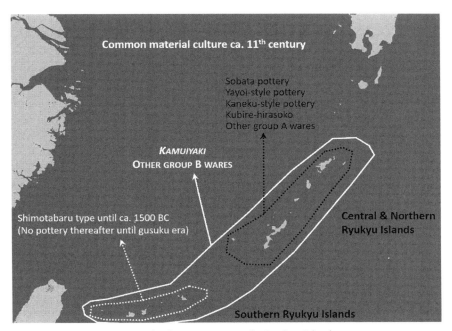

Figure 13.3. Common material culture connecting the Ryukyu Islands.

imply that this common material culture reflected a degree of self-conscious Ryukyuan identity.[4] I would argue, however, that a common material culture is not a prerequisite for state formation and that pottery is not capable of causing ethnogenesis.

Ethnogenesis is the creation or appearance of an ethnic group. It can occur when a group of people begin to recognize themselves as sharing a common culture (and possibly other attributes) and/or when other people recognize a group as possessing a distinctive common culture (and possibly other attributes). In either sense, when did ethnogenesis occur with respect to "Ryukyuans" or some similar group of denizens of the Ryukyu Islands? In other words, when did a significant number of people living in the Ryukyu Islands begin consciously to see themselves as distinctively Ryukyuan (or some equivalent term such as "southern islander")? Conversely, when did other people around the East China Sea region begin to recognize a culturally distinctive Ryukyuan identity?

Answering these complex questions requires access to people's thoughts. Archaeological evidence can provide suggestions, but written sources are a better window into subjective consciousness. In the context of the shell trade and during the *gusuku* era, people would surely have been aware of cultural differences. Japonic-speaking traders, for example, would have needed to devise ways of communicating with Jōmon local residents, who would not have spoken Japonic languages. Occasional references to interpreters in official documents hint at such situations. Early during the *gusuku* era, indigenous communities and Japonic newcomers coexisted in some areas into the thirteenth century, and newly arrived groups such as Koreans, Mongols, or Alans would have retained cultural coherence for a generation or more before absorption into the larger Japonic culture. *Wakō* groups and other seafarers in the region were typically multicultural because their crews usually included people familiar with the languages and customs of the coastal regions in which they operated (Smits 2019, 40–42). In other words, many people living in the Ryukyu Islands during the time of the shell trade or the *gusuku* era would have interacted with people of different cultures. When, however, did a self-conscious Ryukyuan identity emerge?

We have encountered no strong evidence of Ryukyuan ethnogenesis during the time periods covered in this book. Seafaring groups operating in the Ryukyu Islands were mobile. In the many examples we have seen from the *Omoro sōshi*, identities tend to be both local (e.g., a harbor or a fortress) and broadly regional (harbors connected with points in Korea or Japan). The political geography, harbor-fortress pairs linked to other harbors throughout the region, was not conducive to the formation of an Okinawa-wide or Ryukyu-wide identity that transcended, for example, a Katsuren or an Itokazu identity. Eugene E. Roosens (1989, 13) points out that ethnic groups are "most clearly delineated in areas that have one or another form of overarching political organization." The Ryukyu Islands of the fourteenth or fifteenth centuries were home to a similar form of political organization (harbor-fortress units), but they did not become part of the same state until the early decades of the 1500s.

The Shuri-centered empire, which emerged in the 1520s and 1530s, was mainly concerned with extracting wealth from the other Ryukyu Islands, not imposing cultural unity on them (Smits 2019, 186–189). However, the court did create a standard set of royal rites and standardized some of the core concepts connected with them, such as *niraikanai*. These moves began laying a foundation for potential ethnogenesis.

In my view the crucial factor, in addition to state formation, was the cessation of the flow of people coming into the Ryukyu Islands from the north—that is, the closing off of the Ryukyu Islands from Japan and Korea. Such a state of relative isolation developed in the aftermath of Ryukyu's disastrous 1609 war with Satsuma and continued until the 1870s. Owing to Satsuma's policies, by the 1630s or so Japanese, people of Korean ancestry, and anyone else living in Okinawa or the southern Ryukyu Islands all became "Ryukyuans," at least in a formal sense. For this reason and others, I speculated in *Maritime Ryukyu* that a strong, distinctive Ryukyuan cultural identity developed during the early modern era (Smits 2019, 239–243).

That is still my view, but it is worth mentioning some complicating points. One is that the northern Ryukyu Islands became direct Satsuma territory, even though they sent representatives to pose as part of the Ryukyu Kingdom when Chinese envoys were in Naha. Another is the nature of Meiji-era education and social reforms. In the process of inculcating Japanese identity within the Ryukyu Islands, these reforms created an overdetermined Okinawan or Ryukyuan identity (Smits 2015). Aspects of what I have called the theatrical state are also relevant to this matter.[5] For many elites, Ryukyuan identity, whatever exactly it was, was a performed identity. In any case, ethnogenesis took place at different times, in different locations within the Ryukyu chain, among different social groups, and for different reasons between the seventeenth and nineteenth centuries.

A detailed analysis of ethnogenesis is a topic for a future book. My goal in this one is to establish a firm foundation for future research, both in early Ryukyuan history and in the history of later eras. It is also my hope that some readers will take up one or more of the topics and arguments I have advanced and subject them to further research and thought.

Notes

Introduction

1. In its narrow meaning, "Japonic" refers to a family of languages. However, in this book I use the term to refer to culture and/or people from the Japanese Islands. See the section "Conventions and Key Terms" at the end of this introduction for a more detailed explanation.

2. I use the term "barbarian" as a technical term in the "ironic, tongue-and-cheek sense" of James C. Scott. See Scott 2017., esp. 219–256.

3. For example, Toki argues that the 1879 annexation of Ryukyu and subsequent policies became the template for Tokyo's annexations of Taiwan and Korea. In this context he emphasizes the top-down imposition of standard Japanese in Okinawa, Taiwan, and Korea; military conscription; and assimilationist stances by public intellectuals such as Iha Fuyū and Ōta Chōfu (Toki 2018, 88–102).

Chapter One: A New Model of Early Ryukyuan History

1. Located slightly inland from the port of Hakata in Fukuoka, northwest Kyushu, Dazaifu was a branch of the imperial court. It administered the island of Kyushu from the late seventh century until approximately the twelfth century. One of its functions was to oversee foreign trade.

2. There is also a 1427 Monument to the Garden That Benefits the Country, erected by Kaiki (Ch. Huái Jī), an official from China who appears to have managed trade for Shō Hashi (Smits 2019, 84, 112–113). During the mid-fifteenth century, Buddhist priests from Japan produced approximately thirty inscribed bells for Buddhist temples in Okinawa, which typically portrayed the king (most commonly Shō Taikyū) as a Buddhist avatar (Smits 2019, 94, 117).

3. It is found in the collection *Dana-ke monjo* 田名家文書 3 (1), accessed July 25, 2020, https://www.pref.okinawa.jp/edu/bunkazai/bunka/bunkazaizukan/minbunpdf/documents/2019-03-08.pdf.

4. See Takara 1987a, 262–266 for a complete listing. Several more have been found since Takara's writing, but the broader point is that only about 1 percent of the total writs are extant. In other words, even for the sixteenth century the documentary record of Ryukyuan history is sparse.

5. Writs of appointment all begin with the line "Decree of Shuri." It was "Shiyori no o-mikoto" しよりの御ミ事 in the earliest examples. For an explanation of *jireisho* language and structure, see Takara 1987a, 45–49. The early sixteenth century saw Shuri in Okinawa became the strong center of a bureaucratic state. By approximately 1530 Shuri had conquered all the other Ryukyu Islands and began systematically to extract resources from them. The

Ryukyu Kingdom, as it is usually called, or the Shuri Empire, an arguably more accurate name, was at the peak if its economic and military prosperity during the 1530s. It is in this sense that the earliest extant internal documents perfectly reinforce an Okinawa- and Shuri-centric narrative of early Ryukyuan history.

6. I am not suggesting that the official histories are wholly inaccurate with respect to material prior to the sixteenth century. Legends, for example, are typically based on actual events, as is family and household lore. Read against the grain, the official histories can offer useful hints. However, in my view modern and contemporary historians of early Ryukyu usually lean far too heavily on the sparsely supported early Ryukyu material in these texts. In the modern and contemporary eras, of course, historians rarely take conclusions framed according to the tenets of classical Chinese historiography at face value. So, for example, few modern historians take the alleged moral failings of individuals seriously as causal factors. Moreover, especially in recent decades, modern conceptions of group identities have increasingly influenced writing about Ryukyuan history. Nevertheless, nearly all modern and contemporary histories of early Ryukyu follow the general framework of the official histories.

7. The official histories provide narratives going back to the 1180s in terms of events with specific dates attached to them. Their narrative extends back even earlier with respect to mythic origins, such as the creation of the islands and sacred groves by heavenly deities. Putative lineages of kings in the official histories are based in part on the names appearing in Chinese and Korean records.

8. For a discussion of nearly every historian writing in what I am calling the ancient branch model, with an emphasis on their understanding of the origins and significance of agriculture, see Kurima (2010, 132–147).

9. Elaborating on this point, Nakahara turned to physical and cultural anthropology. He argued that Ryukyuans do not exist as a category external to Japanese. However, the common misconception that Okinawans and Japanese are different still persists. It stems from an ignorance of history, and we need to sweep away this ignorance. Nakahara, writing at the time of U.S. control, warned against readers taking seriously a statement such as "You are not Japanese" or any to that effect. Such declarations, he said, are a ploy to weaken the ethnic consciousness of Okinawans (Nakahara 1969, 216).

10. Yanagita's (1967) fullest development of this idea is found in his book *Kaijō no michi,* originally published in 1961. However, Yanagita proposed the term *kaijō no michi* (ocean road) and the southern origins of the Japanese over a decade earlier. As Oguma Eiji (2002, 192–193) explains, "According to [Yanagita], the Japanese nation did not come from the continent to the north but from the islands to the south through the Okinawan islands, and therefore the ancient Japanese language and religion were preserved in Okinawa. The basis of his argument that the Japanese nation came from the south was the fact that the nucleus of Japanese culture was rice, which was a southern crop."

Writing in the early 1990s in the context of arguing against Yanagita's argument that rice agriculture came into the Japanese Islands from the south, archaeologist Shirakihara Kazumi stated that there is no archaeological proof of rice agriculture in the Ryukyu Islands during the Yayoi era. Especially noteworthy is the lack of agricultural tools or any lifestyle adaptation commensurate with wet rice cultivation (Shirakihara 1992, 117; Kurima 2010, 160). No evidence has subsequently turned up. Aleksandra Jarosz et al. (2022, 3) points out, "Despite its influence in Japanese studies, there is no archaeological evidence to support Yanagita's theory; it is clear that cereals spread south [into the Ryukyu islands] from Japan."

11. Nakahara (1969, 219) pointed out that rice cultivation methods are the same in Okinawa and Japan. So the only question is whether rice agriculture and agriculturalists came from the north and swept south or vice versa. If south-to-north, it would have been before the common era; if north-to-south, after the common era.

12. Although some prewar scholars claimed that the Japanese people were of a single origin, the majority view held that they were of mixed origins. For a detailed discussion, see Oguma 2002.

13. According to Higa, initially anyone bold, daring, strong, and/or lucky enough could become an *aji*. As time went on, however, the sons of *aji* became *aji,* and the sons of commoners remained commoners. Social niches hardened, and legends about local rulers like Satto having divine origin emphasized the growing gap between the elites and the commoners (Higa Shunchō 1971, 48).

14. Higa cited the work of castle expert Toriba Masao, noting that as residences for *aji,* Okinawan *gusuku* were castles, fulfilling the same function as mainland Japanese warrior residences. However, because stone was so plentiful in Okinawa, castles appeared there approximately 150 years before they did in Japan. After the last castles were built in Okinawa, 70 or 80 years passed before stone castles started to appear in Japan. Higa also noted that Okinawan castles are unlike those found in China (Higa Shunchō 1971, 50).

15. I have had to leave most of this material out for brevity.

16. In 1978, NHK Broadcasting Company published a survey of the attitudes and ideas of the residents of each prefecture (*Nihonjin no kenminsei: NHK zenkoku kenmin ishiki chōsa*). Okinawa Prefecture emerged as the most distinctive. In the context of this survey, Araki Moriaki noted that Okinawans are racially, ethnically, culturally, linguistically, archaeologically (etc.)—in every respect—related to the larger Japanese group. However, environmental conditions caused Okinawan history to evolve differently. Having been located at the edge of the south seas, Okinawans evolved in a distinctive manner, especially in the context of the Ryukyu Kingdom (Araki 1981, 4). Araki's view, with its emphasis on distinctiveness, is typical of those working in the internal development model. Also typical is a vague implication that a maritime environment was the main reason for this distinctiveness, without specific details.

17. I should also note that Takara was extremely helpful in my research and early career, for which I am most grateful.

18. In this context it is important to note that the mainstream interpretation of the start of a Ryukyu kingdom is 1429, the year Shō Hashi became the sole king according to the 1725 version of *Genealogy of Chūzan.* Some scholars would push the date back to 1372 and the start of the tribute trade. In either case the problem is the tendency to equate the title "king" (Ch. *wáng*) with the existence of a centralized state (or several small centralized states). As I explain in detail in later chapters, the 1429 date is almost one century earlier than the actual emergence of a centralized state in Okinawa.

19. The myth of Ryukyuan pacifism and the ways it has played out in scholarly circles and mass media is a complex topic, about which I plan to write a book in the future. For a shorter discussion, see Smits (2010a, 2010b).

20. The term "stoneware" refers to nonporous pottery fired at relatively high temperatures. It can be glazed or unglazed. *Kamuiyaki* is named after the pond in Isen Town in southern Tokunoshima around which the kilns were located. Prior to the discovery of the kilns, *kamuiyaki* was referred to as *rui-sueki* 類須恵器 (*sue* ware-like) because of its resemblance to *sue* pottery.

21. Following defeat in the war with Satsuma in 1609, Ryukyu's new Shimazu overlords initiated policies that to a large extent isolated the Ryukyu Islands. During this period of isolation from approximately 1630 to 1880, many aspects of culture that came to be regarded as characteristically "Ryukyuan" developed. See Smits 2019, 239–243.

22. Scott notes that from the Bronze Age until the seventeenth century, or even later, non-state peoples ("barbarians") interacted with established agrarian civilizations in a variety of symbiotic or competitive relationships. At different points in this book, I use Scott's insights to shed light on the interactions of Ryukyu Islanders with agrarian states such as China, Korea, and Japan.

23. Much of the content of Kerr's book (though not the writing style) is similar to portions of a collection of material in English about Ryukyuan history and culture prepared by the Research and Analysis Branch of the Office of Strategic Services in anticipation of the Battle of Okinawa and its aftermath. See *The Okinawans of the Loo Choo Islands: A Japanese Minority Group* (Okinawa Kenritsu Toshokan Shiryō Henshūshitsu 1996, 1–148). Kerr ([1958] 2000, 493) acknowledged this source and others like it in his bibliography.

24. In Chinese documents of this era, the term "Liúqiú" (J. Ryūkyū) often referred to Taiwan. However, Akamine assumes that all such mentions refer to Okinawa or the Ryukyu Islands (cf. Akamine 2017, 17–18).

25. Sixteenth-century *wakō* included many Chinese, and they, too, appear in the pages of *Maritime Ryukyu*. However, the majority of that book's discussion concerns earlier *wakō*, who mostly raided the Korean coast and consisted mainly of Japanese and Koreans.

Chapter Two: Well-Traveled Routes

1. This geographic area is nearly the same as the zone I call the East China Sea Network in *Maritime Ryukyu* (cf. Smits 2019, 16). The difference is that here I leave out southern China. As a source of wealth, China eventually became a major force in the development of Ryukyuan history. However, except for an influx of Mongol and Alan refugees into the Nakijin area during the late fourteenth century, China was not a major source of people for the Ryukyu Islands.

2. As Murai Shōsuke (2019, 184) notes in the context of exchanges between Korea and the Ryukyu Islands, "Via the maritime route of the Amami islands, western Kyushu, Iki, and Tsushima, contact has taken place since ancient times [prior to] the advent of a Ming-centered international order."

3. The name literally means "rope pattern" and comes from the striking appearance of certain forms of Jōmon pottery; according to a recent genetic study, "There is still lack of ancient genome data in East Asia critical to understand the peopling history of East Eurasians. Although our data support the idea that [Jōmon skeleton] IK002 was the direct descendant of the Upper-Paleolithic people, how/where those Upper-Paleolithic people migrated to the Japanese archipelago remains unanswered" (Gakuhari, Nakagome, and Rasmussen et al. 2020, discussion).

4. "Our newly analyzed Korean genomes are notable in that they testify to the presence of and admixture with Jōmon-related ancestries outside of Japan" (Robbeets et al. 2021, 620). Later farming migrants replaced this Jōmon and partial-Jōmon population in the Korean Peninsula.

5. Called *kushimemon doki* or *setsumon doki* in Japanese, the earliest comb-pattern pottery appeared in roughly 8000 BCE, and the final stage of its production took place from

approximately 2000 to 1500 BCE. Around 1300 BCE, a new Korean-derived style of plain (K. Mumun) pottery began to appear in the Japanese Islands (Habu 2004, 208–209).

6. These goods were mostly decorative items attached to horses. Although the cone snails came from the Ryukyu Islands, the precise sites of manufacture and the route(s) by which these products came to Korea are uncertain.

7. The modern word for "turbo shells" is *yakōgai*. In some early documents, it was *yakugai* (Yaku shells) because Yaku or Yakushima often stood for all the islands in the Ryukyu arc from Yakushima southward. The worldwide range of turbo shells is limited. They are found only in the central and northern Ryukyu Islands, in the Philippines, and in the Andaman Sea around Nicobar Island (Takanashi 2008b, 218; Yamazato Jun'ichi 2012, 94; Yoshinari 2018, 62–63). In other words, the raw material for turbo shell products anywhere in East Asia almost certainly came from the Ryukyu Islands.

8. A2-B61-DRB1-0405. It is found in 2.7 percent of Okinawans and 0.5 percent of Koreans and is absent in mainland Japanese, Ainu, and northern Chinese populations. Given the large number of haplotypes, these percentages are significant.

9. The arrival of a group from Korea bearing the haplogroup O2b in the southern Ryukyu Islands, whose population was sparse prior to the *gusuku* era, probably had a large genetic impact in relative terms.

10. Xué wèi wōrén yányǔ yīfú, qīnlüè cǎi hǎi rénmín 學爲倭人言語衣服、侵掠採海人民.

11. With respect to language, Hudson notes, "The most likely location for the development of a trading creole in the Yayoi period is in Okinawa, where an extensive trade in tropical shells developed with Kyushu. There is, however, no linguistic evidence for such creolization in the formation of the Ryukyuan languages" (Hudson 2022, 9).

12. Liúqiú guó zhě nánhǎi shèngdì, ér zhōng Sānhán zhī xiù, yǐ Dàmíng wèi fǔchē, yǐ Rì yù wèi chún chǐ 琉球國者 南海勝地 而鍾三韓之秀 以大明爲輔車 以日域爲唇齒.

13. Writing in 1924, linguist Miyanaga Masamori affirmed the hypothesis that the Ryukyuan word for "north," *nishi*, came from ancient Japanese *inishi* 過去, meaning "the past." In other words, the north was Ryukyu's past (Miyanaga 1924).

14. On January 24, 2016, between 1:13 and 1:18 p.m., snow was briefly observed falling at two different times in Amami-Ōshima. The previous sprinkling of snow there took place in 1901. "Amami-Ōshima de 115-nen buri ni yuki," *Huffington Post,* https://www.huffingtonpost.jp/2016/01/24/amami-observes-snow_n_9062930.html.

15. Not counting Kuninaka grove, established in the wake of Shuri's 1500 invasion of Yaeyama. Not surprisingly, its deity came from Okinawa, spelled 悪鬼納 (*Origins* [1713] 1988, 604–605).

16. The deity of the Hazama grove came from Yakushima. The deity of the Kontō grove came from Kumejima, and the deity of the Hariwaka grove arrived from Tokunoshima. The deities of the Nakasuji, Kumabaru, and Hanagusuku groves came from Okinawa (*Origins* [1713] 1988, 603–604).

17. *Origins* lists a Tomori grove in Ahacha-son, Urasoe district. The name of its deity is Yamato Yashiro Sedo-den Ganashi. 大和ヤシロ船頭殿ガナシ. The explanation is that it was the site where the bones of a Japanese man were believed to be buried. The biographical details are not clear, but the person was well regarded in his time. The name "Yashiro" suggests Yatsushiro in Higo (*Origins* [1713] 1988, 384; Tanigawa 2010, 178–179; Smits 2019, 31–32, 73–74, 258n72).

18. Barbara Seyock (2005, 101) notes that most of the tropical commodities from the South China Sea area exported to Korea via Tsushima during the early fifteenth century were purchased in northern Kyushu and the Ryukyu Islands.

Chapter Three: The Land, First Peoples, and the Shellmound Era

1. Marl or marlstone (泥灰岩 *dorohaiiwa*) is a calcium carbonate or lime-rich mud or mudstone that contains variable amounts of clays and silt; *jaagaru* is possibly from the place-name of the same pronunciation, Jagaru or Jaagaru 謝苅 (Nagatsuka 2007, 79).

2. For a detailed description of Ryukyu soils, see Pearson (2013, 24–27).

3. Doi (1998, 99, image 9) includes a photo with a Yayoi, Jōmon, and Hirota skull side by side. All three are clearly different from each other.

4. According to Doi Naomi (2018, 141–142), the prehistoric human remains from the central and northern Ryukyu Arc with the small, round skulls resemble the Yami people of Orchid Island (Lányǔ), just to the southeast of Taiwan. If Doi's observation is accurate, these prehistoric remains suggest that some Austronesian peoples may have resided in the northern Ryukyu Islands. In 2012 the team of Shinoda, Kakuda, and Doi attempted a mitochondrial DNA analysis of dental samples from fourteen of the Yomitan samples and from fifteen samples from a cliff burial site of similar vintage near Gushikawa Gusuku (Uruma City, Okinawa). The team succeeded in extracting haplogroups from only nine of the Gushikawa samples and six of the Yomitan samples (Shinoda, Kakuda, and Doi 2012, 54–56). The total sample was so small that "unfortunately, we could not make any major conclusions on the basis of these results" (Shinoda, Kakuda, and Doi, 2012, 59).

5. Not all archaeologists state the matter this way. According to Rhee and Aikens (2021, 47), for example, "The Yayoi did not come from the Korean Peninsula, as is sometimes stated. Yayoi as a culture and as a people developed within the Japanese Archipelago through cultural interaction and intermarriage among indigenous Jomon [Jōmon] and the immigrant Mumun [Korean] peoples. North Kyushu served as an incubator of this new Yayoi culture." Transposing this view to Hanihara's hypothesis, Mumun (J. Mumon 無文, people named after their plain pottery) immigrants coming into the Japanese Islands were the main cause of the dual structure. The essential point is the same.

6. One recent study of the demographic history of Ryukyu Islanders, for example, notes the presence of skeletal remains in Miyako as old as 26,000 years—that is, during the Pleistocene (approximately 2,580,000 to 11,700 years ago). It concludes that large-scale migrations into the Ryukyu Islands occurred during the Holocene Epoch (ca. 11,700 years ago to the present) "and that these migrations could not be assigned to a particular period" within that epoch (Sato et al 2014, 2936). The entire Holocene epoch is too broad a time interval to be of use to historians, at least for most purposes.

7. The authors point out that "any trace of a Jomon-era common ancestor would have been eliminated" by "recent migrations from Honshu to main-island Okinawa, and from main-island Okinawa to Sakishima [the southern Ryukyu Islands]" (Matsukusa et al. 2010, 221). This conclusion contradicts part of the dual structure hypothesis. Because the authors do not define "recent," anyone unfamiliar with early Ryukyuan history might take this term to indicate the early modern or modern era. Perhaps that is what the authors meant as well. However, the only large-scale, population-altering migration during the Holocene was the *gusuku*-era influx from Kyushu and other northern locations beginning in the eleventh century.

8. For example, Sato et al. 2014, 2933. Summarizing the genetic data, Thomas Pellard (2015, 29) concludes that there is no evidence in the Ryukyu Islands of long-term isolation or population size reduction.

9. Shinoda and Doi (2008) analyzed mtDNA in fifteen dental samples from a tomb in Yonaguni from the early modern era. They concluded that those buried there originated "from Northeast Asia, and they may have migrated into the study area via [the] Japanese mainland and Okinawa Island" (16). Moreover, "It is therefore possible that the similarities in the haplogroup composition between the [Yonaguni] Suubaru population and the contemporary population of the main island of Okinawa is the result of the arrival of immigrants, who almost replaced the indigenous population and brought along with them a new haplogroup distribution" (17).

10. The 20–25 percent Jōmon component in modern Ryukyuan genomes is roughly comparable to the 10 percent component in mainland populations given the recent (eleventh–twelfth centuries) arrival of Japanese (i.e., mostly Yayoi) migrants into the Ryukyu Islands, compared with the much earlier arrival (starting ca. 1000 BCE) of Yayoi migrants into the main Japanese Islands from the continent.

11. The practice of postpartum sweat baths has been reported in a few areas of mainland Japan and is connected with Ninigi in *Chronicles of Japan* (*Nihon shoki*).

12. The short section about Liúqiúguó (the Ryukyu Islands and/or Taiwan) in the official history of the Sui dynasty (581–618) explains that after a woman gives birth, "she engages in self-moxibustion with fire to make her sweat and heal after five days" (*Suíshū* 636). Although described as moxibustion in the text, the relevant practice was a postnatal sweat bath.

13. During the 1920s and 1930s, a mostly Japonica hybrid from Taiwan called Hōrai-mai (Pénglái rice) replaced the varieties previously grown in Okinawa. The cultivars in use before the arrival of Hōrai-mai were collectively called *zairaitō*. Around 1917 an agricultural survey took a total of twenty-two samples of *zairaitō* from different regions in Okinawa plus Miyako and Yaeyama. There was some variation in the samples, but most featured very tall plant size, long ears, few stalk joints, difficult-to-remove husks, and larger plants compared to mainland varieties. In other words, most varieties of *zairaitō* resembled *bulu*. Moreover, there is a chemically distinctive subtype of *zairaitō* in Yonaguni, which is exactly the same as one found in Halmahera Island (Indonesia) and Southeast Sulawesi (Morinaga and Mukai 1969, 12–14; Watabe 1990, 395–397).

14. In Ryukyuan languages and dialects, the term *aman,* or variations of it such as *amamu,* means hermit crab (Yamashita 2003, 86; Yoshinari 2018, 36–37). In the old custom of tattooing hands and arms by women in the Ryukyu Islands (*hajichi*), one tattoo pattern for the left arm was that of a hermit crab. According to an informant in Okinoerabu circa 1960, the reason for this tattoo is that humans are all descendants of Amamu—that is, humans are all descendants of a primordial hermit crab. The term "Amamu" and its variants may be related to proto-Austronesian *(k)umang* (hermit crab), with the *-ng* sound at the end changed to *-n* (Yoshinari 2018, 32–35). In two locations in Amami-Ōshima and two locations in nearby Kakeroma Island, the word for "terrestrial hermit crab" in the local language is *amami.* The place-name Amami is related to this term, as are the names of the deities Amamiku and Amamikyo. The oldest stratum of their names mean "hermit crab" with the honorific *-ko/-ku* attached, and the sense that these names impart is temporal. They are the primordial deities of the mythical age of the hermit crab (Kojima 1983, 206–207; Yoshinari 2018, 36–37, 41).

15. Recall from earlier discussion in this chapter that skeletal remains resembling neither Jōmon nor Yayoi people have been found extensively in Tanegashima. The Tanegashima remains reveal an important clue to their identity in the form of tooth ablation, the ritual removal of one or more healthy teeth. This practice was widespread in ancient populations around the region. Hirota and other Tanegashima sites practiced the same distinctive ablation practice: removing teeth only from one side of the upper jaw. According to Ikehata Kōichi, this form of tooth ablation closely resembles that performed in Taiwan, and it does not resemble ablation practices in Kyushu, Amami-Ōshima, or Okinawa (Ikehata 1990, 129–130). In other words, evidence from physical remains indicates that an ancient Austronesian group may have been present in Tanegashima.

16. For an extensive analysis of this trade based on Chinese and Korean official records and records in *Rekidai hōan,* see Murai (2019, 179, 183–252).

Chapter Four: Kikaijima and the Start of Japonic Ryukyu

1. Physical anthropologist Doi Naomi (1998, 101, 102) points out that the *gusuku* era marked a major change in human morphology: "The present-day people of the Ryukyu islands [Nansei shotō] can trace a continuous connection back only as far as the gusuku era."

2. Adopting a computer metaphor with the islands themselves as the hardware and the people and culture as the software, it is as if a Japonic operating system overwrote the previously existing Jōmon one. Despite the overwrite, some traces of the previous Jōmon code remained. Nevertheless, the change in base culture was profound.

3. I discuss the details of fortresses in later chapters, but over 300 *gusuku* were scattered throughout the Ryukyu Islands. The majority (223) were in Okinawa and the surrounding islands: 45 in northern Okinawa; 65 in central Okinawa; 113 in southern Okinawa (Hokama 2015b, 75).

4. For an image of *kamuiyaki* and a *yamuiyaki* kiln, see Kokushitei Bunkazai nado deetabeesu 国指定文化財等データベース, "Tokunoshima *kamuiyaki* tōki kama ato" 徳之島カムィヤキ陶器窯跡, accessed October 17, 2022, https://kunishitei.bunka.go.jp/heritage/detail/401/00003518. Kilns of the same type are also found in Sagariyama, in Kuma-gun, in Kumamoto Prefecture, and in the Mujang-ri kiln site in Seosan, South Korea. *Kamuiyaki* more closely resembles unglazed Goryeo pottery than medieval Japanese *sue* ware, although some bowls were made in imitation of Chinese trade ware. Both the Sagariyama kilns and those in Tokunoshima shared the same Korean-derived technology base (Shinzato 2017, 133–137, 139; Yotsumoto 2008, 247, 152–253).

5. In earlier work he called it the "Kikaijima–Amami-Ōshima orbit of power."

6. *History of Song* records in 988 a Tōdaiji priest offering gifts to the Chinese emperor that featured MOP inlay. Japanese MOP inlay was so advanced that Fāng Sháo (1066–?) mistakenly declared in his book *Pōzháibiān* that MOP-inlaid utensils originally came from Japan (Yamazato Jun'ichi 2012, 91–92).

7. As for *kamuiyaki,* the most likely scenario is that people from Kikaijima carried the pottery with them as they migrated (Yoshinari 2020, 29–31). Based on its distribution, which is mainly the Ryukyu Islands, *kamuiyaki* was produced not as a trade good for the Hakata-based Japan-Song market but to supply the northern migrants moving southward with necessary daily life products (Ikeda 2019, 22).

8. Much of that evidence is discussed in the previous paragraphs, but one quantity is particularly telling. Excavated soapstone cauldron sherds from the mid-eleventh through the

late twelfth centuries (the start of the *gusuku* era) total 373 in Gusuku (out of 480 for the northern Ryukyu Islands as a whole), 328 in Okinawa and surrounding islands, and only 34 from the southern Ryukyu Islands. In other words, Gusuku played the major role in initiating the southward migrations (Yoshinari 2022, 29, following Shinzato Akito).

9.   Grid R-68 of the site consists of seven strata, the seventh being the oldest. In strata six through four, older group A *kubire-hirasoko* pottery is predominant. From stratum three onward, newer group B *gusuku* pottery has been consistently excavated. Below stratum four, there is no trade pottery or *kamuiyaki*. These items are found only in strata three to one. Stratum three corresponds to the period of the late twelfth or early thirteenth century to the mid-thirteenth century (Ikeda 2019, 27–29). In other words, the older group A and the newer group B pottery coexisted during the early *gusuku* era. These two types of pottery would have been crafted by entirely different groups of people. The group A wares faded out during approximately the end of the thirteenth century. This pattern indicates that an outside group took up residence and gradually absorbed and/or displaced the previous local population, although we cannot know the details of that process from pottery (Ikeda 2019, 41).

10.   Looking at consumption patterns, there was a division of labor between *kamuiyaki* and higher-quality Chinese ceramics. The two pottery sets had similar utilitarian functions, but their quantity typically varied inversely in any particular site. In Okinawa especially, sites in which Chinese ceramics were more numerous corresponded to sites of large *gusuku*. Outside these areas, *kamuiyaki* tended to predominate. In other words, differences in pottery quality were markers of increasing social diversity during the late *gusuku* era, especially in Okinawa (Shinzato Akito 2018, 130, 155, 161). Unfortunately, the archaeological record is not able to reveal details about the societies developing on Okinawa. It is common for scholars to assume that social stratification intensified during the late thirteenth century, which may have been the case. Even so, however, we do not know what the social strata were. What is clear is that wealth was accumulating at the large *gusuku* sites relative to other locations.

11.   As Wayne Farris points out, "Beginning in 1050 . . . trade and towns rebounded, as seen in overseas trade with Sung China internationally and the growth of new ports such as Hakata and Hyōgo domestically" (Farris 2006, 10). Of course, 1050 was precisely the start of the *gusuku* era.

12.   The southern islands were sources of valuable raw material, but between 996 and 1054 the northern Ryukyu Islands, or some of them, were also involved in marauding along the coast of Kyushu (chapter 3). Although a speculative point, Dazaifu may have encouraged merchants from Kyushu to migrate to the Ryukyu Islands as a way of ensuring a supply of southern island products while reducing the danger of violence. Conversely, it is possible that in the context of increasing dysfunction of the *ritsuryō* state, Heian officials lost their ability to control foreign travel or emigration.

13.   Adolphson notes "a general escalation of the difficulties the capital elites faced in controlling the provinces. These problems reached a critical juncture in the early part of the tenth century—described in a recent collaborative work as 'something of a quiet revolution'—when the imperial court, facing challenges in the countryside, made important adjustments to bolster its supremacy" (Adolphson 2007, 26–27).

14.   The consumption of MOP remained high during the thirteenth and into the fourteenth centuries, but demand for turbo shells eased slightly during this time. One reason was improved technology such that what would have required a 2-millimeter-thick shell in the

twelfth century needed only a 0.5-millimeter shell in the thirteenth. Moreover, abalone began to be used for MOP in addition to turbo shells (Takanashi 2008b, 228–229).

15. The last embassy to China from the Heian court took place in 836. Although Buddhist priests occasionally sought to travel abroad, there are no records of Japanese merchants doing business in other countries until the eleventh century. The court occasionally punished Japanese who conducted trade abroad or officials who condoned it. For example, a merchant from Hizen Province was arrested in 1047 for having sailed abroad and had his goods confiscated. In 1093 a Japanese monk selling arms to the Khitans led to the firing of a Dazaifu official and the demotion of the governor of Tsushima. Such measures indicated that the court continued to maintain its prohibition of Japanese conducting commerce abroad. Nevertheless, by the late eleventh century Japanese did go abroad to trade, often without penalty (von Verschuer [1988] 2006, 43–46).

16. More generally, according to James C. Scott, "The conventional 'subspecies' of subsistence modes—hunting, foraging, pastoralism, and farming—make . . . little historical sense. The same people practiced all four, sometimes in a single lifetime; the activities can and have been combined for thousands of years, and each of them bleeds into the next along a vast continuum of human rearrangements of the natural world" (Scott 2017, 71).

17. Even within Mesopotamia, there were major, protracted retreats of agriculture. "From roughly 1,800 until 700 BCE—more than a millennium—settlements in Mesopotamia covered less than a quarter of their previous area, and urban settlements were only one-sixth as frequent as during the previous millennium" (Scott 2017, 188).

18. For a discussion of the many examples, see Bellwood (2005, 37–39).

19. In this case, one reason for the decline was a slightly reduced cereals package (emmer and einkorn wheat plus one or two types of pulses), compared to the more varied Mesopotamian agricultural package. A vicious cycle led to the population becoming "increasingly narrow and uniform," leaving the farmers ever more susceptible to raiding, soil exhaustion, and disease. "Neolithic farming was an experiment that could fail" (Graeber and Wengrow 2021, 271–273).

20. As a typical example, among the Kelabit people of highland Borneo today "rice-growing is described as *lema'ud,* hard work, and is seen as burdensome and tiring, whereas hunting and gathering are regarded as enjoyable." The Penan, who live in the same region, have rejected rice agriculture and mainly obtain their livelihood from the forest. In Kelabit eyes, the Penan rejection of agriculture is "a refusal to grow up" (Barker and Janowski 2011, 11). The broader point is simply that the presence of agriculture does not inevitably lead to agricultural societies.

21. According to David Graeber and David Wengrow, "The systematic rejection of *all* domesticated foodstuffs is even more striking when one realizes that many Californians and Northwest Coast peoples did plant and grow tobacco, as well as other plants—such as springbank clover and Pacific silverweed—which they used for ritual purposes or as luxuries consumed only at special fests. In other words, they were perfectly familiar with the techniques for planting and tending to cultigens" (Graeber and Wengrow 2021, 166).

22. Scott notes that only recently in human history, when the world was in a sense fully occupied, was it possible for state elites to own or control the means of production (land) and, by this means alone, bring forth a surplus. Before then—for example, before about 1600 or 1700—states often had to apply active legal coercion to force peasants to remain in place and on the job. For this reason, in ancient agrarian states it was population, not territory, that mattered most for state power (Scott 2017, 153–154).

23. Raiding, if carried to an extreme, is self-defeating, like a virus that kills its host. For this reason most barbarian groups preferred to extract tribute from states in a sustainable fashion, in the manner of a protection racket. It was also possible for symbiotic alliances between states and barbarian groups to sometimes advance the interests of both (Scott 2017, 240–243).

24. In arguing that Ryukyuan languages came from a Kyushu-Ryukyuan branch of the Japonic tree, Jarosz et al. (2022, 16) point out, "The assumption that the Ryukyuan language spread and dispersed from a common ancestor situated in southern Kyushu indicates that escape from state control may have also been a factor in the dispersal of Ryukyuan."

25. For details on the emergence of a centralized state during the early sixteenth century, see Smits (2019, 161–187).

Chapter Five: Spokes and Hubs

1. Noting the difficulty in reconstructing pots or parts of them from excavated sherds, the widespread local manufacturing of pottery with soapstone powder mixed into the clay, and other reasons, Ikeda Yoshifumi (2019, 20) has argued that many cauldrons probably arrived in the Ryukyu Islands as pieces, not as finished products.

2. Perhaps it was not that local powers in Okinawa pulled away from Gusuku's control but that traders at Gusuku relocated to Okinawa. According to Ryukyu's official histories, the first king, Shunten, ascended the throne in 1187 (d. 1237). The purported start of his kingship nearly matches the 1188 invasion of Kikaijima. Yoshinari Naoki points out that while Shunten was almost certainly a fictional character, it is possible he represented the memory of a trading group that lost its base in Kikaijima and relocated to Okinawa. With respect to the decline in Gusuku pottery from the late twelfth century, it is difficult to imagine that the traders there simply disappeared. At least some of them probably moved southward. Moreover, given that southern island products remained valuable commodities vis-à-vis the Japanese mainland, Okinawa would have been a good location from which to continue commerce. If indeed Shunten was an artifact of the memory of a relocated trading group, it makes sense that he later became joined to the Tametomo legend (Yoshinari 2020, 93–94). Regarding the Tametomo legend, see Smits (2019, 29–31, 153–157).

3. The group that possessed the *kusuha* tile ware bowls was probably associated with the main power holder in the region, Ata Tadakage. He was allied with the Ise Taira, who became prominent officials in Dazaifu. Tadakage was exiled to "Kikaigashima" (Kikaijima or an island in the Satsunan group) by the imperial court in the wake of the Hōgen Disturbance (1156), in which his son-in-law Minamoto Tametomo went down in defeat. Tadakage ended up in the Satsuma Peninsula (present-day Ata-gun), and his economic base there was newly reclaimed land of the Satsuma-kuni Ichinomiya Shinden Hachiman Shrine. This land was the only significant parcel in the area that was not part of the Satsuma no Shō estate. The Ichinomiya land was under nominal Dazaifu jurisdiction, and Tadakage's main economic activity was trade. Incidentally, the legend of Tametomo traveling to Okinawa and spending time in various Kyushu locations may be connected with the close association between Tametomo and Tadakage (Kurima 2013a, 226–227, 231–232).

4. The sites are as follows: in Ishigaki at the Chōmangei (Inoda) site, in Hateruma at the Arabuchi and Buribuchi sites, at Gaijihama Shellmound in Taketomi Island, and at other sites dating from the eleventh through thirteenth centuries. Large stone tuyeres have been found at Ishigaki's Nakasuji Shellmound, at the Motofukai-son (Yamabaree) site, at the

Kidakusuku-son and Takana-son sites in Iriomote, at Yonaguni's Dunanbara site, and at the Kitamura site in Hateruma (Ōhama 2008, 255–356).

5. These sites were the Tokoname and Atsumi kilns in eastern Japan (Pacific coast) and the Suzu and Tōban kilns in western Japan.

Chapter Six: Sacred Groves, Fortresses, and More

1. For a discussion of this complex dynamic, see Smits (1999, 15–49).

2. The term *utaki* is common in academic writing and official names. It probably originated at the Shuri court and literally means "venerable mountain peak." In Okinawa, *utaki* are commonly called *uganjo, ugan,* or *haijo.* In Miyako they are *mutu* and in Yaeyama, *on, wan,* or *waa* (Okaya 2019, 14).

3. In order, the sites that Amamiku created were Asumori in Hedo, Kanahiyabu in Naki-jin, Chinen *mori,* Seifaa *utaki,* Yabusatsu no Urahara, Tamagusuku Amatsuzu, Kudaka Kobau *mori,* and the pair Shuri *mori*/Madama *mori* (*Reflections* [1650] 2011, 31).

4. One of these sites is the coral rock called Yahara-zukasa, located just offshore from Hyakuna beach. According to mythology, Amamiku first made landfall at Yahara-zukasa after arriving from the distant sea (*niraikanai*). Nearby is Hamakawa *utaki* (figure 6.2), where Amamikyo rested in a cave, two springs where rice was first planted (Usanju and Hainju), and Minton Gusuku, where Amamiku first resided. For details, see Yoshinari 2018, 260–262 and Okaya 2019, 126, 128.

5. According to *Origins,* both of the sacred spaces in Yabusatsu *utaki* were the sites of official rites during the Second Shō dynasty (*Origins* [1713] 1988, 360). Priestesses, commonly called *noro* (*tsukasa* in the southern Ryukyu Islands), would have conducted these official rites.

6. The oldest stoneware (*sueki*) in Japan dates to about 400 CE and was excavated from the Obatera site in Sakai. It is "strikingly similar to" Korean stoneware of the time and was introduced into northern Kyushu and the Inland Sea area by Korean immigrants (Rhee and Aikens 2021, 133).

7. Other pronunciations include *garan* and *garo.* In 1969 there were 172 such sites (Shimono [1969] 1995, 477–480).

8. In Shimono's analysis, by the time they became established in Tanegashima all three of these grove types became subsumed under the *garō* mountain label (Shimono [1969] 1995, 503).

9. Confucian officials during the Joseon era (Yi dynasty, 1392–1897) regarded worship at groves led by women as a debased form of religion. In 1702, for example, the Korean court sent out officials to destroy sacred groves and Buddhist temples in 130 locations. Some 400 priestesses and shamans were punished and forcibly returned to farming (Okaya 2019, 156). The 1970 New Village Movement, other infrastructure modernization, and the spread of Christianity also reduced the number of groves and, in many cases, altered their ostensible purpose (Lee 2011, 122–124; Okaya 2019, 142–143, 166–167).

10. The island of Shimokoshiki is offshore from Ichiki-kushikino City in Kagoshima Prefecture. There, a *yabusa* shrine is located in the village of Sasenoura. Local people are aware, however, that the original site was a bamboo grove just above where the waves washed the sand. That grove was feared as a haunted mountain (Eguchi 2008, 113–114). Even in places where Yabusa is now understood to be the name of a deity, few local people claim to understand its characteristics. In some parts of Kyushu, Yabusa's name has become Yakusa or

Yakusasa because of a tendency to conflate Yabusa with Yakushi, the healing Buddha (Eguchi 2008, 99–100).

11. These sites are Nakijin-jō, Zakimi-jō, Katsuren-jō, Nakagusuku-jō, and Shuri-jō. I call them "castles" because in the context of the official registration documents, their titles all contain the suffix -jō 城. Moreover, as I explain in detail in chapter 8, large *gusuku* functioned as castles by any reasonable definition of the term. See Okinawa Prefectural Education Bureau 2001.

12. They are Samnyeon Sanseon, Sangdang Sanseong, Mireuk Sanseong, Chungju Sanseong, Jangmi Sanseong, Deokju Sanseong, and Ondal Sanseong, all located in central South Korea. Chungcheongbuk-do Province in cooperation with the Korea Fortress Academy has prepared a general volume on mountain fortresses plus a detailed volume for each of the seven World Heritage candidates. The series title is Mountain Fortresses of Inland Korea. As examples, see Korea Fortress Academy 2007, 2008a, 2008b.

13. "In Korea, people constructed sanseongs on high mountains near them, but separated from their cities and villages in preparation of wartime. They saved food, water, salt, and charcoal in the fortress in normal times, and when enemies invaded, they moved all remaining resources to the sanseong, so that the enemies could not use them. Then Koreans stayed in the sanseong and waited for the enemies to withdraw because of starvation" (Korea Fortress Academy 2008a, 39).

14. "Koreans regarded sanseongs as sacred places where the holy god helped and protected people, so many religious ceremonies were held there, and myths and legends related to the sanseong were made and passed down. The government performed religious services, praying to nature and gods at fortresses or fortress gates, and the local government also performed unique services in prayer for its peace and welfare. Sometimes, a historical character was deified" (Korea Fortress Academy 2008a, 39).

15. In Japan, there "remain sanseongs [J. *Yamashiro*] to defend against the allied forces of the Tang Dynasty and the Silla Dynasty, constructed after the Baekje Dynasty, which Japan supported, was defeated by the allied forces. Documentary records inform us that Japan built *mizuki* (fortresses with [an] underground waterway) with the help and supervision of the Baekje people" (Korea Fortress Academy 2008a, 35).

16. Each volume in the Mountain Fortresses of Inland Korea series includes a chapter 2, "Features of Mountain Fortresses in Central Inland Korea," with identical content. The pagination is slightly different from one volume to the next.

17. "Archeologically, Chinese fortresses have several features," according to the Korea Fortress Academy (2008a, 33):

(1) The cities were established on plains near rivers or streams. (2) The cities were virtually surrounded by walls. (3) The walls of the cities were made by the stamped earth method. (4) Almost all of the cities were made in the shape of a square or rectangle, but a few of them did not have a regular shape. (5) Palace and graves were built in the cities based on their belief of directions, considering the meridian line from north to south. (6) Earthen altars and great graves were politically or traditionally the most important constructions, so they were made to attract the eye. (7) Chinese people made special areas in the shape of a square in every city, which has not changed.

None of these characteristics apply to *gusuku* or to mountain fortresses.

18. In Japanese these three types of wall construction are called *nozurazumi, aikatazumi,* and *nunozumi,* respectively. For photos of each type, see Okinawa Prefectural Education Bureau 2001, 36.

19. Similarly, Okinawan portrayals of the Three Principalities often associate each with an essential function (Sanhoku, military power; Sannan, economic prosperity; Chūzan, spiritual power). The same tendency is found in Korean portrayals of the first three Silla kings (Yoshinari 2018, 199; Smits 2019, 85–87, both following Georges Dumézil and Ōbayashi Taryō).

20. There appear to have been at least two people with the name Shōsatto, in part because it is likely that the "-satto" part of the name was generic. See chapter 10 for much more on this matter.

21. Recall from chapter 2 the genetic evidence linking the Korean Peninsula and the Ryukyu Islands, specifically Y chromosome haplotype O2b and a human leukocyte antigen (HLA) haplotype that only Koreans and Ryukyu Islanders have in common.

22. In the *Omoro*, following tradition, modern translators almost always render Yashiro as Yamashiro (a province near Kyoto). In *Maritime Ryukyu* I present extensive evidence that the Yamato-Yashiro pair refers to Satsuma and Yatsushiro, respectively (Smits 2019, 31–32, 73–74, 258n72).

Chapter Seven: Agriculture

1. The oldest site showing genuine agriculture (large-scale farming) is Naazakibaru in Naha, dating from the ninth and tenth centuries. The large quantity and variety of carbonized grain found in soil samples there make it unlikely that the grain arrived via trading. Agricultural tools have been excavated from the area, and no nuts (*kara*), a common Shellmound-era food, were found. All evidence points to this community having supported itself primarily by agriculture (Morimoto 2008, 272–273; Hokama 2015a, 57).

2. Similarly, considerable evidence shows that some Jōmon groups practiced small-scale agriculture during the late and final Jōmon eras or that they actively cultivated certain plants (Habu 2004, 69–71). There is also a vigorous debate among Japanese scholars about the extent to which rice cultivation, or even full-fledged agriculture, developed in certain Jōmon communities. For a detailed discussion, see Kurima 2010, 24–88.

3. The main evidence for agriculture is the presence of carbonized grain, cereal grain impressions in pottery sherds, agricultural tools, and skeletons of livestock and, more rarely, the excavation of plots of land that had been cultivated. Evidence of ancient diets from human bone collagen samples is also useful in dating the arrival of agriculture.

4. I argued briefly in *Maritime Ryukyu* that agricultural surpluses cannot account for Okinawa's many fortresses (Smits 2019, 36).

5. In the context of contemporary Southeast Asia, Barker and Janowski (2011) note, "Rather than a simple dichotomy between 'foraging' and 'farming' today . . . there is a continuum between the forest at the one end of the spectrum and wet-rice fields at the other end, with various practices in between."

6. Data from human bone collagen samples indicate the contribution of agriculture to the food supply. "Around AD 1000 there is a decrease in $\delta^{15}N_{coll}$ values for the Ryukyus with values similar to Hirota, or even lower, suggesting an increased dependence on plant foods and lower consumption of marine protein. This is supported by zooarchaeological evidence showing that fish consumption declined with the introduction of farming" (Jarosz et al. 2022, 10).

7. Asato has explicitly come to reject the influential "late historical development hypothesis" advanced by Shinzato Keiji in the 1960s and 1970s. Shinzato contrasted Okinawa and mainland Japan with respect to eleven criteria, including the time of Okinawa's appearance in the records of other countries, the arrival and use of writing, the arrival of Buddhism, unification of the state's territory, and the compilation of its own histories. Shinzato concluded that

Okinawa developed roughly eight centuries later than Japan on average. Because iron and wet-rice cultivation developed late, a primitive society persisted in Okinawa into the thirteenth century. In terms of Marxist historical evolution, Okinawa did not become an ancient state (*kodai kokka*) until the early fifteenth century, and it did not reach the feudal society stage until the seventeenth century (Shinzato Keiji 1970, 36–37; Asato 2010, 12). In 1987 Takara Kurayoshi criticized the late development idea, noting the rapid appearance of a kingdom following the *gusuku* era. He argued that Ryukyuan history got off to a late start but, once started, developed rapidly (Takara 1987b, 372–373; Asato 2010, 13–14).

8. An excellent map of soil distribution can be found at Okinawa no Dojō/Soils of Okinawa, http://www.okinawa-nougyou.net/OkinawaSoils.html, accessed September 23, 2022.

9. *Kunigami-maaji,* the main soil in the north of Okinawa, corresponds mostly to G1, with some areas of G2. The areas that Hokama lists as both *Shimajiri-maaji* and *jaaguru* in southern Okinawa (Hokama 2015a, 59) correspond roughly to J4 in the inventory. However, in parts of Hokama's finely detailed discussion, it appears that he regards F3 (gray lowland soil) as a variety of *jaagaru* (Hokama 2018a, 38–42).

10. Hokama sometimes calls *jaagaru* "gray lowland soil," which is type F3.

11. Selecting the E, F, and J soil types and eyeballing the map, roughly one-third of the land of the Ryukyu Islands (not evenly distributed) could have served some kind of agricultural purpose (Japan Soil Inventory), assuming proper tools, labor, know-how, and, in most cases, fertilizer. It is important to bear in mind that tools, labor, and fertilizer appear to have often been in short supply.

12. Indica (Champa) rice (J. *senjōtō* 占城稲 or *chanpatō* チャンパとう) originated in India and spread from Vietnam to southern China. It had arrived in Fújiàn by 1012, and it eventually spread to some parts of western Honshu along the Inland Sea. This type of rice matures relatively quickly and does not require intensive cultivation. Specifically, no large plows or iron tools would have been required, and the ears came off easily at harvest. The Okinawan *taitōmai* was an Indica variety. It was easy to cultivate but regarded as a low-quality variety (Kurima 2013a, 123–127).

13. This idea seems to have originated from a 1376 entry in *Ming Veritable Records* (*MVR* 2001, 1:12 [#8]).

14. The situation in the Yaeyama Islands fits Xú's observations. Until the mid-twentieth century, rice cultivation began in the ninth month, with harvesting in the fifth month. The cultivation cycle typically began with oxen trampling the fields. More broadly, from before the seventeenth century and well into the twentieth, there was no summer cultivation. Today, summer cultivation is limited to gourds and related crops such as *goya* (Kurima 2010, 119–120).

15. According to the Centers for Disease Control and Prevention (CDC), "Four kinds of malaria parasites infect humans: *Plasmodium falciparum, P. vivax, P. ovale,* and *P. malariae.* In addition, *P. knowlesi,* a type of malaria that naturally infects macaques in Southeast Asia, also infects humans, causing malaria that is transmitted from animal to human ("zoonotic" malaria). *P. falciparum* is the type of malaria that is most likely to result in severe infections and if not promptly treated, may lead to death" (https://www.cdc.gov/malaria/about/, accessed February 22, 2023).

16. At temperatures below 20°C (68°F) *Plasmodium falciparum* cannot complete its growth cycle and thus cannot be transmitted (CDC, https://www.cdc.gov/malaria/about/distribution.html, accessed February 22, 2023).

17. In the early Taishō era, approximately twenty people per year died of malaria in Okinawa, and during a major outbreak in 1916, approximately 60–70 percent of the rural residents of Kunigami on northern Okinawa became infected. During the 1920s and 1930s in Miyako, villages whose members cleared away nearby trees and vegetation did not contract malaria, and the reverse was true for those who did not clear vegetation (Inafuku 1995, 488–489, 493).

18. According to Majikina Ankō, "It appears that a taxation system in Okinawa developed after the Keichō era [1598–1615], along with the surveying of land" (Majikina [1923] 1993, 328). In response to Kurima (who cited Majikina) stating that Okinawa had no tax system until the seventeenth century, archaeologist Takamiya Hiroto asserts that *gusuku*-era Okinawa was a hierarchical society (*kaisō shakai*). Moreover, it was a sophisticated society despite a lack of writing. Noting that nearly all societies develop a tax system, Takamiya (2021, 199) argues that archaeological findings do not rule out the possibility that a tax system existed during the *gusuku* era. I find Takamiya's argument unconvincing on several levels. First, I disagree with his characterization of *gusuku*-era society as hierarchical, for reasons that the following two chapters will make clear. Moreover, *gusuku*-era Okinawa was not a single society, at least in terms of political geography. Second, the speculation that a tax system may have existed because most societies have tax systems is too weak a claim to be convincing in the complete absence of any positive evidence.

19. Sugarcane and pineapples are the most abundant edible crops today. Tropical flowers and foliage plants are also significant agricultural products. For details, see Japan CROPs, https://japancrops.com/en/prefectures/okinawa/crops, accessed September 28, 2022).

Chapter Eight: Trading and Raiding Intensify

1. Yaeyama place-names provide an indication of militarization. There, residences surrounded by stone walls often have "warrior" (*bushi,* often as *busu*) in their names. For example, in Ishigaki there is Busuyashiki (J. *bushi no yashiki* [warrior residence]), Busunuyaaishigaki (J. *bushi no ie no ishigaki* [stone fence of a warrior residence]), Busunuyaa (J. *bushi no ie* [warrior household]), and Busunuyama (J. *bushi no yama* [warrior mountain]). On Hatoma Island there is Bushinyaa (J. *bushi no ie* [warrior household]) and on Aragusuku Island, Nishinubushinuyaa (J. *nishi no bushi no ie* [northern (or western) warrior household]) (Ōhama 2008, 254).

2. Writing in the late 1960s, Inamura Kenpu noted that places such as Nago Gusuku, Nejame Gusuku, Amami Gusuku, and many other sites in northern Okinawa called "gusuku" were not castles. Unaware that they were fortresses of a different type, Inamura (1969, 414–415) regarded them as the ruins of old settlements located on high ground.

3. The prominent influence of *gusuku* on geography persists to the present. Local place-names that include cardinal directions, such as Nishihara (西原, also Nishibara or Nishibaru, meaning "northern community") or Haebaru (南風原, also Haebara, indicating a community located south or southeast of something) usually make sense in relation to a nearby *gusuku,* either one that still exists or one that existed in the past (Inamura 1969, 227).

4. In Korean mountain fortresses, "small stone" (K. *soseog*) construction resembles field stone stacking, "plank shape" (K. *pansang*) construction resembles cloth stacking, and fitted stacking walls correspond to the use of "diverse" (K. *dayanghan*) stones (Gungnip Munhwajae Yeonguso 2012, 1300–1301).

5. Takanashi (2015, 260–261) notes that the prominence of trench-and-earthworks *gusuku* in most of the northern Ryukyu Islands indicates that the medieval (chūsei) history of Okinawa and the northern Ryukyu Islands differed significantly. However, there are also many trench-and-earthworks *gusuku* in Okinawa, especially on the northern part of the island.

6. For summaries, see Tōma 2012, 74–76; Kurima 2013b, 141–144.

7. For complete summaries, see Naka 1992; Tōma 2012, 59–83; Kurima 2013b, 137–156.

8. Quoting *Origins of Ryukyu,* Yamazato acknowledged that Iō Gusuku in Naha harbor had a military function vis-à-vis possible pirate attacks. Even in that case, however, he emphasized that the main purpose of the *gusuku* in Naha harbor was support of commerce (Yamazato Eikichi 1963, 239).

9. Such discussions typically note the many places called "-gusuku" that were not walled fortresses and focus on their religious significance or function. This rhetoric is not convincing because, as we have seen, many military *gusuku* were trench-and-earthworks fortifications without stone walls. Moreover, all military *gusuku* included religious facilities in the belief that they would augment military power. Because fortresses, and warfare, were so common, a variety of nonmilitary place-names contain the element *-gusuku*.

10. The first type is centered atop a rise or other elevated area. Examples include Shuri Castle, Uegusuku (Kumejima), Iha Gusuku, Zakimi Gusuku, Katsuren Gusuku, Nakagusuku Gusuku, Urasoe Gusuku, Tamagusuku Gusuku, Sunja Gusuku (Tonaki Island), and Omonawa Gusuku (Tokunoshima). Second are those built atop isolated mountains. Examples include Dana Gusuku (Iheya), Izena Gusuku (Izena), Chibana Gusuku, Yonamine Gusuku (Kumejima), and Agena Gusuku. In the third type, one or two sides are atop cliffs. Examples include Nakijin Gusuku, Ishikinawa Gusuku (Kumejima), Gushikawa Gusuku (Itoman City), Chinen Gusuku, Uezato Gusuku, Itokazu Gusuku, Tomigusuku, and Iso Gusuku. The fourth type is trench-and-earthworks fortresses without stone walls. They include Jana Gusuku, Chatan Gusuku, Gushikawa Gusuku (Kumejima), Gushikawa Gusuku (Gushikawa City), and locations in Amami-Ōshima such as Toguchi Hirakiyama Gusuku, Ōgachi Gusuku, En Gusuku, Itsubugachi Gusuku, Urakami Gusuku, Beru Gusuku, and Akagina Gusuku (Naka 1992, 148).

11. Amid a lengthy technical study of *gusuku,* Tōma Shiichi somewhat whimsically observes that the "sweet taste of walking through *gusuku* lies in the romance of history such that one can feel the tense situation within Ryukyuan society during the era of state formation, pursuing the soldiers' dreams" (Tōma 2012, 426). Tōma's romanticizing of the battles fought at *gusuku* is an interesting counterpoint to the more common practice of romanticizing a fictitious peaceful Ryukyuan past.

12. Sulfur and horses, along with weapons, were also among the most important items that Tsushima merchants (with *wakō* roots) provided to Korea during the first half of the fourteenth century (Seyock 2005, 100). The Joseon court pursued a strategy similar to that of the Ming court with respect to taming *wakō* by making trading more profitable than raiding.

13. As Barbara Seyock (2005, 95–96) notes, in a 1380 Jeju Island battle with pirates and local residents, Goryeo military forces captured sixteen hundred horses. *Wakō* forces could move quickly on land because of the large quantities of horses accompanying them, with as many as two thousand head on the island of Jeju.

14. To mention a few examples, Richard Pearson argues for 1273, citing similar tiles in a Korean castle that was in use between 1270 and 1273. He also states that "radiocarbon determinations . . . support the date of AD 1273" but provides no citation or further details

(Pearson 2013, 173–174). Some scholars arguing for 1333 note that although the initial 1986 survey of Urasoe Castle ruins dated the tiles' manufacture to the mid-thirteenth century, it was later determined that tiles were used only in buildings with foundations. Those buildings date to the first half of the fourteenth century (Yoshinari 2018, 290n29). Shimizu Nobuyuki (1998, 39) argues for 1333 based in part on comparison with tiles of the same type from a Korean temple of similar vintage. Ikeda Yoshifumi (2019, 30) places the dates for all three Korean tile castles in Okinawa as within the fourteenth century. He also notes that Chinese ceramics found with the tiles date from the end of the thirteenth to the early fourteenth century, thus making 1333 more likely than 1273 (Ikeda 2012b, 335).

15. See also Takahashi 2008, 176–177; Tōma 2012, 15; Hokama 2018, 61–62.

16. Based on its depiction in maps, Kenneth R. Robinson describes Hakata as "the pivot in the maritime routes. . . . This port city was a central place for economic interaction where ships from or en route to central Japan, Chosŏn [Korea], northeastern Kyushu, Tsushima, and Ryukyu ported" (Robinson 2000, 97).

17. During the fourteenth century, Akagina Gusuku developed multiple trenches, earthworks, and enclosed spaces (Nakayama 2008, 188–193; Takanashi 2015, 261). Akagina featured three lines of trenches dug out around the northern earthworks to augment their defensive function. This use of trenches was common in castles in northern Kyushu during the fourteenth and fifteenth centuries (Kasari-chō 2003, 31). During the late fourteenth and early fifteenth centuries, this type of fortress became common in both Amami-Ōshima and northern Okinawa. Moreover, Shō Hashi's fortress at Sashiki in southern Okinawa was of similar Japanese design (Yoshinari 2020, 182–186).

18. Other significant fortresses in northern Amami-Ōshima include Beru Gusuku and Minato Gusuku (both near Akagina), Ōgachi Gusuku, and En Gusuku (in Tatsugō), Koshuku Gusuku, Chinaze Gusuku, Itsubugachi Gusuku, and Urakami Gusuku (all in Amami City).

19. There are equally viable explanations for the pottery distribution at this time, such as traders based at Nakijin importing whiteware and distributing it to the southern Ryukyu Islands.

20. Yoshinari (2020, 114–152) also summarizes Uema's arguments and evidence.

21. They were known as Āsù 阿速, also written Ālán 阿蘭 and Āsī 阿思.

22. Han'anchi ruled until 1416 according to official sources, but his sudden reappearance in Chinese records as having sent tribute in 1416 followed nearly ten years of complete silence and inactivity. Almost certainly the 1416 tribute sent in Han'anchi's name was from a party other than Han'anchi, who probably died in 1406 at the hands of Shō Hashi.

23. There are three types of *birōsuku* ware. The first two (B1 and 2) came into the Ryukyu Islands at approximately the same time, the late thirteenth and early fourteenth centuries. Although found in moderate quantities in the southern Ryukyu Islands, the majority of it has been excavated from Nakijin Gusuku (Shinzato 2018, 80). Of the large *gusuku*, only Nakijin was closely connected with these Fújiàn ceramics (Yoshinari 2020, 119–120). The third type (B3) replaced B1 and B2 in the mid-fourteenth century, continuing into the early fifteenth century.

If there had been a direct trade route from Fújiàn up through the southern Ryukyu Islands, Okinawa, and the northern Ryukyu Islands, we would expect to find a large increase in B3 in the southern Ryukyu Islands. However, the quantity of B3 relative to B1 and B2 decreased in the southern Ryukyu Islands (Shinzato 2018, 80, fig. 37; Yoshinari 2020, 120). It is possible, therefore, that merchants based at Nakijin conducted the trade in Fújiàn whiteware. They procured the pottery, stored it, and sold it to other localities. Nakijin traders obtained the whiteware via two possible routes: sailing up to Hakata or sailing to Fújiàn (Yoshinari 2020, 120–122). Whiteware probably did pass through or near the Ryukyu Islands from Fújiàn, but we cannot be sure whether the terminus point was somewhere in the Ryukyu Islands or in Hakata or whether Chinese ships stopped along the route to trade (Yoshinari 2020, 117–118). In any case the appearance of Fújiàn whiteware indicates a significant new trade route involving the southern Ryukyu Islands, Nakijin, and southern China.

Chapter Nine: The Geopolitical Landscape

1. This lord of Tedokon may have been Shō Hashi's father, known as Shō Shishō. According to Nakamatsu Yashū's interpretation, the term "Nihon" here refers to an entity that encompasses both Yamato (the main Japanese Islands) and Ryukyu (Yoshinari 2020, 196–197, 302–303).

2. Inamura Kenpu came up with a different list of powerful locations in central and southern Okinawa by using *Origins of Ryukyu* and locating sacred groves (*utaki*) whose names indicate rulership or control of territory. He hypothesized that these groves were the tombs of powerful local rulers and that such rulers, or their descendants, later coalesced into the Three Principalities (Inamura 1969, 44–45). Inamura's hypothesis is based on an assumption that the account of the Three Principalities in the official histories is basically accurate.

3. Other examples from the early and middle fourteenth centuries include Guraru (Goran) Magohachi and Waja Masaburō in Okinoerabu (*Yononushi yuisho sho* [1850] 1968, 180; Smits 2019, 71).

4. The Nakijin count here is probably low, and the high Urasoe count reflects accumulation since the middle or late fourteenth century. Nakijin was the earliest large *gusuku* in Okinawa to trade in Chinese ceramics, possibly directly with China but more likely obtaining the wares from Hakata merchants. This early trade is the likely reason for its relatively high count.

5. In *Maritime Ryukyu* I translated this *omoro* slightly differently, with the second line as "Should the many lords think to come north from Shuri" (Smits 2019, 82). I used "Shuri" based on the headnotes in Hokama and Saigō (1972, 32). However, the key term is simply "upward" (*kami*), and it could indicate any southern power or powers moving north toward Nakagusuku.

6. Itokazu Gusuku is 189 meters in height. The next seven highest are Tamagusuku Gusuku (181 meters), Nakagusuku Gusuku (167 meters), Ōzato Gusuku (150 meters), Shuri Castle (130 meters), Zakimi Gusuku (127 meters), Nago Gusuku (103 meters), and Katsuren Gusuku (98 meters) (Okada 2000, 136).

7. The white horses of Makabe were widely desired by other warlords. The lord of Makabe refused their requests for horses, whereupon the lord of Kunigami led a large force southward and laid siege to Makabe, taking the lord of Makabe by surprise. Makabe *aji* sent word to his younger brother, Kakihana *aji*, asking for help. Kakihana *aji* was unable to save the horses, which all died in the battle. Makabe *aji* was so saddened by the loss that he killed himself. As a result, the villagers around Makabe lost the means and know-how for raising white horses (Shinjō 1982, 350; Okinawa-ken 1983, 150).

8. Examples include Aman Gusuku, Okuma Gusuku, Kijoka Gusuku, Tsuha Gusuku, Hana Gusuku, Kouri Gusuku, Jin Gusuku, Ama Gusuku, Uugusuku, Uigusuku, Uegusuku, Uezato Gusuku, Oyagawa Gusuku, and Jana Gusuku (Okinawa-ken 1983, 24–39; Takanashi 2015, 253).

9. A technical term for these trench-and-earthworks fortifications built into the side of mountains is *chūsei jōkaku* 中世城郭. Noting the fourteenth-century appearance of Japanese-style fortresses in northern Okinawa, Yoshinari (2020, 184–185) points out that this part of Okinawa became occupied mainly by outside arrivals, especially *wakō*, who had connections with powers in the northern Ryukyu Islands.

Chapter Ten: Many More than Three

1. In some of the secondary literature, Sannan is also known as Nanzan, and Sanhoku is also known as Hokuzan.

2. This basic teleology, with a centralized kingdom as the end point and agriculture as the main economic driver, partially informs the official history accounts. Additionally, personality strengths and (more often) flaws play a prominent causal role in historical events. Shō Hashi's legendary biography is an example. Hashi of Chūzan knew that Tarumi of Sannan coveted beauty and wealth. Hashi persuaded Tarumi to cede valuable territory, the Kadeshi Spring, in return for a gold-plated screen (*byōbu*). Hashi's control of this water source crippled agriculture in Sannan, whose farmers rebelled. By understanding the importance of agriculture as well as Tarumi's character flaws, Hashi deposed Tarumi and gained control of Sannan (*Kyūyō* [1743–1876] 1974, 1978, 119–120 [84]; Smits 2019, 86).

3. According to the narrative in the official histories, between 1314 and roughly the 1420s the island of Okinawa consisted of three small kingdoms or principalities, literally "Three Mountains" (Sanzan). Sannan (or Nanzan) was the southern principality, Chūzan was roughly in the center and included the Shuri-Naha-Urasoe area, and Sanhoku (or Hokuzan) was roughly the northern two-thirds of Okinawa, with its capital at Nakijin. In the official narrative, Urasoe was the capital of Chūzan, and nearby Ōzato was the capital of Sannan.

4. In *Maritime Ryukyu* I mistakenly stated that Ryukyu sent more tribute embassies to China than any other country (Smits 2019, 65). However, Korea sent the largest number of embassies, with Ryukyu in second place. I thank Kirk Larsen for this information.

5. Sin's map was based on a 1453 map of Hakata, Satsuma, and Ryukyu presented to the Korean court by Dōan, a Hakata merchant and Buddhist priest who worked as an envoy to Korea from Ryukyu (Robinson 2000, 94, 97; Hashimoto 2008, 292–294; Murai 2019, 296).

6. Although *East Sea Countries* was drafted in 1471, it was periodically revised until 1501 (Robinson 2000, 88).

7. *Omoro-sōshi* 14–982 is about "Janamoi" (the beloved son of Jana), portraying him as a magnificent person who opened up the storehouses of the many lords. Because the official histories claim that Satto was born in Jana, this Janamoi is conventionally regarded to be Satto. It is possible that this passage is a reference to Satto initiating tribute trade, but it is not necessarily about Satto. In any case this song is the only possible reference to any of the trade kings of the Three Principalities other than Shishō and Hashi.

8. While some of the trade kings lack tombs, an excess of tombs is also possible. For example, the legendary king Gihon has three tombs in the Kunigami region of northern Okinawa (Inamura 1969, 42–43).

9. Sūn Wěi (2015, 61–102) makes extensive use of local genealogies and mortuary tablets to identify lineages of Sannan trade kings.

10. Several Okinawan pronunciations of Eiso's name are possible: Iizu, Izu, Ueezu, Eezu, and Eesu. Moreover, there are several sets of Chinese characters used in written sources to gloss the

"-eiso" element, either in Eisoʼs name or in the names of several Sannan trade kings containing this same element. Reading these sets of characters as Chinese results in (1) 惠祖 Huìzǔ, (2) 應[応]祖 Yīngzǔ, (3) 英祖 Yīngzǔ, (4) 英紫 Yīngzǐ, and (5) 英慈 Yīngcí. Names 2 and 3 are typically pronounced ōso and eiso, respectively, in Japanese, but they are identical in Chinese. Names 4 and 5, while not identical in Chinese, are similar (Yoshinari 2018, 189; 2020, 164).

11. In their translation of the Omoro, Hokama Shuzen and Saigō Nobutsuna gloss the "Iizu" in this song with the same set of characters as Iizu (Iso) Gusuku because this person, whom they regard as Eiso, is clearly one warrior among many, albeit a superior one. In other words, this Iizu was Eiso before he became king. Because they assume that the official history accounts of Eiso are basically accurate, Hokama and Saigō gloss Iizu-niya, which literally means "person of Iizu," with the same characters for Eiso found in the official histories (Hokama and Saigō 1972, 517). If the official history accounts of Eiso are not basically accurate, as I would argue, then that gloss is not warranted.

12. For example, Eisoʼs remains would have to have been reburied there after the tile-roof structures were built in the fourteenth century. Furthermore, it would have been necessary for the warlord who controlled Urasoe Castle to have preserved Eisoʼs remains. Almost certainly that warlord was Satto, a person who disappeared without a trace, as we will see. It would be strange for Satto to have preserved Eisoʼs remains and tomb but not to have made any arrangements for himself (Yoshinari 2018, 183–184; 2020, 162–163).

13. Tobutono is 兔武登能, and the exact pronunciation is uncertain. Assuming the -tono part is an honorific, then the name means Lord Tobu.

14. Many modern sources leave off the final character 氏 and refer to him as Ōeiji or Ōeishi 汪英紫. This shorter name better fits a contemporary sense of pronunciation because in modern Japanese usage -shi -氏 is a formal title appended to surnames. However, this king clearly appears as 汪英紫氏 in Chinese sources, with the final character part of the sound of his name. Moreover, 氏 does not appear at the end of any other royal names. In Chinese the full name would be Wāngyīngzǐshì.

15. The original text of Ming Veritable Records lists Urasoe Satto as Sato 查都 (Zhādōu). Later texts used Satto 察度 (Chádù; Yoshinari, 2018, 196).

16. There are, of course, rumors and discussions of this matter on websites. The typical approach is to use biographical information in the official histories combined with information about Urasoe to speculate about which extant tomb site might house Sattoʼs remains.

17. Contrary to the general consensus that Shōsatto and Onsado were two names for the same person, Sūn Wěi (2016, 58–60) has argued that they were different and, moreover, that they constituted different lineages. My view is that they might well have been different people, if indeed they were specific individuals. However, the key point is that they were both part of the Satto/Sato/Sado group.

18. According to the traditional story, in 1392 or 1393 the Ming emperor ordered thirty-six families from Fújiàn Province to relocate to Okinawa. They settled in what would become Kumemura (e.g., Kerr [1958] 2000, 75). However, there is no record of such an order or migration at that time. The earliest mention of the thirty-six families occurred in investiture envoy Chén Kǎnʼs 1534 record, Shǐ Liúqiú lù (Shi Ryūkyū roku 1534, 67). There does not appear to have been any large, sudden influx of Chinese to the Naha area. Instead, merchant-officials came to Naha as needed, with some remaining, others returning to China, and newcomers taking their place. Their residence area became Kumemura. The term "thirty-six families" appears to have been shorthand for all Chinese who came to reside in Kumemura during the fourteenth and early

fifteenth centuries. In 1607 King Shō Nei invoked the (invented) memory of the thirty-six families in requesting the Ming court to once again order a group of Chinese to settle in Okinawa to revive Kumemura, which was in decline. Ming authorities declined the request (*MVR* 2006, 3:17 [#56]).

19. For example, someone called Ubama (步馬 or 阿勃馬)-utchi served twice as tribute envoy under the auspices of Tarumi of Sannan before 1425. In 1425 he returned to Okinawa but as an envoy of Chūzan's Shō Hashi. He soon set out again as Hashi's envoy to Siam (Thailand), and in 1428 and 1429, he again served as a tribute envoy of Tarumi. Between 1430 and 1440, he was again back in the service of Shō Hashi and Hashi's Chinese prime minister, Kaiki (Ch. Huái Jī), as a tribute envoy and as an envoy to several locations in Southeast Asia (Murai 2019, 103, 2-1-202).

20. In 1423 an envoy of Shō Hashi, Asato, Afusato, or Ōsato 阿不察都, appeared (*MVR* 2001, 1:24 [#94, #95], and most likely the same person, glossed 阿蒲察都, appeared as an envoy in 1430 and 1433 (*MVR*, 28 [#46, #47], 30 [#77, #79]. This name is probably a coincidence because -*sato* was a common element in Okinawan names. However, there is a slight chance it indicates a remnant of the Satto group.

21. Although thoroughly conventional in her general view of the Three Principalities era, Sūn Wěi (2016, 160) notes that although Satto and the other trade kings who appear in Chinese and Korean records dominate the narratives of the era, many other "heroes" (i.e., warriors) appear in the songs of the *Omoro* (Sūn 2016, 160).

Chapter Eleven: Era of the First Shō "Dynasty"

1. Terms like *aji, satonushi, ueekata, peechin/peekumi,* peasants (*hyakushō*), etc., date from the sixteenth century or later. One term we do find commonly in Chinese records from this time is *utchi* (J. *okite*), often written 結致, indicating the head or chief of a harbor or similar unit. Undoubtedly, there were people who fulfilled specialized tasks or functioned as leaders within each seafaring group, but there appears to have been no general, codified Okinawa-wide or Ryukyu-wide formal social hierarchy during the fifteenth century.

2. Writing in the early sixteenth century, Portuguese merchant Vasco Valvo noted that Ryukyuans sail first to Fújiàn and from there "go secretly" to carry on trade further south. For details, see Ptak 2005, 309–311.

3. As S. M. Hong-Schunka (2005, 148) notes regarding a Ryukyuan embassy to Korea in 1500, "there were only twenty-two native Ryūkyūans out of a total of 470 traders, less than five percent. Furthermore, Ryūkyūan missions to Korea sailed in Japanese ships owned by Japanese captains, who assumed the senior functions such as chief and vice ambassador. Of altogether ca. fifty official missions from Ryūkyū to Korea between the late fourteenth and to the early sixteenth century, only four missions were headed by ethnic Ryūkyūans." It should be noted that many of these fifty or so embassies were spurious, as I explain later in the chapter.

4. Scholars writing in Japanese have proposed a variety of hypotheses for the origin of the Shō name. For a summary, see Tanigawa and Orikuchi (2012, 40–43).

5. On this basis Hokama and Saigō speculate, unconvincingly in my view, that two of the four instances in which the *Omoro* mentions Agarui-no-Ōnushi (Great Lord of the East) refer to Shō Chū. This is because the sun rises over the Sashiki area of Okinawa and eventually extends to northern Okinawa as it rises higher in the sky (*Omoro sōshi* 5-238, 14-1030; Hokama and Saigō 1972, 497). Even if this speculation is accurate, the passages provide no information about Shō Chū.

6. In *Maritime Ryukyu* I suggested the migration took place circa 1400, but a better time frame would be circa 1385–1390. In either case, Hashi would have been born in Kyushu.

7. Of the twenty-two known Buddhist temple bells cast before the seventeenth century, eighteen were cast during Shō Taikyū's reign by Japanese technicians from northern Kyushu, Fujiwara Kuniyoshi of Chikuzen and Fujiwara Kunimitsu of Buzen (Murai 2019, 187; Takahashi Yasuo 2015, 378). Kuniyoshi cast Taikyū's Sea Bridge to the Many Countries Bell.

8. The records of Korean observers found mainly in the *Joseon Veritable Royal Records* (*JVRR-r*) and that they have been widely reproduced in secondary literature. For a thorough summary, see Murai 2019, 147–168. See also Smits 2019, 41–42, 49–50, 92–96.

9. Circa the 1930s, the former mayor of Kikai Village, Orita Noboru, wrote down the battle lore that had been passed down in the oral tradition in Kikaijima. In his account the island's beaches and cliffs were well defended. One tactic was to deploy dummies, at which the invaders shot arrows. The Kikaijima defenders then took those arrows and shot them back at the invaders. Moreover, the defenders hid themselves in the shadows of boulders to surprise the attackers. When at last the attackers overwhelmed the defenders at Araki beach and went ashore, the carnage was immense on both sides (Takeuchi 1960 [1933], 80–81). It is impossible to verify any of these details. The point is simply that even into the twentieth century, Shō Toku's conquest of Kikaijima lingered in local folk memory as an especially awful event.

10. The reading of the names is based on Takahashi Ichirō (2008, 162).

11. Inamura also interprets "Agaru-mochizuki" as "Mochizuki-aji," the male ruler of Katsuren. However, every other instance of "Agaru-mochizuki" in the *Omoro* refers to a shamanic priestess, possibly the daughter or sister of the male ruler Mochizuki.

12. Another route, starting early in the fifteenth century, was for a tribute ship to sail from Naha to China and then from China to Thailand to obtain sappanwood and other tropical products and then back to China to sell or exchange the tropical products. Ships from Thailand also sometimes came to Naha (Murai 2019, 109–110). In this way, nominally "Ryukyuan" ships based at Naha provided a legal way to circumvent the Ming government's Maritime Prohibitions. See also Smits 2019, 61, 66, 74–75.

13. Hashimoto Yū (2008, 290) has identified four patterns of envoys during this era: 1) authentic envoys with authentic documents; 2) a false envoy with authentic documents; 3) an authentic envoy with forged or manipulated documents; and 4) a false envoy with false documents.

14. According to Hashimoto (2008, 296), the main reason spurious "Ryukyuan" envoys to Korea did not renew the names of Ryukyuan kings in their documents was because once the Korean court had accepted a particular king, changing the king's name would incur official suspicion.

15. As S. M. Hong-Schunka (2005, 127) points out regarding the period 1392–1527, "Many of the ambassadors allegedly from Ryūkyū were in fact Japanese merchants from Tsushima and Hakata interested in commerce but without any authorization by the Ryūkyūan king."

16. Two later embassies from Jiŭbiǎn arrived, one in late 1481 or early 1482 and another in 1482. None succeeded in establishing formal relations with the Korean court. Japanese merchants also created the fake country of Ezogachishima. Although creating an entirely new country may seem overly troublesome, a major goal in both the Jiŭbiǎn and Ezogachishima charades was to obtain the 6,805 volumes of the *Goryeo Tripitaka* (Robinson 1997, 59, 64). Presumably, they reasoned that the Korean court would be more likely to give such a large, expensive item to a new country.

17. Commenting on this era, Kenneth R. Robinson notes with respect to the territories of warlords based at fortresses, "In the early 1450s, the Ryukyuan king seems to have lacked sufficient means to extend royal authority deeply into these communities" (Robinson 2000, following Miyagi Eishō).

Chapter Twelve: The Second Shō Dynasty and the Creation of a Centralized State

1. I have, of course, left out many details. At Munakata, Hetsumiya 辺津宮 enshrines Ichikishimahime 市杵島姫; at Ōshima, Nakatsumiya 中津宮 enshrines Tagitsuhime 湍津姫; and at Okinoshima, Okitsumiya 沖津宮 enshrines Tagorihime 田心姫. For a thorough analysis of the shrines, their origins, their rituals, and so forth, see Munakata (2017). I thank Akiko Smits for bringing the Munakata Shrine to my attention.

2. Makishi notes that this change in Sasukasa's character corresponded to changes in the nature of the royal government (Makishi 2023, 277).

3. Leaving out the technical details, Makishi Yōko argues convincingly that Shō Shin's conquest of Kumejima must have taken place sometime before Shuri's 1500 conquest of Ishigaki. Her reason is that *Omoro sōshi* 1–33, a lengthy song about the 1500 conquest, presupposes the existence of the *hiki* system and mentions a Kumejima *ibe* name as a paired term for the high priestess (Makishi 2023, 254). It is also possible that Okinawan forces invaded Kumejima both in 1506 and at some time before 1500 (Smits 2019, 167).

4. For example, according to *Mawashi-shi shi,* when Shō Shin was campaigning in Kunigami, he encountered trouble in the Motobu Peninsula. A younger brother of Shō En, Uema Ōya, risked his life in battle and saved the day. Uema Ōya became lord of Nakijin district as a result, and two of his sons were permitted to move from Gushiken in Motobu to the Shikina heights on the outskirts of Shuri. Their village was called Shiken (from Gushiken), which transformed into Shikina (Inamura 1969, 19).

5. Rekihaku, https://www.rekihaku.ac.jp/outline/press/p210316/index.html.

6. During Sai On's time in office, and for some time thereafter, it was common for the central government to force people in the countryside to relocate, sometimes great distances, to facilitate more efficient agricultural production. While these relocations were rational in some sense, they caused great human suffering. The most notorious example was the forced relocation of people from Okinawa to Yaeyama. Although it is unclear whether Sai On personally ordered all such relocations, they took place while he was in power. Looking only at the Yaeyama Islands, here are examples of relocations during Sai On's time. The numbers indicate people:

1722: 400 from Kuroshima-son to Nosoko 野底 in Miyara-son to create Nosoko-son.

1722: 700-plus drawn from five villages in Ishigaki to create Tōzato-son 桃里村.

1722: 600-plus drawn from Kohama and other small islands to form Takana-son 高那村 in Iriomote.

1734: Seventy-four from Taketomi-son in Iriomote sent to Yarabu-mori to create Haemi-son 南風見村 (vicinity of the Nakama river in Iriomote).

1737: 533 drawn from a village in Tōnoshiro (Ishigaki; today's Banna Park area) and combined with 87 of the original inhabitants of Nagura-son 名蔵村 to create a village of 600+.

1750: 960 from Ishigaki-son to create Arakawa-son. Then 1,500 from Tōnoshiro to form Ōkawa-son; 185 from Hirae-son to establish Maezato-son; 400 more from

Hirae-son plus 400 from Ōhama-son to establish Nakahara-son; 686 from Shi-raho-son to establish Maja-son真謝村.

1753: 48 from Ibaruma-son, 100 from Shiraho-son, plus 200 from Taketomi-son to establish Ara-son 安良村.

1755: 200 from Hateruma to establish Sakiyama-son 崎山村 in Iriomote.

(Data from Tamura [1927] 1977, 146–149)

Chapter Thirteen: Early Ryukyu in Regional History

1. As Scott (2017, 243) points out, "One-time plunder raiding is likely to kill the host alto-gether, while a stable protection racket mimics the process of state appropriation and is com-patible with the long-run productivity of the [state's] grain core."

2. Stated concisely: "The key to the nexus between grains and states lies . . . in the fact that only the cereal grains can serve as a basis for taxation: visible, divisible, assessable, storable, transportable, and 'rationable.' Other crops—legumes, tubers, and starch plants—have some of these desirable state-adapted qualities, but none has all these advantages" (Scott 2017, 129).

3. As Jarosz et al. (2022, 16) note, "The assumption that the Ryukyuan language separated and dispersed from a common ancestor situated in southern Kyushu indicates that escape from state control may also have been a factor in the dispersal of Ryukyuan."

4. For example, according to Richard Pearson (2013, 167): "The regional exchange system of *kamuiyaki* is evidence of commercial communication throughout the islands from the Northern Ryukyus to the southernmost islands of Sakishima and can be seen as a prelude to the emergence of regional political unity. . . . A sense of regional Ryukyu identity was created through the circulation of local products to every corner of the archipelago."

Here, Pearson is expressing a consensus view. I have read nearly identical statements many times in the Japanese literature, and I have always found them puzzling. In my view they attri-bute too much ethnocultural power to pots, plates, and bowls—items that nearly anyone in the world at that time would have recognized, understood, and been able to put to good use.

5. The term "theatre state" is associated with Clifford Geertz (1980).

WORKS CITED

Note: The place of publication for Japanese books is Tokyo unless otherwise indicated.

Adolphson, Mikael. 2007. *The Teeth and Claws of the Buddha: Monastic Warriors and Sōhei in Japanese History*. Honolulu: University of Hawai'i Press.

Akamine, Mamoru. 2017. *The Ryukyu Kingdom: Cornerstone of East Asia*. Translated by Lina Terrell. Edited by Robert Huey. Honolulu: University of Hawai'i Press.

Anma Kiyoshi 安間清. (1952) 1995. "'Niso no mori' chōsa"「ニソの杜」調査. In *Nihon minzoku bunka shiryō shūsei, dai nijūichi kan: Mori no kami no minzokushi* 日本民族文化資料集成, 第二十一巻: 森の神の民族誌, edited by Tanigawa Ken'ichi 谷川健一, pp. 76–98. San'ichi shobō.

Araki Moriaki 安良城盛昭. 1980. *Shin, Okinawa-shi ron* 新・沖縄史論. Naha: Okinawa taimusu sha, 1980.

———. 1981. "Ryūkyūshi no tokushitsu ni tsuite" 琉球史の特質について. *Gekkan, Rekishi techō* 月刊, 歴史手帳, April, 4–11.

Arashiro Toshiaki 新城俊昭. 2010. *Okinawa kara mieru rekishi fūkei* 沖縄から見える歴史風景. Naha: Henshū kōbō, Tōyō kikaku.

Asahi Shinbun Digital. "Miyakojima senshi no hitobito 'kitagawa no Okinawa shotō kara' 'Minami kara' setsu o kutsugaesu" 宮古島先史の人々「北側の沖縄諸島から」「南から」説を覆す, November 13, 2021.

Asato Susumu 安里進. (2006) 2010. *Ryūkyū ōken to gusuku* 琉球王権とグスク. Yamakawa shuppansha.

———. 2010. "Sōron: 'Ko-Ryūkyū' gainen no saikentō" 総論:「古琉球」概念の再検討. In *Okinawa kenshi, kakuronhen dai-sankan (Ko-Ryūkyū)* 沖縄県史, 各論編第3巻(古琉球), edited by Okinawa-ken Bunka Shinkōkai 沖縄県文化振興会, pp. 3–19. Naha: Okinawa-ken kyōiku iinkai.

Asato Susumu 安里進 and Doi Naomi 土肥直美. 2011. *Okinawajin wa doko kara kita ka: Ryūkyū-Okinawajin no kigen to seiritsu* 沖縄人はどこから来たか: 琉球=沖縄人の起源と成立. Rev. ed. Naha: Bōdaainku.

Azuma Yasuyuki 東靖晋. 2008. "Nissō kōeki no michi: Ojika, Hakata, Munakata" 日宋交易の道: 小値賀・博多・宗像. In *Nichi-Ryū kōeki no reimei: Yamato kara no shōgeki* 日琉交易の黎明: ヤマトからの衝撃, edited by Tanigawa Ken'ichi 谷川健一, pp. 27–52. Shinwasha.

Barker, Graeme, and Monica Janowski. 2011. "Why Cultivate? Anthropological and Archaeological Approaches to Foraging-Farming Transitions in Southeast Asia." In

Why Cultivate? Anthropological and Archaeological Approaches to Foraging-Farming Transitions in Southeast Asia, edited by Graeme Barker and Monica Janowski, pp. 1–16. Cambridge: McDonald Institute for Archaeological Research.

Batten, Bruce L. 2003. *To the Ends of Japan: Premodern Frontiers, Boundaries, and Interactions*. Honolulu: University of Hawaiʻi Press.

———. 2006. *Gateway to Japan: Hakata in War and Peace, 500–1300*. Honolulu: University of Hawaiʻi Press.

Bellwood, Peter. 2005. *First Farmers: The Origins of Agricultural Societies*. Malden, MA: Blackwell.

Bendjilali, Nasrine, Wen-Chi Hsueh, Qimei He, D. Craig Willcox, Caroline M. Nievergelt, Timothy A. Donlon, Pui-Yan Kwok, et al. 2014. "Who Are Okinawans? Ancestry, Genome Diversity, and Implications for the Genetic Study of Human Longevity from a Geographically Isolated Population." *Journals of Gerontology Series A: Biological Sciences and Medical Sciences* 69 (12): 1474–1484.

Chang Chu-keun 張壽根. 1973. *Kankoku no minkan shinkō: Saishūtō no fuzoku to fuka (Ronkō hen)* 韓国の民間信仰: 済州島の巫俗と巫歌 (論考編). Kinkasha.

Chūzan seifu 中山世譜. (1701) 1998. *Sai Taku bon Chūzan seifu* 蔡鐸本中山世譜. Translated by Harada Nobuo 原田禹雄. Ginowan, Japan: Yōju shorin.

Chūzan seifu 中山世譜. (1725) 1988. *Sai On bon Chūzan seifu* 蔡温本中山世譜. In *Ryūkyū shiryō sōsho* 4 琉球史料叢書 4, edited by Yokoyama Shigeru 横山重. Hōbun shokan.

Dana Masayuki 田名真之. 1992. *Okinawa kinseishi no shosō* 沖縄近世史の諸相. Naha: Hirugisha.

———. 2008. "Ryūkyū ōken no keifu ishiki to Minamoto Tametomo torai denshō" 琉球王権の系譜意識と源爲朝渡来伝承. In *Kyōkai no aidentitii* 境界のアイデンティティ, edited by Kyūshū Shigaku Kenkyūkai, pp. 181–195. Iwata shoin.

Denshinroku 傳信録. (1721) 1982. Xú Bǎoguāng 徐葆光. *Chūzan denshinroku* 中山傳信録 (Zhōngshān chuánxìn lù). Translated by Harada Nobuo 原田禹雄. Gensōsha.

Dodo Yukio 百々幸雄, ed. 1995. "Mongoroido no chikyū 3: Nihonjin no naritachi" モンゴロイドの地球 3: 日本人のなりたち. Tōkyō daigaku shuppankai.

Doi Naomi 土肥直美. 1998. "Nansei shotō-jin kokkaku no keishitsu-jinruigakuteki na kōsatsu: Hone karamita Nanseishotō no hitobito" 南西諸島人骨格の形質人類学的な考察: 骨からみた南西諸島の人々. In *Okinawa no rekishi to iryōshi* 沖縄の歴史と医療史, edited by Ryūkyū Daigaku Igakubu Fuzoku Chiiki Iryō Kenkyū Sentā, pp. 89–103.

———. 2018. *Okinawa honegatari: Jinruigaku ga semaru Okinawajin no rūtsu* 沖縄骨語り: 人類学が迫る沖縄人のルーツ. Naha: Ryūkyū shinpōsha.

Doi Naomi 土肥直美 and Kudaka Ken 久高健. 2017. *Kinkyū kōkai: Shiraho-Saonetabaru dōkutsu iseki 1–4 gō jinkotsu* 緊急公開: 白保竿根田原洞穴遺跡1〜4号人骨. Okinawa kenritsu maizō bunka sentaa.

East Sea Countries. (1471) 1991. Sin Sugju 申叔舟. *Account of East Sea Countries (Haedong jegukgi)*. *Kaitō shokokuki: Chōsenjin no mita chūsei Nihon to Ryūkyū* 海東諸国紀: 朝鮮人の見た中世日本と琉球. Translated and edited by Tanaka Takeo 田中健夫. Iwanami shoten.

Eguchi Tsukasa 江口司. 2006. *Shiranuikai to Ryūkyūko* 不知火海と琉球弧. Fukuoka-shi, Japan: Gen shobō.

———. 2008. "Nantō kōeki to yabusa: Shiranui-kai engan o chūshin ni" 南島交易とヤブサ: 不知火海沿岸を中心に. In *Nichi-Ryū kōeki no reimei: Yamato kara no shōgeki* 日琉交易の黎明: ヤマトからの衝撃, edited by Tanigawa Ken'ichi 谷川健一, pp. 91–119. Shinwasha.

Farris, Wayne. 2006. *Japan's Medieval Population: Famine, Fertility, and Warfare in a Transformative Age*. Honolulu: University of Hawai'i Press.

Fujita, Masaki, Shinji Yamasaki, Chiaki Katagiri, Itsuro Oshiro, Katsuhiro Sano, Taiji Kurozumi, Hiroshi Sugawara et al. 2016. "Advanced Maritime Adaptation in the Western Pacific Coastal Region Extends back to 35,000–30,000 Years before Present." *Proceedings of the National Academy of Sciences* 113, no. 40 (October 4): 11185–11189.

Fuku Hiromi 福寛美. 2008. *Kikaijima, oni no kaiiki: Kikaigashima kō* 喜界島・鬼の海域: キカイがシマの考. Shintensha.

———. 2021. *Kazan to take no megami: Kiki, Manyō, Omoro* 火山と竹の女神: 記紀, 万葉, おもろ. Shichigatsusha.

Gakuhari, Takashi, Shigeki Nakagome, Simon Rasmussen, Morten E. Allentoft, Takehiro Sato, Thorfinn Korneliussen, Blánaid Ní Chuinneagáin et al. 2020. "Ancient Jomon Genome Sequence Analysis Sheds Light on Migration Patterns of Early East Asian Populations." *Communications Biology* 3:437. https://doi.org/10.1038/s42003-020-01162-2.

Geertz, Clifford. 1980. *Negara: The Theatre State in Nineteenth-Century Bali*. Princeton, NJ: Princeton University Press.

Gi Tomihiro 義富弘. 2007. *Shimanuyu 1: 1609-nen Amami, Ryūkyū shinryaku* しまぬゆ1: 1609年, 奄美・琉球侵略. Kagoshima, Japan: Nanpō shinsha.

Goryeo History. 2005. Vols. 1 and 2 of *Kōraishi Nihonden* 高麗史日本伝 (Goryeosa, Ilbonjeon). Translated and edited by Takeda Yukio 武田幸男. Iwanami shoten.

Gotō Akira 後藤明. 2010. *Umi kara mita Nihonjin: Kaijin de yomu Nihon no rekishi* 海から見た日本人: 海人で読む日本の歴史. Kōdansha.

Graeber, David, and David Wengrow. 2021. *The Dawn of Everything: A New History of Humanity*. New York: Farrar, Straus and Giroux.

Gungnip Munhwajae Yeonguso 國立文化財研究所 (National Research Institute of Cultural Heritage, Korea). 2012. *Hanguk gogohak jeonmun sajeon, seonggwak bongsu-pyeon* 韓國考古學專門事典: 城郭, 烽燧 篇. Daejeon, South Korea: Gungnip munhwajae yeonguso.

Gushikami-son shi daishikan sonraku hen 具志頭村史第四巻村落編. 1993. Edited by Gushikami-son Shi Henshū Iinkai 具志頭村史編集委員会. Naha: Taiyō.

Gushikami-son shi dainikan tsūshi hen 具志頭村史第二巻通史編. 1991. Edited by Gushikami-son Shi Henshū Iinkai 具志頭村史編集委員会. Naha: Yūgen kaisha.

Habu, Junko. 2004. *Ancient Jomon of Japan*. New York: Cambridge University Press.

Haneji shioki 羽地仕置. (1673) 1981. In *Okinawa-ken shiryō, zenkindai 1* 沖縄県史料, 前近代1, edited by Okinawa-ken Okinawa Shiryō Henshūjo 沖縄県沖縄史料編集所. Naha: Okinawa-ken kyōiku iinkai.

Hanihara, Kazuro. 1991. "Dual Structure Model for the Population History of the Japanese." *Japan Review*, no. 2, 1–33.

Harada Nobuo 原田信男. 2017. *Yoshitsune densetsu to Yoritomo densetsu: Nihonshi no kita to minami* 義経伝説と頼朝伝説: 日本史の北と南. Iwanami shoten.

Harajiri Hideki 原尻英樹. 2012. "Saishūtō no dan (dō) to Ikinoshima no o-dō: Higashishina kaiiki ni okeru kyōyūka sareteiru bunka to 'kami'" 済州島のダン(堂)と壱岐島のお堂: 東シナ海域における共有化されている文化と「カミ」. In *Higashi Ajia no kanchihō kōryū no kako to genzai: Saishū to Okinawa, Amami o chūshin ni shite* 東アジアの間地方交流の過去と現在: 済州と沖縄・奄美を中心にして, edited by Tsuha Takashi 津波高志, pp. 79–104. Sairyūsha.

Hashimoto Yū 橋本雄. 2005. *Chūsei Nihon no kokusai kankei: Higashi-ajia tsūkōken to gishi mondai* 中世日本の国際関係: 東アジア通行圏と偽使問題. Yoshikawa kōbunkan.

———. 2008. "The Information Strategy of Imposter Envoys from Northern Kyūshū to Chosŏn Korea in the Fifteenth and Sixteenth Centuries." In *The East Asian "Mediterranean": Maritime Crossroads of Culture, Commerce and Human Migration*, edited by Angela Schottenhammer, pp. 289–315. Wiesbaden, Germany: Harrassowitz Verlag.

Hay, Simon I, Carlos A. Guerra, Andrew J. Tatem, Abdisalan M. Noor, and Robert W. Snow. 2004. "The Global Distribution and Population at Risk of Malaria: Past, Present, and Future." *Lancet: Infectious Diseases* 4, no. 6 (June): 327–336.

Heo Namchun 許南春. 2012. "Saishū to Ryūkyū no shinwa hikaku: *Omoro sōshi* o chūshin ni" 済州と琉球の神話比較: 『おもろさうし』を中心に. Translated by Kamiya Tomoaki 神谷智昭. In *Higashi Ajia no kanchihō kōryū no kako to genzai: Saishū to Okinawa, Amami o chūshin nishite* 東アジアの間地方交流の過去と現在: 済州と沖縄・奄美を中心にして, edited by Tsuha Takashi 津波高志, pp. 301–321. Sairyūsha.

Higa Chōshin 比嘉朝進. 2006. *Okinawa sengoku jidai no nazo* 沖縄戦国時代の謎. Naha: Naha shuppansha.

Higa Shunchō 比嘉春潮. 1971. *Higa Shunchō zenshū*. Vol. 1 of *Rekishi-hen 1* 比嘉春潮全集 第一巻歴史編I. Naha: Okinawa taimusu sha.

Higashionna Kanjun 東恩納寛惇. 1980. *Higashionna Kanjun zenshū 7* 東恩納寛惇全集 7. Edited by Ryūkyū Shinpōsha 琉球新報社. Daiichi shobō.

Hokama Kazuo 外間数男. 2015a. "Tsuchi kara mita gusuku jidai 1: Okinawa ni bunpu suru dojō no shurui to seishitsu" 土からみたグスク時代1: 沖縄島に分布する土壌の種類と性質. *Okinawa nōgyō* 沖縄農業 47 (1): 57–70.

———. 2015b. "Tsuchi kara mita gusuku jidai 2: Okinawatō no iseki, gusuku no bunpu" 土からみたグスク時代2: 沖縄島の遺跡, グスクの分布. *Okinawa nōgyō* 沖縄農業 47 (1): 71–77.

———. 2018a. "Tsuchi kara mita gusuku jidai 3: Shō Hashi no taitō kiban" 土からみたグスク時代3: 尚巴志の台頭基盤. *Okinawa nōgyō* 沖縄農業 49 (1): 31–49.

———. 2018b. "Tsuchi kara mita gusuku jidai 4: Gosamaru no tenpū" 土からみたグスク時代4: 護佐丸の転封. *Okinawa nōgyō* 沖縄農業 49 (1): 51–68.

Hokama Shuzen 外間守善 and Saigō Nobutsuna 西郷信綱. 1972. *Omoro sōshi* おもろさうし. Iwanami shoten.

Hokama Shuzen 外間守善 and Tamaki Masami 玉城正美. 1980. *Nantō kayō taisei 1* (Okinawa-hen, jō) 南島歌謡大成1 (沖縄編 上). Kadokawa shoten.

Hong-Schunka, S. M. 2005. "An Aspect of East Asian Maritime Trade: The Exchange of Commodities between Korea and Ryūkyū (1389–1638)." In *Trade and Transfer across the East Asian "Mediterranean,"* edited by Angela Schottenhammer, pp. 125–161. Wiesbaden, Germany: Harrassowitz Verlag.

Hudson, Mark J. 1999. *Ruins of Identity: Ethnogenesis in the Japanese Islands.* Honolulu: University of Hawai'i Press.

———. 2017. "The Ryukyu Islands and the Northern Frontier of Prehistoric Settlement." In *New Perspectives in Southeast Asian and Pacific Prehistory,* edited by Philip. J Piper, Hirofumi Matsumura, and David Bulbeck. Canberra: ANU Press.

———. 2020. "Language Dispersals and the 'Secondary Peoples' Revolution." In *The Oxford Guide to the Transeurasian Languages,* edited by Martine Robbeets and Alexander Savelyev. Oxford: Oxford University Press.

———. 2022. "Re-thinking Jomon and Ainu in Japanese History." *Asia-Pacific Journal: Japan Focus* 20, no. 15 (August 1).

Iha Fuyū 伊波普猷. 1974a. *Iha Fuyū zenshū 1* 伊波普猷全集, 第一巻. Heibonsha.

———. 1974b. *Iha Fuyū zenshū 2* 伊波普猷全集, 第二巻. Heibonsha.

———. 1974c. *Iha Fuyū zenshū 3* 伊波普猷全集, 第三巻. Heibonsha.

Ikeda Yoshifumi 池田榮史. 2012a. "Ryūkyūkoku izen: Ryūkyū, Okinawa-shi kenkyū ni okeru gusuku shakai no hyōka o megutte" 琉球国以前: 琉球・沖縄史研究におけるグスク社会の評価をめぐって. In *Nihon kodai no chiiki shakai to shūhen* 日本古代の地域社会と周辺, edited by Suzuki Yasutami 鈴木靖民, pp. 277–303. Yoshikawa kōbunkan.

———. 2012b. "Ryūkyū rettō to Kan-hantō: Busshitsu bunka kōryū, kōeki shisutemu no kaimei" 琉球列島と韓半島: 物質文化交流・交易システムの解明. In *Higashi Ajia no kanchihō kōryū no kako to genzai: Saishū to Okinawa, Amami o chūshin ni shite* 東アジアの間地方交流の過去と現在: 済州と沖縄・奄美を中心にして, edited by Tsuha Takashi 津波高志, pp. 325–346. Sairyūsha.

———. 2019. "Ryūkyū rettōshi o horiokosu: Jūichi-jūyon seiki no ijū, kōeki to shakaiteki henyō" 琉球列島史を掘りおこす: 十一~十四世紀の移住・交易と社会的変容. In *Ryūkyū no chūsei* 琉球の中世, edited by Chūseigaku Kenkyūkai 中世学研究会, pp. 13–44. Kōshi shoin.

Ikehata Kōichi 池畑耕一. 1990. "Kai no michi: Kai no bunka to Hirota iseki" 貝の道: 貝の文化と広田遺跡. In *Hayato sekai no shimajima* 隼人世界の島々, Ōbayashi Taryō 大林太良 et al., pp. 111–138. Shōgakkan.

Ikeya Machiko 池谷望子, Uchida Akiko 内田晶子, and Takase Kyōko 高瀬恭子. 2005. *Chōsen ōchō jitsuroku, Ryūkyū shiryō shūsei, genbun hen* 朝鮮王朝実録 琉球史料集成, 原文編. Ginowan, Japan: Yōju shorin.

Ikuta Shigeru 生田滋. 1984. "Ryūkyūkoku no 'Sanzan tōitsu'" 琉球国の「三山統一」. *Tōhō gakuhō* 65, no. 3–4: 175–206.

———. 1992. "Ryūkyū Chūzanōkoku to kaijō bōeki" 琉球中山王国と海上貿易. In *Ryūkyūko no sekai* 琉球弧の世界, edited by Tanigawa Ken'ichi 谷川健一, pp. 265–296. Shōgakkan.

Inafuku Seiki 稲福盛輝. 1995. *Okinawa shippeishi* 沖縄疾病史. Daiichi shobō.

Inamura Kenpu 稲村賢敷. 1957. *Ryūkyū shotō ni okeru wakō shiseki no kenkyū* 琉球諸島における倭寇史跡の研究. Yoshikawa kōbunkan.

———. 1969. *Okinawa no kodai buraku makyo no kenkyū* 沖縄の古代部落マキョの研究. Naha: Shirono insatsu.

Japan Soil Inventory (Nihon Dojō Inbentorii) 日本土壌インベントリー. https://soil-inventory.dc.affrc.go.jp/index.html.

Jarosz, Aleksandra, Martine Robbeets, Ricardo Fernandes, Hiroto Takamiya, Akito Shinzato, Naoko Nakamura, Mark J. Hudson et al. 2022. "Demography, Trade and State Power: A Tripartite Model of Medieval Farming/Language Dispersals in the Ryukyu Islands." *Evolutionary Human Sciences* 4:e4.

Jinam, Timothy, Nao Nishida, Momoki Hirai, Shoji Kawamura, Hiroki Oota, Kazuo Umetsu, Ryosuke Kimura et al. 2012. "The History of Human Populations in the Japanese Archipelago Inferred from Genome-Wide SNP Data with a Special Reference to the Ainu and Ryukyuan Populations." *Journal of Human Genetics* 57:787–795.

Jūhen shi Ryūkyū roku 重編使琉球録. (1561) 2000. Guō Rǔlín 郭汝霖, *Zhòngbiān shǐ Liúqiú lù*. Translated by Harada Nobuo 原田禹雄. Yōju shorin.

JVRR-d (*Joseon Veritable Royal Records* [Joseon wangjo sillok]) 朝鮮王朝實録. Academia Sinica digital version. http://hanchi.ihp.sinica.edu.tw/mql/login.html.

JVRR-r (*Joseon Veritable Royal Records* [Joseon wangjo sillok]). 2005. *Chōsen ōchō jitsuroku Ryūkyū shiryō shūsei, yakuchū hen* 朝鮮王朝実録 琉球史料集成, 訳注編. Translated and edited by Ikeya Machiko 池谷望子, Uchida Akiko 内田晶子, and Takase Kyōko 高瀬恭子. Ginowan, Japan: Yōju shorin.

Kamei Meitoku 亀井明徳. 1993. "Nansei shotō ni okeru bōeki tōjiki no ryūtsū keiro" 南西諸島における貿易陶磁器の流通経路. *Jōchi Ajia-gaku* 11 (1993): 11–45.

Kamimura Toshio 上村俊雄. 1990. "Minami Kyūshū no kōkogaku" 南九州の考古学. In *Hayato sekai no shimajima* 隼人世界の島々, Ōbayashi Taryō 大林太良 et al., pp. 45–110. Shōgakkan.

Kanzawa-Kiriyama, Hideaki, Timothy A. Jinam, Yosuke Kawai, Takehiro Sato, Kazuyoshi Hosomichi, Atsushi Tajima, Noboru Adachi et al. 2019. "Late Jomon Male and Female Genome Sequences from the Funadomari Site in Hokkaido, Japan." *Anthropological Science* 127 (2): 83–108.

Kasari-chō. 1997. *Ushuku kaizuka shutsudo jinkotsuhen* 宇宿貝塚出土人骨編. Edited by Kasari-chō Kyōiku Iinkai 笠利町教育委員会. Kasari-chō.

———. 2003. *Akagina gusuku iseki* 赤木名グスク遺跡. Edited by Kasari-chō Rekishi Minzoku Shiryōkan 笠利町歴史民俗資料館. Kasari-chō kyōiki iinkai.

———. 2006. *Beru gusuku hakkutsu chōsa hōkoku gaiyō* 辺留グスク発掘調査報告概要. Edited by Kasari-chō Kyōiku Iinkai 笠利町教育委員会. Kasari-chō kyōiku iinkai.

Kerr, George H. (1958) 2000. *Okinawa: The History of an Island People*. Rev. ed. Rutland, VT: Tuttle.

Kinoshita Naoko 木下尚子. 1996. *Nantō kai bunka no kenkyū: Kai no michi no kōkogaku* 南島貝文化の研究貝の道の考古学. Hōsei daigaku shuppankyoku.

———. 2003. "Kai kōeki to kokka keisei: 9 seiki kara 13 seiki o taishō ni" 貝交易と国家形成: 9世紀から13世紀を対象に. In *Senshi Ryūkyū no nariwai to kōeki: Amami, Okinawa no hakkutsu chōsa kara* 先史琉球の生業と交易: 奄美・沖縄の発掘調査から, edited by Kinoshita Naoko, pp. 117–144. Kumamoto, Japan: Kumamoto daigaku bungakubu.

Kinoshita, Naoko. 2019. "Prehistoric Ryūkyūan Seafaring: A Cultural and Environmental Perspective." In *Prehistoric Maritime Cultures and Seafaring in East Asia*, edited by Chunming Wu and Barry Vladimir Rolett, pp. 315–332. Singapore: Springer.

Kojima Yoshiyuki 小島瓔禮. 1983. *Ryūkyūgaku no shikaku* 琉球学の視角. Kashiwa shobō.

———. 1990. "Kaijō no michi to Hayato bunka" 海上の道と隼人文化. In *Hayato sekai no shimajima* 隼人世界の島々, Ōbayashi Taryō 大林大良 et al., pp. 139–194. Shōgakkan.

Kokubu Naoichi 国分直一. (1957) 1995. "Mori no shinkō" 森の信仰. In *Nihon minzoku bunka shiryō shūsei, dai nijūichi kan: Mori no kami no minzokushi* 日本民族文化資料集成, 第二十一巻: 森の神の民族誌, edited by Tanigawa Ken'ichi 谷川健一, pp. 128–132. San'ichi shobō.

Kokuritsu Rekishi Minzoku Hakubutsukan 国立歴史民俗博物館 (National Museum of Japanese History). 2021. *Umi no teikoku Ryūkyū: Yaeyama, Miyako, Amami kara mita chūsei* 海の帝国琉球: 八重山・宮古・奄美からみた中世. Nyūkaraa shashin insatsu.

Korea Fortress Academy. 2007. *A Basic Research on Mountain Fortresses in Central Inland Area of Korea*. Chungcheongbuk-do Province, Korea Fortress Academy.

———. 2008a. *Mountain Fortresses of Inland Korea*. Vol 1, *Samnyeon Sansong Mountain Fortresses*. Chungcheongbuk-do Province, Korea.

———. 2008b. *Mountain Fortresses of Inland Korea*. Vol. 2, *Sangdang Sansong Mountain Fortresses*. Chungcheongbuk-do Province, Korea.

Kurima Yasuo 来間泰男. 2010. *Inasaku no kigen, denrai to "Kaijō no michi."* Vol. 2 (ge) 稲作の起源・伝来と "海上の道" (下). Nihon Keizai hyōronsha.

———. 2013a. *Gusuku to aji 1: Nihon no chūsei zenki to Ryūkyū kodai* グスクと按司(上)日本の中世と琉球古代. Nihon keizai hyōronsha.

———. 2013b. *Gusuku to aji 2: Nihon no chūsei zenki to Ryūkyū kodai* グスクと按司(下)日本の中世と琉球古代. Nihon keizai hyōronsha.

Kyūyō 球陽. (1743–1876) 1974, 1978. *Kyūyō yomikudashi hen* 球陽 読み下し編. Edited by Kyūyō Kenkyūkai 球陽研究會. Kadokawa shoten.

Lebra, William P. (1966) 1985. *Okinawan Religion: Belief, Ritual, and Social Structure*. Honolulu: University of Hawai'i Press.

Lee Choon Ja (Li Chunja) 李春子. 2011. *Kami no ki: Nichi, Kan, Tai no kyoboku, rōju shinkō* 神の木: 日・韓・台の巨木・老樹信仰. Hikone-shi, Japan: Sanraizu shuppan.

Majikina Ankō 眞境名安興. (1923) 1993. *Majikina Ankō zenshū*. Vol. 1, (*Okinawa issennen shi*) 眞境名安興全集第一巻 [沖縄一千年史]. Naha: Ryūkyū shinpōsha.

Makishi Yōko 真喜志瑶子. 2023. *Ko-Ryūkyū no ōgū girei to Omoro sōshi* 古琉球の王宮儀礼とおもろさうし. Heibonsha.

Matsuda Kiyoshi 松田清. 1981. *Kodai, chūsei Amami shiryō* 古代・中世奄美史料. JCA shuppan.

Matsukusa, Hirotaka, Hiroki Oota, Kuniaki Haneji, Takashi Toma, Shoji Kawamura, and Hajime Ishida. 2010. "A Genetic Analysis of the Sakishima Islanders Reveals No Relationship with Taiwan Aborigines but Shared Ancestry with Ainu and Main-Island Japanese." *American Journal of Physical Anthropology* 142:211–233.

Matsunami, Masatoshi, Kae Koganebuchi, Minako Imamura, Hajime Ishida, Ryosuke Kimura, and Shiro Maeda. 2021. "Fine-Scale Genetic Structure and Demographic History in the Miyako Islands of the Ryukyu Archipelago." *Molecular Biology and Evolution* 38 (5): 2045–2056.

Matthews, Peter, Emiko Takei, and Taihachi Kawahara. 1992. "*Colocasia esculenta* var. *aquatilis* on Okinawa Island, Southern Japan: The Distribution and Possible Origins of a Wild Diploid Taro." *Man and Culture in Oceania* 8:19–34.

Mishina Shōei 三品影英. (1941) 1995. "Tsushima no Tendō densetsu" 対馬の天道伝説. In *Nihon minzoku bunka shiryō shūsei, dai nijūichi kan: Mori no kami no minzokushi* 日本民族文化資料集成, 第二十一巻: 森の神の民族誌, edited by Tanigawa Ken'ichi 谷川健一, pp. 162–168. San'ichi shobō.

Miyagi Eishō 宮城栄昌 and Takamiya Hiroe 高宮廣衞, eds. 1983a. *Okinawa rekishi chizu, rekishi hen* 沖縄歴史地図 <歴史編>. Kashiwa shobō.

———. 1983b. *Okinawa rekishi chizu, kōko hen* 沖縄歴史地図 <考古編>. Kashiwa shobō.

Miyanaga Masamori 宮良當壮. 1924. "Waga kodaigo to Ryūkyūgo to no hikaku" 我が古代語と琉球語との比較. *Shigaku* 史学 3 (3): 51–89.

Morimoto Isao 盛本勲. 1992. "Ryūkyūken ni kyōtsū, ruiji suru iseki" 琉球圏に共通・類似する遺跡. *Gekkan kōkogaku jaanaru* 月刊考古学ジャーナル 352 (October): 2–7.

———. 2008. "Gusuku jidai no maku-ake: Bunbutsu to nōkō o megutte" グスク時代の幕開け: 文物と農耕をめぐって. In *Nichi-Ryū kōeki no reimei: Yamato kara no shōgeki* 日琉交易の黎明: ヤマトからの衝撃, edited by Tanigawa Ken'ichi 谷川健一, pp. 263–284. Shinwasha.

Morinaga Shuntarō 盛永俊太郎 and Mukai Yasushi 向井康. 1969. "Okinawa shotō no zairaitō" 沖縄諸島の在来稲. *Nōgyō oyobi engei* 農業および園芸 44 (1): 11–16.

Munakata Yoshiki 宗像善樹. 2017. *Munakata sanjoshin to Okinoshima densetsu* 宗像三女神と沖ノ島傳説. Yūbun shoin.

Murai Shōsuke 村井章介. 1988. *Ajia no naka no chūsei Nihon* アジアの中の中世日本. Kōsō shobō.

———. 2019. *Ko-Ryūkyū: Kaiyō Ajia no kagayakeru ōkoku* 古琉球: 海洋アジアの輝ける王国. Kadokawa.

MVR (Ming Veritable Records 明実録). 3 vols. In "*Min jitsuroku*" *no Ryūkyū shiryō* 「明実録」の琉球史料, edited and translated by Wada Hisanori 和田久徳 et al. Haebaruchō, Japan: Okinawa-ken Bunka Shinkōkai, Kōbunsho Kanribu, Shiryō Henshūshitsu, 2001 (vol. 1), 2003 (vol. 2), 2006 (vol 3).

Nagadome Hisae 永留久恵. (1953–1954) 1995. *Tendō shinkō no kenkyū* 天道信仰の研究. In *Nihon minzoku bunka shiryō shūsei, dai nijūichi kan: Mori no kami no minzokushi* 日本民族文化資料集成，第二十一巻: 森の神の民族誌，edited by Tanigawa Ken'ichi 谷川健一, pp. 206–279. San'ichi shobō.

Nagafuji Yasushi 永藤靖. 2000. *Ryūkyū shinwa to kodai Yamato bungaku* 琉球神話と古代ヤマト文学. Miyai shoten.

Nagatsuka Shizuo 永塚鎮男. 2007. "Dojō yomoyamabanashi 1: Jaagaru no gogen o saguru" 土壌よもやまばなし (1): ジャーガルの語源を探る. *Okinawa nōgyō* 沖縄農業 40 (1): 77–81.

Naka Shōhachirō 名嘉正八郎. 1992. "Gusuku no rekishi to kōkogaku" グスクの歴史と考古学. In *Ryūkyūko no sekai* 琉球弧の世界, edited by Tanigawa Ken'ichi 谷川健一, pp. 130–158. Shōgakkan.

Nakahara Zenchū 仲原善忠. 1969. *Nakahara Zenchū senshū*. Vol. 1 仲原善忠選集上巻. Okinawa taimusu sha.

Nakahashi Takahiro 中橋孝弘. 2005. *Nihonjin no kigen: Kojinkotsu kara rūtsu o saguru* 日本人の起源: 古人骨からルーツを探る. Kōdansha.

Nakamura Kazumi 中村和美. 2008. "Manosegawa ryūiki no iseki: Ibutsu kara miru kōeki no kanōsei" 万之瀬川流域の遺跡: 遺物からみる交易の可能性. In *Nichi-Ryū kōeki no reimei: Yamato kara no shōgeki* 日琉交易の黎明: ヤマトからの衝撃, edited by Tanigawa Ken'ichi 谷川健一, pp. 73–90. Shinwasha.

Nakayama Kiyomi 中山清美. 2008. "Kyōkai'iki no Amami: Akagina gusuku to Kuraki-saki kaitei iseki" 境界域の奄美: 赤木名城と倉木崎海底遺跡. In *Nichi-Ryū kōeki no reimei: Yamato kara no shōgeki* 日琉交易の黎明: ヤマトからの衝撃, edited by Tanigawa Ken'ichi 谷川健一, pp. 183–208. Shinwasha.

Nakayama Tarō 中山太郎. (1929) 2012. *Nihon fujoshi* 日本巫女史. Kokusho kankōkai.

Nanjō-shi 南城市. 2017. *Itokazu jōseki: Kurayashiki chiku hakkutsu chōsa hōkokusho* 糸数城跡: 蔵屋敷地区発掘調査報告書. Edited by Okinawa-ken Nanjō-shi Kyōikuiinkai 沖縄県南城市教育委員会. Naha: Haebaru insatsu.

Nányōngzhì 南雍志 (Ming dynasty). Chinese Text Project. https://ctext.org/library .pl?if=gb&res=2295.

Naze-shi 名瀬市. 1996. *Kaitei Naze-shi shi 1 kan, Rekishi-hen* 改定名瀬市誌 1 巻 歴史編. Edited by Kaitei Naze-shi Shi Hensan Iinkai 改定名瀬市誌編纂委員会. Naze-shi [Amami-shi], Japan, Naze-shi yakusho.

Ōbayashi Taryō 大林太良. 1990. "Gōryū to kyōkai no Hayatosekai no shimajima" 合流と境界の隼人世界の島々. In *Hayato sekai no shimajima* 隼人世界の島々, Ōbayashi Taryō 大林太良 et al., pp. 9–42. Shōgakkan.

Oguma, Eiji. 2002. *A Genealogy of "Japanese" Self-Images*. Translated by David Askew. Melbourne: Trans Pacific Press.

Ōhama Eisen 大濱永亘. 2005. *Oyake Akahachi, Honkawara no ran to San'yō-sei ichimon no hitobito* オヤケアカハチ・ホンカワラの乱と山陽姓一門の人々. Ishigaki, Japan: Sakishima bunka kenkyūjo.

———. 2008. "Yaeyama shotō no kōeki: Suku bunka-ki o chūshin ni" 八重山諸島の交易: スク文化期を中心に. In *Nichi-Ryū kōeki no reimei: Yamato kara no shōgeki* 日琉交易の黎明: ヤマトからの衝撃, edited by Tanigawa Ken'ichi 谷川健一, pp. 347–382. Shinwasha.

Okada Teruo 岡田輝雄. 2000. *Sekai isan, gusuku kikō: Ko-Ryūkyū no hikari to kage* 世界遺産, グスク紀行: 古琉球の光と影. Naha: Ryūkyū shinpōsha.

Okamoto Hiromichi 岡本弘道. 2010. *Ryūkyū ōkoku kaijō kōshōshi kenkyū* 琉球王国海上交渉史研究. Ginowan, Japan: Yōju Shorin.

Okaya Kōji 岡谷公二. 2019. *Okinawa no seichi, utaki* 沖縄の聖地 御嶽. Heibonsha.

Okazaki Masanori 岡崎正規, Kimura Sonoko Dorotea 木村園子ドロテア, Hatano Ryūsuke 波多野隆介, Toyoda Kōki 豊田剛己, and 林健太郎. 2010. *Zusetsu Nihon no dojō* 図説日本の土壌. Asakura shoten.

Okimoto Tsuneyoshi 沖本常吉. (1950) 1995. "Kōjinmori: Iwami, Tsuwanokawa chihō" 荒神森: 岩見津和野川地方. In *Nihon minzoku bunka shiryō shūsei, dai nijūichi kan: Mori no kami no minzokushi* 日本民族文化資料集成, 第二十一巻: 森の神の民族誌, edited by Tanigawa Ken'ichi 谷川健一, pp. 108–111. San'ichi shobō.

Okinawa-ken 沖縄県. 1983. *Gusuku: Gusuku bunpu chōsa hōkoku (1), Okinawa hontō oyobi shūhen ritō* ぐすく: グスク分布調査報告 (1), 沖縄本島及び周辺離島. Edited by Okinawa-ken Kyōikuchō Bunkaka 沖縄県教育庁文化課. Okinawa kyōiku iinkai.

———. 1986. *Kadokawa Nihon chimei daijiten 47: Okinawa-ken* 角川日本地名大辞典 47: 沖縄県. Edited by Kadokawa Nihon Chimei Daijiten Hensan Iinkai 「角川日本地名大辞典」編纂委員会. Kadokawa shoten.

Okinawa Kenritsu Maizō Bunka Sentaa 沖縄県立埋蔵文化センター. 2017. *Shiraho-Saonetabaru dōketsu iseki: Jūyō isei han'i kakunin chōsa hōkokusho 2, sōkatsu hōkoku hen* 白保竿根田原洞穴遺跡: 重要遺跡範囲確認調査報告書2, 総括報告編 (Report no. 86 調査報告書第 86 集). Yaese-chō, Japan: Bunshin insatsu.

Okinawa Kenritsu Toshokan Shiryō Henshūshitsu 沖縄県立図書館資料編集室. 1996. *Okinawa-ken shi, shiryō hen 2* 沖縄県史, 資料編2. Naha: San insatsu.

Okinawa Kōkogakkai 沖縄考古学会, ed. 2018. *Nantō kōko nyūmon: Horidasareta Okinawa no rekishi, bunka* 南島考古入門: 掘り出された沖縄の歴史・文化. Naha: Bōdaainku.

Okinawa taimusu 沖縄タイムス. May 22, 2022. "Okinawa ni Nishi-Yōroppa-kei no jinkotsu: Nanjō-shi no furuhaka-gun" 沖縄に西ヨーロッパ系の人骨: 南城市の古墓群.

Origins. (*Origins of Ryukyu. Ryūkyūkoku yuraiki* 琉球国由来記). (1713) 1988. In Vols. 1 and 2, *Ryūkyū shiryō sōsho* 琉球史料叢書, edited by Yokoyama Shigeru 横山重 (continuous pagination). Hōbun shokan.

Ōshiro Itsurō 大城逸郎. 1992. "Ryūkyūko no chishitsugaku: Ryūkyū rettō no seiritsu to tokushoku" 琉球弧の地質学: 琉球列島の成立と特色. In *Ryūkyūko no sekai* 琉球弧の世界, edited by Tanigawa Ken'ichi 谷川健一, pp. 69–87. Shōgakkan.

Ōshiro Kei 大城慧. 1983. "Okinawa no tetsu" 沖縄の鉄. In *Ine to tetsu: Samazamana ōken no kiban* 稲と鉄: さまざまな王権の基盤, edited by Mori Kōichi 森浩一 et al., pp. 282–300. Shōgakkan.

Ōta Kōki 太田弘毅. 2002. *Wakō: Shōgyō, gunji shiteki kenkyū* 倭寇: 商業・軍事史的研究. Yokohama, Japan: Shunpūsha.

Ōtsuru Masamitsu 大鶴正満. 1998. "Okinawa no mararia" 沖縄のマラリア. In *Okinawa no rekishi to iryōshi* 沖縄の歴史と医療史, edited by Ryūkyū Daigaku Igakubu Fuzoku Chiki Iryō Kenkyū Sentā, pp. 149–155.

Pearson, Richard. 2013. *Ancient Ryukyu: An Archaeological Study of Island Communities.* Honolulu: University of Hawai'i Press.

Pellard, Thomas. 2015. "The Linguistic Archeology of the Ryukyu Islands." In *Handbook of the Ryukyuan Languages,* edited by Patrick Heinrich, Shinso Miyara, and Michinori Shimoji, pp. 13–37. Berlin: De Gruyter Mouton.

Ptak, Roderich. 2005. "The Image of Fujian and Ryūkyū in the Letters of Cristóvão Vieira and Vasco Calvo." In *Trade and Transfer across the East Asian "Mediterranean,"* edited by Angela Schottenhammer, pp. 303–319. Wiesbaden, Germany: Harrassowitz Verlag.

Reflections (*Reflections on Chūzan. Chūzan seikan* 中山世鑑). (1650) 2011. Translated and edited by Moromi Tomoshige 諸見友重. Ginowan, Japan: Yōju shorin.

Rhee, Song-nai, and C. Melvin Aikens. 2021. *Archaeology and History of Toraijin: Human, Technological, and Cultural Flow from the Korean Peninsula to the Japanese Archipelago c. 800 BC–AD 600.* With Gina L. Barnes. Oxford: Archaeopress.

Robbeets, Martine, Remco Bouckaert, Matthew Conte, Alexander Savelyev, Tao Li, Deog-Im An, Ken-ichi Shinoda, Chao Ning et al. 2021. "Triangulation Supports Agricultural Spread of the Transeurasian Languages." *Nature* 599 (November 10). https://doi.org/10.1038/s41586-021-04108-8.

Robinson, Kenneth R. 1997. "The Jiubian and Ezogachishima Embassies to Chosŏn, 1478–1482." *Chōsenshi kenkyūkai ronbunshū* 35 (October): 56–86.

———. 2000. "The *Haedong Chegukki* (1471) and Korean-Ryukyuan Relations, 1389–1471: Part 1." *Acta Koreana* 3 (July): 87–98.

———. 2001. "The *Haedong Chegukki* (1471) and Korean-Ryukyuan Relations, 1389–1471: Part 2." *Acta Koreana* 4:115–142.

Roosens, Eugene E. 1989. *Creating Ethnicity: The Process of Ethnogenesis.* Newbury Park, CA: Sage.

Rots, Aike P. 2019. "Strangers in the Sacred Grove: The Changing Meanings of Okinawan *Utaki.*" *Religions* 10 (5): 298.

Sai On zenshū 蔡温全集. 1984. Edited by Sakihama Shūmei 崎浜秀明. Honpō shoseki.

Saitō Seiya 斎藤成也. 2005. *DNA kara mita Nihonjin* DNAから見た日本人. Chikuma shobō.

Sakitani Mitsuru 崎谷満. 2008. *DNA de tadoru Nihonjin Jūmannen no tabi: Tayō na hito, gengo, bunka wa dokokara kita ka?* DNA でたどる日本人 10万年の旅: 多様なヒト・言語・文化はどこから来たのか? Kyōto-shi, Japan: Shōwadō.

Sakuhō Ryūkyū shiroku sanpen. (1684) 1997. Wāng Jí 汪楫, *Cèfēng Liúqiú shílù sānpiān* 冊封琉球使録三篇. Translated by Harada Nobuo 原田禹雄. Yōju shorin.

Sato, Takehiro, Shigeki Nakagome, Chiaki Watanabe, Kyoko Yamaguchi, Akira Kawaguchi, Kae Koganebuchi, Kuniaki Haneji et al. 2014. "Genome-Wide SNP Analysis Reveals Population Structure and Demographic History of the Ryukyu Islanders in the Southern Part of the Japanese Archipelago." *Modern Biological Evolution* 31 (11): 2929–2940.

Scott, James C. 2017. *Against the Grain: A Deep History of the Earliest States.* New Haven, CT: Yale University Press.

Senda Yoshihiro 千田嘉博. 2004. "Nihon rettō no naka no gusuku" 日本列島の中のグスク. In *Gusuku bunka o kangaeru* グスク文化を考える, edited by Nakijin-son Kyōiku Iinkai, Shakai Kyōiku-ka, Bunkazai-gakari 今帰仁村教育委員会社会教育課文化財係. Nakijin-son, Japan: Nakijin-son kyōiku iinkai.

Serafim, Leon A., and Rumiko Shinzato. 2021. *The Language of the Old-Okinawan Omoro Sōshi: Reference Grammar, with Textual Selections.* Leiden: Brill.

Seto Tetsuya 瀬戸哲也. 2019. "Shūraku kara gusuku e: Gusuku jidai ni okeru kōeki to nōkō no tenkai" 集落からグスクへ: グスク時代における交易と農耕の展開. In *Ryūkyū no chūsei* 琉球の中世, edited by Chūseigaku Kenkyūkai 中世学研究会, pp. 45–67. Kōshi shoin.

Seyock, Barbara. 2005. "Pirates and Traders on Tsushima Island during the Late 14th to Early 16th Century: As Seen from Historical and Archaeological Perspectives." In *Trade and Transfer across the East Asian "Mediterranean,"* edited by Angela Schottenhammer, pp. 91–124. Wiesbaden, Germany: Harrassowitz Verlag.

Shapinsky, Peter D. 2021. "Review of *Maritime Ryukyu, 1050–1650.*" *Journal of Japanese Studies* 47–1 (Winter): 188–193.

Shimamura Kōichi 島村幸一. 2008. "Nantō kayō ni miru kōeki: Miyakojima to Yaeyama o chūshin ni" 南島歌謡にみる交易: 宮古島と八重山を中心に. In *Nichi-Ryū kōeki no reimei: Yamato kara no shōgeki* 日琉交易の黎明: ヤマトからの衝撃, edited by Tanigawa Ken'ichi 谷川健一, pp. 305–326. Shinwasha.

Shimizu Nobuyuki 清水信行. 1998. "Kankoku Ronsangun Kaitaiji shutsdo meibun kawara ni tsuite no ikkōsatsu" 韓国論山郡開泰寺出土銘文瓦についての一考察. *Nihon kōkogaku* 日本考古学5 (5): 19–46.

Shimoji Kazuhiro 下地和宏. 2008. "Tōji kōeki to Miyako: Miyako-jin to Chūzan chōkō nitsuite" 陶磁交易人宮古: 密牙古と中山朝貢について. In *Nichi-Ryū kōeki no reimei: Yamato kara no shōgeki* 日琉交易の黎明: ヤマトからの衝撃, edited by Tanigawa Ken'ichi 谷川健一, pp. 327–346. Shinwasha.

Shimono Toshimi 下野敏見. (1969) 1995. "Garō-yama o meguru shomondai" ガロー山をめぐる諸問題. In *Nihon minzoku bunka shiryō shūsei, dai nijūichi kan: Mori no kami no minzokushi* 日本民俗文化資料集成, 第二十一巻: 森の神の民俗誌, edited by Tanigawa Ken'ichi 谷川健一, pp. 476–505. San'ichi shobō.

———. 2005. *Amami, Tokara no dentō bunka: Matsuri to noro, seikatsu* 奄美, 吐噶喇の伝統文化: 祭りとノロ, 生活. Nanpō shinsha.

Shinjō Tokuyū 新城徳祐. 1982. *Okinawa no jōseki* 沖縄の城跡. Naha: Rokutoseikatsu sha.

Shinoda Ken'ichi 篠田謙一. 2007. "Nihonjin ni natta sosentachi: DNA kara kaimeisuru sono tagenteki kōzō" 日本人になった祖先たち: DNA から解明するその多元的構造. Nihon Hōsō Shuppan Kyōkai.

———. 2018. "DNA kara mita Nansei shotō shūdan no seiritsu" DNA から見た南西諸島集団の成立. In *Amami, Okinawa shotō senshigaku no saizensen* 奄美・沖縄諸島先史学の最前線, edited by Takamiya Hiroto 高宮広土, pp. 69–84. Nanpō shinsha.

Shinoda, Ken-ichi, and Naomi Doi. 2008. "Mitochondria DNA Analysis of Human Skeletal Remains Obtained from the Old Tomb of Suubaru: Genetic Characteristics of the Westernmost Island Japan." *Bulletin of the National Museum of Nature and Science Series D, Anthropology* 34:11–18.

Shinoda, Ken-ichi, and Noboru Adachi. 2017. In *New Perspectives in Southeast Asian and Pacific Prehistory*, edited by Philip. J Piper, Hirofumi Matsumura, and David Bulbeck, pp. 51–58. Canberra: ANU Press.

Shinoda, Ken-ichi, Tsuneo Kakuda, and Naomi Doi. 2012. "Mitochondrial DNA Polymorphisms in Late Shell Midden Period Skeletal Remains Excavated from Two Archaeological Sites in Okinawa." *Bulletin of the National Museum of Nature and Science Series D, Anthropology* 38:51–61.

Shinzato Akito 新里亮人. 2008. "Ryūkyū rettō shutsudo no kasseki-sei ishinabe to sono igi" 琉球列島出土の滑石製石鍋とその意義. In *Nichi-Ryū kōeki no reimei: Yamato kara no shōgeki* 日琉交易の黎明: ヤマトからの衝撃, edited by Tanigawa Ken'ichi 谷川健一, pp. 51–72. Shinwasha.

———. 2018. *Ryūkyūkoku seiritsu zenya no kōkogaku* 琉球国成立前夜の考古学. Dōseisha.

Shinzato Keiji 新里恵二. 1970. *Okinawa-shi o kangaeru* 沖縄史を考える. Keisō shobō.

Shinzato Takayuki 新里貴之. 2010. "Chūbu Ryūkyūken senshi jidai no hensen" 中部琉球圏先史時代の社会の変遷. *Kōkogaku jaanaru* 考古学ジャーナル, no. 597 (March 2010): 9–11.

———. 2018. "Kaizuka jidai goichiki no doki bunka" 貝塚時代後一期土器文化. In *Amami, Okinawa shotō senshigaku no saizensen* 奄美・沖縄諸島先史学の最前線, edited by Takamiya Hiroto 高宮広土, pp. 20–44. Nanpō shinsha.

Shirakihara Kazumi 白木原和美. 1992. "Ryūkyūko no kōkogaku: Amami to Okinawa o chūshin ni" 琉球弧の考古学: 奄美と沖縄を中心に. In *Ryūkyūko no sekai* 琉球弧の世界, edited by Tanigawa Ken'ichi 谷川健一, pp. 88–129. Shōgakkan.

Shi Ryūkyū ki 使琉球記. 1802. Lǐ Dǐngyuán 李鼎元, *Shǐ liúqiú jì*. Translated by Harada Nobuo 原田禹雄. Gensōsha, 1985.

Shi Ryūkyū roku 使琉球録. 1534. Chén Kǎn 陳侃, *Shǐ Liúqiú lù*. Translated by Harada Nobuo 原田禹雄. Ginowan, Japan: Yōjusha, 1995.

Shi Ryūkyū roku 使琉球録. 1579. Xiāo Chóngyè 蕭崇業 and Xiè Jié 謝杰, *Shǐ Liúqiú lù* 使琉球錄. Translated by Harada Nobuo 原田禹雄 and Muira Kunio 三浦國雄. Ginowan, Japan: Yōju shorin, 2011.

Smits, Gregory. 1999. *Visions of Ryukyu: Identity and Ideology in Early-Modern Thought and Politics*. Honolulu: University of Hawai'i Press.

———. 2010a. "Romanticizing the Ryukyuan Past: Origins of the Myth of Ryukyuan Pacifism." *IJOS: International Journal of Okinawan Studies*, premier issue (March): 51–68.

———. 2010b. "Examining the Myth of Ryukyuan Pacifism." *Asia-Pacific Journal: Japan Focus* 8, iss. 37, no. 3, Article ID 3409.

———. 2011. *Ryūkyū ōkoku no jigazō* 琉球王国の自画像. Translated by Watanabe Miki 渡辺美紀. Perikan sha.

———. 2015. "New Cultures, New Identities: Becoming Okinawan and Japanese in Nineteenth-Century Ryukyu." In *Values, Identity, and Equality in Eighteenth- and*

Nineteenth-Century Japan, edited by Peter Nosco, James E. Ketelaar, and Yasunori Kojima, pp. 159–178. Leiden: Brill.

———. 2019. *Maritime Ryukyu, 1050–1650*. Honolulu: University of Hawai'i Press.

Sòngshǐ 宋史. 1346. Chinese Text Project. https://ctext.org/wiki.pl?if=en&res=975976.

Suíshū (*Suíshū* "Liúqiúguó" 隋書 "流求國"). 636. Chinese Text Project. https://ctext.org/wiki.pl?if=en&chapter=584840#流求國.

Summerhayes, Glenn, and Atholl Anderson. 2009. "An Austronesian Presence in Southern Japan: Early Occupation in the Yaeyama Islands." *Bulletin of the Indo-Pacific Prehistory Association* 29:76-91.

Sūn Wěi 孫薇. 2005. "Warigeki jidai no Ryūkyū: Jūyonseiki shichijūnendai kara jūgoseiki nijū nendai ni kakete" 割據時代の琉球: 十四世紀七十年代から十五世紀二十年代にかけて. *Kokusai Nihongaku* 2 (March): 79–126.

———. 2016. *Chūgoku kara mita ko-Ryūkyū no sekai* 中国から見た古琉球の世界. Naha: Ryūkyū shinpōsha.

Suzuki Tōzō 鈴木棠三. 1972. *Tsushima no shintō* 対馬の神道. San'ichi shobō.

Suzuki Yasutami 鈴木靖民. 2020. *Kodai Nihon to Higashi-Ajia: Hito to mono no kōryūshi* 古代日本と東アジア: 人とモノの交流史. Bensei shuppan.

Takahashi Ichirō 高橋一郎. 2008. "Umi no ko-Amami: Higashi-Ajia kaiiki no jūgo seiki o yomu" 海の古奄美: 東アジア海域の十五世紀を読む. In *Nichi-Ryū kōeki no reimei: Yamato kara no shōgeki* 日琉交易の黎明: ヤマトからの衝撃, edited by Tanigawa Ken'ichi 谷川健一, pp. 151–181. Shinwasha.

Takahashi Yasuo 高橋康夫. 2015. *Umi no "Kyōto:" Nihon, Ryūkyū toshi shi kenkyū* 海の「京都」: 日本琉球都市史の研究. Kyoto: Kyōto daigakuu gagujutsu shuppankai.

Takamiya Hiroto 高宮広土. 2005. *Shima no senshigaku: Paradaisu de wa nakatta Okinawa shotō no senshigaku* 島の先史学: パラダイスではなかった沖縄諸島の先史学. Naha: Bōdaainku.

———. 2021. *Kiseki no shimajima no shenshigaku: Ryūkyū rettō senshi, genshi jidai no tōsho bunmei* 奇跡の島々の先史学: 琉球列島先史・原史時代の島嶼文明. Naha: Bōdaainku.

Takanashi Osamu 高梨修. 2005. *Yakōgai no kōkogaku* ヤコウガイの考古学. Dōseisha.

———. 2008a. "Gusuku isekigun to Kikaigashima: Ryūkyū-ko to Kikaijima seiryokuken" 城久遺跡群とキカイガシマ: 琉球弧と喜界島勢力圏. In *Nichi-Ryū kōeki no reimei: Yamato kara no shōgeki* 日琉交易の黎明: ヤマトからの衝撃, edited by Tanigawa Ken'ichi 谷川健一, pp. 121–149. Shinwasha.

———. 2008b. "Yakōgai kōeki: Ryūkyū-ko to kodai kokka" ヤコウガイ交易: 琉球弧と古代国家. In *Nichi-Ryū kōeki no reimei: Yamato kara no shōgeki* 日琉交易の黎明: ヤマトからの衝撃, edited by Tanigawa Ken'ichi 谷川健一, pp. 209–235. Shinwasha.

———. 2015. "Chūsei Amami no jōkaku iseki" 中世奄美の城郭遺跡. In *Ryūkyūshi o toinaosu: Ko-Ryūkyū jidairon* 琉球史を問い直す: 古琉球時代論, edited by Yoshinari Naoki 吉成直樹, Takanashi Osamu 高梨修, and Ikeda Yoshifumi 池田榮史, pp. 243–266. Shinwasha.

Takara Kurayoshi 高良倉吉. 1980. *Ryūkyū no jidai: ōinaru rekishizō o megutte* 琉球の時代: 大いなる歴史像をめぐって. Chikuma shobō.

———. 1987a. *Ryūkyū ōkoku no kōzō* 琉球王国の構造. Yoshikawa kōbunkan.

———. 1987b. "Ryūkyū, Okinawa no rekishi to Nihon shakai" 琉球・沖縄の歴史と日本社会. In *Nihon no shakai shi, daiikan: Rettō naigai no kōtsū to kokka* 日本の社会史, 第一巻, 列島内外の交通と国家. Iwanami shoten.

Takeuchi Yuzuru 竹内譲. (1933) 1960. *Shumi no Kikaijima shi* 趣味の喜界島史. Rev. ed. Kuroshio bunka kai.

Tamura Hiroshi 田村浩. (1927) 1977. *Ryūkyū kyōsan sonraku no kenkyū* 琉球共産村落の研究. Sōgensha.

Tanigawa Ken'ichi 谷川健一. 1992. "'Ko-Ryūkyū' izen no sekai: Nantō no fūdo to sei-katsu bunka" 「古琉球」以前の世界: 南島の風土と生活文化. In *Ryūkyūko no sekai* 琉球弧の世界, edited by Tanigawa Ken'ichi 谷川健一, pp. 9–66. Shōgakkan.

———. 2008. "Jo: Nissō bōeki to Nichi-Ryū kōeki" 序: 日宋貿易と日琉交易. In *Nichi-Ryū kōeki no reimei: Yamato kara no shōgeki* 日琉交易の黎明: ヤマトからの衝撃, edited by Tanigawa Ken'ichi 谷川健一, pp. 8–25. Shinwasha.

———. 2010. *Rettō jūdan, chimei shōyō* 列島縦断, 地名逍遥. Fuzanbō intaanashonaru.

Tanigawa Ken'ichi 谷川健一 and Orikuchi Shinobu 折口信夫. 2012. *Ryūkyū ōken no genryū* 琉球王権の源流. Ginowan, Japan: Yōju shorin.

Toki Naohiko 土岐直彦. 2018. *Tatakau Okinawa, hondo no sekinin: Takakuteki ronten maru-wakari* 闘う沖縄, 本土の責任: 多角的論点丸わかり. Kyoto: Kamogawa shuppan.

Tokunaga Katsushi 徳永勝士 and Jūji Takeo 猛夫. 1993. "HLA kara miru Nihonjin no kigen to keisei" HLA からみる日本人の起源と形成. In *Nihonjin to Nihon bunka no keisei* 日本人と日本文化の形成, edited by Hanihara Kazurō 埴原和郎, pp. 343–355. Asakura shoten.

Tōma Shiichi 當眞嗣一. 2012. *Ryūkyū gusuku kenkyū* 琉球グスク研究. Naha: Ryūkyū shobō.

Tomiyama Kazuyuki 豊見山一行. 1991. "Tōitsu ōkoku keiseiki no taigai kankei" 統一王国形成期の対外関係. In *Shin Ryūkyūshi, ko-Ryūkyū hen* 新琉球史, 古琉球編, edited by Ryūkyū Shinpōsha, pp. 141–162. Naha: Ryūkyū shinpōsha.

———. 2003. "Kinsei Ryūkyū shakai no tokuchō to shoronten" 近世琉球社会の特徴と諸論点. In *Ryūkyū, Okinawa no sekai* 琉球・沖縄の世界, edited by Tomiyama Kazuyuki 豊見山和行. Yoshikawa kōbunkan.

———. 2004. *Ryūkyū ōkoku no gaikō to ōken* 琉球王国の外交と王権. Yoshikawa kōbunkan.

Tonaki Akira 渡名喜明. 1992. "Aji, noro, ō: Monogatari no kōzō to ronri" アジ・ノロ・王: 物語の構造と論理. In *Ryūkyūko no sekai* 琉球弧の世界, edited by Tanigawa Ken'ichi 谷川健一, pp. 159–192. Shōgakkan.

Tsukuda Seisaku 塚田清策. 1970. *Ryūkyūkoku hibunki* 琉球國碑文記. 4 vols. Keigaku shuppan.

Uehara Kenzen 上原兼善. 1992. "Ryūkyū ōchō no rekishi: Daiichi, daini Shōshi no sei-ritsu to tenkai" 琉球王朝の歴史: 第一・第二尚氏の成立と展開. In *Ryūkyūko no sekai* 琉球弧の世界, edited by Tanigawa Ken'ichi 谷川健一, pp. 195–264. Shōgakkan.

Uema Atsushi 上間篤. 2018. *Chūsei no Nakijin to sono seiryoku no fūbō: Genchō ni tsu-kaeta Aranjin to Han'anchi* 中世の今帰仁とその勢力の風貌: 元朝に仕えたアラン人と攀安知. Naha: Bōdaainku.

UNESCO World Heritage Convention. 2001. *World Heritage: Gusuku Sites and Related Properties of the Kingdom of the Ryukyus* [*Sekai isan: Ryūkyū ōkoku no gusuku oyobi kanren isangun* 世界遺産: 琉球王国のグスク及び関連遺産群]. Culture Department, Okinawa Prefectural Education Bureau. Naha.

von Verschuer, Charlotte. (1988) 2006. *Across the Perilous Sea: Japanese Trade with China and Korea from the Seventh to the Sixteenth Centuries.* Translated by Kristen Lee Hunter. Ithaca, NY: East Asia Program, Cornell University.

Watabe Tadayo 渡部忠世. 1990. "Hōmitsu jinja no akagome to tōkō: Ōsutoroneshia-teki inasaku no hokujō" 宝満神社の赤米と踏耕: オーストロネシア的稲作の北上. In *Hayato sekai no shimajima* 隼人世界の島々, Ōbayashi Taryō 大林太良 et al., pp. 378–404. Shōgakkan.

Yamagiwa, Kaishi, Shingo Fujimoto, Hiroaki Aoyama, Jin Izumi, and Shingo Kameshima. 2019. "A Possible New Oldest Pottery Group in the Southern Ryukyu Islands, Japan: Comparative Analysis of Elemental Components of Potsherds from the Shiraho-Saonetabaru Cave Site." *Journal of Archaeological Science: Reports* 26, 101879. https://doi.org/10.1016/j.jasrep.2019.101879.

Yamaguchi Matarō 山口麻太郎. (1941) 1995. "Iki ni okeru Yabosa-jin no kenkyū" 壱岐に於けるヤボサ神の研究. In *Nihon minzoku bunka shiryō shūsei, dai nijūichi kan: Mori no kami no minzokushi* 日本民族文化資料集成, 第二十一巻: 森の神の民族誌, edited by Tanigawa Ken'ichi 谷川健一, pp. 285–316. San'ichi shobō.

Yamasaki Shinji 山崎真治. 2018. "Okinawa no kyūsekki-jin to sono bunka" 沖縄の旧石器人とその文化. In *Amami, Okinawa shotō senshigaku no saizensen* 奄美・沖縄諸島先史学の最前線, edited by Takamiya Hiroto 高宮広土, pp. 45–46. Nanpō shinsha.

Yamashita Kin'ichi 山下欣一. 2003. *Nantō minkan shinwa no kenkyū* 南島民間神話の研究. Dai'ichi shobō.

Yamazato Eikichi 山里永吉. 1963. *Kochū no tenchi: Ura kara nozoita Ryūkyū shi* 壺中の天地:裏からのぞいた琉球史. Naha: Asahidō insatsujo.

Yamazato Jun'ichi 山里純一. 2012. *Kodai Ryūkyūko to Higashi-Ajia* 古代の琉球弧と東アジア. Yoshikawa kōbunkan.

Yanagita Kunio 柳田國男. 1925. *Kainan shōki* 海南小記. Ōokayama shoten.

Yano Misako 矢野美沙子. 2014. *Ko-Ryūkyūki Shuri ōfu no kenkyū* 古琉球期首里王府の研究. Kōsō shobō.

Yonami Takeo 与並岳生. 2005. *Shin Ryūkyū ōtō shi 6: Miyako, Yaeyama; Shō Sei ō, Shō Gen ō, Shō Ei ō* 新琉球王統史 6: 宮古・八重山／尚清王・尚元王・尚永王. Naha: Shinsei shuppan.

Yononushi yuisho sho 世乃主由緒書. (1850) 1968. In *Okinoerabujima kyōdoshi shiryō* 沖永良部島郷土史資料, compiled by Nagayoshi Takeshi 永吉毅, pp. 177–180. Wadomari-chō, Japan: Wadomari chōyakuba.

Yoron-chō. 1990. *Uigusuku ato, Uigusuku iseki* 上城跡・上城遺跡. Edited by Yoron-chō Kyōiku Iinkai 与論町教育委員会. Asahi insatsu.

Yoshinari Naoki 吉成直樹. 2009. "Gusuku jidai izen no Ryūkyū no zaichi shūdan: Gengo, shinwa, DNA" グスク時代以前の琉球の在地集団: 言語・神話・DNA. In *Okinawa bunka wa dokokara kita ka: Gusuku jidai toiu kakki* 沖縄文化はどこから

来たか:グスク時代という画期, edited by Takanashi Osamu 高梨修, Abe Minako 阿部美奈子, Nakamoto Ken 中本謙, and Yoshinari Nakoki 吉成直樹. Shinwasha.

———. 2015. *Ryūkyūshi o toinaosu: Ko-Ryūkyū jidai ron* 琉球史を問い直す: 古琉球時代論. Shinwasha.

———. 2018. *Ryūkyū ōken to taiyō no ō* 琉球王権と太陽の王. Shichigatsusha.

———. 2020. *Ryūkyū ōkoku wa dare ga tsukutta no ka? Wakō to kōeki no jidai* 琉球王国は誰がつくったのか: 倭寇と交易の時代. Shichigatsusha.

———. 2022. *Ryūkyū kenkoku shi no nazo o otte: Kōeki shakai to wakō* 琉球建国史の謎を追って: 交易社会と倭寇. Shichigatsusha.

Yotsumoto Nobuhiro 四本延宏. 2008. "Tokunoshima Kamuiyaki tōki yōseki: Yōseki hakken to sono ato no chōsa seika" 徳之島カムイヤキ陶器窯跡: 窯跡発見とその後の調査成果. In *Nichi-Ryū kōeki no reimei: Yamato kara no shōgeki* 日琉交易の黎明: ヤマトからの衝撃, edited by Tanigawa Ken'ichi 谷川健一, pp. 237–262. Shinwasha.

Yuánshǐ 元史. Chinese Text Project. https://ctext.org/wiki.pl?if=en&res=603186.

Index

Page numbers in boldface type refer to illustrations

Agarui-no-ōnushi, 294n5

Agaru-mochizuki, 238, 295n11

Agena Gusuku, 160, 289n10

agriculture, 3, 9–10, 55, 66–67, 90, 96, 99–100, 101–105, 137–155; carbonized grain, 90, 96, 141, 143, 154, 174, 193, 286n1, 286n3; cereal grains, 46, 102, 137, 141, 146–147, 153–154, 256, 258, 262, 297n2; Chinese envoys' reports on, 150–151; documentary record of, 148–150; environmental constraints on, 46, 64, 151, 154–155, 262; *jaagaru* (soil type), 66–67, 140, 143–144, 146–147, 278n1; Japan Soil Inventory (Nihon dojō inbentorii), 146–147; *Kunigami-maaji* (soil type), 66, 146, 287n9; *Shimajiri-maaji* (soil type), 66, 140, 143–144, 146, 149; problems explaining, 37–38, 40–41, 142–143, 223, 266–267; rejection of, 102, 268, 282n20, 282n21; sweet potatoes, 149, 151, 153; and state formation, 3, 17, 29, 40, 44, 139, 154–155, 180, 194, 257, 263, 266; and taxation, 149, 154, 235, 265, 268, 288n18; tools for, 29–30, 31, 33, 67, 90, 103, 114, 140, 141, 143–144, 145–146, 148, 150–151, 154, 164–165, 194, 206, 230, 266–267, 274n10, 286n1, 286n3, 287n11, 287n12; wet rice cultivation, 30, 102, 143–144, 146–147, 154, 193–194, 274n10, 287n7. *See also* tubers

agricultural rites, 256

agricultural society, 9, 28, 31–32, 34, 38, 101–102, 137, **138**–142, 144–145, 149–150, 153, 155, 206, 223, 256, 258, 265

aji. See warlords

Akagina Gusuku, 154, 157, 171, 289n10, 290n17

Akamine, Mamoru, 49–51, 165, 176, 276n24, 290n21

Akibatsu, 173. *See also* Yi Seonggye

Alan people, 6, 16, 46, 174–175, 261, 270, 276n1

Amami interpreters, 82–83, 203, 270

Amami (southern barbarian) pirate raids, 83–85

Amamikyo (Amamiku), 32, 60–61, 118, 279n14, 284n3, 284n4

Amami-Ōshima. *See* Northern Tier islands

Amamiwainoro, 238. *See also* Ezu Gusuku

Amawari, 177, 233, 238–240. *See also* Katsuren Gusuku. *See also* Tomoi group (Otomoi group)

ancient branch model, 12, 17, 25–27, 35–38, 41–42, 44, 47, **48**–49, 72, 86, 89, 138, 180, 196, 266, 268, 274n8

Aoriyae, 249, 251, 256, See also Kumejima. *See also* Sasukasa

Araki Moriaki, 39, 275n16

arrowheads. *See* warfare

Asato Susumu, 38, 40, 143–144, 267, 286n7. *See also* agriculture

Ata Tadakage, 283n3

banana fiber cloth (*bashōfu*), 77, 81, 150, 172

barbarian zone, 9, 101–103, 153, 162, 257, 265, 268. *See also* Scott, James C.

Baten priestess 229, 237. *See also* Samekawa, Lord. *See also* Yamato Banta (Harbor)

Bellwood, Peter, 102
Benzaiten, 256
birōsuku ware, 176, 290n23
bishopwood (*akagi*), 80, 81, 98
black writing pottery, 109
blacksmiths, 114, 251–252
bone cults, 236
bone tools and arrowheads, 143–144, 175
Bōnotsu, 91, 112, 114, 170
Bora (Boranomotojima), 61–62, 79, 171, 241. *See also* Miyako (Island)
Bunei, 209–**214**, 215. *See also* Muryeong of Baekje
Busan, Korea, **107**, 115, 124, 248

cavalry forces, 114, 162, 174–175, 230. *See also* Sashiki in Okinawa. *See also* warfare
Chén Kǎn, 150, 293n18
Chéng Fù (J. Tei Fuku), 176–177, 210
Chikama Tokiie, 169–170
Chinatown place names, 112
Chinzei Hachirō. *See* Minamoto Tametomo
Chiyoganemaru (sword), 174
Choku Karo (Zhí Jiālǔ), 211
Chūzan. *See* Three Principalities (Sanzan)
cloth stacking (*nunozumi*), 158, 191, 288
collagen, human bone, 67, 286n3, 286n6
cone snail shells (*imogai*), 54, 58–59, 80, 277n6
core cultural zone, 52–**53**, 56–57, 59, 63, 84

Dana Masayuki, 39
dang (*dangsan*). *See* sacred groves
Dazaifu, 21, 80, 82, 83–85, 91–93, 100, 106, 264, 273n1, 281n12, 283n3
discontinuities, historical, 5–6, 7, 27, 36, 41, 44, 51, 68, 89, 103, **104**, **178**, 179. See also *gusuku* era
DNA evidence, 1, 6, 16, 53, 67, 72–**76**, **77**–78, 152, 278n4
Dōan, 166–167, 243, 292n5, 280n1
Dodo Yukio, 70
Doi Naomi, 278n4, 279n9
dual structure hypothesis (Hanihara hypothesis), 6, 17, 68, 70–**71**, 72–73, 76–**77**, 87, 261, 278n5, 278n7. *See also* Hanihara Kazurō

East China Sea Network, 4, 276n1
East Sea Countries, Account of (1471), 125, 135, 200, 238, 292n6
eastern Okinawa, characteristics of, 199–200, 221
Eiso (line), 30, 32, 40, 140, 180, 191–192, 202–**205**, 206, 213–214, 216, 292n10, 292n11, 292n12; Ōeijishi, 201, **205**–206, **214**; Ōōso, 201, **205**–206, 211–212, 214–215; Tamagusuku, King, 198, 204–**205**, 216. *See also* Satto (group)
embassies to China (*kentōshi*), 81–82. See also southern islands route (*nantōto*)
environment as driver of history, 9, 10, 20, 25–27, 31, 46–47, 64, 154, 259, 266–268
ethnogenesis. *See* Ryukyuans as ethnic group
eunuch incident (1406), 213, 217
external agents model, 13, 17, 25, 26–27, 40, 42–**45**, 46–47, **48**, 259, 265–267
Ezogachishima, 295n16
Ezu Gusuku, 185, 233, 238, 244. *See also* Katsuren Gusuku. *See also* Tomoi group (Otomoi group)

Fāng Guózhēn, 173, 175
field stone stacking (*nozurazumi*), 158, 288n4
firearms, 160, 187, 188, 191
fitted stacking (*aikatazumi*), 158, 288n4
fortresses. See *gusuku* (fortresses)
Fuku Hiromi, 44
Furi, 232–234, 244. *See also* Shiro (and Shiro-Furi war). *See also* warfare
Futaoi Island, 120

Gaja (K. Wasa) and Gajajima, 166. *See also* Tokara Islands
genetic diversity, 73
geography. *See* environment as driver of history
Gihon, 202, 292n8
Goeku (Castle), 186, 200, 231–233
golden age of barbarians, 47, 103, 141. *See also* barbarian zones. *See also* Scott, James C.

Gongmin (Goryeo king), 172–173. *See also*
    mùhú pastoralists (in Jeju Island)
Goryeo History, 57, 108, 162
Goryeo Tripitaka, 295n16
Gosamaru, 168, 183, 189, 233. *See also*
    Nakagusuku Gusuku
Graeber, David, 282n21
grain mills, portable, 174
group A pottery, 95–96, 269, 281n9
group B pottery, 95–96, 103, 141, 269, 281n9
Guō Rǔlín, 150
Guraru (Goran) Magohachi, 147, 223, 228,
    240, 245, 291n3. *See also* Okinoerabu
    (Island)
Gushikawa gusuku (in Kumejima), 250, 253
gusuku era, 12, 15, 17, 30, 36, 38, 49–50, 55,
    79, 80, 85, 89–**94**, 95–**104**, 105–106, 117,
    125, 134, 137–139, 142, 145, 148–150,
    152–154, 156–157, 161, **178**, 179; as
    discontinuity, 5–6, 26, 30, 36, 41, 51, 68,
    69–70, 72–73, 75–76, 83, 85–89, 140, 179;
    regional trade networks during, 106–116,
    168–**169**. *See also* discontinuities,
    historical
gusuku (fortresses), 128–**131**, 132–133,
    157–161, 200, 289n10; debate (*gusuku
    ronsō*), 129, 158–160; functions of,
    160–161; stone-walled, 15, 34, 60, 129,
    131–133, 157, 160, 165, 188, 262;
    trench-and-earthworks (*chūsei jokaku*),
    15, 128–129, 157–158, 189n5, 194, 195,
    237–238, 289n9, 290n17, 292n9. *See also*
    Korean mountain fortresses. *See also*
    warfare
Gusuku Site Group (Gusuku), 15, 21, 42,
    55–56, 65, 84, 90–94, 95–96, 100, 105,
    106, 110–111, 113–116, 158, 261–262,
    266–267, 281n8, 283n2. *See also*
    Kikaijima

hajiki ware, 91, 111
Hakata, 46, 52, 91, 99, 106–108, 110–112, 115,
    120, 243, 248, 292n5, 295n15; as conduit
    for Chinese products, 93, 108–110,
    168–**169**, 170, 173, 281n11, 290n16,
    291n23, 291n4

Hakata Site Group, 109
hammer (*hetsu*), 165
Han'anchi, 174, 198, 201, 212–**214**, 216, 243,
    290n22. *See also* Nakijin. *See also* Three
    Principalities (Sanzan)
Hanagusuku (Tatanagusuku), 185, 189–190
hand cannon. *See* firearms
Haneji shioki, 149
Hanihara Kazurō, 6, 68, 71–72, 77, 87, 261
haplogroup M7a, 74, 76
harbor-fortress units, 7–8, 13, 20, 34, 152,
    154, 158, 181–**182**, **185**, 186–**195**,
    196–198, 200, 221–222, 240, 244,
    262–263, 265–266, 268–271. *See also*
    nekuni (base)
Hashimoto Yū, 244, 295n13, 295n14
Hateruma, 30, 65, 283n4, 296n6
hawksbill sea turtles, 80–81
hermit crab mythology, 79, 279n14
heroes, era of (*eiyū jidai*), 199, 240–243
Higa Chōshin, 212, 217, 228
Higa Shunchō, 27, 32–35, 89, 158, 275n13,
    275n14
Higashionna Kanjun, 23
high priestess (*Kikoe-ōgimi*), 247, 296n3. *See
    also* three sister deities
Higo Province. *See* Kumamoto Prefecture
hiki system, 235, 247, 296n3. *See also*
    Kumejima
Hirota site (Tanegashima), 58, 68–69, 260,
    278n2, 280n15, 286n6. *See also*
    Tanegashima
History of Song (*Sòngshǐ*), 114, 280n6
Hokama Kazuo, 142–144, 147–148, 193–194,
    287n9, 287n10. *See also* agriculture
Hokama Shuzen, 293n11
Hokkaidō, 57–59, 63, 70–71, 89, 264
Hong-Schunka, S. M., 133, 294n3, 295n15
Hóngwǔ emperor (Zhū Yuánzhāng), 173,
    175, 177
Honkawara. *See* Oyake Akahachi
Hú Wéiyōng. *See* Lín Xián and Hú Wéiyōng
    Incident
hub-and-spoke model, 7, 17, 106–**107**,
    108–116, 168–**169**, **185**, 266
Hudson, Mark, 43, 71, 277n11

human leukocyte antigen (HLA), 55–56,
    286n21
human trafficking, 14, 85, 117, 135, 162,
    165–168, 177–179, 208, 261, 264. *See also*
    Naha, port of
hunter-gatherer society, 28, 31, 102, 137, 138,
    260
huŏcháng (ship captains), 225–226

ibe (sacred space), 61, 120
Iha Fuyū, 23, 29–30, 60–61, 139, 226, 273n3
Iheya Island, 64, 229–230
Iizu/Iizu-niya. *See* Eiso
Iizu (Iso) Gusuku, 203–204, 293n11. *See also*
    Eiso
Ikeda Yoshifumi, 43–44, 90, 95, 161, 163,
    283n1, 289n14
Iki (Island), 4, 52, 56–57, 83–84, 108, 120,
    122, 125–126, 162, 199, 276n2
Ikuta Shigeru, 196, 200, 256
illicit trade, 62, 85, 162, 172–173, 208, 216,
    220, 242–243, 253, 262, 265
Inamura Kenpu, 27, 31–34, 36, 44, 140,
    189–190, 230, 241, 288n2, 288n3, 291n2,
    295n11
Indica (Champa) rice, 148, 154, 287n12
indigenous population(s) (Shellmound era),
    6, 51, 72, 74, 86, 96, 179, 258, 270, 279n9;
    crash of 85–**86**, 101, 105, 260
internal development model, 10, 12, 13, 17,
    21, 25, 26, 28, 30–31, 37–44, 46–**48**,
    49–50, 72–73, 86, 89, 129, 138–139, 141,
    180, 196, 266–268, 275n16
invasion of Ishigaki (Yaeyama). *See* warfare.
    See also Ishigaki (Island). *See also*
    Yaeyama
investiture envoys, Chinese, 145, 150–151,
    293n18. *See also* agriculture
iron and iron tools, 29–33, 43–44, 50, 91–92,
    103, 111, 114–115, 134, 140–141, 143–144,
    146, 148, 150, 154, 161, 164–165, 192–194,
    206, 230, 247, 266–267, 286n7
Ishigaki (Island), 61, 64, 65, 68, 70, 74, 76, 79,
    82, 114, 125, 146–147, 172, 176, 241–242,
    248, 251, 252–253, 259, 283n4, 288n1,
    296n3, 296n6. *See also* Nagura Bay

Ishikinawa (of Kumejima), 253
Island smashing (*shima-utchi*), 228. *See also*
    warfare
Iso Gusuku. *See* Eiso
Itokazu Gusuku (Castle), 132, 184, 186, 191,
    192, 204, 205, 298n10, 291n6
Itoman fishermen, 57
Izena Island, 120, 246, 250, 251, 289n10

Japonic languages, 82–83, 89, 96, 262, 270
Japonica rice, 148, 279n13
Jeju Island, 7, 56–57, 78, 122, 124, 126–**128**,
    135, 156, 164, 172–173, 175, 289n13
Jeonglu, 167
Jōmon era, 52–54, 63, 73, 84–86, 94, 117, 133,
    175, 264, 278n7
Jōmon people, 6, 16, 46, 54, 68, 70–**71**, 72,
    74–**75**, **76**, **77**, 87, 102–103, 260, 261, 269

Kaiki (Ch. Huái Jī), 231–232, 273n2, 294n19.
    See also Shō Hashi
kaijō no michi (ocean road), 274n10. *See also*
    Yanagita Kunio
Kamakura, city of, 92, 100, 156, 186, 239
kamuiyaki (grey stoneware), 42–**43**, 50, 55,
    84, 90–93, 95, 103, 112–115, 121, 134, 141,
    171, 192, 193, 262, 264, 269, 275n20,
    280n4, 280n7, 281n10, 297n4. *See also*
    Korean technology and technicians
Kanagusuku chikudun-peichin Wasai, 148.
    See also agriculture
Kanahiyabu, 174, 284n3
Kaneku pottery, 91
Kanemaru. *See* Shō En. *See also* Kawara *wakō*
Kanemaru of the north, 250–251. *See also*
    Kawara *wakō*. *See also* Shō En.
Kaneyoshi, Prince, 179, 198
Kanzaki no Shō (estate), 106–107
Kasari Peninsula (of Amami-Ōshima), 65,
    90, 92, 94, 100, 147, 167, 171, 234, 262
Katsuren Gusuku (Castle), 20, 128, 132, 157,
    163–164, 168, 177, **182**, 184–**185**, 186–187,
    190, 194, 200, 222, 226, 232–234,
    237–240, 244, 266, 271, 285n11, 291n6,
    295n11. *See also* Ezu Gusuku. *See also*
    Tomoi group (Otomoi group)

Kawara *wakō,* 246–247, **252**–254, 256–257. See also *wakō. See also* warfare

Kerr, George H., 47, 49, 276n23. *See also* Ryukyuan pacifism, myth of

Kikaijima. *See* Northern Tier islands. *See also* Shuri conquest of Kikaijima

Kikaijima orbit of power, 92

Kimihae priestess, 247–**248**, 252–253. *See also* Kumejima. *See also* three sister deities

king, the title (*wáng*). *See* trade kings

knife coins, 33, 54

Kokubu Naoichi, 120

komibune, 241

Korean mountain fortresses (*sanseong*), 15, 128–**130**, 285n12; compared with Chinese fortresses, 131–132, 285n17; compared with *gusuku,* 128–133, 158–159, 188, 192, 262, 288n4; functions of, 129,159–160, 285n13, 285n14, 285n18. See also *gusuku* (fortresses)

Korean-style roof tiles, 132, 134, 163–164, 186, 208

Korean technology and technicians, 54, 56, 84, 93, 115–116, 121, 132–134, 208, 262. See also *kamuiyaki*

kubire-hirasoko earthenware, 95, 281n9

Kudakajima, 136, 236, 256

Kumamoto Prefecture (Higo), 55, 91, 121, 280n4

Kumejima, 28, 60, 64, 146, 228, 247–**248**, **249**–251, **252**–253, 256, 289n10, 296n3. See also *hiki* system. *See also* Kimihae priestess. *See also* three sister deities

Kumemura, 135, 225, 254, 293n18; Korean community in, 136. *See also* thirty-six families

Kundagusuku, 236. *See also* bone cults

Kurakizaki Undersea Site, 109, 112

Kurima Yasuo, 44, 90, 144–145, 148, 154

Kuroshima, 81, 241, 296n6

kusuha tile ware bowls, 112, 283n3

kyoda. See *makyo*

Larsen, Kirk, 292n4

Lebra, William P., 77, 127

Legends from the Elders (Irō setsuden), 23

Lèlàng Commandery, 54

Lín Xián and Hú Wéiyōng Incident, 173

Lóngquán kilns, 62, 109

M7a haplotype, 74, 76

Maegata harbor, 109

Magatama (jewels) 114, 161

Majikina Ankō, 288n18

Makishi Yōko, 247, 296n2, 296n3

makyo, 31, 140

malaria, 145, 151–152, 154, 287n15, 287n16, 288n17

Mannyeon, 167–168

Manose River. *See* Mottaimatsu

mantic arts, 80, 174

Mashifuri, 184, 232–233

Michinoshima, 52, 65

migration, 3, 15, 29, 40–41, 54, 61, 74–75, 79, **94**–101, 106, 278n7

Minamoto Tametomo, 23, 25, 30, 161, 283n2, 283n3

Minatogawa people, 41, 67–68, 87, 89, 259

Ministry of Justice, Chinese, 172

Miyako (Island), 28, 31, 61–63, 64–68, 70, 73, 75–**76**, 78–79, 87, 95, 113, 125, 147, 168, 171, 241–242, 251, 255, 259, 261, 278n6, 288n17. *See also* Bora (Boranomotojima). *See also* Nagabaka site

Mochizuki (of Katsuren), 177, 186, 238, 240, 295n11. *See also* Tomoi group (Otomoi group)

Momotofumiagari, 233. *See also* Oni-Ōgusuku. *See also* Shō Taikyū

Mongols, 6, 16, 46, 173–176, 261, 270; Yuan dynasty remnants, 173–177, 195, 199, 216

mother-of-pearl (MOP), 93, 99–100, 280n6, 281n14. *See also* turbo shells

Mottaimatsu, 106, 109, 111–113

Mount Omoto, **248**, 252. *See also* Kimihae priestess. *See also* three sister deities

mùhú pastoralists (in Jeju Island), 172–173. *See also* Gongmin (Goryeo king)

Munakata Shrines, 248, 251, 296n1. *See also* three sister deities

Muryeong of Baekje, 209. *See also* Bunei

Nagabaka site, 68, 75–**76**. *See also* DNA
  evidence
Nagafuji Yasushi, 147–148
Nagura Bay, 172, 241–242. *See also* Ishigaki
  (Island). *See also* Shitadaru Seafloor Site
Naha, port of, 4, 5, 60, 65, 79, 98, 135, 162,
  183, 196–198, 200, 210, 215, 232,
  246–247, 250, 264, 289n8, 295n12; as
  center of human trafficking, 135,
  162–163, 165–166, 177, 225, 242. *See also*
  human trafficking
Naka Shōhachirō, 161
Nakagusuku Bay, 187–**188**, 190, **193**–194
Nakagusuku Gusuku, 128, **131**–132, 160,
  168, 185, **187**–190, 233, 289n10, 291n6
Nakahara Zenchū, 27, 28–33, 35–36, 42, 89,
  274n9, 275n11
Nakamatsu Yashū, 158, 161, 291n1
Nakasone of Miyako, 241–242, 255
Nakijin Gusuku (Castle), 35, 46, 131–132,
  157, 163, 165, 174–176, 186, 190, 217, 261,
  285n11, 290n23. *See also* Han'anchi
Nakijin priestesses and deities, **249**,
  251–**252**, 256. See also Kumejima. *See
  also* three sister deities
nard (Persian board game), 175
Nawa of Yatsushiro (Nawashiro), 183, 230.
  See also Samekawa, Lord. *See also* Shō
  Hashi
nekuni (base), 181–**182**, 183–184, 190,
  193–194. *See also* harbor-fortress pairs
Níngbō, 108–109, 170, 173
niraikanai (horizontal orientation), 127, 256,
  271, 284n4
noro. See priestess
northern frames of reference, 60. *See also*
  snow, references to
Northern Tier islands, 3, **104**, 106, 110–112,
  115, 168; Amami-Ōshima, 3, 21, 55, 58,
  61, 64–65, 90–94, 100, 106, 109, 112, 124,
  147, 153–154, 157–158, 167–168, 170,
  183–184, 234, 237–238, 240, 244, 262, 264,
  277n14, 279n14, 290n17; Kikaijima, 3–5,
  15, 21–22, 26, 46, 55, 64, 83–85, 89–**94**,
  95–100, 103–105, 106, 111, 113, 115, 147,
  167–168, 170–171, 184, 234–237, 244, 254,
  261–262, 267, 280n7, 283n2, 283n3,
  295n9; Tokunoshima, 3, 42, 55–56, 64, 78,
  82–84, 90–**94**, 100, 106–**107**, 113, 115, 121,
  134, 146–147, 154, 170–171, 183–184, 237,
  262, 264, 275n20, 280n4. *See also* Gusuku
  Site Group (Gusuku). See also *kamuiyaki*
  (grey stoneware)

Ōeijishi (Ōeiji, Ōeishi). *See* Eiso (group)
official histories, 2, 3–4, 8, 17, 23, 26, 28–29,
  35, 39–42, 49, 62–63, 117, 133–134, 141,
  143, 179, 180–181, 191, 194, 196, 198,
  202–206, 209, 213, 216, 222–223, 229,
  232–234, 236, 242, 246, 250–252,
  254–255, 266–267, 274n6, 274n7, 283n2,
  291n3, 292n3, 292n7, 293n11; absence of
  Korea in, 8, 17, 117, 133, 206; *Kyūyō*
  (1743–1876), 230, 232–233, 242, 252;
  Reflections on Chūzan (Chūzan seikan,
  1650), 41, 60, 118, 198, 202–203, 209,
  228–229, 232–233, 235, 254; Sai On
  Genealogy of Chūzan (1725), 41, 174, 191,
  198, 203, 209, 222–223, 228–229,
  232–233, 236, 275n18; Sai Taku
  Genealogy of Chūzan (1701), 41, 203–204,
  209, 222, 228–229, 232–233, 236;
  Shuri- or Okinawa-centric bias in, 3, 35,
  41, 194, 196, 233
official students (Ch. *guānshēng*; J. *kanshō*),
  210–212, 217
Ōhama Eisen, 101
Ōhira Satoshi, 159
Okinoerabu (Island), 64, 80, 147, 158, 170,
  184, 223, 228, 240, 245, 279n14, 291n3.
  See also Guraru (Goran) Magohachi
Okuma blacksmith, 251–252. *See also* Satto
  (group). *See also* Shō En
Omoro sōshi (the Omoro), 4, 5, 14, 16, 22–23,
  28, 30, 32, 40–42, 60, 112, 121, 135–136,
  140, 165, 181–186, 188–189, 190, 194, 196,
  200–204, 219, 226, 228–230, 232,
  237–239, 240, 246–247, 249–251, 254,
  257, 270, 286n22, 292n7, 293n11, 294n5,
  294n21, 296n3. *See also* Shō Shin
Oni-Ōgusuku, 233. *See also*
  Momotofumiagari
Onsado. *See* Satto (group)
Ōōso. *See* Eiso (group)

open-air burials, 118, 126
origin tales, Ryukyuan, 60, 164–165, 241
Original Nakagusuku Group, 189, 220
Origins of Ryukyu (*Ryūkyūkoku yuraiki*, 1713), 61, 114, 117, 125, 277n17, 284n5, 289n8, 291n2
Orikuchi Shinobu, 118–119
Orita Noboru, 295n9
Ōshiro Kei, 148
Otomoi (see Tomoi group)
outsiders or newcomers as drivers of Ryukyuan history, 5, 6, 20, 44, 156, 162, 165, 206, 257, 259, 265, 267
Oyagawa Gusuku, 194, 291n8
Oyake Akahachi, 241, 253. *See also* warfare
Ōyama Ringorō, 233
Oza (in Yomitan), 219. *See also* Taiki
Ōzato, 35, 125, 148, 206, 291n6, 292n3

palm fronds (*biro, binrō, kuba*), 24, 80–81, 98, 114
Pearson, Richard, 43, 147, 186, 194, 254, 289n14, 297n4
physical environment. *See* environment as driver of history
Plasmodium (malaria parasite), 151, 287n15, 287n16
population crash, indigenous, 85–**86**
postnatal sweat baths, 78, 279n11, 279n12
priestesses, 121, 161, 164–165, 181–182, 190, 247, 252, 284n5
proto-Ryukyuan, 72, 97, 103, 262

ramie, 80–81, 167, 172
red bowls (*akawan*), 136
red rice, 78. *See also* treading cultivation
Red Turban revolts, 173
Robinson, Kenneth R., 290n16, 296n17
royal seal, 216, 232
Ryang Seong, 132, 135, 143, 211
Ryukyuan pacifism, myth of, 31, 37, 49, 275n19. *See also* warfare
Ryukyuans as ethnic group, 7, 26–27, 32–33, 36, 84, 89, 179, 270–271; ethnogenesis, **178**–179, 270–271, 297n4; notions of continuity of, 32–33, 36, 68, 86, 89, 259–260

sacred groves (*utaki*), 9, 60–61, 117–**128**, 129, 160, 236, 247, 291n2; characteristics of, **123**, 126–**128**; *dang* (*dangsan*), 56, 119, 122, 124–127; dates of, 124–126; distribution of, **119**–**124**; *garō/garan* mountain, 122–124; *kōjin no mori/yabu*, 120, 122–123; Korean origins of, 9, 17, 56, 117, 119, 125–126, 127–128, 262, 274n7; *moidon*, 122–123; Mount Soto, 56; *niso no mori*, 120, 122–123; *obotsu* mountain, 122–124; *o-dō*, 56, 60; *shigechi*, 122– 123; *tendō/tendōchi*, 120–121, 123; and tourism, 126; *yabusa/yabosa*, 118, 120–126, 284n10
sado (local officials), 135, 206
Sai On, 49, 155, 223, 233, 258, 296n6
Saigō Nobutsuna, 238, 291n5, 293n11, 294n5
Sakihara, Mitsugu, 49
Sambyeolcho Rebellion, 156, 164
Samekawa, Lord, 193, 229–230, 237. *See also* Nawa of Yatsushiro (Nawashiro)
Sangurumii, 210–211, 226
Sanzan. *See* Three Principalities
sanzan tōitsu (unification of the Three Principalities), 220, 224
sappanwood, 62–63, 99, 108, 208, 242, 295n12
Sashiki in Kyushu, 118, 147, 193, 229–230, 247
Sashiki in Okinawa, 60, 118, 147, 184, 193, 229–230, 237
Sashiki (Ui) Gusuku, 129, 147, 157, **182**, 184, **193**–194, **195**, 230, 290n17, 294n5
Sasukasa, **249**, 251, 256. *See also* Aoriyae
Satto (group), 46, 117, 135, 143, 165, 176–177, 189, 191, 197–198, 200, 204–**207**, 208–210, 211, 212–213, 216–**218**, 219–220, 223, 230, 236, 243, 251–252, 261, 275n13, 286n20, 292n7, 293n12, 293n15–17, 294n20–21; Jana, 206, 230, 292n7; -sato named envoys, 219, 294n20; Onsado, 201, 206–207, 209, 212, 219, 293n17; Shōsatto, 135, 201, 206–**207**, 208–210, 219, 286n19, 293n17; Taiki (Taichi), **218**, 219–220. *See also* Okuma blacksmith. *See also* Oza

Scott, James C., 3, 47, 101, 103, 153, 268, 273n2, 276n22, 282n16, 282n22, 297n1. *See also* barbarian zone
Sea Bridge to the Many Countries Bell (Bankoku shinryō no kane), 11, 22, 59–60, 134, 234, 295n7. *See also* Shō Taikyū
sea cucumbers, 81, 172
Seifaa utaki, 256, 284n3
Seoul, 136. *See also* red bowls
Serafim, Leon, 181
Serikaku priestess, 165
Seto Tetsuya, 144, 157, 200
Seyock, Barbara, 278n18, 289n13
Shapinsky, Peter D., 14
shell trade, 57–**59**, 69, 84, 89, 92, 97, 270
Shellmound Era, 17, 33, 41–42, 56, 64–88, 95, 113, 134, 260, 264, 269
shige/shigechi, 121–124, 126
shikyoma (*mishikyoma*) rites, 256
Shimono Toshimi, 124–125
Shin-sarugaku ki, 99
Shinzato Akito, 95, 141, 171
Shinzato Keiji, 286n7
Shinzato, Rumiko, 181
ship captains (Chinese). See *huǒcháng*
Shiraho-Saonetabaru Cave Site, 68, 74
Shirakihara Kazumi, 86–87, 161, 274n10
Shiro (and Shiro-Furi war), 232–234, 244. *See also* warfare
Shitadaru Seafloor Site, 172, 241. *See also* Nagura Bay
Shō Chū, **227**, 229, 232, 294n5
Shō Ei, 150
Shō En (Kanemaru), 165, 206, 234, 236, 246–247, 251, **252**–254, 256–257, 296n4
Shō Gen, 150
Shō Hashi, 5, 10, 30, 46, 128, 143, 147, 165, 180, 183, 193–194, 196, 198–199, 201, 206, 213, 215, 217, 220–226, **227**–232, 237–238, 240, 244, 246, 256, 273n2, 275n18, 290n17, 292n2, 294n19, 294n20. *See also* Sashiki in Kyushu. *See also* Samekawa, Lord. *See also* Sashiki in Okinawa
Shō Kinpuku, 167, **227**, 229, 231–232
Shō Sei, 20, 150, 215, 240, 246–247, 256–258

Shō Sen'i, 254, 257
Shō Shin, 2, 5, 14, 20, 22, 20, 46, 134, 220, 223, 246–247, 250–251, 253–258, 265, 296n3, 296n4
Shō Shishō, 196, 201, 206, 211, 229, 291n1
Shō Shitatsu, **227**, 229
Shō Shōken (Haneji Chōshū), 149, 155, 233, 258
Shō Taikyū, 11, 20, 46, 59, 134–135, 185, 211, 222–**227**, 228, 231–236, 238, 240, 244, 246, 253, 256, 273n2, 295n7. *See also* Sea Bridge to the Many Countries Bell (Bankoku shinryō no kane)
Shō Tei, 151
Shō Toku, 223, **227**–228, 234–236, 244, 246, 256, 295n9
Shōsatto. *See* Satto (group)
Shunten, 23, 30, 35, 165, 191, 283n2
Shuri as strong center of a maritime empire, 5, 20, 22, 223–224, 243, 254–255, 265, 271, 273n5
Shuri Castle, 13, 131–132, 165, 193, 194, 211, 226, 228–229, 231–232, 256, 289n10, 291n6
Shuri Conquest of Kikaijima, 167, 234–236, 244, 254, 295n9. *See also* warfare
slave trade. *See* human trafficking
Smits, Akiko, 296n1
smuggling. *See* illicit trade
snow, references to, 60, 183, 194, 277n14. *See also* northern frames of reference
soapstone cauldrons (*kasseki-sei ishinabe*), 42, 50, 90–91, 95, 103, 110–111, 113–114, 262, 283n1
Sobata-type pottery, **54**
soil. *See* agriculture
southern islands route (*nantōro*), 81, 109, 170, 177, 208. *See also* embassies to China (*kentōshi*)
spades (*hera*), 143–144, 148, 151. *See also* agriculture, tools for
spurious envoys, 243–244, 295n13–14
standard narrative, 2–11, 134, 196, 215. *See also* internal development model
state(s), 3, 8–15, 20, 25–27, 29–30, 35, 38, 41, 47, 62, 89–90, 98, 101–105, 119, 134,

138–139, 153, 155, 162, 179, 180–181, 194,
196–198, 209, 212, 217, 220–221, 235,
241–242, 253, 254–258, 263, 265–268,
271, 273n5, 275n18, 276n22, 282n22–25,
286n7, 289n11, 297n1–3; absence of, 116,
145, 152–154; control, 99, 105, 153, 268,
283n24, 297n3; definition of, 13;
formation, 3, 4–5, 17, 21, 29, 40, 44, 134,
139, 154–155, 180, 194, 257, 263, 266,
270–271, 289n11. *See also* agriculture.
See also barbarian zones. *See also*
harbor-fortress units
stone-walled *gusuku*. See *gusuku* (fortresses)
sue ware, 91, 111, 275n20, 280n4
sulfur, 80, 99, 108, 162, 164, 173, 176, 208,
242, 289n12
Sūn Wěi, 135, 292n9, 293n17, 294n11
Suzuki Tōzō, 121, 125

Taiki (Taichi). *See* Satto (group)
Taiwan, 6, 16, 50, 62, 75, 77–79, 114, 175,
273n3, 278n4, 279n12–13, 280n15; Liúqiú
as, 16, 114, 175, 276n24, 279n12
Takahashi Ichirō, 166, 237, 295n10
Takamiya Hiroto, 85–86, 153–154, 288n18
Takanashi Osamu, 92, 158
Takara Kurayoshi, 39, 275n17, 287n7
Taketomi, 61, 65, 283n4, 296n6
Tamagusuku Gusuku, 132, 204–205, 289n10,
291n6
Tamagusuku, King. *See* Eiso (line)
Tametomo legend. *See* Minamoto Tametomo
Tanegashima, 58, 64, 68–69, 78–79, 81–83,
92–93, 97, 122, 124, 260, 284n8, 289n15.
See also Hirota site
Tanigawa Ken'ichi, 43
Tarumi (Tarumai), 197, 201, 213–**214**, 215,
292n2, 294n19
tax system, 154, 235, 288n18
Thailand, 294n19, 295n12
thirty-six families, the, 293n18
Three Principalities (Sanzan), 2, 4–5, 8, 20,
35, 41–42, 139, 180, 192, 195, 196–221,
222–224, 228, 240, 243–244, 258,
265–266, 286n19, 291n2, 292n7, 294n21;
Chūzan, 4–5, 35, 62–63, 196–198, 200,

206–213, 215–217, 219, 220, 222, 226, 233,
238, 242, 252, 286n19, 292n2–3; new
model of, 216–**218**; Sanhoku (Hokuzan),
4–5, 134, 174, 186, 196–197, 210, 212–213,
215–217, 220, 229, 292n1, 292n3; Sannan
(Nanzan), 4–5, 134–135, 189, 192,
196–197, **205**–206, **207**–209, 210–212,
213–219, 222, 242, 292n1–3, 292n9–10,
294n19; warfare connected with, 35, 195,
197, 199, 205, 212, 214, 217, 226, 228, 231.
See also Han'anchi. *See also* Mongols
Three sister deities, 247–**248**, 251. *See also*
high priestess (*Kikoe-ōgimi*). *See also*
Kimihae priestess. *See also* Mount
Omoto
Toba Masao, 158
Toguchi Castle, 170, 289n10
Tokara Islands (Wasa/Gaja Islands), 52, 61,
78, 97, 112, 121, 124, 166, 170, 247, 249,
251; as maritime commons, 166–167
Tokunoshima. *See* Northern Tier islands
Tōma Shiichi, 131, 188, 189n11
Tomari harbor, 183, 203
Tomiyama Kazuyuki, 39, 144
Tomoi group (Otomoi group), 223, 228,
236–**239**, 240, 244–245, 266, 268. *See also*
Amawari. See also Katsuren Gusuku. *See
also* Mochizuki (of Katsuren)
Tóng'ān kilns, 109, 113
tōngshì (trade manager), **225**–226
Torii Ryūzō, 70
trade kings, 14, 46, 150, 153, 162–163, 166,
194–195, 197, 201–202, 211, **214**, 222–223,
224– **225**, 228–229, 235, 243–244,
256–257, 265, 292n7–10, 294n21. *See also*
king, the title (*wáng*)
treading cultivation, 78–89, 143, 147, 154.
See also red rice
trench-and-earthworks *gusuku*. See *gusuku*
(fortresses)
tribute trade, 4–5, 8, 35–36, 62, 79, 141, 156,
172, 176–179, 186, 189, 191, 194–195,
197–200, 202, 212, 215–217, 220,
222–224, 226–229, 231–233, 236, 238,
241–242, 244, 246, 255– 256, 265,
275n18, 292n7

trumpet shells (*gohoragai*), 80
Tsukishiro shrine, 183. *See also* Sashiki in
   Okinawa. *See also* Shō Hashi
Tsushima (Island), 4, 52, 56–57, 83–84, 108,
   115, 120–122, 124–27, 162, 199, 243, 248,
   276n2, 278n18, 282n15, 289n12, 290n16,
   295n15. *See also* Iki (Island)
tubers, 78, 149, 154; taro type, 78–79
turbo shells (*yakōgai*), 54, 55, 59, 80, 93–94,
   99–100, 108, 112, 263, 277n7, 281n14. *See
   also* mother-of-pearl (MOP). *See also*
   shell trade
tuyeres (bellows valves), 91–92, 114, 283n4

Uema Atsushi, 174, 175
Ukeshima, 184. *See also* Yoroshima
Urasoe Castle (Gusuku), 163, 177, 186,
   191–192, 202–206, 208, 228, 289n14,
   289n10, 293n12
Urasoe yōdore (mausoleum), 69–70, 191,
   202–204
Uruka ships, 241
utaki. See sacred groves
-*utchi* (J. *okite*), 215, 226, 293n18, 294n1. See
   also *wan-okite* (harbor chief)

Vasco Valvo, 294n2

wakō, 4, 14–15, 26, 31–32, 34, 36, 40, 44, 51,
   56–57, 62, 85, 97, 117, 126, 128, 133, 135,
   141, 147, 156, 161–163, 165–167, 172–173,
   175, 177–179, 182, 186, 189, 195, 197–199,
   208, 213, 216–217, 219, 220–221, 228, 230,
   236, 240–243, 245, 246–247, 251–253,
   256, 261– 262, 264–265, 270, 276n25,
   289n12–13, 292n9
wan-okite (harbor chief), 167. See also -*utchi*
   (J. *okite*)
warfare, 5, 8, 11, 13, 20, 26–27, 29–31, 33–37,
   42, 49, 65, 83–85, 99, 114, 129, 149,
   156–162, 172, 179, 185, 192, 195, 197, 199,
   203–205, 209, 212, 214–215, 217, 220, 222,
   224, 226, 228, 230, 231–236, 240–245,
   247, 249, 251, 253–255, 257, 265–266, 271,
   289n9, 291n7, 295n9, 296n3; arrowheads,

156–157, 161, 165, 175, 191, 193; conquest
   of Kikaijima, 234–236, 295n9; invasion
   of Yaeyama (Ishigaki), 161, 172, 241–242,
   252–253, 277n15. *See also* Ryukyuan
   pacifism, myth of. *See also* Three
   Principalities, warfare connected with
warlords (*aji*), 13, 14, 25, 28, 29–36, 38,
   139–140, 142, 158–159, 163–164, 180,
   188, 195, 197, 210, 241, 256, 266,
   275n13–14, 291n7, 296n17. See also *wakō*
Wasa (islands). *See* Tokara Islands
Wengrow, David, 282n21
Writs of appointment (*jireisho*), 22, 39,
   273n5

Yà Lánpáo, 210, 231
yabusa/yabosa. See sacred groves
Yabusatsu *utaki,* 117–118, 120–121, 126,
   284n3, 284n5. *See also* sacred groves
Yaese, 140, 206
Yaeyama (Islands), 28, 30, 57, 61–62, 65, 70,
   74–76, 81, 95, 100–101, 113–114, 127, 161,
   168, 172, 241–242, 255, 262, 277n15,
   279n13, 284n2, 287n14, 288n1, 296n6.
   See also invasion of Ishigaki (Yaeyama).
   See also Ishigaki (Island)
Yagi (anchorage), **188**–189. *See also*
   harbor-fortress units. *See also*
   Nakagusuku Gusuku
Yakushima, 64, 81, 92–93, 97, 170, 277n7,
   277n16
Yamaguchi Matarō, 125
Yamashita-chō Cave Site 1, 67, 87
"Yamato" as southern Satsuma peninsula,
   112, 136, 286n22. *See also* Yatsushiro
   (Yashiro)
Yamato Banta (harbor), 183, 229. *See also*
   Sashiki in Okinawa
Yamato court envoys to the southern
   islands, 82
Yamazato Eikichi, 159
Yamazato Jun'ichi, 82–83
Yàn, Chinese state of. *See* knife coins
Yanagita Kunio, 29, 118, 274n10
Yano Misako, 39

Yatsushiro (Yashiro), 112, 118, 136, 183, 193, 224, 230, 239, 247, 277n17, 286n22. *See also* Nawa of Yatsushiro (Nawashiro). *See also* Samekawa, Lord.

Yayoi, 9, 16–17, 57, 58–**59**, 63, 69–72, **76**, 80, 86–88, 90, 260–261, 274n10, 277n11, 278n3, 278n5, 279n10, 280n15. *See also* dual structure hypothesis (Hanihara hypothesis)

Y-chromosome haplogroup O2b, 56, 277n9, 286n21

Yi Seonggye, 173, 208. See also Akibatsu

Yonaguni (Island), 5, 61, 64, 78, 146–147, 242, 254, 279n9, 279n13

Yǒnglè emperor, 213

Yoron (Island), 64, 158, 170

Yoroshima, 184–185. *See also* Ukeshima

Yoshinari Naoki, 44, 79, 83, 98, 145, 153, 175, 191, 202, 283n2

Zakimi Gusuku (Castle), 132, 168, 183, 285n11, 289n10, 291n6

Zhāng Shìchéng, 175

Zhū Yuánzhāng. *See* Hóngwǔ emperor

ABOUT THE AUTHOR

Gregory Smits is professor of history and Asian studies at Pennsylvania State University. He is the author of *Visions of Ryukyu: Identity and Ideology in Early-Modern Thought and Politics; Seismic Japan: The Long History and Continuing Legacy of the Ansei Edo Earthquake; When the Earth Roars: Lessons from the History of Earthquakes in Japan;* and *Maritime Ryukyu, 1050–1650.*